PRAISE FOR *MANSON EXPOSED*

"The most detailed behind-the-scenes account of the Manson trial that I have ever read. Fascinating."
— Stephen Kay, deputy prosecutor, Charles Manson and
Charles Watson murder trials

"A compulsively readable back-porch memoir about all the amazing reach the Charlie Manson murder case had into the celebrity world of 1960s-'70s Los Angeles—in both the movie and music industries. In his years as a Hollywood writer, Ivor Davis came to know most of its famous characters personally, and revisits them with a wicked eye for detail and an astonishingly detailed memory—it helps that he was usually taking notes. He brings a sometimes disturbing, often brilliant era to life."
— Mark Bowden, author of best seller *Black Hawk Down* and *The Last Stone: A Masterpiece of Criminal Interrogation*

"This compelling book combines the skills of a Truman Capote plus the genuine 'I was there' Zelig/Forrest Gump sensibilities. More than just a murder story spanning half a century, *Manson Exposed* is a scarily fast personal ride told with insight and a soupçon of gallows humor."
— Marshall Terrill, author of *Steve McQueen: The Life and Legend of a Hollywood Icon*

"An insider's riveting, detailed account of how the criminal justice system struggled with a sensational tragedy—and with a diabolical defendant battling to discredit the system. Davis will convince you that in many respects the tumultuous Manson case still deserves its longstanding 'Trial of the Century' title."
— Martin Kasindorf, journalist/attorney who covered the Manson trial for *Newsweek*

"*Manson Exposed* is a piercing, original look at a crime that shocked the world. Davis, in this mix of personal memoir, criticism, and riveting reportage, delves into the heart of the case—and offers much that is new and perceptive about a crime that terrified and obsessed a nation."
> — Simon Wells, author of the best seller *Charles Manson: Coming Down Fast*

"This is a true-life story about everyone who knew the victims and the defendants—the investigators, the prosecutors, and all the leading players—and delivers a fresh, vivid picture of what witnesses, reporters, and showbiz figures thought and said about the murders. A helluva read."
> — Sandi Gibbons, City News Service and former media director for the Los Angeles District Attorney

"Davis, who was on the scene from day one and never stopped reporting, offers new facts and fresh insights in this revealing and thorough account. *Manson Exposed* lives up to its title—and then some."
> — Steve Oney, author of *And the Dead Shall Rise: The Murder of Mary Phagan and the Lynching of Leo Frank*

"Competing on fast-breaking big American news stories in the pre-Internet era, Davis stayed ahead of the pack, particularly on the frenetic Manson murder story. Take my word: his new version of how it all came down is the way it really was."
> — Anthony Delano, author of *Joyce McKinney and the Case of the Manacled Mormon* and *Slip-Up: How Fleet Street Found Ronnie Biggs And Scotland Yard Lost Him*

"Ivor Davis was the first reporter to write a book about the Tate killings. As an expert on the spot, he entertainingly serves up the bizarre inside story of one of the craziest trials I ever covered."
> — Linda Deutsch, Associated Press Special Correspondent

MANSON EXPOSED

A Reporter's 50-Year Journey into Madness and Murder

IVOR DAVIS

MANSON EXPOSED: A Reporter's 50-Year Journey into Madness and Murder
Cockney Kid Publishing, Ventura, California

For a complete list of photo credits, please see *Photo and Illustration Acknowledgments* at the end of the book.

Author services by Pedernales Publishing, LLC.
www.pedernalespublishing.com

Cover design: Dave McTaggart

Library of Congress Control Number: 2019906412

ISBN 978-0-9903710-2-1 Paperback Edition
ISBN 978-0-9903710-3-8 Hardcover Edition
ISBN 978-0-9903710-1-4 Digital Edition

Printed in the United States of America

In memory of Sally Ogle Davis—who lived through all of this madness with me

ALSO BY IVOR DAVIS

Five to Die

Five to Die: The Book That Helped Convict Manson

The Beatles and Me On Tour

Ladies and Gentlemen...The Penguins!

MANSON EXPOSED

CONTENTS

ASSIGNMENT MURDER

"Tip the world over on its side, and everything loose will land in Los Angeles."
—Frank Lloyd Wright

In 1969, I was the West Coast correspondent of the *London Daily Express*, one of the most widely read newspapers in Europe with an impressive 4 million readers a day. I was a one-man bureau, headquartered in West Los Angeles and my job was a foreign correspondent's paradise—never a dull moment, never a slow day, never a shortage of lively or provocative assignments, or sunshine for that matter.

But, in August of that year, the world—and particularly Southern California—was shocked beyond belief by a series of events that petrified residents in an affluent Los Angeles neighborhood. The illusion that their luxurious homes were insulated from commonplace crime was well and truly shattered.

From the moment the series of savage murders exploded onto the front pages of newspapers around the world in early August 1969, I jumped on the case, did my own sleuthing and learned more than anyone ever wanted to know about the Charles Manson Family. I became intimately familiar with all the gruesome details of the carnage and what they were capable of. The moment Manson was identified as the architect of the killings, I went to a courthouse in Inyo County, California on the edge of Death Valley where he was being held. Then to the Spahn Ranch in Los Angeles's sprawling San Fernando Valley where they lived. And I began interviewing Family members. Much to my surprise, many of the leftover members who had not been arrested or indicted for murder, were still sacking out on a sea of ratty old mattresses on the tarpaulin-covered dirty floor of a fake and decaying Western saloon bar.

And they were just dying to spill their guts. While they were mostly silent about the murders, they offered vivid stories, detailing chapter and verse the lifestyle that culminated in the bloodbath of seven innocent people on two awful nights.

Even as a seasoned reporter, I had a hard time separating fact from fiction. With my seen-it-all, cynical editors 6,000 miles away in London screaming for stories, and with deadlines to meet, I filed a series of tales that caused those hardened editors of mine on London's Fleet Street to question the veracity of my outlandish narratives.

Nine months later, I wrote *Five to Die*, the first book about the infamous murders which was published three months before the trial began. It was a damning indictment of Manson and his mindless followers. It laid out in graphic detail for the very first time, the bizarre lifestyle, the drugs, the orgies and the violence which had become the daily routine of that raggle-taggle band of young men and women who were worshipping at Manson's feet. And it detailed Manson's most outrageous and fiendish gospel, served up with regular doses of assorted psychedelic drugs fed to them daily, claiming that the lyrics to songs on the Beatles' 1968 *White Album*, specifically "Helter Skelter," were secret messages to Charlie and only Charlie.

The Gospel According to Manson declared that the Beatles were warning of a coming racial Armageddon which the Family would survive by fleeing on a flotilla of dune buggies to a secret refuge in Death Valley, California, where they would live happily ever after.

In my mind it was total, unadulterated garbage—absolute poppycock for the delusional Manson to interpret the Beatles lyrics in the way he supposedly did. While I am in no way a musicologist, by pure chance I was extremely familiar with the Beatles, their music, and their lyrics. In 1964, I traveled with them on their first North American tour and saw them again in 1965 when they returned to the USA. I knew with absolute certainty that there was no subliminal warning of a black-white conflagration hidden in their songs.

In *Five to Die* I didn't hold back castigating Manson's demented worshippers for following a diabolical madman. Not surprising, this did not endear me to the remnants of Manson's crackpot army of young women who were to keep a year-long vigil outside the Los Angeles courthouse. They had all pledged to remain loyal to their ruler forever. And do whatever was necessary, "until Charlie walks out a free man." And "whatever was necessary," I quickly discovered, was pretty chilling.

I will never forget my brief encounter with Manson devotee Lynette "Squeaky" Fromme when I saw her squatting on the street outside the courtroom on the first day of the trial in July 1970. She recognized me right away. We had talked at the Spahn Ranch seven months earlier and now my book, which painted Manson and his gang as a depraved band of killers, had been published.

She greeted me with a friendly wave—and an angelic smile. "Hi, Ivor," she called out, in that sing-song, butter-wouldn't-melt-in-her-mouth, emotionless voice. "Do you know what it feels like to have a razor-sharp knife slid down your throat?"

Her comment sent shivers down my spine. I didn't respond. No quip or rebuttal readily came to mind. So I quickly moved past her into the courthouse.

My sojourn into the lifestyle and inner workings of the Family grew, as weeks turned into months and then years. Manson and his mob just wouldn't go away. My pursuit of the story was to sweep me up on a strange and unique personal odyssey that stretched over almost half a century. As time went by and the threats subsided, the trials came and went, the case continued to obsess me like no other story I have ever encountered.

I could not rid myself of those ghastly images. I carefully followed the circuitous trail of those convicted of the killings after spending almost a year covering the trial. I revisited the case, interviewing leading players in California, London and Paris.

My unending assignment took me through a House of Horrors—a journey that began with the destruction of the innocent lives of the pregnant actress Sharon Tate, fashionable Hollywood hairstylist Jay Sebring, and their friends at a mansion hidden away on Cielo Drive off Benedict Canyon, and then a day later moved to a Los Angeles residential neighborhood where the lives of Los Angeles businessman Leno LaBianca and his wife Rosemary were senselessly cut short. There were other corpses strewn along the path, as well—some who died, innocents whose lives were forever scarred beyond repair by those heinous two nights: the internationally acclaimed movie director, the rock legend, the Hollywood superstar, the music-industry giant.

Feel free to come along on this journey with me.

DAILY EXPRESS

No. 21,517   MONDAY AUGUST 11 1969   Weather: Dry, sunny; very warm   Price 5d.

FIND THE RED FERRARI!

Midnight: New hunt for mass killer

IVOR DAVIS
Los Angeles
Sunday

A NATION-WIDE hunt for a man who may be in a red Ferrari was under way tonight as police investigated the macabre ritual murder of five at a Hollywood party.

THE MAN is a friend of 19-year-old William Garretson who is charged with the murders.

THE CAR belongs to Roman Polanski, husband of "Valley of the Dolls" star Sharon Tate, who was stabbed to death at her £80,000 Bel Air home.

Tonight police admitted that Garretson may be released soon if a detective had cleared him.

Weird

Lieut. Robert Helder said: "There is no physical evidence to tie the boy's living quarters to connect him with the crime.

"The case is weird. There is no indication that there were any odd parties going on.

None of the victims, he added, was sexually molested.

One aspect puzzling police remains: Why didn't any one of the victims have time to flee?

THE MURDERS were discovered last night when a maid came to the house and then ran out screaming: "There's bodies and blood everywhere."

On the front door, written in blood: "Pig."

In the living-room, strung by her neck from a nylon rope: MISS TATE, aged 26, in nightdress and brassiere. She was five months pregnant. She had been stabbed to death.

At the other end of the rope, which was flung over a wooden beam: JAY SEBRING, aged 26, a hair stylist to the stars and Miss Tate's former fiancé. Over his head, a hood. He had been stabbed too.

Trimmed

On a lawn at the ranch-style house: VOYTECK FROKOWSKI, aged 37, who worked with Polanski in their native Poland. He had been shot.

Also on the neatly trimmed lawn: ABIGAIL FOLGER, aged 26, in nightgown. Heiress to a coffee fortune. She had been stabbed.

Near the car: STEVEN PARENT, aged 18, from Los Angeles, not known to Miss Tate's set. He had been shot.

Draped over a couch in the living room — an American flag.

A policeman summed it up: "It all seemed ritualistic. Almost a battlefield in the house."

When the maid gave the alert, police raced to the secluded cul-de-sac and entered the house with guns drawn.

A dog barked and police heard a man's voice call for help. They entered a guest house and found caretaker Garretson. He wore pin-striped, bell-bottom trousers and no shirt.

There were no drugs found in the house and apparently nothing missing.

MOTHER: Mrs. Mary Garretson, of Lancaster, Ohio, described her son as "a quiet, gentle boy," adding: "That kid can never been violent. He could never have done this."

She said he told in letters of entertaining young friends in his caretaker's quarters.

One letter told of a young veteran back from Vietnam whom he entered.

PAGE TWO, COL. FOUR

PICTURE BY HENRY GRIS

ROMAN POLANSKI
Leaving yesterday

WHAT SHARON TATE WANTED FOR HER BABY

"THIS is one of the last photographs taken by London of Sharon Tate."

She met photographers and talked to Jackie in this quiet, beautiful room, and spoke of the baby she was going to have.

"I'll have a nursery for the baby. And that is why we want whatever I leave to be for a child."

They talked of ordinary things — of life and love.

Franc: Europe faces farms crisis

MICHAEL GILLARD
SQUARE BARRACLOUGH

JOHN ELLISON
IN PARIS

THE effect of France's devaluation will hit Britain today after a weekend of speculation.

TEACHING

LATEST

WHITE-HAIRED

TV-Radio programmes Page 8

STUNTMAN KILLED

PHONE INFO CODE 011
353 8000

Moon men 'free'

RICHARD MILLAR
HOUSTON, Sunday

Sea search for family

Angus Ogilvy ill in church

Prince 'not well'

Killer peaks

Even the *London Daily Express* front page headline of August 11, 1969, got it all wrong. It turned out that Sharon's red Ferrari was in the garage repair shop.

PART I

THE CRIME

TIMELINE

- *July 25, 1969:* Musician Gary Hinman murdered in his Topanga Canyon, Los Angeles home.

- *August 1, 1969:* Charles Manson shoots drug dealer Bernard Crowe in Hollywood apartment.

- *August 6, 1969:* Robert Beausoleil, Manson Family member, arrested for Hinman murder.

- *August 9, 1969:* Murders at 10050 Cielo Drive, off Benedict Canyon, Beverly Hills.

- *August 10, 1969:* Murders at 3301 Waverly Drive, Los Angeles.

- *August 16, 1969:* Los Angeles Sheriff Special Enforcement Bureau raid Spahn Ranch, Chatsworth, California, and arrest Charles Manson and Family members on suspicion of car theft. No link made to Hinman/Tate-LaBianca murders.

- *August 18, 1969:* All arrested are released because of bureaucratic mistakes.

- *August 26, 1969:* Stuntman Donald "Shorty" Shea murdered by Manson gang and his body buried at Spahn Ranch.

- *October 10-12, 1969:* Manson and Family members arrested for destroying a government earth mover at the Barker Ranch in Death Valley and held in Inyo County, California.

- *October 20, 1969:* Inyo County DA notes that a Susan Atkins in his custody is wanted for the murder of Gary Hinman. She is returned to LA and while an inmate at the Sybil Brand Institute confesses to cellmates about the Sharon Tate murders.

- *December 1, 1969:* Los Angeles Police Chief Edward Davis announces the murder case has been solved after Atkins's prison confessions are revealed to LAPD.

- *December 3, 1969:* Manson arraigned for car theft in Inyo County, California before being handed over to Los Angeles police.

- *December 5, 1969:* Susan Atkins gives a full confession to the Los Angeles Grand Jury.

- *June 15, 1970:* Tate-LaBianca murder trial begins.

THE KILLINGS

"I felt absolutely nothing for her as she begged for her life and the life of her baby...there was nothing I could do...no turning back. It was like I was caught in something I had no control over...it was like I was a tool in the hands of the devil."
—Susan Atkins, 1976 ABC TV interview

"The swirling hallucination of the sixties had climaxed in the ultimate 'summer bummer,' and it all made a grotesquely twisted sense,"
—Barney Hoskyns, *Waiting for the Sun, Strange Days, Weird Scenes, and The Sound of Los Angeles,* 1996

Saturday, August 9, 1969, was undoubtedly the most horrifying day in Winifred "Winnie" Chapman's life.

The sun was trying hard to burn through the early morning Los Angeles haze as the fifty-five-year-old housekeeper stepped off the bus at Santa Monica Boulevard and Canon Drive in Beverly Hills. Those early morning buses were often called the "Maids' Specials" because housekeepers, cooks, and babysitters would leave at sunrise to travel the twenty-odd miles to serve affluent Westside families. The trip from her home on East 46ᵗʰ Street in South Central LA took about forty-five minutes.

As she stepped off the bus shortly before 8:00 a.m., Chapman caught sight of a familiar face. It was a friend of her employers—the Polish-born film director, Roman Polanski, and his eight-months-pregnant wife, actress Sharon Tate. The couple was renting a ranch-style, barn-red house in remote Benedict Canyon, surrounded by pine trees, lawns, and well-manicured shrubbery. The "dream house" had been built in 1941 by the French actress Michelle Morgan, and it had previously been home to actors Henry Fonda and Cary Grant, as well as record producer Terry Melcher (son of Doris Day) and Melcher's actress-model girlfriend, Candice Bergen. At $1,500 a month, it was the perfect property for showbiz people seeking privacy.

Indeed, the Benedict Canyon area had been a popular hotspot through the years. Rudolph Valentino once had a home there, as did Doris Duke, the tobacco heiress. And just a few doors away was Joseph Stefano, screenwriter for the chilling landmark movie *Psycho* and close friend of Alfred Hitchcock.

Chapman had been looking after the Polanski housekeeping needs for more than a year and was equally as thrilled as Tate to watch the spare bedroom being turned into a nursery. The Polanskis' Good Samaritan friend offered Chapman a ride to the gated house, some two miles up the road on an easy-to-miss side street off Benedict Canyon Drive. The address was 10050 Cielo Drive. She gratefully accepted the offer; it saved her cab fare.

Minutes later, shopping bag in hand, the slender housekeeper, who some said resembled singer Eartha Kitt and who was affectionately called "Winnie Pooh" by the white families in the San Fernando Valley where she earned extra money doing nanny duties, walked briskly up the driveway to the estate gate. She pushed the button, and the gate immediately opened. She noted a broken telephone wire hanging above the house but assumed it had been felled by the wind.

She picked up the morning copy of the *Los Angeles Times* from the red mailbox and hurried to the house. Even with the quicker than normal bus ride and car lift, she was still tardy for work, and Chapman didn't like being late.

She noted a car in the driveway—a white Rambler, which she didn't recognize as belonging to the Polanskis or to their long-term houseguests. She was, however, familiar with the black Porsche, which belonged to Tate's friend, Beverly Hills hairstylist Jay Sebring, a frequent visitor at the house. Though the Rambler looked odd and out of place—jutting out, half sideways in the driveway, as if hurriedly parked—she barely gave it a second glance as she hurried to the front door.

"I snapped out the outside lights, which someone had left on, unlocked the back door, and went in," she was to haltingly recount later to a Los Angeles grand jury. "I went to the kitchen phone and picked it up. It was dead. Since our electric was on, I surmised it was the telephone wires that had fallen. Then I started up front to waken someone. That is when I saw the bodies and the bloody clothes and…what-have-you."

She stepped inside…and froze. All around her were unrecognizable bodies, looking artificial, like mannequins covered in blood, strewn around the house. It was a scene straight out of a horror movie—only this was real. Paralyzed by fear, she felt faint, her heart began to palpitate. She could hear it pounding. And then she began screaming.

"Murder…murder!" she screamed, as she ran back down the driveway to get help at the next-door neighbor's house. She hammered her small fists on the front door until her hands began to hurt.

"Call the police, murder!" she shrieked again and again to no one in particular. "There's blood, bodies everywhere."

No reply. She raced to a second house further down the hill, still howling, her brain spinning wildly, unable to comprehend what she had witnessed just moments earlier.

At the lower house on Cielo, fifteen-year-old Jim Asin, a member of the local Law Enforcement Troop 800 Boy Scouts, part of a police-sponsored troop, was standing in the driveway. He calmly alerted his father Ray. They phoned the West Los Angeles police station, in whose jurisdiction Cielo Drive fell. The teenager shrewdly noted the time was 8:33 a.m. Then the Asins did their best to try to calm the hysterically sobbing woman. But she was inconsolable and collapsed on the floor in a heap.

Minutes later six squad cars, sirens wailing, came racing up the narrow winding canyon road, screeching to a halt at the half-opened Cielo Drive estate gate.

"It was like a battlefield," one of the uniformed officers was later to remark. "There was a bullet-riddled young guy in the Rambler. Another man with no face left, on the lawn in the back of the house. And just a few feet away, another body—a barefooted woman—further down on the grass." They sent out an urgent call for homicide detectives and, guns drawn, carefully entered the house. Who knew if the killers might still be lurking somewhere?

There was no sign of life anywhere on the grounds, but suddenly the officers heard barking from the guest house. Three of the officers—Jerry Joe DeRosa, William Whisenhunt, and Robert Burbridge—cautiously approached. There were noises and definite movement inside, just steps from the lawn and the boulder-lined swimming pool area. Then more barking.

Was the killer hiding? A decision had to be made; so they smashed down the front door. A barking Weimaraner leapt at one of the cops; then from behind the dog stepped a skinny, young, bare-chested man with a thick mop of curly black hair, looking as though he had just gotten out of bed. He was still rubbing sleep out of his eyes as the three officers pointed a rifle, a shotgun, and a pistol into his chest. He seemed totally confused, facing the heavy artillery gun barrels pointed just inches from his flesh.

The young man identified himself as William Garretson. He was nineteen and had been hired as a resident caretaker by the owner of the property, Rudi Altobelli. Altobelli was manager to a slew of stars, including Henry Fonda, Katherine Hepburn, and newcomer British actress Samantha Eggar. Garretson explained that he lived in the guest house with three of Altobelli's dogs while the owner was away in Europe on business.

Altobelli had purchased the estate for $86,000 in the early sixties because he fell in love with what he called the property's "magical views," which on a clear day stretched all the way to Santa Monica and the Pacific Ocean. But because he traveled extensively on business, he frequently rented the main house out to showbiz tenants; when he was home, he lived in the guest house. It was an idyllic setup—until "Helter Skelter" was unleashed.

The police took no chances. They handcuffed the terrified Garretson, then frog-marched him over to the back-garden lawn—and to the bodies of the man and woman. "Do you know them? Who are they?" snapped Whisenhunt.

Garretson was barely able to fix his eyes on the mutilated corpses. He was scared out of his wits, possibly hungover. He wasn't making much sense, mumbling almost incomprehensibly. The woman, he said looked like Winnie Chapman, the Polanskis' housekeeper. Or maybe not; he couldn't be sure. And the male could be a relative or friend of Roman Polanski. He was certain of nothing.

He said that he had been home in the guest cottage all night long, listening to The Doors on headphones, and that he finally fell asleep somewhere around 5:30 a.m.—he had tried to make a phone call to check the time, but the phone had no dial tone. Almost like a mantra, he kept repeating that he had heard nothing until the cops kicked his door down.

Despite his insistence that he was innocent, Garretson was carted off to jail. It gave him no comfort when, while being booked, he overheard an officer say, "There's the guy who killed all those people in Beverly Hills."

Intuitively, the cops working the investigation doubted he was a killer. Still, he looked like he was coming off a bad drug trip, leading them to surmise that maybe some of his "hippie" friends might be responsible.

On Cielo Drive, more LAPD officers had arrived at the scene, many off duty and still in plain clothes. They fanned out, grimly searching every inch of the meticulously landscaped property for any piece of evidence that might reveal what had gone down. Cautiously—with guns drawn—several inched toward the main house where they were to find two more bodies butchered even more heinously than those already found on the lawn. The warm afternoon sun bounced off the sparkling blue-tiled swimming pool water. Just a few feet away, the automatic pool cleaner hummed quietly as if it were just another day in paradise.

Within hours, a new army of LAPD homicide detectives descended. One of them, Michael McGann, vividly remembers everything he saw. For an oral history of the murders given to *Los Angeles* magazine writer Steve Oney, he described what he had seen:

> *There was a car parked in the middle of the driveway, and there was a body in the car. That was Steven Parent. He was slumped over to the side on the front seat. He'd been shot (three times). As I approached the house, I noticed that the word "pig" was written in what appeared to be blood on the front door. Then I went inside. Sharon Tate and Jay Sebring were lying on the living-room floor, both with multiple stab wounds. A rope was tied around Sharon's neck and draped over a rafter. The other end of the same rope was affixed to Jay Sebring's neck. They were probably about four feet apart. Sharon was in a bikini-style nightie. She was eight and a half months pregnant, and I could tell she had been stabbed 15-plus times. Sebring had been stabbed and beaten over the head.*
>
> *There was blood everywhere. I went through the house and down a long hallway leading out to the back door where the pool was, and*

I went out onto the lawn and found Abigail Folger. She was in a nightgown, and she'd been stabbed numerous times. Her gown was soaked in blood. Then a little bit farther on was Voytek Frykowski. He had numerous head wounds, like he'd been hit with some kind of object. He also had many stab wounds and had been shot several times. He was fully clothed, and he was covered in blood. In the space of ten minutes I saw all five bodies. I'd worked homicide for five years and seen a lot of violence. This was the worst.

Shortly after 11:00 a.m. on that Saturday, I got a call from my London office. Reuters was reporting that five people had been murdered in a private Hollywood enclave, and they were saying it was drug related. I needed to get on the story, fast. I checked the local City News Service ticker tape for the address and raced the fifteen miles over the canyons from my home in Studio City to Cielo Drive. By the time I arrived, it was already a crazy and hectic scene. TV cameras, radio, and print media had set up shop, confined to the road leading up to the front gate. From time to time, LAPD media-relations officer Dan Cooke tried to answer questions without giving too much away. As new reporters arrived, they would get their information from the others. Fact mixed in with heavy doses of fiction and speculation—not a regimen to guarantee journalistic accuracy. That first day we got only sparse details about what had gone down and who the victims were. Outside the house, as bedlam grew, I recognized Hollywood gossip columnist Rona Barrett.

"What are *you* doing here?" I inquired. "Have they got you covering the police beat now?"

"Don't you know who lives at this house?" she asked, knowingly. And then she told me.

I was shocked. I had interviewed Sharon Tate a couple of years earlier on the 20th Century-Fox set of *Valley of the Dolls*, and she was a lovely lady. Based on Jacqueline Susann's bestselling novel, the movie had attracted an eclectic cast, including Susan Hayward, who stepped in when Judy Garland dropped out, and Oscar-winner Patty Duke. Songs were penned by Dory and Andre Previn—with music by a then-unknown composer named John Williams.

Raquel Welch, who had just come off *Fantastic Voyage*, was also to have starred, but Welch—or, more likely, her controlling husband/manager Patrick Curtis—turned the role down claiming that she didn't want to play sexpots anymore. So they offered the part of Jennifer North, the young actress with limited talent, to the sexy new girl on the block: Sharon Tate. We all knew that Tate's husband of twenty months was the hotshot director Roman Polanski. It didn't take a genius to realize that this story was not going to go away.

In the early afternoon, with the temperature edging toward the 90s, as the increasingly large media army waited desperately for any actual facts to beef up the paucity of information, a forlorn looking man stepped out of the guarded front gate. It was obvious he wasn't a cop because he wore white tennis shorts, tennis shoes, and a light sweater.

"That's Roman's manager," Barrett whispered.

It was, in fact, Bill Tennant, the twenty-eight-year-old Hollywood super-agent who meticulously oversaw Polanski's career and had become close friends with his client and his wife. He had been summoned from a Saturday morning game of tennis for the ugly task of identifying the bodies. As he walked out of the estate to climb into his car, his head was bowed and he was grim- faced and ashen.

"Is it Sharon, Bill?" Barrett shouted to him. Tennant looked startled. "Oh, Rona," he snapped back angrily, "don't be such an asshole." And he kept walking.

Because the cops still weren't talking for the record, I spoke to several neighbors who were milling around to observe the media disruptions, but who were also both agitated and intrigued by the violence that had invaded their quiet, respectable community. Several filled me in the best they could, confirming that the home's current occupants were indeed Polanski and Tate, and possibly a few other showbiz types staying with them. I was not alone in wrongly assuming that both Polanski and Tate had been killed—details were sparse and rumors were rampant, although police did confirm that the body count stood at five. But who exactly were they?

Gradually the names and the identities of the victims were revealed, and odd bits of information leaked out. Was it a drug murder? Yes, some drugs had been found at the scene: three ounces of marijuana, just over an ounce of hashish, a gram of cocaine, and ten capsules of MDA—a hallucinogenic drug. Some of it was found in Tate's bedroom, and some in a car belonging to her friend Sebring.

But that still didn't explain *why* the mass murder? Did everyone go berserk during a bad acid trip? Was it a Mafia hit? Had a drug deal gone bad? They even had a suspect—a drug-crazed teenager, who was deeply involved in the peddling of LSD. How was he the only survivor?

Satanism was tossed into the mix after one cop on the scene described the killings as "ritualistic." That sort of made sense. Didn't Polanski direct *Rosemary's Baby* just a year before? A blood-stained American flag had been found, according to one reporter who was monitoring the police-radio waveband in his car. What the heck could that mean? Sharon and Roman were said to be involved in the production of raunchy sex tapes. Drugs and orgies were rumored to be part and parcel of Sebring's lifestyle, which reportedly included sadomasochism. Another rumor was that the killers were wearing Ku Klux Klan garb, hence the hoods over some of the bodies.

As was common practice on murder investigations, detectives deliberately withheld details about the precise way the victims died, and particularly the gruesome details of the carnage. But we soon learned the names of those who had perished atop the remote canyon.

First identified was Tate, whom Polanski had met while he was casting the 1967 horror spoof *The Fearless Vampire Killers—or Pardon Me, Your Teeth Are in My Neck*. She was a beautiful, blonde twenty-six-year-old actress pegged as the next Marilyn Monroe. One of her bridesmaids at the high-profile wedding at the London Playboy Club in January 1968 was Canadian-born actress Barbara Parkins, whom she had met when they worked together on *Valley of the Dolls*.

In the summer of '69, Tate put her career on hold to have a baby. She was just days away from delivering her first child, a son. In fact, a baby shower had been set for a few days later; and the day before violence struck, painters had put the finishing touches on the house's spare bedroom, turning it into a nursery.

It later came out that Tate had been stabbed sixteen times, and five of those wounds could have been fatal because they had penetrated her heart and lungs, causing massive hemorrhaging. She was dressed in a nightgown, and had a rope tied around her neck, which had caused severe rope burns on her cheek. Polanski, we quickly learned, was not a victim but, at that very moment, heavily tranquilized on a jet flying back to Los Angeles from London, comforted by his good friend Warren Beatty.

Also among the dead was the thirty-five-year-old Sebring. He had been stabbed seven times and shot once. Born Thomas John Kummer, his claim to Hollywood fame was that he had invented a new, more natural way of cutting men's hair, and he was well-compensated for his technique. He charged $25 at a time when barbers were getting $1.50, and a tad more, $350, for celebrity toupees. He also extracted $2,500 a day, plus expenses, from the studios for on-set visits. The stars loved what he could do with a pair of scissors. His client list included the likes of Beatty, Steve McQueen, Paul Newman, Kirk Douglas, Frank Sinatra, Sammy Davis, Jr., and Jim Morrison of The Doors.

Sebring had the reputation as a playboy, with a taste for beautiful women and kinky sex. He was also a former fiancé of Tate, and even when they broke up and she had married Polanski, Sebring stayed in the picture. Polanski was never jealous—in fact, he liked Sebring well enough to invite him to regularly hang out on Cielo Drive.

The corpses on the lawn first spotted by Winnie Chapman included Frykowski, thirty-two, who had been shot four times, stabbed fifty-one times, and had suffered thirteen blows to his head with a blunt instrument. He was an old friend of Polanski's from Poland and a wannabe screenwriter with a penchant for hard drugs. He not only partook of them but sold them on the side to make pocket money. He had no visible means of support and sponged off the generosity of his live-in girlfriend, "Gibby" Folger, the twenty-five-year-old heiress to the famous coffee empire. Now her body lay a few feet away from his. She had been stabbed twenty-eight times.

Polanski had felt sorry for his Polish compatriot, inviting him and Folger to become near-permanent guests at Cielo.

Slumped over the wheel of the white Rambler in the driveway was Steven Parent, an eighteen-year-old delivery boy, who worked part time in a Los Angeles stereo shop and who simply happened to be in the wrong place at the wrong time. He was visiting Garretson, having stopped by late at night to try to sell him a radio. Hailing from the blue-collar Southern California neighborhood of El Monte, Parent's timing was tragic. He was at the wheel of his car and about to drive away when he was shot three times.

I left the murder scene three times to call in my story to my editors in London. But I didn't have to go far to find a phone. I knew Cielo Drive. I had been there before. By a weird coincidence, a close friend actually lived on the street—a British friend who played for the same Los Angeles soccer team as I did. Phillip Freed, an executive for Volkswagen of America, and his American wife, Joyce, had a home a few steps away at 10210.

Freed was also able to confirm with absolute certainty that his neighbors were the Polanskis and that they were notorious partygoers and party throwers. The father of two young daughters, he told me there were frequent loud parties at the estate with music resounding throughout the canyon and scores of cars parked all the way down the long driveway almost reaching Benedict Canyon. "We never got invited and they kept to themselves," he said. "They did their own thing. This was not the kind of place where we had neighborhood block parties. In fact, it was a bit of a revolving door. Lots of new faces. Many of the houses seemed to have new tenants every few weeks."

Somewhat surprisingly, Freed did not know a huge criminal investigation was unfolding under his very nose until his brother-in-law showed up around 10:45 a.m. and told him that scores of media were milling around the Tate driveway. "That Saturday around 9:30 a.m. I was trying to get a last-minute suntan at my pool because I was due to fly home to London on Tuesday to visit my mother," he told me. "Suddenly a whole bunch of police and TV helicopters were swooping low over my house. I thought they were going to attack me. And I wondered what the hell was happening. And why were they taking pictures of me?"

After hanging out for a few hours outside the gates, I knew I had to file a story for my London paper's first edition. So I walked over to the Freed house—it was to become the perfect central headquarters for me and some of my colleagues who desperately needed to find a telephone in the days before we carried them around in our pockets. It helped me tremendously in getting a leg up when reporting the story. I was able to finally confirm the identities of those living at the Cielo estate to my London editors.

"Stay around," deputy foreign editor Jim Nichol told me. "This is our front-page splash… we'll take everything you can give us. Your first-edition story runs to over seventy inches." For those unfamiliar with the newsroom term, it meant that my story was going to be three times the normal length of what I usually filed.

As the sun began to set, the 90-degree weather had cooled to the high 60s, and most of the media, having been kept mostly at bay, were ready to call it a day. But the crime team still had lots of work to do. Homicide detective Danny Galindo, who had worked on LA's legendary 1947 Black Dahlia case, took charge of the investigation; he was ordered to remain at the house all night long to make sure the crime scene was not tampered with. "I was told to stay and guard the interior," he told *Los Angeles* magazine. "I couldn't find a good area to lean against or lie down on or relax against because of all the blood. I tried to find a spot at the front door, but it was too bloody. I tried to find a place inside, but when you opened the door, there was so much blood on the wall. I finally found a place in back. And fell asleep."

THE WORST MURDER rampage in Los Angeles history was barely twenty-four hours old when news agencies began to clatter out more awful news. Another massacre, barely fifteen miles away from the affluent mansions of Cielo Drive, had gone down on the night of Sunday, August 10th.

This time, the location was 3301 Waverly Dr. in the respectable suburb of Los Feliz, in the hills not far from downtown Los Angeles, and just around the corner from the popular Griffith Park Observatory, where home prices were a fraction of what they were in rarified Beverly Hills.

Fifteen-year-old Frank Struthers was dropped off by friends in the driveway at the home of his stepfather, businessman Leno LaBianca, at around 8:30 p.m. He thought it was unusual that their speedboat was still attached to their Thunderbird and parked on the long concrete driveway leading to the house. It struck him as odd because he knew that LaBianca, who owned a chain of grocery stores, didn't like to leave the boat out at night. He and his second wife, Rosemary, lived in a white, old Mission-style stucco house set well back from the street. It had rounded portals, a red tile roof, a large well-kept lawn, and nicely trimmed hedges.

Struthers noted that the window blinds were drawn, and behind them, the lights were on in the house. He knocked firmly on the front door. There was no response. He shouted out their names. Again, silence. Worried, he contacted his sister Suzanne, who soon showed up with her boyfriend, Joe Dorgan. Again they knocked. Again, no reply. She found a set of door keys hidden under a flower pot and they entered through the back door.

"Stay in the kitchen," Joe told Suzanne. "Don't worry. Everything's okay. We'll check things out."

They stepped into the living room and immediately made their grisly discovery. Steps away, the Struthers' forty-four-year-old stepdad lay on his back, a bloodstained pillow over his head, a cord around his neck, and something that looked like a knife sticking in his stomach, "WAR" carved on his chest. On the refrigerator scribbled in blood was "Death to Pigs" and "Healter Skelter." Upstairs in the master bedroom police found Rosemary LaBianca. The thirty-eight-year-old was face down in a pool of blood. She also had been stabbed many times and had a pillowcase over her head.

As he was two-finger typing his reports about the Tate murders at police headquarters at Parker Center in downtown Los Angeles, detective Galindo took a phone call from City News Service police beat reporter, Norman "Jake" Jacoby. "Danny, listen to this. They got another one of those bloody ones just like the one you're working on," he said. "And there's a knife stuck in the throat of the victim."

Once again, Galindo was called into action. "So I drove to Los Feliz," he recalled. "When I walked in, Leno LaBianca's body was lying on the floor in front of the couch on the left side, and it was sitting in a huge pool of blood. The couch was full of blood. They bled him dry. I noticed that his head was covered with a pillow slip all the way down over his chest, and I'm thinking about the knife that's supposed to be stuck in his throat. I couldn't see it. Somebody on the premises—maybe an ambulance crewman or another policeman—had seen something and leaked it to the press.

"Rosemary LaBianca's body was in the bedroom," Galindo said. "She had fallen over the far side of the bed. There was a pillowcase over her head, too, and around her neck was an electric cord connected to a bed lamp that had toppled over—not, in my opinion, by a struggle but by Mrs. LaBianca pulling herself into a cavity between the wall and the bed. That's where she died. She was on the floor, partially disrobed, and she had a lot of puncture wounds—there were forty-odd wounds. She bled inwardly. She drowned in her own blood."

On one wall in the living room, written in blood, was "Death to Pigs." On another wall, also written in blood, was the word "Rise." Scraped into Leno's stomach with a fork—a bifurcated carving fork—was the word "War." The fork was stuck in his stomach. It was concluded that the word had been etched into him while he was still alive, because he'd bled through the letters.

In the kitchen, "Death to Pigs" and "Healter Skelter" were scribbled in blood on the refrigerator—of significance was the misspelling of the word "Helter."

"That night I was interviewed by a television reporter," Galindo recalled. "He pointedly asked me, 'Do you think this case is connected to the other one?' He meant Tate. I told him, 'I think it's more of a copycat case.' I introduced that expression, and I've lived with it forever. It was a helluva mistake on my part, because it wasn't until much later that things would begin to fall into place."

Indeed, they would, and it turned out to be far more bizarre than anyone, including this inquisitive and cynical news reporter, could ever have imagined.

YOUNG CHARLIE

"He's not insane. His moral values are extremely twisted and warped, but we shouldn't confuse that with insanity. He's crazy the way Hitler was crazy. He's able to assess his weaknesses and strengths and know exactly what he's doing."

—Vincent Bugliosi, June 10, 2015, interview with
Los Angeles Times writer Patt Morrison

"Other writers have portrayed Mom as a teenage whore. Because she happened to be the mother of Charles Manson, she is down-graded. I prefer to think of her as a flower-child in the 30s, thirty years ahead of her times."

—*Manson In His Own Words,* 1986, Grove Press

"The most compelling, but in some ways the most understandable, member of the family is Manson himself, a man whose life stands as a monument to parental neglect and the failure of the public correctional system."

— Steve Roberts, *New York Times,* January 1970

It is with no relish whatsoever that I consider myself a contemporary of Charles Manson. Just the word "contemporary" somehow conjures up visions of closeness, affinity, kinship, or maybe even intimacy.

Not so.

Without stretching it, a reasonable case could be made for the fact that we are of the same generation and children of the thirties. However, born on continents 4,000 miles apart, our family circumstances and our childhoods couldn't be more dramatically different.

Manson was born November 12, 1934, in Cincinnati General Hospital in Ohio to Ada Kathleen Maddox. She was a peppy but unworldly fifteen-year-old woman-child, who had been reared in a devout, always-obey-your-parents home by her mother, Nancy, and father, Charlie, who worked as a conductor for the Chesapeake & Ohio railroad. But Kathleen possessed a wild streak and got pregnant with the first man she ever dated.

"I was a dumb fifteen-year-old girl who got pregnant," she admitted to the *Los Angeles Times* in January 1971, adding, "I had a tendency to be a little wild, the way kids will."

There was some uncertainty, even mystery, surrounding who actually was the father because the newborn at first had been listed as "No Name Maddox." But barely a month later, the new mother registered a birth certificate listing the child's father as William Manson, who at twenty-five was working for a local dry cleaner and resided simply in Cincinnati. Local gossip suggested the teenager had somehow persuaded him to marry her merely for show: a baby bastard born into a Bible-thumping home invited disgrace to that kind of community.

Thousands of miles away on another continent, I showed up in July 1938 in the London Hospital, in Whitechapel, a working-class neighborhood in the city's blue-collar East End. My father, Oscar Davitsky (who, shortly after arriving in London from Poland, changed his name by deed poll to Davis), claimed to be forty, although family members said he had knocked ten years off his age when he sneaked into England as an illegal immigrant. My mother, Rachel, born in England in

1909, was twenty-eight. Rumor was that her parents, nervous that their plain-looking daughter was getting on in years and might be left on the shelf, called in the local matchmaker to find her a husband.

It worked. They had a big wedding in 1937 and a year later I showed up. Then in September 1939 all hell broke loose when a one-time Austrian house painter with a strange mustache started World War II.

Not surprising, I have no memories of the day the deadliest conflict in human history broke out. However, it took only a few years before the tendrils of that conflagration, which was to stretch on for six more years, came to impact me. Big time.

Beginning in September of 1940, Der Fuhrer ordered his merciless Luftwaffe Air Force to unleash 57 nonstop nights of bombing on old London town. The aim of the blitz was to devastate England, bring it to its knees, and force an immediate surrender. It was a ferocious onslaught, and the citizens of England had seconds only of warning as air raid sirens screeched day and night. Thousands died in the bombings, and thousands of children were swiftly evacuated away from London and Liverpool and the larger British towns, which were home to international shipping ports, to the more, supposedly safe, tranquil countryside. I, however, remained in the densely populated East End of London, as it—along with other strategic shipping centers—came under constant barrage that left our streets with smoldering craters large enough to swallow a red double-decker bus.

Then, as I was about to turn six, and following five long years of war, the heat intensified with a new, terrifying onslaught. Every night in the nine months from June 1944 until March 1945, London again became a city under siege. I vividly recall that, with paraffin lamp in hand, I retired to a bunk bed in the Mickey Mouse of a concrete bomb shelter that my family had built in our back garden. I say "Mickey Mouse" because everyone knew that if a bomb were to make a direct hit, our puny concrete makeshift shelter would have collapsed like a house of cards, burying all within.

The pilotless V-1 "buzz bombs," or doodlebugs as they were called, rained over London with deadly, monotonous regularity. Some nights when I couldn't sleep, I stood with my father on our garden steps as these pilotless drones moved eerily overhead. "Keep moving, keep moving," I screamed into the night because, even at my young age, I knew that once the bombs stopped buzzing, it meant they had run out of fuel and would fall to earth, destroying everything below.

After the war ended in September 1945, my stressed-out parents, I, and my three siblings who were born as war raged on, emerged from the long shellacking and blitzkrieg and desperately tried to find some semblance of normalcy.

On another continent, halfway across the world in the American Midwest, unbeknownst to me, another child was fighting his very own war for survival.

BY THE TIME PEACE was declared in Europe, Harry S. Truman, the 33rd president of the United States, had taken over in the White House from Franklin D. Roosevelt, who had died on April 12, 1945. No bombs had fallen in his neighborhood, but the personal devastation of eleven-year-old Charles Milles Manson had already begun, causing wounds that would never heal.

To many, the story of the Manson childhood reads like a sappy tearjerker. Almost a cliché. Cue the violins. Send in the clowns.

But there was to be no happily-ever-after ending as a backdrop for the final credits. As Manson himself often told it, Oliver Twist toiling in the London workhouse had it cushy compared to *his* life as an abandoned child, bounced coldly from reform school to reform school. Manson was to become the perfect victim. The system in which he was trapped from an early age totally failed to divert the skinny, parentless kid from the shocking but inevitable road mapped out before him.

Here, indeed, was a child who got no normal love and attention, who grew up in a poor, broken home. Neglected. Battered, brutalized, and sodomized in reform schools, leaving him a young man, scarred for life.

In the voluminous literature penned about Manson's beginnings, as well as tomes purportedly in his own words, the conventional wisdom was that the teenage Kathleen Maddox was already pregnant by the time she slept with William Manson. In fact, most agree that the father of her first born was actually a twenty-three-year-old with a smooth line of patter called "Colonel" Walker Henderson Scott from Ashland, Ohio. No officer and gentleman was he—merely an affable young farmer's son who had a silver tongue and an eye for a pretty girl. Part of his *shtick* was to claim he was a real army colonel. Hard to swallow considering his age, but the naïve, virgin Kathleen Maddox bought it hook, line, and sinker.

Besotted by the smooth talking "Colonel," she fell in love, surrendered her virginity, and became pregnant. She never saw him again. Then claiming to be twenty-one and hoping to save her reputation, the pregnant Kathleen quickly hooked up with a dry-cleaning chap. The couple wed on August 21, 1934. By the time the healthy baby showed up some three months later, the new mother had earned a degree of respectability—brief as it was to be—with the arrival of her son.

But the marriage of convenience didn't work. Manson sought a divorce, charging his young wife with "gross neglect of duty," often used to describe behavior that included infidelity, drunkenness, or abandonment during their marriage. So, no longer fettered by marriage and in pursuit of funds, Kathleen and her brother, Luther, who was three years older, launched a nefarious career: she lured men to her room where Luther separated them from their cash and wallets. Shortly, both were jailed for beating up and robbing one of the johns she had picked up in a seedy downtown bar. And baby Charles became motherless.

Then fatherless. William Manson made a swift divorce exit, leaving his son to become an innocent pawn in the grimy game his mother was playing. For most of his childhood, the toddler was shunted from family member to family member. He moved to a new home with his grandmother,

Nancy Maddox, in Ashland, Ohio, some sixty miles from the big smoke of Cleveland. Years later, he was to talk fondly of the only person he said showed him some affection—the doting Nancy. "My grandma was a mountain girl from Kentucky. She never did smoke or drink or cuss or lie...she cooked for the Salvation Army, and she was a human being...I'd go to church...and sweep the floor for her," he told NBC's Tom Snyder in 1981. Then he added, "I did good in reform school."

On the morning of December 7, 1941, shortly after young Charlie's seventh birthday, Japan bombed Pearl Harbor and America jumped into World War II. A year later, as war continued to rage in the Pacific and European theaters, the youngster was feeling like a shuttlecock—bounced once again from his grandmother Nancy in Ashland to his railroad worker uncle Bill Thomas, and his aunt Glenna, who lived in the grimy West Virginia blue-collar town of McMechen on the Ohio River.

Moving in with his aunt and uncle was convenient, for they lived just a few miles from the West Virginia Penitentiary—the grim, Gothic-style prison in Moundsville, where Kathleen and Luther were reluctant residents. The big house was famous for another reason. From time to time, locals could gain access for the area's hottest ticket: watching inmates hang on the local gallows near the prison's North Wagon Gate. Manson was too young to attend those frequent gruesome sideshows, but no doubt he heard about them.

Whenever the kid became too troublesome to handle, he was shunted to the next relative or odd acquaintance who could be persuaded to babysit, until he was reclaimed by Kathleen when she was finally released early for good behavior from her ten-year sentence. Free, and with Charles in tow, she moved to Indianapolis where she quickly shacked up with a traveling salesman. When that didn't last, she shared her bed with an assortment of men, moving from one slummy apartment to another. Nights she often spent away from her son; when she did come home, worse the wear from a night of heavy drinking and carousing, the boy found himself on the receiving end of a beating for one reason or other.

At one point, she felt helpless enough to seek the help of urgent-aid social workers. They took one look and decided she was a danger to herself and her son.

In 1947, the thirteen-year-old Charles took another big step on the well-worn road to abandonment. He had become too difficult a child for his struggling mother to cope with because he kept running away from home and getting up to nefarious things while running wild. Kathleen didn't tell her son, but she decided to make him a county ward, turning the youngster over to the Gibault School for Boys in Terre Haute, Indiana, seventy-odd miles from where the family had been living in Indianapolis. The "school" was run by an order of Catholic priests and founded on a mean-spirited policy that decreed troubled young men could only find the road to salvation with hard beds, cold showers, and frequent beatings, plus daily doses of force-fed religion. Much later, he was to recount his time at Gibault with a series of mostly horrendous stories of beatings until he bled and sexual attacks that left him a whimpering pile on the floor.

So he ran away. Time and again. And each time his mother—despite her son's protestations about turning over a new leaf—sent him back to Gibault. He fled again, and at fourteen, showing remarkable independence for one so young, he moved into a rundown rented room, surviving on odd jobs and frequent small-scale pilfering, plus car theft. Arrested yet again for larceny, the local judge, on being told by Kathleen that her son was completely out of control, suggested that the youngster might benefit from a stay at Boys Town, the well-known school for juveniles located in the suburbs of Omaha.

The place had become famous following the release of the 1938 movie *Boys Town*, with Spencer Tracy playing the devout priest trying to teach tough love to the reprobate Mickey Rooney. A priest at Boys Town remembered the teenage Manson as "a beautiful kid for his age, a warm and friendly boy constantly smiling who won over all of us within days."

Warm or not, he fled from Boys Town after just three days,

accompanied by another resident named Blackie Nelson. When they were picked up in Peoria, Illinois, for stealing food, Manson received the first sentence of what was to become a tradition in his young life: incarceration at the Indiana Boys School Reformatory in Plainfield. Again, he made a habit of escaping. Eighteen times he ran away—and eighteen times he was recaptured, until frustrated authorities turned him over to the feds, who sent him to the National Training School for Boys in Washington, D.C. Benign as the training school sounded, Manson hated the place that offered another dose of the harsh treatment he had experienced at Gibault.

For the next three years, he was shuttled through an assortment of federal reformatories, and was described by those who crossed his path as "ingratiating, but totally unreceptive to training."

STRUGGLING TO FIND his place in the white-bread American Midwest, the twenty-year-old Manson was paroled in May 1954 from the latest of his "residences," the Federal Reformatory in Chillicothe, Ohio, a community best known for its diverse prison system. In the nearby men's jail, Dr. Albert Sabin paid inmates to play guinea pig for a new vaccine he was working on to cure a horrible disease known to the world as polio.

Manson was ill-prepared for the outside world, and the future looked bleak. Now a young adult, he was unschooled and uneducated in the ways of life on the outside. Graduation from the schools of savage knocks left him qualified for nothing. But the one skill he had honed and dedicatedly learned behind bars was one that was to serve him well: the skill of survival.

So Manson continued the only way he knew how—on the petty criminal path. But even in his pock-marked life, there were to be brighter interludes, moments of relief from the harshness of a young, wastrel life spent mostly trying to survive the revolving door of reform schools; a sad existence that had already turned him into a conniving youngster who often felt it was him against the world.

Manson journeyed 170 miles back to the familiarity of the small town of McMechen, where he had once lived with his aunt and uncle.

At first, he seemed to adapt remarkably well, and for a while he led what can only be described as a "normal" lifestyle. Decked out in a crisp clean shirt and tie, the twenty-year-old began attending Nazarene church services with his grandmother Nancy. There, he was exposed to the wild and woolly book of Revelation. It included sermons stressing how God had decreed the importance of women obeying the men in their lives. Or else. Lo and behold, the lad also showed up for Sunday school classes.

Work was poorly paid and hard to come by as he tried his hand at several jobs, including shoveling shit in the stables of Wheeling Downs racetrack. Still, he managed to stay out of trouble. His daily routine was so ordinary, in fact, that as 1955 was in its infancy, the one-time troublemaker landed a role he'd never played before: dutiful husband.

Rosalie Willis was the girl who caught his eye. She was the fifteen-year-old daughter of a Manson friend named Clarence "Cowboy" Willis who had scandalized the town by divorcing his wife and abandoning his three daughters. Rosalie worked in a local grocery store, and when they took out a marriage license in January 1955, she said she was seventeen. It was winkingly acknowledged that she was at least two years younger. The almost clichéd standard wedding photo revealed a happy, clean-cut and handsome young man with a well-coiffed head of hair, nattily dressed in light jacket and tie. He was clasping the hand of his pretty, smiling brunette bride—a good three inches taller—who was wearing a sleeveless, white, ankle-length dress, adorned with flowers.

They posed smiling, cutting a two-tiered wedding cake.

In the months after his marriage, Manson, for the first time in his life, tried to earn a legal living as a normal newlywed. In McMechen, they rented an apartment and Manson took whatever part-time jobs he could find to boost his income. He even bought a guitar and began strumming as he taught himself to play. Years later Manson was to make the marriage sound like a storybook romance. And maybe it was: "It was a good life, and I enjoyed the role of going off to work every morning and coming home to my wife," he told Nuel Emmons, author of *Manson in His Own Words: The Shocking Confessions of "The Most Dangerous Man Alive."* "She was a super girl who didn't make any demands, but we were both just a couple of kids."

The new Mrs. Manson became pregnant. Earlier, with a view to supporting this burgeoning family, he began to hone some of the other skills he had learned at reform schools. Stealing cars proved particularly profitable, as he grabbed them in one state and sold them in another for a fast buck.

His on-again, off-again mother Kathleen didn't show up for the wedding because she had moved to California. In July 1955, Manson headed to the West Coast to show off his new bride. Unfortunately, and true to form for young Charlie, LA cops ran a check on the out-of-state license plate and discovered the car was stolen. He was once again in a real mess—and facing a battery of interstate legal problems.

Pleading mercy and leniency claiming his wife was expecting their first child—she did give birth in March 1956 to a son, Charles Jr., but Manson was in jail at the time—he claimed that he took his impending fatherhood responsibilities quite seriously. He conned the court into giving him five years probation.

But driving stolen cars over state lines still dogged him. Rather than willingly go to California to face the music, he fled once again, this time to Indianapolis where, after a brief interlude as a fugitive, he was arrested again in late 1956 on the California warrant and extradited to Los Angeles for arraignment.

This time there was no mercy. He was now twenty-one and an adult, and the judge—ignoring pleas of family responsibilities—hit him with a three-year sentence.

Strangely for Manson, being sent to prison in Southern California turned into something of a blessing in disguise.

For his new home was to be Terminal Island Prison in San Pedro, on the outskirts of Los Angeles. And Manson made the best of it. During his incarceration, he learned that his wife Rosalie had divorced him, taking his son with her.

The abandonment, yet again, stung badly; however, Terminal Island turned out to be Charles Manson's finishing school, and he discovered there were hidden benefits to be obtained behind the walls of that prison.

He was now a veteran of the U.S. prison system, and having tasted life on the West Coast, albeit most of the time locked up as a guest in Terminal Island, he was to leave the jail much wiser. The institution was to eventually become his gateway to San Francisco where he was to savor a new lifestyle, which included lots of drugs, endless women, and free love.

CURTAIN CALL FOR
THE SIXTIES

*"The smog was heavy, my eyes were weeping from it, the sun was hot,
the air stank, a regular hell is L.A."*
—Jack Kerouac, *The Dharma Bums*

In 1956 at age twenty-one, Charles Manson moved to the Coast.
Or, rather, he had been unwillingly moved. His new home was the
low-security Terminal Island federal prison in balmy San Pedro, just
twenty-odd miles from California's fabled golden beaches. Even Manson
was impressed with his new digs compared to the other sleazy joints
he had inhabited. His roommates included pimps, drug peddlers, and
white-collar criminals—inmates not considered violent. And it had a
separate wing for women. Compared to his other residences, Manson
called it "paradise."

It also meant he wasn't far from his mother when she deigned to visit
him, which became more and more rare. And while Rosalie's visits with
their new baby Charles, Jr. also quickly diminished, and he was later to
discover that she had divorced him while he was incarcerated, he found
benefits he had never anticipated. The education of Charles Manson was
about to get quite a boost, compliments of the U.S. government; prison
became a finishing school and college for surviving behind bars without
damage to life and limb. He was able to improve his musical skills, and

he began singing and composing songs; and somewhere along the way, he discovered there was more to life than the con game. He was particularly intrigued by books about assorted mystical philosophers, diverse and strange religious sects, even dabbling early with L. Ron Hubbard's soon-to-be-controversial Scientology.

He hit the jackpot when he signed up for every Terminal Island convict's most wanted topic: a Dale Carnegie correspondence course, based on his bestselling 1936 book, *How to Win Friends and Influence People*. For Manson, it was like striking gold. He thrived on it and couldn't get enough. Though he'd had no formal education, he quickly glommed onto the writer-lecturer's simple philosophy—that anyone's behavior can be changed by one's behavior toward them. As Carnegie wrote, "Make the other person feel important" and, "The only way to get the best of an argument is to avoid it."

It was to be his master class on the basic rules for manipulating people without resorting to threats or brute strength, and it resonated strongly. In fact, he already had been practicing it with some degree of success by the mere fact that he had survived his tortured jailhouse life. It would serve him well almost a decade later when he was able to convince his acolytes to commit a series of heinous murders—and then, with outraged, wide-eyed innocence, declare that he was no killer because he had wielded neither gun nor knife.

One edict, lifted straight from the book, was to become his mantra as he bathed in the media spotlight after *Life* magazine labeled him "The Most Dangerous Man Alive" more than a decade later, in June 1970: "You have to use showmanship. The movies do it. Radio does it. And you will have to do it if you want attention—dramatize your ideas."

And there was one other topic at Terminal Island that never offered a formal correspondence course but might have been titled, "Pimping 101." Manson sat at the feet and picked the brains of some of the most successful pimps who had stumbled their way to the top, and now with lots of time to kill, were only too happy to pass on their accumulated wisdom about mastering the art of managing hookers to a keen student like Manson. Techniques he learned in these sessions were to serve him in good stead when it came to managing his own Family.

"Make them love you—as well as fear you," was a favorite Manson dictate.

Manson was released early for good behavior in September 1958 after serving two years and five months of his three-year sentence. Given his freedom, the graduate of Pimping 101 began his new life rounding up a small harem of women and selling sex. He hooked up with a prostitute, who gave birth to his second child, and they eventually split up. He worked at finding jobs that paid in cash and didn't require tax returns, but less than a year later he landed in trouble again, this time for forging a check for less than fifty bucks. But worse, for violating the federal Mann Act—transporting women across state lines for prostitution purposes. This time, freedom lasted just three years, for in June 1961, he was convicted and sentenced to ten years for violation of the Mann Act. This time his accommodation was not so convenient, nor close to the attractions of the Los Angeles entertainment capital. His new digs: a cell at McNeil Island Penitentiary in Washington.

McNeil was Washington's answer to Alcatraz, without offering inmates top-tier celebrity mobsters like Al Capone or Mickey Cohen, or even the scenic skyline of San Francisco seemingly just a short swim away. Still, utilizing everything he had learned from the Carnegie course, he was better able to cope with the McNeil environment, claiming time in the library and again becoming an avid student of Scientology. Many times he read from front to back L. Ron Hubbard's *Dianetics: The Modern Science of Mental Health*. Hubbard's techniques, like Carnegie's tome, seemed to make absolute sense to him.

Jail also allowed him time to practice on his guitar, even compose music. He received musical tutelage from McNeil's resident high-profile mobster, Alvin "Creepy" Karpis, a Depression-era gangster and an able guitar-plucker to boot. Karpis, once the FBI's Public Enemy No. 1, earned his nickname from his weird and sinister smile; he earned time in prison for heading up one of the most formidable gangs of the 1930s, known for killing, shooting, robbing, stealing, and kidnapping.

Listening to the radio was also permitted, which brought him the current crop of hit singers like the pure, clear, clarion-voiced Frankie Laine, whose hits like *High Noon* and *Rawhide* particularly appealed to Manson, and whom he tried to emulate. But in particular, he was drawn to a new group of singers from Liverpool, England, who had taken America by storm in February 1964, when they appeared on the tube's top variety show, featuring a wooden-faced host by the name of Ed Sullivan. It is likely that Manson, as an inmate at the jail, had access to a communal TV, and was one of the 73 million TV viewers who was charmed by the Beatles' TV appearance. He certainly had become enamored by their beat, their funny accents and clever witticisms, and as an avid listener to pop stations, he became addicted to their music. But, above all else, he was impressed and also mystified by the ceaseless screaming from overwrought and passionate young girls in the audience who flew into endless fits of hysteria at the very sight of those skinny young men in their tight suits and their mop-like haircuts. Accents and haircuts aside, he was much taken by their music.

The Sixties, of course, offered Manson more than just the sensational success of the Beatles invasion. But for the most part, the inveterate prisoner and his fellow inmates were fighting for their own kind of survival, cloistered as they were, against the daily insanities making the front pages of newspapers around the world. And in the Sixties, much was coming down fast in the outside world.

In October 1962, the nation watched in horror as the Cuban missile crisis unfolded, and the world teetered on the brink of nuclear annihilation until a heroic John F. Kennedy faced down Russia's Nikita Khrushchev. Nikita blinked first, and the world marched forward. That same month, James Meredith became the first African American to enroll in Ole Miss—escorted to his classes by 500 (yes, 500!) US marshals. It was a big news story and as a young reporter I was smuggled onto the campus, posing as a student, and got a frontline view as the campus was turned into a battleground of riots, fires, and gunfire. When dawn broke there were two dead and the National Guard crushed protesters while trying to restore order.

On November 22, 1963, JFK was killed in broad daylight in Dallas. His assassin, Lee Harvey Oswald, was captured, taken into police custody, and then killed two days later on live TV with nightclub owner Jack Ruby pulling the trigger at point-blank range in the basement of the Dallas police station. How Jack Ruby was running free in the innards of the cops' lair was open to speculation. Ruby swore he did it—with a straight face and oodles of righteous indignation—because he was so distraught by Oswald's evil act. A mere three months later, in February 1964, those four mop-topped young men from far-off Liverpool entranced viewers from coast to coast on *The Ed Sullivan Show*. The British rock invasion had begun.

And then, in March 1965, America sent combat troops to Vietnam, and the country was soon embroiled in an unpopular war in godforsaken, never-heard-of-the-place-before, spots like Hue or the Ia Drang Valley. Vietnam was geographically far away, yet on our doorstep thanks to the nightly news as network anchors, almost by rote, offered us the latest American body counts.

For escape, there was a new drug in town: lysergic acid diethylamide—better known as LSD. The guru of this doozy of a hallucinogenic was a slightly bombastic, high-profile Harvard psychologist named Timothy Leary who delightedly extolled the virtues of dropping acid: "Turn on, tune in, drop out." In an ironic twist, according to an article Leary penned for *Oui* magazine in August 1976, the high priest of LSD found himself a neighbor of Charles Manson in 1972. Their lodgings were cells in Folsom Prison.

The emergence of acid perfectly coincided with the growing popularity of a group in the outer fringes of California, the "hippies."

They were tuning in, all right—into sex, drugs, and all sorts of bizarre philosophies. Birth-control pills had come into the picture, which meant that copulation didn't necessarily lead to childbirth. And while all this was being played out, Manson was switching jails: Terminal Island to McNeil Island and then back to Terminal Island.

UNAFFECTED BY THE OUTSIDE WORLD, happily distracted by music, library time, and already dreaming of becoming a rock star, Manson impressed some of his jailers, who quoted his passion for music as the sole reason for his good behavior. So, in May 1966—with the rest of America still roiling ferociously about the war in Southeast Asia, and young men and women marching in the streets of America to protest the unwinnable war thousands of miles from their doorstep—Manson, after finishing six years of his ten-year prison sentence, was given something of a reprieve. As a result of his good behavior at McNeil, he was transferred back to Terminal Island in June 1966.

For Manson, arriving back at Terminal Island that summer was, strangely, a homecoming of sorts. There were many new faces, including a live-wire thirty-one-year-old inmate serving time for dealing drugs. Nashville native Phil Kaufman was also in the record business, and in him Manson quickly found a musical kindred spirit. Kaufman, who was later to serve as a gofer for the Rolling Stones and road manager for the Flying Burrito Brothers and Emmylou Harris, hit it off with Manson, who was desperately looking for the right connections into the rock world. In Kaufman, he found someone who might indeed be his passport.

Kaufman talked about the time he first set eyes on Manson in his 1993 autobiography, *Road Mangler Deluxe*. "There was this guy playing guitar in the yard one day at Terminal Island. And it was Charlie, singing his ass off," Kaufman recalled. "He had an old guitar with all kinds of writing on it, all kinds of songs. And the guards kept taking it away from him, saying, 'If you play it in this place at this time, you are violating this rule.' They had these rules, so you'd continually know that you were captive."

Kaufman opined that Manson was a very bad guitar player but capable enough as a singer/songwriter to have a chance of getting a record contract.

"Charlie had done seven and a half years on a ten-year sentence for a $15.00 postal check, and when he got out, I sent him to (producer Gary Stromberg) a friend at Universal to record him. And they did record him," Kaufman wrote. "He went in and did three hours of tapes, and they wanted him to do some more, but he just split one day. He and the girls. He had a big black bus at the time, and they traveled a lot. This was in 1967. He showed up a year later in another studio, but after he recorded, he split again and never signed anything. We tried to sell Charlie's music a long time ago, but we never could get him to sit down and do it. Now at least, we got him sitting down."

As soon as Kaufman was sprung from jail, he went looking for Manson, who had been paroled from Terminal Island a year earlier.

I got out of jail in March 1968 and joined Charlie a couple of weeks later in Topanga. By that time he had gone to San Francisco and was back. The Family was pretty much the same as now except none of the same guys were there. The original girl was Mary [Brunner], then Lyn [Fromme]. There was Patty Krenwinkel. Sandy [Good] came right after I did in '68. Sandy came with a friend of Charlie's and never went back. The friend went back alone. There were about 12 girls. Every time Charlie saw a girl he liked, he'd tell someone, 'Get that girl.' And when they brought her back, Charlie would take her out in the woods and talk to her for an hour or two. And she would never leave.

After the Manson murder story broke and the names of those indicted were published, Kaufman declared: "When I looked at the papers and read the names of the perpetrators and their accomplices, I realized that I'd had sex with every one of those murderesses."

Kaufman was a keen observer of Manson's style in jail and said he was like a chess master among the inmates. "In lockup you have to be aware of everything, and so when Charlie came out he was like a caged tiger. Nothing got by him," Kaufman said.

If something happened within 100 miles of him, he made sure he knew about it. Whenever he came into a new room, he made sure to case it. He always sat with his back to the wall, making sure where the windows were and how to get out fast.

Prison was his training ground. He was a tiny guy and the target of all the biggest, bullying jail shits, the guys on power trips who wanted to trample you to death within a week. Charlie was a midget physically, so skinny he could have slipped through the cell bars. But he soon developed the gift of the gab that gave him power over the six-foot brutalizers.

Later Kaufman was to tell the story—apocryphal or not—of a guard who once taunted Manson that he would never get out. Manson barely blinked, kept strumming his guitar and softly said: "Get out of where?"

"Prison," Kaufman explained, "either makes you very weak or strong, and Charlie learned the ropes. And you quickly discover your explosion point—and the kind of power you can wield."

Eventually, Kaufman was to fall foul of the wrath of Manson over the release of *Lie: The Love and Terror Cult*, a 1970 album of Manson's self-penned songs. Manson said he had been ripped off by Kaufman and had never seen a penny from the producer. Kaufman said he never made any money off the album, which was a gigantic flop—only 3,000 copies were pressed. Today, of course, it's become a pricy collector's item in the world of Manson memorabilia.

When Manson finally walked out of Terminal Island a free man, he was brimming over with all the psychological claptrap he'd absorbed behind bars, and the youth of Aquarius were ripe for the picking. This after all, was The Summer of Love.

Freedom appealed to him and he travelled from San Francisco to Los Angeles in a school bus with windows painted black, recruiting discontented women into his growing movement. In between, according to a December 1969 *Los Angeles Times* story after his arrest, Manson had actually held a few jobs. One was as a bartender in Hollywood, another as a door-to-door refrigerator salesman. A third—which beggars belief—was as a ballroom dance instructor, although where the ex-con might have acquired skills enabling him to become a convincing Fred Astaire sounded like a figment of someone's fevered imagination.

In 1968 America was once again plunged into violent political chaos. In April 1968, Martin Luther King was assassinated at a Memphis hotel, and the same month Manson was behind bars—albeit briefly. He had crashed his bus in a ditch in Point Mugu, California, and soon after there were reports that several naked women were running wild on the local beach with a tiny newborn baby. Ventura County cops arrested Manson and several of the women with him on charges of "disorderly conduct and not having proper identification." The week-old baby belonging to Mary Brunner was placed in protective custody. When cops discovered the bus was not stolen, Manson and his entourage hit the road again.

Two months later, in June 1968, another national figure was murdered. John Kennedy's brother Bobby was gunned down in the kitchen pantry of the Ambassador Hotel in Los Angeles on June 6 by Jordanian citizen Sirhan Sirhan. It was a scene forever etched in my mind as I followed Bobby into the kitchen as a foreign correspondent covering his fateful presidential campaign.

Manson, the perpetual offender against society and scarred by a lifetime of hard knocks and brutality, was about to finally and irrevocably opt out of a society in which he had never fit—a society that he said had turned him into a human garbage bin. He quickly realized that, much to his amazement, this was a whole new world where his jailhouse education would make him king of any particular castle he chose. Manson, fresh out of the pen, bore absolutely no resemblance to the wild-eyed, scraggly bearded, self-proclaimed prophet who was to etch himself into our memories. The man licking his lips as he surveyed the scantily clad young ladies of Haight-Ashbury was a clean-shaven, good-looking in an emaciated way, soft-voiced stranger, who appeared much younger than his thirty-two years.

Empowered by a lifetime behind bars and more and more aware of his own ability to master other human beings who had not benefited from the survive-or-die prison structure, he arrived in Berkeley and San Francisco and quickly found it was just too easy to manipulate this army of youthful hippies, throwaways and runaways who were seeking—not sure what, other than a good time.

Suckers, easy prey, waiting to be conned. His prison education was not going to waste, especially when it came to matters of his libido.

In the spring of '67, Charles Milles Manson discovered a new Wonderland, his very own Garden of Eden. And lots of confused Eves queuing up to offer plenty of bites of the apple.

The Sixties had become a tantalizing elixir to anyone willing to sip and sup. Down south in Los Angeles was where all the music action was; however, it came with the stinking, gray, polluted air called smog, not unlike London's very own pea-soup fog, only not quite as thick. Each day, summer and fall, it settled in the Los Angeles basin—foul air and exhaust fumes, trapped by the surrounding mountains with its lid of hot air. When it got so thick, and "smog alerts" were declared, locals donned masks, and schoolchildren and oldsters were advised to stay home.

And then the terrible topper: In the Summer of 1969, in the rarified precincts of Benedict Canyon where someone once observed, "It was so quiet you could hear the sound of ice tinkling in martini glasses," there was the gruesome mass murder involving a beautiful, blonde, and very pregnant film actress, along with her friends, including one of Hollywood's most famous hairstylists.

David Brinkley, one half of the Huntley-Brinkley News on the NBC TV network, invaded the living rooms of America to announce in December 1969 the abrupt conclusion to the free-for-all Sixties.

"In California, five members of a so-called religious cult including Charles Manson, the guru or high priest, have been indicted for the murder of Sharon Tate and six others," he intoned. And the perpetrators: "The involvement of a mystical hippie clan which despised the straight, affluent society. Young girls supposedly under the influence of a bearded Svengali, who allegedly masterminded the seven murders...."

A brutal curtain had slammed down on the most tumultuous decade in centuries.

Director Roman Polanski's life was filled with tragedy.

POLANSKI: THE
HOMECOMING

"That's all. I am sorry for being so long…but I have to tell you what has been on my mind."

—Roman Polanski, August 19, 1969, press
conference

Just a few days after Roman Polanski first stepped over the threshold of his own "House of Blood" on Cielo Drive, I was on hand to witness an extraordinary event which unfolded on August 19, 1969. It was the emotional, self-imposed, near self-immolation of Roman Polanski, played out dramatically in front of a packed house of journalists.

It was high drama. Ignoring the advice of every one of his friends and advisors, the wan-faced thirty-six-year-old director decided to place himself on the torture rack. The chamber he chose was weird: under several ornate chandeliers in the thickly carpeted, elegant ballroom of the tony Beverly Wilshire Hotel in the heart of Beverly Hills. His audience was to be some fifty-plus TV, radio, and print reporters who had hurriedly assembled to see Polanski and hear what he had to say.

As I look back today, Polanski was in serious grief, but this was a weird manifestation. His presence fanned the flames. And his words threw gasoline on the fire.

The tension was high as Polanski slowly stepped in front of a lectern with microphones spilling over it and began to speak softly, almost incomprehensibly at first. Although *speak* didn't quite describe it. He talked in a strangled, anguished voice, barely able to deliver his words.

Wearing a smart gray double-breasted suit and tie, hands dug deeply into his pockets, he had decided to face the press in what he viewed as an odd kind of rebuttal to the "Live Freaky, Die Freaky" school of journalism accusations that had been flung his way since the grisly discovery of August 9.

Since the murder story broke, there had been little for the media to sink their teeth into. The crumbs, however, were tantalizing: drugs, orgies, wild sex parties, ritual slaughter. It led to that "Live Freaky, Die Freaky" assessment, which basically suggested that the killings were the inevitable penalty one paid for living a lewd, lascivious, and dissolute kind of life.

It was "Hollywood Babylon" revisited. The media smelled blood, and were relentless in pursuit of finding proof.

The stories had played out all over the globe, rattling on the wire services and running on the front pages of the *London Daily Express*, *The New York Times*, and *Le Monde*, touting drug-fueled orgies and the recovery of vast caches of illegal contraband. You name it, they printed it.

Polanski brushed back his dark, tousled hair and nervously fingered his deep sideburns, staring blankly like a zombie.

He began slowly, ever so cautiously, with a soft voice: "Frykowski and Jay Sebring smoked (he paused, having a hard time uttering their names) pot sometimes. I saw them doing it...in my house there were parties. They did smoke pot...and I must tell you, furthermore, I was not at a Hollywood party where someone didn't smoke pot. But not Sharon. She did not use drugs; she didn't touch alcohol; she didn't smoke cigarettes. The last film she made was not a happy experience for her, but her greatest pictures she was doing...was her pregnancy...I have never seen anyone so preoccupied with it." He choked yet again.

Confronting the ravenous media horde was probably not a wise choice given his emotional fragility—that and the fact that he had been pumped full of added doses of tranquilizers ever since he landed at Los Angeles International Airport a week earlier, accompanied by pals Warren Beatty and Victor Lownes, the American-born boss of Europe's Playboy empire. The pain was clearly etched on his pale face, yet he somehow felt he had to get it out. He targeted the media—awaiting every word.

"Shame on those for writing those horrible things," Polanski scolded. Fighting back the tears, he continued, "I spoke to Sharon a few hours before the tragedy. It was the only time of true happiness I had in my life. And the last few years I spent with her." Overwhelmed by tears, he stopped again.

"You all know how beautiful she was. But only few of you know how good she was. Sharon was vulnerable. She couldn't refuse any friendship. There was always Sharon and the dogs and friends waiting for me when I was coming back from the studio."

He talked glowingly of his wife's pregnancy and said anyone visiting the house would see "innumerable books on natural birth...baby clothes...and the room she was painting for the child."

No matter how tragic the circumstances were, what had further exacerbated the media-versus-Polanski aggressive vibes was that a story broke hours earlier that on Polanski's return to his rented home he was not alone: the grieving widower was accompanied by Tommy Thompson, the Texas-born *Life* magazine writer, who went on to become a bestselling true crime author with his book, *Blood and Money*.

As Polanski ushered Thompson through the Cielo front door, he cynically told the writer, "This must be the world famous orgy house."

Also along for the home visit was the magazine's young photographer, Julian Wasser, who took a series of photos of the inside of the house, as well as a bunch of Polaroid pictures.

Polanski was documenting his most intimate grief in a very public way to a bunch of strangers, and it was just flat-out incomprehensible. And it only got more bizarre.

When Polanski approved the Polaroids that had been taken, Wasser handed them over to another member of the exclusive group of visitors that included Hollywood psychic Peter Hurkos. The Dutchman living in California, after studying the Polaroids, was later to announce: "Three men killed Sharon Tate and the other four, and I know who they are. I have identified the killers to police and told them the men must be stopped soon; otherwise, they will kill again."

Hurkos claimed that they were friends of Sharon who killed under the influence of LSD. And the killings took place while participants were involved in some kind of black magic rituals. Polanski might have blamed the press for writing horrible stories, but his new friend didn't help matters in the image department.

Much later, police revealed that Mr. Hurkos had not communicated with them, offering them his predictions; and if he had, they most likely would have shown him the door. On August 27, another celebrity got in on the act. Truman Capote, author of the acclaimed 1959 true crime best seller *In Cold Blood*, popped up with Johnny Carson, host of the popular *The Tonight Show* on NBC, to offer his expert opinion on whodunit. Admitting his version was based solely on everything he had gleaned from press reports, Capote declared the killings were the work of one person—young, enraged and paranoid—who held a grudge against the residents, adding, "Something happened to trigger a kind of instant paranoia."

Sometime after, photographer Wasser offered his version of what happened at that photo shoot: "When I went up there for *Life* magazine, Roman asked me to take Polaroid shots of the scene as well and give them to a psychic who could study them and find out who the killers were. You can see my Polaroid on the chair beside Roman.

"At that point, no one knew the murders had been committed by the Manson Family. The police couldn't figure out anything. The knives and the bloody clothes were found by an ABC camera crew. There was this kind of New Age belief at the time: 'The cops aren't up to it; we'll get psychic vibrations instead. The police, the establishment, they're not like us—we're artistic; we're special. We'll do it our special way.'

"I went with Roman through all the rooms, all the belongings, all the photographs, and shot him looking at it all. When he went into the nursery, he opened a drawer and it was full of beautiful pictures of Sharon. She was such a good-looking girl. And he started crying. It really hit him, the loss. I felt awful, like, my God, why was I there? What an invasion of privacy. But that's what being a professional is. You feel terrible, but you still shoot. You're a journalist, an observer—you're not a participant, you can't be someone's pal.

"Hollywood was afraid because they didn't know what was going on. They thought it was a strange cult that was going to kill everybody. It led to security mania, everybody putting in special alarm systems. If you said hi to someone in the street, they'd think you were another Manson. Total paranoia.

"But I didn't hear anyone say, 'Oh, that poor Polanski. He's been through so much.' I used to live in Paris and I still visit there a lot. I see Polanski around, but I don't talk to him. I don't want to remind him of how he knows me. Hopefully, he's forgotten all that."

But worse was to come. Days later those same Polaroids given to Hurkos popped up in a story about the murders and Hurkos's "crucial" involvement in helping police solve the case in the pages of the *Hollywood Citizen News*.

All the media, excluded from the murder house, perceived the appearance of the prestigious *Life* magazine on the scene as a Polanski sellout. What was he playing at? What normal grieving husband would behave like that? It was disgusting that this "aggrieved husband" was peddling this most private of personal stories to the highest bidder. Whatever sympathy he had from the media soon dissipated.

Life did run the "exclusive" story and pictures from inside and outside the house in its August 29, 1969, edition, and a spokesman categorically declared: "*Life* did not buy the photographs from the film director, nor did they have any contractual agreement with Polanski for the pictures." I felt it was a case of he doth protest too much.

Polanski was to explain later that he was friends with Thompson and thought that by allowing Hurkos to study the Polaroids of the interior of the house, the psychic might be able to lead cops to the real killers. That excuse was hard to swallow; but Polanski obviously was not thinking with any kind of logic.

Back in the packed hotel ballroom, Polanski, still facing the battery of microphones, soldiered on: "The house is open now…you can go and see the orgy place….he said cynically, his voice laced with irony. "You will see lots of blood all over the place…and baby clothes. That's all. I am sorry for being so long, but I have to tell you what has been on my mind."

He said he had planned to fly back to Los Angeles the following week in time for the baby's arrival—and to celebrate his 36th birthday on August 18. "Sharon told me, 'a little kitten came from the hills' and they were trying to feed it with an eyedropper."

He vehemently claimed there was no party planned the night of the murders. "Police found a few glasses—maybe six—used. Does that look like a party?"

Polanski should have ended his press conference, but he kept on talking. He said when he and his wife first went to Europe four months earlier, they decided to let Frykowski stay at the house and care for their dogs. Sharon, he said, had made a movie in Rome called *The Thirteen Chairs* and then went to London for a film he was prepping.

"By that time she was six months pregnant," Polanski said. "I put her on the boat, the Queen Elizabeth Second, and that's the last time I saw her."

Polanski said he called his wife frequently—so much so, "that my telephone bill is reaching astronomical figures.

"Sharon started to attend natural childbirth classes—and I was going to go with her. I don't know too much about it," he said as tears rolled down his cheeks, "but she said I had to go to those classes."

Unprompted, he spoke briefly of his friend Wojciech Frykowski who, like Polanski, had escaped from Poland as a child. They met in Paris where Polanski was establishing a career as a movie maker and he gave Frykowski a job on his film set. He was blunt about his friend: "Wojciech was a very nice human being who wanted success but had little talent. There was little I could do for him except give him money and encouragement."

He said Frykowski and Folger had lived on Cielo Drive for around four months and were there while both he and Sharon were overseas.

And though Polanski's criticism of Frykowski and the sensationalized news coverage of the murders were harsh, he had only praise for another group of people.

After almost twenty-five minutes of talk, he paused and his voice lifted: "People who show me the most heart and understanding…and change a lot of my opinions what in certain circles, we call 'fuzz.' The cops were really very, very good…thank you, gentlemen."

And that was it.

No follow-up questions allowed, although the hostility in the room toward him was very palpable. When it was all over, as he was about to leave the hotel, Polanski walked past Mary Neiswender, a crime reporter for the *Long Beach Press Telegram*.

She would later recall that Beverly Wilshire Hotel conference in her 2012 book, *Assassins, Serial Killers…Corrupt Cops*. To her, it seemed that Polanski might have put on a big act.

She told me, "When I saw Polanski leaving the hotel, his tears were all gone. I saw him turn to a friend and inquire, 'How did I do?' as if looking for some kind of applause at the end of a convincing performance."

I didn't see what she saw; but based on what I had seen play out in the ballroom, I believe Neiswender's evaluation was slightly off. Watching in the room, I can state categorically it was not an act. Sure, Polanski took time to castigate the media—and rightly so in many cases because, in pursuit of new angles daily, many published stories exaggerated beyond belief, with complete disregard for the suffering or sensitivities of loved ones like Polanski. I had carefully observed his anguish and viewed it as a sad and plaintive cry for help from a man in a deep state of shock.

Later, Mia Farrow, his *Rosemary's Baby* leading lady, who knew the couple well, explained it this way: "Roman was so insecure about so many things," she said. "About his childhood and his family. He didn't have a blueprint for life that others had.

"We loved them both. His future was her and them. Then suddenly he was disintegrating and everything in his life just collapsed."

And the same could be said for the police investigation into the murders.

FEAR AND LOATHING
IN HOLLYWOOD

"This hit the movie community very deeply. On a 10-point scale, it disturbed me at around a 27. Jay Sebring, Sharon, Abigail and Voytek were friends of mine. It was something that happened, and no one knew why... The collective response to these killings was what you might expect if a small nuclear device had gone off."
> —Warren Beatty, to Steve Oney, *Los Angeles* magazine

"Whispers that a psychotic killer was after wealthy residents of isolated homes in the Hollywood Hills continued after the murder of Miss Tate and the four others was followed a day later by that of a rich supermarket owner and his wife in a plush home 12 miles away."
> —Bruce Russell, West Coast Bureau Chief, Reuters

Just days after the slaughter on Cielo Drive, I went to the only place I knew where I might take the true pulse of the Hollywood community—The Daisy. The unofficial "village pump," it was located at 326 North Rodeo Drive in Beverly Hills, and the nightly gossip and innuendo there was fierce.

Back in the Forties and Fifties, Number 326 was Romanoff's, the flashy and popular eating place of such top stars as Gable, Cooper, Garbo, Tracy, and Hepburn, run by a likable con man named Michael Romanoff. Romanoff claimed he was from Russian royalty, but in reality he was a shrewd pants-presser from Brooklyn named Hershel Geguzin.

In the early sixties, the location was taken over by a charismatic salesman named Jack Hanson, who parlayed a modest *schmatta* business into high-end fashions for women. Hanson was the creator of Jax Slax—tight pedal pushers that zipped up the back—and thigh-high mini-skirts, popular because they emphasized the female derriere. Hanson's client list included Marilyn Monroe, Katharine Hepburn, and Jackie O, and he ran his profitable business on the prime real-estate corner of Wilshire Boulevard and Bedford Drive with his wife Sally, a shrewd fashion designer. He opened The Daisy as a "veddy, veddy" private, members-only nightclub for his pals, and his 1934 Rolls Royce was always parked outside the front door.

It had food, music, and a great bar, as well as an upmarket pool hall, and it flourished from day one, drawing Movieland's power brokers seeking the refuge to boogie far from the prying eyes of the paparazzi who were allowed only as far as the front curb. Nancy Sinatra once declared: "The most important men in America are my father, Hugh Hefner, and Jack Hanson." Indeed, on any given night, even during the week, you'd see Steve McQueen, Robert Redford, Natalie Wood, or Omar Sharif. Producer Aaron Spelling (*The Love Boat*, *Charlie's Angels*) and his wife Candy, whose later claim to fame was the construction of a 123-room house just a mile away, were also regulars. I went there one night to confirm that there was a tight relationship between Warren Beatty and the beautiful *Darling* British star, Julie Christie. John Derek liked to show off his new bride Linda Evans. Even fussy Zsa Zsa Gabor liked the place, as did Joan Cohn (widow of the fearsome ex-Columbia boss, Harry), who often showed up with her boy toy paramour, Brit actor Laurence Harvey, whom she later married. The Brits liked The Daisy as well—Twiggy, the fashion beanpole; Michael Caine, still in his *Alfie* bachelor mode; Joan Collins, not long out of Warren Beatty mode and, at the time, married to actor/singer Anthony Newley, all made it their unofficial home away from home.

Sinatra frequently showed up with his entourage and when he brought Mia Farrow along one night, it signaled something more serious was afoot. It was at The Daisy that writer Gay Talese centered his landmark piece, "Frank Sinatra Has a Cold," for *Esquire* in April 1966. It was also at The Daisy in the Seventies where O.J. Simpson took a shine to an eighteen-year-old waitress named Nicole Brown.

And Jay Sebring used to take Sharon Tate there before her marriage to Roman Polanski. Hanson, always the epitome of discretion as far as his famous clients and customers were concerned, confided in me after the murders: "Both I and Sally were friends with Roman, and I know it was the crowd from the Daisy that went in and out of the house on Cielo Drive."

Robert Evans, the head of Paramount Pictures, told me shortly after the murders: "Everyone I know—me included—who lived within a couple of square miles of that house went into immediate anaphylactic shock. They were shitting bricks."

Evans was a close pal of Polanski, who had directed *Rosemary's Baby* at his studio in 1968. And when the distraught Polanski, jet-lagged and zonked out on tranquilizers, flew back into Los Angeles from London twenty-four hours after learning of the death of his wife, it was Evans who arranged for him to hide out, first at Evans's mansion off Coldwater Canyon, and then in Julie Andrews' dressing room on the Paramount lot.

"Jack is freaking out," said Evans, referring to his buddy Jack Nicholson, who lived in isolated splendor just a couple miles up Benedict Canyon, on the remote Mulholland Drive. Nicholson had bought his three-acre property in July 1969—just days before the murders. His next-door neighbor was Marlon Brando, who, if he wasn't working on a movie, was ready to flee to the safety and isolation of Tetiaroa, his Tahitian island retreat.

And it didn't help that the mighty Los Angeles Police Department seemed clueless. For weeks, nay, months, it had little to say about two crimes that were obsessing homicide investigators at headquarters in Parker Center. Mostly following drug leads, investigators were flying hither and thither to Jamaica and Canada in search of suspects, one of whom was a boyfriend of Cass Elliot of the Mamas and the Papas. But each time, they came back empty-handed and none the wiser. They were, quite frankly, unable to link the crimes, confused and baffled by the fact that murder number one was in a canyon, tucked away in Beverly Hills, and the second, a dozen miles away. Despite some similarities, including the telltale victims' blood daubed on walls, it was a case of never the twain shall meet.

From August to December 1969, until members of the Manson family were arrested, Tate and Polanski's friends were asking numbly: "Who is gonna be next?" Nervous friends like Warren Beatty and Peter Sellers, who lived not far from the murder house, gathered a bunch of showbiz buddies to offer a $25,000 reward for information leading to the capture of the killers. Sellers, uncharacteristically, made his plea to the media. "It's inconceivable that the amount of blood on clothing would have gone unnoticed," and with frustration in his voice he added, "So where is the blood-soaked clothing, the knife, the gun, the getaway car? Someone must be able to help, please!"

But perhaps the most freaked out of them all was Tate and Sebring's pal, Steve McQueen. He went wildly off the rails, imbibing cocaine and other chemicals as though there was no tomorrow, becoming totally paranoid and installing an expensive security system at his Brentwood mansion, carrying a gun with him at all times (even to Sebring's funeral, where he gave a eulogy) and weaving in and out of traffic when he thought someone was after him. And he later learned through a front-page story in the *Los Angeles Herald Examiner* that he was at the top of a purported Manson "hit list." Susan Atkins was later to tell a cellmate that she did not like McQueen because she "felt he was getting too politically inclined" and this, "went against her grain."

Tate's and Sebring's deaths hit McQueen very hard. He adored them both. He had gotten to know them well when they double-dated—McQueen with his first wife Neile, and Sebring with Tate. While they had never worked together, in late 1964, he tested with Tate for *The Cincinnati Kid* and thought she was perfect for the part. But director Sam Peckinpah (the film's original director) overruled him, preferring Tuesday Weld. A year later, Tate did a screen test for *The Sand Pebbles*. Again, McQueen said yes, but director Robert Wise opted for an up-and-comer named Candice Bergen. In a 1980 deathbed interview, McQueen admitted Tate was a "girlfriend" and Sebring was his "best friend."

But what shattered McQueen's fragile equilibrium was the fact that on the night of the murders, he had been invited to dinner on Cielo Drive.

According to Marshall Terrill, author of several books about McQueen, as well as biographies of Elvis Presley, Johnny Cash, and basketball star "Pistol" Pete Maravich, McQueen always had a wandering eye for beautiful women, even though he was married. On that summer's night in August 1969, he set out on his motorbike for Tate's house, but he got sidetracked. "He picked up a female hitchhiker on his bike, and, instead of ending up on Cielo Drive, he ended up in bed with the mystery woman." Terrill said in 2019, "Cheating saved his life, and stories at the time referred to his near brush with death as *The Great Escape*."

And there's more. Months before the slaughter, according to an *Esquire* story in 2017, Charles Manson approached McQueen outside his Solar offices in San Francisco with a script he thought Solar should produce. According to *Esquire*, an altercation took place between the two, resulting in McQueen breaking Manson's nose. I don't buy that story; however, there were published reports and an eyewitness account based on fact about an incident that happened in the summer of 1968 when Manson visited McQueen's sometime playground—the Whisky a Go-Go on Sunset. Along with him was Beach Boy Dennis Wilson, record producer Terry Melcher, and talent scout Gregg Jakobson. Jeff

Guinn, author of the authoritative 2013 Manson biography, *Manson: The Life and Times of Charles Manson*, details the visit by the quartet in his book, which concludes with Manson taking to the crowded dance floor alone and entertaining watchers with a one-man frenzy of dancing. Waitress Corrine Maglieri was later to add another intriguing fact to that evening, telling Terrill what she had told no one else. She was concerned that Manson was doing lines of cocaine on one of the tables. She called over her future father-in-law, Mario Maglieri, an Italian from Chicago, who was the club's manager, to take out the trash.

McQueen never outran his obsession with the murders. In his book *The Family*, Ed Sanders recounted that in August 1970, the actor was on location in France while shooting *Le Mans:* "The trial of the Manson family had just begun, and he and a pal began drinking heavily at a local watering hole. Suddenly, the conversation turned to Tate, and McQueen, still furious and full of hate about Manson, said, "I'm gonna kill that Charlie Manson. If it ain't me, I'll hire some dude to get him.""

A few months later, on October 17, 1970, in the midst of the Manson trial, the actor wrote to his lawyer, Edward Rubin, at the law firm of Mitchell, Silberberg, and Knupp, with a request:

Dear Eddie:

> *As you know, I have been selected by the Manson Group to be marked for death, along with Elizabeth Taylor, Frank Sinatra and Tom Jones. In some ways I find it humorous, and in other ways frighteningly tragic. It may be nothing, but I must consider it may be true both for the protection of myself and my family.*
>
> *At the first possible time, if you could pull some strings and find out unofficially from one of the higher-ups in Police whether, again unofficially, all of the Manson Group has been rounded up and/or do they feel that we may be in some danger.*
>
> *Secondly, if you would call Palm Springs and have my gun*

permit renewed, it was only for a year, and I should like to have it renewed for longer as it is the only sense of self-protection for my family and myself, and I certainly think I have good reason.

Please don't let too much water go under the bridge before this is done, and I'm waiting for an immediate reply.

My best,
[Signed "Steve"]
Steve McQueen

The murders had a lingering emotional impact. McQueen drank and drugged for years, and, according to biographer Terrill, slept with a shotgun underneath his bed for the rest of his life. He wasn't alone—just days after the murderous weekend, celebrities were rushing to their local gun shops and paying $200 and upwards for weapons that the day before sold for less than $50. Gun sales rocketed, and many stores sold out over a twenty-four-hour period. The demand for attack dogs and round-the-clock security guards quadrupled overnight. Children were sent out of town for safety.

In the guarded beachfront enclave of Malibu Colony, twenty-five miles away, Tanya Sarne, the twenty-four-year-old London-born, pregnant wife of British director Michael Sarne, who was close friends of the Polanskis, went to extraordinary lengths to protect herself. In a 2018 interview she told me: "I was very pregnant and stuck home alone because Michael was at 20th Century Fox studios from dawn till sometimes the early hours of the morning. Or he was out drinking and drugging with (singer) John Phillips. I was terrified. So, each night before I went to bed, I moved a huge chest of drawers behind the bedroom door so no one could get in. And I got a rope ladder that went from my bedroom window some 30 feet down to the sandy beach. That was to be my escape if any strangers tried to get into my bedroom."

"We were all running around with guns in our purses," Michelle

Phillips of the Mamas and the Papas recalled. "We all suspected each other. It was the most bizarre period of my life. I didn't trust anyone. It could have been anyone, as far as I was concerned. The last conversation I ever had with Sharon was about wallpaper for her nursery. Do you remember Peter Hurkos, the psychic? He put his hand on my stomach and said, 'You have to carry a gun at all times, loaded and cocked.' I carried one for three months. The police were questioning everyone. Everyone was flushing drugs down the toilet. For some reason, they suspected my husband, John Phillips. 'Would your husband have any reason to have any animosity toward anyone in that house?' they asked me. I told them I had spent a night in London with Roman. I felt bad about that because of Sharon. And John was furious when he found out. In fact, he held a knife to Roman's throat and threatened to kill him."

Not long after the killings, Michelle showed up at The Daisy and began waving a gun at the disco bar. Sally Hanson stepped in and quietly said, "Darling, please put the gun away."

Others also felt threatened. Gossip columnist Rona Barrett told me in 2018: "My home was on Angelo Drive, right around the corner from Cielo. I got a call saying something bad had happened at Sharon and Roman's place. I got up to the driveway and into the parking area. I saw a sedan there. There was a dead body behind the steering wheel. Then a whole group of detectives converged on the property. I saw them covering another body on the lawn. Then the police said, 'Please, leave.' There were quickly rumors of a hit list of famous people. Next day Metromedia gave me a private guard."

Actor George Hamilton, who lived within a half mile of Cielo Drive, close to the fabled Douglas Fairbanks-Mary Pickford estate "Pickfair," was in Palm Springs with Peter Lawford and Alana Collins—who later became Hamilton's wife—when the murders occurred. He telephoned author Dominick Dunne and said, "We used to think no, drugs aren't bad, life is great—but it all ended that day. Everyone felt personally involved because so many people from all walks of life had passed through the house on Cielo Drive in the short time that Roman and Sharon lived there. Roman brought a dark energy to the house."

Dark was the operative word.

A LAPD cop stands watch at the Cielo Drive murder house.

Aerial shot of Cielo Drive, 1969.

GUESS WHO'S *NOT* COMING TO DINNER

"After we all lived in the Chateau Marmont, Roman asked Michael and me if we would like to share his house on Cielo Drive. We were newlyweds, and I didn't want to live in a film star's house and have to ask permission to make a cup of tea. Also, I was just Mrs. Mike Sarne—a nobody. I wanted my own house. So I refused. Gibby and Voytek moved in instead."

—Tanya Sarne, wife of British film director
Michael Sarne

"I went up to look at the house and thought, Yeah, I'll stay for a while, because I wanted to get out of the Beverly Wilshire Hotel. But then Abigail and Voytek walked out from another part of the house and said that Roman had told them to take the house. There's plenty of room for everybody, they told me. But I thought, No, I don't want to be in a house with other people."

—Warren Beatty

Just hours after news broke big about the carnage on Cielo Drive, a macabre lament emanated from the mouths of some of Hollywood's most famous denizens. Shell-shocked friends of the glamorous couple revealed that, like Steve McQueen, they, too, had been invited to the Polanski home on the night of the killings. "People scrambled to get on the 'I-almost-got-killed' bandwagon," comedy writer Buck Henry told friends at the time. "If half the people who were supposed to have been there that night had been there, it would have rivaled Jonestown." In her 1984 memoir *Knock Wood,* actress Candice Bergen wrote, "It was hard to find anyone in the LA Basin who didn't boast about being invited to drop by the house that night, mystically deciding, at the last minute, not to go." Another cynic wryly observed that those spurious stories—apocryphal or not—had become a "Guess Who's *Not* Coming to Dinner?" game in the jaded film town.

Exaggerations or not, I don't doubt that a few of the stories have some veracity. For, in fact, security was a vague, even dirty, word in the Age of Aquarius, where "California Dreamin'" was the innocent signature tune. Tate and Polanski always had the welcome mat out for genuine stars like Warren Beatty, Dennis Hopper, John Phillips, and screenwriter Robert Towne, as well as a raggle-taggle band of social-climbing wannabes looking for a friendly nightcap…or something more stimulating. "We'd often drop in unannounced. You never knew who might be having a drink or sharing a joint," Julie Payne, Townes' wife and the daughter of actor John Payne, told me. And it was slap-bang in the middle of a showbiz neighborhood. "Warren and Marlon and Jack all lived within yodeling distance," she said. "Peter Sellers was a regular at the house. He starred as a gay shopkeeper in *A Day at the Beach,* an obscure little 1968 film that was written and produced by Polanski. This, after all, was the hang-loose Sixties—love, peace, and all that kind of thing. In Roman's circles, the formality of invitations was never required."

There was no butler at the door to take your sweatshirt or private security force sitting in a booth by the front gate like they had down the road in nearby Bel-Air. Sure, there was an electric gate at the Cielo Drive house, but electric gates are easy to circumnavigate. And inside the Polanski compound, doors were never locked. When Charles "Tex" Watson, Susan Atkins, and the others with murder on their mind, showed up at the house, Folger and her Frykowski barely blinked at the strange faces. Maybe it was Sebring's or Voytek's drug dealer of choice dropping in at an unearthly hour with fresh supplies.

Folger, who, with her boyfriend, had been camping out in the Polanski house for several months, smiled at the handsome stranger who strolled into their room. His presence failed to arouse suspicion. But noting the unresponsive look in the blank eyes of the six-foot intruder Charles Watson, she finally inquired, almost matter-of-factly, "Who are you?"

"I'm the devil, here to do the devil's work," he replied.

There are stories I heard that strained credibility. Most recently, in 2018, I met a lady at a Venice, California, book signing who claimed she had bought a baby-shower gift for Tate, but, because she was unable to attend the shower—scheduled for August 11, the Monday following the murders—she had planned to drop it off on that tragic Saturday night, but simply ran out of time and wasn't able to make her delivery.

Then there was Polish actress/model Ava Roosevelt, whose fourth husband was William Donner Roosevelt—the Harvard-educated investment banker and one of FDR's twenty-five grandchildren, who died in December 2003. Ava moved to Los Angeles in 1969 from her native Poland to pursue a career in modeling. She soon reached out to Polanski, whom she'd first met in Poland after *Knife in the Water* came out, she told *Town and Country* magazine in May 2017. "He introduced me to Sharon, who was already pregnant when I met her." Roosevelt, twenty-one at the time, said she and Tate hit it off right away. "She was the most loving and beautiful human being I had ever encountered," she was to recall. "I regarded her as a sister; it was like she adopted me and took me under her wing."

Roosevelt said she was invited to have dinner at the popular Mexican restaurant El Coyote at 7:30 p.m. on the fateful night. "I'll try," Roosevelt said. But she missed dinner and was driving to the house later that evening for a post-dinner drink when she noticed the gas gauge on her 1955 Silver Dawn was flickering. Worried that she might break down and wind up stranded, she turned around and went home.

"I survived and they didn't, and it's haunted me for years," she told friends. "I never stop thinking about Sharon."

Dennis Hopper was a frequent visitor to Cielo. In late 2009, just months before he died, I met Hopper for afternoon tea in his suite at a hotel in Pasadena where he had come to talk about his role in the TV series *Crash*—a spinoff of the hit movie of the same name. Prostate cancer had slowed him down. He was thin, clean-shaven, with neatly combed silver hair. He wore an open-necked shirt and blazer, looking more like an aging movie executive than Hollywood's notorious *enfant terrible*.

Somehow, talk turned to the Manson murders. He told me he still had vivid memories of the night he failed to keep his appointment with Tate and Sebring. "That Friday night, we started off drinking at The Daisy. I hung out with Mia (Farrow), and I drank with Ryan (O'Neal). They all said they were going on to Sharon's for drinks. We knew she was very pregnant and Roman was in England, but that didn't seem to bother anybody. By the time we left The Daisy, we were fit for nothing."

In Peter Biskind's informative book, *Easy Riders, Raging Bulls*, which perfectly captures the film factory mood of that era, Hopper recounts that in 1970, once the Manson gang was arrested, he became increasingly intrigued by the cult leader. "Manson wanted me to play him in a movie version of his life," Hopper told Biskind, "so one day I went to the courthouse where he was in a cell and all the little girls were camping in tents outside." (Not quite accurate: while every day those Manson women not involved in the trial did sit in the street outside the courthouse, they never actually pitched tents in downtown Los Angeles, although the vision of girls popping out of their canvas sidewalk retreats might make for a better movie script.) Another time, Hopper's buddy Jack Nicholson, intrigued by the Manson theatrics, sneaked into the courtroom to eyeball Manson. "He was fascinated by Manson's persona and the crazy way he looked," wrote Nicholson biographer Marc Eliot. "It amounted to courtroom pornography, and Jack, who was there almost every day, couldn't get enough of it."

Hopper also claimed he somehow was allowed to visit Manson, who had seen the actor in an episode of the TV series *The Defenders*. "He'd cut himself a cross on his forehead. I asked him why. 'Don't you read the newspapers, man? All my followers have cut themselves like this so when the black revolution comes, they'll know which ones are mine.'"

Another "escape" story was told to me recently by British director Michael Sarne, confirmed by his ex-wife Tanya. Sarne was living in the gate-guarded Malibu Colony while making *Myra Breckinridge*, based on the Gore Vidal novel. The star-studded cast included current sex symbol Raquel Welch, aging sex symbol Mae West, and John Huston. Sarne was a bosom buddy of John Phillips—they both had shared the favors of Genevieve Waite, a South African actress who starred in Sarne's first film, the low-budget *Joanna*. So captivated was Phillips by Waite that he made her his third wife in 1968, only to divorce thirteen years later. Phillips was also writing some of the music for Sarne's film, and they all became members of the Polanski inner circle.

The Sarnes had first met Tate and Polanski in London. "When I came to America to make *Myra Breckinridge*," he told me, "we became even closer, and we all lived together at the Chateau Marmont on Sunset." He said he frequently dropped by Cielo Drive, and Tate and Polanski visited him in Malibu. In fact, when the distraught Polanski returned to California after the murders, one of the pals he sought refuge with was Sarne. First, Polanski hid out on the Paramount lot, then at the home of Paramount studio boss Bob Evans. Then, looking to escape the media madness, he moved into Sarne's beachfront guest house.

Here's what he told me happened on the night of the murders: "Roman was still in London, prepping *Day of the Dolphins*, so we kept in close touch with Sharon who was expecting. My own wife, Tanya, was also pregnant. On that Friday in August, I called earlier in the day and said we were going out for dinner in LA and would drop by after our meal. So off we set from the Colony. Me, Tanya, John, and Genevieve. John was driving his 1952 Rolls, which could be a bit dangerous. But at least he knew LA better than I, a visiting Londoner, did. So, despite his passion for drugs, we let him drive. We went to a Japanese restaurant near Century City. On the way we smoked some joints, and at the café we all took our shoes off and started drinking sake. Lots of sake. By the time we finished eating and had found our shoes, which believe me was a merry riot, I was six or seven sheets to the wind. I was so pissed out of my mind that it took John and the girls and one of the waiters to literally carry me to John's Rolls and dump me in the back seat. We were just a couple of miles from Sharon's place, but I was in no shape to visit anyone, even though I'd promised Roman to look in on her. But I couldn't walk. John was in slightly better shape. And so we decided to head home to the beach. The grunion were running that night. I collapsed into bed, and the more sober ones went hunting for grunion."

The next day, Sarne switched on the radio to hear the news. "Roman flew back to LA. Then, a couple of days later, we drove from the Colony, after he'd moved into our guesthouse, and he gave us a tour of his Cielo place. I know that sounds awful. He took us to the bloody rooms, the nursery—a horrible guided tour. I know it sounds so crass and so diabolical, but I think Roman did it because everything was so unbelievable. He somehow thought that by revisiting that house and seeing the blood and what had happened to their gilded life, everything would turn out to be a movie. Utter make believe. It would be just a terrible nightmare, so that the next morning he would wake up and things would be back to normal again. It was, in a weird kind of way, his therapy.

"Going to the house," he continued, "was something I'll never forget. He took us from room to room and pointed out where all the bodies were found, as if he didn't believe it himself. In the freshly painted nursery, he collapsed and said none of it would have happened if he had been there. That's the way his mind works. Don't forget this was a period when many of us had a hard time sorting fact from fiction. I was making a crazy film, running around Hollywood in a big fucking limo, being treated like a prince. And making this horrible Gore Vidal book, this disgusting crap, into some semblance of a film. We were all living in a kind of weird netherworld—exacerbated no doubt by drugs and drink and the feeling that we were in a strange world all of our own which bore little resemblance to reality."

Another Hollywood personality who claimed he had promised to visit Cielo on the night of the murders was Robert Evans, the larger-than-life former actor who ran Paramount during its most successful years—and in doing so became a master of self-promotion. In July 2002, I interviewed Evans after his bestselling 1994 memoir, *The Kid Stays in the Picture*, had been turned into a documentary. We had a wide-ranging discussion over a long, leisurely lunch, overlooking the tennis court at his sixteen-room French Regency estate Woodland, which was once owned by Greta Garbo. Lunch was served by his longtime British butler David Gilruth. At the time I wrote:

> He talked a mile a minute as he thumbed through *The Kid Stays in the Picture*, offering me dramatic readings straight from the pages of his book, interspersed with chunks of dialogue.
>
> *Just about the only really happily married couple I knew in Hollywood were Roman and Sharon. Coming from a childhood horror in Nazi-occupied Poland, Roman couldn't believe he was the husband of this milk-fed American beauty. Sharon's movie career was just beginning to heat up after* Valley of the Dolls. *In Roman's eyes she was already the brightest star in the world. Around his gentle, sun-kissed bride he was like a child who's just seen his first Christmas tree light up. I was in London with Roman in the Summer of 1969—and before I took off for L.A., Roman said, 'Look after Sharon for me, will you, Bob?' Tell her I love her. I'll be home in a few days.'*
>
> *Now Sharon was on the phone from the house in Benedict Canyon. She loved feeling the baby kick, but she felt cooped up. How about joining her and a few friends on Friday night? It*

would just be her houseguests, Gibby Folger and Gibby's boyfriend, 'Voytek' Frykowski, a Polish rogue and great friend of Roman's. Dinner with Jay Sebring—her ex-boyfriend who was still devoted to her—at a nothing place like El Coyote on Beverly.

'Sounds great, baby. I'm working in the editing room. I might be a little late.' I was still in the editing room. I called Sharon. 'I'm stuck, baby. Count me out. Sorry.'

'Sweet dreams.'

'You too.'

On Saturday morning, Evans said he was having a meeting at his house with the head of Paramount, Charlie Bluhdorn, when butler David interrupted. "'Joyce Haber (the LA Times gossip queen) must speak to you,'" he said. "'No calls this morning,'" I said. "She said it's urgent, Mr. Evans. She sounded terrible."

I took the call in my bedroom. When she heard my voice, Joyce started wailing. "You aren't dead!"

'Joyce, what are you talking about? Of course I'm not dead!'

'You didn't hear? It's on the radio. Last night at Sharon and Roman's house on Cielo. They're all dead…Sharon, Jay Sebring, Gibby Folger, that Polish Voytek what's-his-name . . .'

'I was supposed to be there.'

'They've all been killed!'

My body went numb. 'A landslide?'

'No, they were murdered. Some kind of massacre.'

I started to cry. Charlie came over, and put his arm around me. 'Bob—what happened?'

I told him, and we went out to sit under the tree. When Roman arrived from London, I arranged for him to be driven to Paramount and installed in the suite that had recently been Julie Andrews' dressing room for Darling Lili. *There, he hibernated for a few days, heavily sedated by a Paramount doctor. Not wanting to leave him alone at Paramount, Roman moved into my guesthouse. Sounds simple; it wasn't. Every crackpot in the state wanted to get a jab in. It necessitated having around-the-clock guards for the duration of his stay. The LAPD put their own tap on my phone, which became an integral instrument in their investigation. How I remember cradling Roman as if he were a child. I loved him. I felt his pain.*

Roman's good friends— Warren Beatty, Richard Sylbert, I and a few others—took turns keeping him company.

Leaving Holy Cross Cemetery, he said something that would come back to haunt me: 'The only one of Sharon's good friends who didn't come, Bob, is Steve McQueen. Sharon loved that cold son of a bitch.'

Aug 12, 1969. Reporters went with the erroneous "copycat" killings after the LaBianca murders as Hollywood was hit by a tsunami of terror.

PART II

THE INVESTIGATION

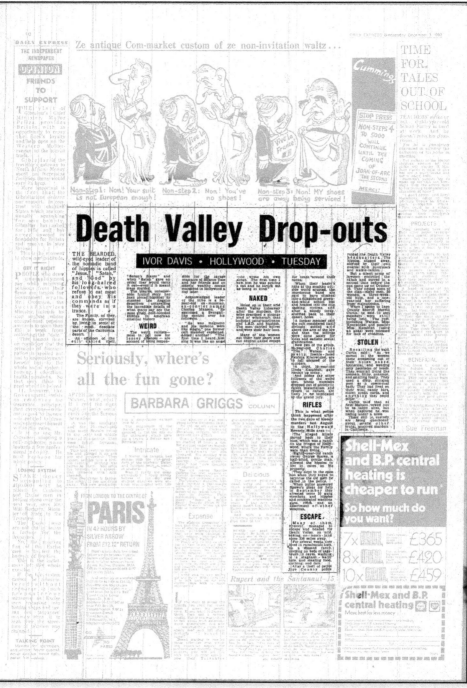

Dec 3, 1969, Story chronicles Manson and his Family, following their Death Valley arrests.

LOOSE LIPS SINK SHIPS

Vincent Bugliosi: *What did Susan Atkins tell you with respect to the Tate murders?*

Veronica Howard: *She said that after she entered the Tate house, she proceeded toward the bedroom. She noticed a girl sitting in a chair reading a book; the girl didn't look up and notice her. She continued toward the bedroom and reached the bedroom door. Sharon Tate was sitting in bed with a pillow propped up behind her, and Jay Sebring was sitting at the side of the bed, and they were engrossed in conversation, and at first, she [Atkins] wasn't noticed.*

Q: *Did you ask her how Sharon Tate was dressed?*

A: *Yes, I did. She said she had a bikini bra and pants on.*

Q: *Did she identify the person who was seated at the bed with Sharon?*

A: *Yes, she did.*

Q: *What name did she give?*

A: *Jay Sebring.*

Susan Denise Atkins, a.k.a. "Sadie Mae Glutz," was twenty-one years old when she arrived at the Sybil Brand Institute, a jail for women in Downtown Los Angeles, in October 1969. She was wan and looked like a pasty-faced child desperately in need of care and attention. She was not a well woman—her feet covered in sores and her face with acne, her hair falling out in clumps, and her digestive system a mess. But worse, she was suffering from a severe case of diarrhea...*vocal* diarrhea. It was a symptom that no amount of medication could cure, and one that would lead to disaster for her and those close to her. It was Atkins' propensity for boasting that brought the downfall of all those she considered precious in her short, damaged life, as well as the eventual destruction of the man she worshipped: Charles Manson.

Atkins had been arrested, along with the rest of the Manson clan at the Barker Ranch, on October 10, for willful damage of a government vehicle and was sitting in a jail cell in Inyo County. And when Inyo deputy district attorney H. L. "Buck" Gibbons, punched her name into his system it rang all sorts of bells. He discovered she also was wanted in connection with the July 1969 Topanga Canyon murder of musician Gary Hinman, implicated by the key suspect, Robert Beausoleil. She quickly found herself incarcerated at the Sybil Brand Institute, separated from Family members, while the Hinman murder trial quietly unfolded in a Santa Monica courthouse, with no one making the connection between that murder and those that had occurred barely a fortnight later. It was an embarrassing dilemma: One of the most notorious murder cases in California history, and the armies of detectives had hit a brick wall. Luckily for them, the loose lips of Sadie Mae Glutz soon came to their rescue.

Atkins was housed in a section of the jail known simply as "Block 8000," a large dorm with two dozen beds lined up opposite each other. Next to Atkins, also waiting disposition on their cases, were two women. One was the voluptuous Veronica "Ronnie" Howard, accused of forging prescriptions; next to her was a dazzling actress-turned-escort, Virginia Graham, who proudly told anyone who would listen that she had dated some of the biggest names in Hollywood, including (on and off for ten years) the legendary Frank Sinatra. Howard and Graham were longtime friends and rivals—both had assorted run-ins with the vice squad over their involvement in the party-girl-escort-hooker scene. Howard even married Graham's ex-husband; they were that close.

Girl talk began quickly with the petite, 105-pound, undernourished Atkins. She was bored stiff, suffering from cabin fever and feeling abandoned. After all, dammit, she was in lockup because a Family member had ratted her out. From time to time she met with her lawyer, Richard Caballero, a former district attorney now in private practice, who took her case when she was implicated in the Gary Hinman murder trial; but, mostly she was stuck in a cell, feeling like a caged animal, with little to do except gossip with her cellmates to prove she was on equal terms with them—that anything they could do, she could do better.

Atkins was hard to miss, said Howard. "The other girls used to make fun of Sadie because she would do exercises in the yard without any underclothing underneath. She would sing and dance go-go all the time. It wasn't the kind of behavior that fitted in," recalled Howard.

"What are you in for?" Graham asked.

"First-degree murder," Atkins proudly shot back.

They were stunned by that response.

"She was very young and real sweet," said the thirty-seven-year-old Graham, who had been around the block a few times and felt that there was not much left that could surprise her. "She looked like a little girl who should be in school, and I thought, *Oh, you poor little kid.* I felt sorry for her because she was also being teased mercilessly by the others because of her last name—Glutz." Indeed, it was the kind of word or name you'd find in the pages of the then-popular *MAD* magazine. This immature, bisexual hippie chick was ripe pickings for the rough-and-tumble jail crowd.

At lights out, Atkins was nowhere ready for shuteye. So she talked. And talked. Long and late into the night she began whispered conversations with Howard. First, she boldly suggested they start having sex, and Howard said she politely declined, saying she preferred to talk. Eventually the dialogue turned into a long, monstrous, one-way confessional. "We were talking about many things, and then the conversation drifted on to LSD, which I, myself, had taken one time, and so we discussed LSD for a while," Howard later told police. "And then I warned Sadie that she talked entirely too much. I told her that I didn't care particularly what she had done, but I didn't think it was advisable for her to talk so much. She also told me that she could tell by looking at me, my eyes, that I was a kind person, and that she wasn't worried about it anyway. And that the police were on the wrong track about some murders. 'What do you mean?' I asked."

Atkins said, "The murders at Benedict Canyon."

"And just for a moment, I didn't quite snap to what she meant, and I said, 'Benedict Canyon?' And she said, 'Yes. The Tate murders. You know who did it, don't you?'"

"No, I don't."

"Well, you are looking at her."

At first, Howard thought Atkins was just bragging. Seeing the confusion on Howard's face, Atkins added: "I was the one who killed *her*."

Still, Howard thought she might be boasting or parroting something she picked up from the newspapers. Then, knowing the effect longtime use of LSD can have on the mind, she assumed her cellmate must be suffering from some kind of delusion—especially when Atkins added, almost matter-of-factly, that she and her friends had killed Tate and her companions, "in order to release the souls of the victims."

What the hell is she talking about? Howard thought.

The conversations resumed over the next few nights, with Atkins elaborating. "She said she and her cohorts had already killed nineteen people," said Howard, becoming increasingly frightened. Especially when her cellmate coolly declared: "When I plunged the knife into Sharon Tate, it felt so good going in."

Atkins saw she had her audience entranced, and so she skipped from the Tate murders to the Gary Hinman killing. "What a feeling to stab someone," she bragged. "You can't describe the thrill. Everything in life is in and out and in and out. Everything, eating and even killing. In and out, in and out goes the knife. I stabbed Hinman and I came." Howard didn't know what to make of this skinny, strange girl who didn't look tough enough to fight her way out of a paper bag, but was spinning these grotesque tales. As they talked, Atkins boasted about her sexual conquests—men, women, men and women—and about orgies with the man she said was Jesus.

Each night, Atkins tossed new facts into the confessional pot, elaborating not just on the Tate murders, but on the killings of Rosemary and Leno LaBianca. And there was *another* murder—that of a stuntman named Shorty Shea, although she claimed she wasn't in on that one; she was merely reporting what other Family members had told her.

As days of confessions turned into weeks, Howard conferred with her friend Graham, who slept a few beds away and who, it turned out, had been hearing similar horror stories. "What impressed me was Sadie's amazing details," Graham later told investigators. "By strange coincidence I had visited the Cielo Drive house with my husband when I looked at it as a rental. Sadie confirmed many the details about furnishings and stuff like that as I had remembered the place. And she was so cool and coherent. She was excited as she told me the story. It was like a child that runs to its mother and says, 'Oh Mommy, I have to tell you something fast' type of thing."

Finally, Howard and Graham became true believers—terrified by their kid-roomie, who they now agreed was some kind of psychotic monster. But there was their jailhouse dilemma: to snitch or not to snitch; that was the question. "I heard that snitches often ended up with a shiv in the ribs—or even worse," Howard said.

Finally, after a long discussion with Graham, Howard decided to go to the authorities with her story. Easier said than done. For days she ran into red tape and roadblocks from low-level jailers who brushed her aside, possibly assuming she was just another wack-job inmate trying to game the system. They told her they were not qualified to pass the information on to higher levels within the prison system. But just when the frustrated Howard thought her crucial information was to be lost by bureaucratic bungling, Graham made a breakthrough. After more than two weeks at Sybil Brand, she was transferred to the California Institute for Women, then called Corona Prison, and got someone in authority to listen to her story. And on November 26, LAPD homicide detective Michael Nielsen, who worked on the LaBianca murders, eagerly showed up to tape record both women's versions of the Susan Atkins jail confessions.

Five days after their interviews, Police Chief Edward Davis would step in front of the world press and introduce the world to Charles Manson, proudly declaring that LAPD had cracked the case.

But until these loose lips dropped the bomb that sank the Manson Family ship, the LAPD would chase a few more rabbits.

CLUELESS

"Could the killers strike again? Personally, I suspect not. Professionally, I couldn't rule it out."
— Deputy Los Angeles Police Chief Robert Houghton, September 1969

Three months into the investigation of the worst series of murders in Los Angeles history, public interest was waning. It was 1969, after all, and there was no shortage of distractions on the nightly news. British troops arrived in Northern Ireland to intervene in sectarian violence between Protestants and Roman Catholics; the New York Mets, led by future Hall of Fame pitchers Nolan Ryan and Tom Seaver, defeated the Baltimore Orioles for the World Series title; North Vietnamese President Ho Chi Minh died, as did Beat Generation chronicler Jack Kerouac; more than half a million people showed up for the Woodstock Music Festival in a small town near Bethel, New York; the "Chicago 8" trials commenced in the Windy City; Col. Muammar Gaddafi deposed King Idris in the Libyan revolution; a group of eighty American Indians occupied Alcatraz Island in the name of "Indians of all Tribes"; the US government held its first draft lottery since World War II in 1942; the Rolling Stones staged a rock concert at the Altamont Speedway in Livermore, California, for some 300,000 fans. Despite their good intentions, fans were beaten, and one person, Meredith Hunter, was stomped and stabbed to death by a Hells Angel during the show. One man also drowned in a nearby canal and two people were crushed to death by a runaway car.

But on the Tate-LaBianca murders, the silence from our boys in blue was deafening. They were seriously stumped, which left reporters scrambling for new angles. The frustration showed in my discussions with colleagues, including Australian-born Bruce Russell, bureau chief of the prestigious Reuters News Agency, whose stories serviced clients all over the world. "Editors all over the place are screaming for news," he said, "and there's nothing, absolutely nothing, I can give them."

In September, I went to Parker Center, where newly installed Police Chief Edward M. Davis, who, with his neatly combed silver hair and a dark business suit, looked more like the CEO of a Fortune 500 corporation than a cop who had climbed the ranks, accompanied by his deputy Robert A. Houghton, were to provide us with "updates." But they kept sidestepping key questions about the case. At least they didn't try to bullshit us. "We have no murder weapon," Davis admitted. "We have no motive and we have no suspects. The killer or killers didn't leave a calling card…so we had to start with two million suspects." He kept insisting—and rightly so—that details of the crime could not be disclosed because it might hamper the probe and subsequent criminal proceedings. He noted that seventeen sergeants, two lieutenants, a captain, and an investigator were doing "as good a job as can humanly be done." A few scraps were tossed our way. Houghton did confirm that narcotics were found "in more than one place" on the secluded Benedict Canyon estate, which triggered another spurt of "decadent druggies" speculation, but he denied reports that the victims had been mutilated.

We asked about fingerprints, motives, modus operandi, anything to run with but, again, there was nothing useful they could give us. I thought it strange that they cryptically refused to respond to questions about Polanski and whether they had confirmed the whereabouts of the director at the time of the crime. Outrageous as it seemed, could he really be a "person of interest"? They hedged on other issues: the blood type of Tate's unborn son, whether the caretaker William Garretson had definitely been cleared, or if they had ruled out a Canadian narcotics ring involvement in the murders. Houghton refused to give any description of the murder weapons other than to say that firearms and cutting tools were involved. The murder time, the detective confirmed, had been established and "could be" between midnight—the time caretaker Garretson said his friend Steven Parent left—and 2:00 a.m., when some neighbors claimed they had heard screams. Chomping at the bit and pursuing our own selfish newspaper agendas and deadlines, it was a frustrating period.

But it was not as if armies of investigators had been standing idly by. My notes of the period indicated that they had conducted more than 600 separate interviews, including every person known to have been acquainted with the victims or ever to have stepped over the threshold of the house on Cielo Drive. That list included tradesmen, friends, and employees—even the mailman and employees of their answering service. Since many of these people moved in a world that scattered them all over the globe, thousands of miles were traveled, hundreds of teletypes exchanged with law-enforcement officials around the world and many in-person interviews conducted. More than forty officers were assigned to the case, and they painstakingly checked out more than 100 other murders in Southern California for possible connections, however slight.

Unfortunately, their fine-tooth comb missed one. On July 31, 1969, days before the Tate killings, Los Angeles County Sheriff's detectives were called to a gruesome crime scene in Topanga Canyon—a rustic, woodsy canyon that spilled out onto Pacific Coast Highway between Santa Monica and Malibu. It was definitely a case for the Sheriff's office; they handled crimes within the county, but outside the city limits of Los Angeles. Those in the city fell into the bailiwick of the LAPD. And while both organizations had headquarters in downtown Los Angeles just a few blocks apart—the Sheriff's at the Hall of Justice and the LAPD at Parker Center—the two entities functioned totally separately. Robbery homicide cops in LAPD did not drink or mingle with their county compatriots. Or share information. It was a macho turf thing.

The murder scene was in an idyllic setting in the westernmost part of Topanga Canyon, literally within spitting distance of the surf hitting the sand on the busy corner of Topanga Canyon Boulevard and Pacific Coast Highway. The canyon itself offered an intriguing alternative lifestyle—a favorite hangout for Los Angeles's ever-changing "flavor of the month" cults and communes, and primo real estate for hippies, longhairs, and granolas—it wound scenically through picturesque countryside for some twenty or more miles straight, changing as it threaded its way through the middle-class suburbs and burgeoning, crowded shopping centers of the San Fernando Valley. It ended abruptly back in rural territory at the spread of property known as the Spahn Ranch.

Strangely, the Topanga Canyon murder, despite its gruesome nature, garnered little attention at first. It had taken place at 964 Old Topanga Canyon Boulevard, in an isolated, two-story, barn-like house tucked into a steep hill surrounded by trees and undergrowth. Police, alerted by neighbors, arrived after dark to be met by three friends of the owner who said the occupant was a Gary Allen Hinman. They described the thirty-four-year-old as an intellectual and a kind man. He worked at a music shop, taught bagpipes, piano, trombone, and drums, had a gentle nature, along with a passion for Buddhism. So much so that he was excitedly looking forward to heading to Japan in a few days to visit Buddhist centers. What they didn't tell Sheriff's detectives was that when there was a paucity of paying students, Hinman liked to supplement his income by cooking up a little mescaline in the kitchen and selling it to a steady clientele who came calling all hours of the day and night. Hinman always had the welcome mat out. In fact, a few weeks prior, he had played host to a small army of visitors that included a charismatic singer-guitarist named Charlie Manson and his omnipresent band of nubile young women. Hinman happily invited them to stay, giving them the run of his house until they finally moved on.

Seen-it-all detectives gagged when they entered the barn-like structure and encountered what was left of Mr. Hinman. It was a scene straight out of a gruesome Grand Guignol production: The stench of death was overpowering; armies of flies buzzed round a rotting, bloated corpse that was half-eaten by maggots and had turned black with decay. The barefooted Hinman wore a blood-drenched T-shirt, and in the pocket of his blue jeans they found a wallet. It was empty. A shattered wristwatch was on his left wrist. It had stopped at 10:07. They reckoned the body had been decomposing for maybe a week or more. Closer examination indicated six severe knife wounds and signs of torture. His ear had been cut off and then crudely sewed back on. But what struck them as even odder was the signage written in what appeared to be the dead man's blood. On the wall in the living room someone had daubed the words "Political Piggy." And close by on another wall was what looked like a paw mark in blood. The body had something partially covering the head; closer inspection revealed it was a pillow used as a towel.

Astounding as this may seem in retrospect given the bloodthirsty nature of the two murders, neither set of investigators thought to break policy and later check with their brethren. The only people who knew about the "Pig" blood daubings at Cielo were at the LAPD; the only ones who knew about "Piggies" in Topanga were in the County Sheriff's office. The crime scenes had screaming similarities, and yet none of these territorial investigative teams were able to put two and two together.

Or, perhaps their failure to communicate was not so astounding. At the time, the vast, sprawling County of Los Angeles was policed by a dozen different agencies. The Los Angeles City Police Department, staffed by more than 5,000 officers, covered an area of 464 square miles and handled 40,000 crimes in an average two months, including murders, rapes, armed robberies, assaults, and burglaries, not to mention drunks, quarreling lovers and spouses, and traffic violations. At the time, the Sheriff and the LAPD co-existed in some kind of jealous brother relationship. Then there were the two dozen or so jurisdictions within or connected to the greater Los Angeles area, each with its own separate, independent police force. The City of Beverly Hills—under the twenty-six-year iron rule of Chief Clinton Anderson—preferred to keep it in the family. So they notoriously micro-managed their very own brand of justice, often favoring the town's more celebrated residents. Other smaller cities contracted for law enforcement, usually with the County Sheriff. And there was the California Highway Patrol, cruising the more than 140 miles of freeway that crisscrossed the city, mostly handing out moving violations.

And yet, if just a cursory exchange of details had taken place between the Sheriff's office and the LAPD, alarm bells would most surely have rung. Instead, they remained clueless. Some time later, deputy DA Stephen Kay recalled that early in the investigation, two Sheriff's homicide detectives working the Hinman murder told LA detectives, "Look, we have this Hinman murder and there's writing in Hinman's blood on the wall. We think this could be connected to your case. And the LA police sent them away saying, 'No...they're not connected.'"

But while detectives beat the bushes looking for leads, a surprising candidate volunteered his services to the LAPD and was given surreptitious and unofficial support by the baffled cops who were desperate for new leads and eager to enlist anyone with special connections to Hollywood's inside track to help them crack the case. Armed with forensic kits and warned that this one-man Mission Impossible did not come with their official blessing, this private sleuth launched what might have been perceived as a crackpot investigation. He desperately hoped he could reach deep into the heart of Hollywood and unmask who was behind the brutal murder of Sharon Tate and her friends.

The unofficial investigator was an actor-director by the name of Roman Polanski, and he was seeking vigilante justice.

Obsessed with trying to find out who and why his wife and friends had been killed, Polanski embarked on his very own mission to find out if anyone in his tight, inner showbiz circle might be responsible for the slayings.

He told no one, but did confer with local police, who, with no leads whatsoever, still did not encourage him to embark on this private odyssey...but were willing to supply whatever technical support they could legitimately offer him. Anything he might dig up was better than the nothing sandwich they had.

Another thing that none of us members of the media covering the case realized was that at the time Polanski embarked on his one-man Sherlock Holmes probe, Sharon's forty-six-year-old father, Colonel Paul Tate, was thinking along similar lines.

Sharon's distraught father, who had worked in military intelligence for much of his career, had also become suspicious of his son-in-law's motivations. The rigid and precise military man had never quite adjusted to his daughter's unconventional husband and the showbiz-influenced behavior changes he noticed in his darling, unblemished daughter. And what kind of father-to-be was Polanski—the absentee husband, living halfway across the world on another continent while his wife was about to deliver their first child? Tate and his wife, Doris, did not approve of the hard-drinking, hard-drugging motley crew that flocked around the Pole and his entourage. Tate had grown a long beard and tried to pass himself off as a hippie, trolling the streets around Sunset Boulevard until the wee small hours of the morning, mingling with the locals, and questioning the druggie crowd that frequented the Strip. Intelligence was his forte, and he too was desperately looking for anything that could cast light on who might have murdered his daughter. But weeks of night-long pavement pounding on the Strip led to naught.

I remember learning of Colonel Tate's masquerade in search of some truth while I was covering the murder trial. It led to bizarre wisecracking and jollity—black humor—from those of us desperately looking for something to lighten up the grim mood. The very idea of this clean-cut officer with his firm, lifelong militaristic bearing, trying to pass as a dozer, a scruffy and unwashed hippie on the Strip—bushy beard or not—seemed outlandishly comical. And frankly, it absolutely was.

But Polanski's one man "Sherlock" campaign, which I learned about a few years later from Polanski, seemed much more tied to reality.

"They (the police) had treated me with great sensitivity and respect," Roman told me in 1994 in a Paris restaurant. "And from the very beginning I instinctively felt something didn't fit. I felt it had to be someone I knew or who knew me. At the time I wasn't thinking straight, but from the moment I went to bed to the moment I woke up all I could think about was to find who had done this to Sharon."

Polanski said in order to clear his mind and reputation, he first volunteered early on to take a lie detector test. By the time the long interrogation had finally finished, Polanski had come to a decision of his own. He was passionate about finding the killers and he decided he would do whatever he could, even if it meant interrogating many in his inner circle.

HE LATER RECALLED, "They never told me I was off the hook. But they did say they thought it was definitely a case of personal revenge. Nothing was stolen from the house."

"Maybe you have a friend who is a psychopath," police Lt. Robert Helder, who was in charge of the investigation, told Polanski.

The *Life* magazine controversy still burned Polanski, although that half-baked idea was of his own volition. "I thought I might find something of Sharon still in the house—and I wanted to do something to end all the malicious stories."

Afterwards, he said he approached Helder and team members and volunteered to help them as best he could—particularly in checking out some of the alibis of his friends.

"Most of them had been to my house for dinner and at parties," Polanski said. "They knew the place inside out. And I really felt that the killer might be someone I knew. Helder agreed. He said he too leaned towards a personal revenge motive."

"Treat your personal friends as suspects," Helder told Polanski, who took it to heart.

The director later observed: "I was looking for someone who knew us, or was connected with us—who mixed in our circles. I know it sounds strange, but I had better access to them than the police. I had become close to the police and wanted to help them. They too thought it was someone we probably knew, who hung out in our social circles, and Helder thought they would be much less guarded if I talked to them. So I was to be an amateur sleuth."

One of the leads, which turned out to be a dead end, was a pair of glasses found at the Cielo House. Detectives believed it might have belonged to the killer, so Polanski acquired a lens measuring device—a small gadget that was small enough to slip into his pocket. Whenever he visited friends' houses, he surreptitiously measured their spectacles. At that time, martial arts expert Bruce Lee came into his "suspect" focus. Lee knew them both. He had taught Tate for her role in the 1968 Dean Martin spy spoof movie *The Wrecking Crew*. In addition, Polanski had flown Lee to Switzerland to give him martial arts lessons. When Polanski heard that Lee told friends he had lost his glasses, he rapidly checked him out. Roman's blind reasoning went like this: Only a person who had the deadly martial arts skills of a Bruce Lee could have managed to kill them all so quickly and so silently.

Next ex-Marine Danny Bowser, then head of the Los Angeles Police Department's top secret Special Investigations Section (SIS), gave Polanski a state-of-the-art tiny microphone, which was easily concealed, plus bugs that he could plant in friends' houses.

They also gave him a complex device to help him take blood samples. It was complicated, particularly for someone who was ham-handed or inexperienced in forensics. It was also unwieldy and required taking two glass vials with chemicals in them and swabbing the suspected areas with a Q-tip in an area that he believed might contain a blood stain. Then the swab sample had to be dipped into another vial—and if the vial turned blue it indicated that blood was present.

Unwieldy as it was, Polanski snuck into friends' garages, particularly those living in the Malibu Colony, to play scientific sleuth. But all of his experiments were either bungled or came up negative. Polanski recalled that one day his friend Victor Lownes frantically telephoned him from London and pointed out that their mutual pal, the brilliant writer Jerzy Kosinski (*Being There*), had a character in one of his novels that perfectly fit the profile of the killer and that he should be viewed as a suspect. Oh, to be Polanski's friend at this time in his life.

On one occasion, the suspicious Polanski sneaked into the garage of John Phillips and frantically combed through the singer's Jaguar looking for bloodstains. He found none, but he did find a machete in the trunk—which turned out not to match any of the weapons used at Cielo Drive. But Polanski had another big reason for focusing on the oft-drugged-out singer.

Phillips knew that Polanski had had a one-night stand with his wife, Michelle, in London. How did he know? Turns out that Michelle confessed to him! So the reasoning went that John could have gone berserk and killed Sharon in the ultimate savage act of revenge.

Roman had admitted to the affair and said it took place a year or two earlier in England, not while Polanski was in London filming and Sharon was at home awaiting the birth of her first child.

Michelle Phillips, the Mamas and Papas California bombshell singer, was not an innocent party in all of this promiscuity. Never a shrinking violet, she was kryptonite to a series of famous men: in between her relationship with the volatile Phillips—which had begun when she was just seventeen—she enjoyed the company of men and went on to have liaisons with Mamas and Papas group member Denny Doherty, Jack Nicholson, Warren Beatty, and plastic surgeon Steven Zax. There had also been that whirlwind (no doubt chemically induced) marriage to Dennis Hopper in 1970—the duration of which was just seven days.

Polanski's somewhat tortured mind envisaged that John, the dope fiend of all dope fiends, before he went on to marry South African actress-model Genevieve Waite (who had come off a relationship with his good buddy, pop singer-turned-director Michael Sarne), might have killed Sharon in a fit of anger over his dalliance with his Michelle.

Phillips never forgot the wrath of Polanski post the murders: "We were just talking in the kitchen. He picked up a knife and grabbed me from behind. He was a madman. I just managed to talk him out of slitting my throat."

Later, friends who saw him at the time in the throes of grief and despair, including director Sarne, remembered, "We talked about his utter sense of loss, of despair and bewilderment and shock and love—a love he had lost."

Not surprising, Polanski must have also lost his mind.

December 3, 1969, Manson's first court appearance in Inyo County, California, where he was arraigned for stealing cars and damaging government property. He sits next to his public defender Fred Schaefer. Lynette "Squeaky" Fromme sits behind Manson.

POLANSKI: ON THE HOT SEAT

"As far back as I can remember, the lines between fantasy and reality have been hopelessly blurred."
—Roman Polanski, from *Roman by Polanski*

In the summer of 1969, close friends of Roman Polanski agreed that he had become a suitable case for treatment and indeed could easily have been diagnosed by any psychiatrist as suffering from temporary insanity.

It was not surprising. Polanski had survived a childhood wracked with horror, but had turned his life into the storybook happy ending. Or so he thought.

Rajmund Roman Thierry Polanski was born in Paris in 1933, but was just four years old when his parents returned to Poland. Their timing was inopportune because the Nazis invaded Poland and began their pogrom against anyone Jewish—or with Jewish blood in their veins.

Roman's mother, Bula, was reared Catholic but was half-Jewish and she suddenly disappeared. Roman never saw her again. She died in the Auschwitz gas chamber. His father, Ryszard, a painter, was sent to Mauthausen but survived the war.

Young Roman had a horrendous childhood, dodging the Nazis, escaping from the ghetto at the age of ten. He had vivid memories of being used for target practice by the Nazi occupiers and foraging desperately for food. In order to survive, the young Polanski changed his name to Romek Wilk and was hidden and protected by some local Catholic families who knew his father and had promised his father to look after the boy.

After the war, his father reclaimed his son; but when he remarried, young Roman left home and decided to strike out on his own, pursuing his passion for movies. After landing the leading role in a stage version of *Son of the Regiment* in Poland, he was accepted at the National Film School in Lodz. He directed a couple of short movies, then became a hot property in 1962 after directing his first feature length film, *Knife in the Water*. He moved to Paris, and then to London, and followed up with two more acclaimed pictures. Polanski was on a roll. In Paris he directed *Repulsion* in 1965 and a year later, *Cul-de-sac*. The much-in-demand director moved to London where he starred in and directed his first color movie, *The Fearless Vampire Killers*, a horror spoof. Much against his will he agreed to hire a young American actress to play a small role as the innkeeper's daughter. Her name was Sharon Tate. The two initially couldn't stand each other, but soon got over that hurdle by marrying in London in January 1968.

ARRIVING BACK IN HOLLYWOOD in the summer of 1969, the newly widowed Polanski was feeling nothing—paralyzed, almost numb, walking around in shock, filled with prescription meds. His about-to-be first-born son was dead, along with his blonde goddess wife of just eighteen months. Polanski was coping on a diet of tranquilizers and sleeping pills washed down by wine—not exactly a healthy diet. And he looked like a zombie, functioning like a man trapped in his very own nightmare.

To further exacerbate the pain and anguish, Los Angeles homicide detectives had not completely ruled him out—as outlandish as it might appear—as the possible architect of the bloodshed. With media outlets still touting the by now "live freaky, die freaky" accusatory line of reasoning, Polanski's life had turned into yet another nightmare in a life already packed with personal disasters.

It was almost as if, even with the support and sympathy of his intimate buddies who knew him well and tried so desperately to protect him from himself, with this latest tragedy, Polanski saw himself as a latter day Job.

Was he suicidal or hell-bent on self-destruction?

After walking a *Life* magazine writer and photographer through his death house, Polanski tried to explain away his decision by saying he was desperately looking for reasons why the Grim Reaper had visited his family, yet again. And the media exposure was his way of trying to understand what had happened, and trying to make sense of it.

The controversial August 29, 1969, issue of *Life*, which hit the newsstands a few weeks after the murders, did little to salvage his tainted reputation, even though it may have helped him find a strange kind of redemption. The story was rushed into print to capitalize on the sensational elements of the murders, but was too late to make the magazine's cover. In that issue the Pulitzer prize-winning author, Norman Mailer, adorned the front page. Mailer had penned part one of a lengthy two-part series about the US space program in an article titled "A Fire on the Moon."

The Polanski murder house story also vied for readers' attention with the magazine's glossy ads that touted, "Men in Space" commemorative medals along with the joys of mixing Gordon's gin with Fresca. Also vying for readers was another story in the same issue illustrated by a slew of vivid photos taken by staff photographers John Dominis, a veteran of the Vietnam War, and Bill Eppridge, who had taken dramatic shots of Bobby Kennedy as he lay dying in the Ambassador Hotel kitchen.

This spread also showed young, naked "hippies" bathing in local water holes following torrential downpours, which brought a sea of mud and utter chaos and devastation to the region. But none of the half-million people who showed up seemed to care. They had come for a three-day music festival held on Max Yasgur's dairy farm in New York's Catskills district in the village of Bethel, some forty miles from better known Woodstock. It was a rollicking, drug-infused celebration, as the photos attest. Young people frolicked in the mud as they were entertained day and night by a veritable who's who of the rock world. It was a doozy of a live happening. Artists including Joan Baez, Arlo Guthrie, Richie Havens, Janis Joplin, and Joe Cocker, along with groups such as The Grateful Dead, Country Joe and the Fish, Jefferson Airplane, and Crosby, Stills and Nash, provided the music.

Despite torrential rains, no real shelter, limited food, and catch-as-catch-can accommodations, it was hailed as one of the milestones of the decade. Two people died and there was reportedly one birth, but no one complained. Woodstock instantly became an overnight rock history legend.

Deeper into the *Life* magazine pages, Polanski finally made his appearance. Grim and unsmiling in a white T-shirt, black slacks, white loafers with no socks, he sat at the doorstep of Cielo Drive. There was a blank look on his baby face and he posed at the front door, which clearly showed the dried bloodstained daubing that read "Pig."

The guided tour got worse.

Roman looked in at the master bedroom where he and Sharon slept, and at the creased bedroom pillows and the lime green and orange double-bed sheets.

"She hugged the pillows instead of me," he softly told reporter Tommy Thompson.

When first questioned by police, Polanski tried to give detectives his version of what he thought might have happened. Although it was pure speculation, it raised early suspicions from investigators.

Later he tried to make certain that detectives knew it was pure theory:

"I didn't say I thought she was asleep. I said I thought she must have been in bed because of the way the bed was set—indicating that she was already in bed. That day the bed was made by our housekeeper. I could see the way the pillows were set along the bed, the thing she was doing. When I wasn't with her she would line the pillows and cuddle those pillows; especially when she was pregnant, she found the best position for her was lying on her side. There was a pattern of this type of thing. I know that Jay would hang on a long time and Sharon would go to bed. You know, he would talk to Voytek and sit with him and have a beer. I know that Sharon was going to bed early every night since she was pregnant; she was tired, she was in her eighth month. So, I assume that either Voytek or Jay were sitting and talking, maybe accompanied by Gibby. Sharon was already in her bed. That's how I see the thing, I don't know why."

He continued his commentary in a low voice as he ushered them through the house, and then into the living room.

"They hit her here," he said. "She tried to get out of that door...and they dragged her into the living room...and...did...it."

Sharon's and Jay's bodies were gone, of course, but, in the living room, Roman—this time having switched his wardrobe to a blue long-sleeved shirt—was photographed crouched in front of Sharon's favorite rocking chair, and below him a huge zebra-skin bedspread on the floor. He averted his gaze from the still visible gigantic bloodstains, which seemed to fill the room and grimly marked where Sharon's mutilated body had lain just days before. Clearly visible in the photo were huge swaths of carpet where he stood, still stained with his wife's and unborn baby's blood.

For Polanski, re-imagining what went down had to be emotional self-mutilation. A twisted self-flagellation, or his own brand of therapy, though I don't think he was there to get better. Whatever he was there for, bringing along a photographer and reporter was just bad taste.

"Roman kept muttering to himself," Tommy Thompson recalled. "There is something here...I can feel it...something the police missed. I must find the thread."

He pulled open a drawer and it contained publicity stills of the gorgeous Sharon, both before her pregnancy and as she glowed with health, her stomach bump growing bigger. Ah, those utterly photogenic Tate high cheekbones, almond eyes, and sun-kissed blonde hair. Cameras adored and embraced her. She melted all comers with her classic doll-like beauty.

Like someone sleepwalking through life, Polanski aimlessly wandered into the spare bedroom, now decorated as a nursery, and randomly pulled open drawers and cupboards. Out of an armoire spilled blankets, diapers, formula bottles, and a bassinet. On the shelf were books: *Naming Your Baby, Let's Have Healthy Children*, and *How to Teach your Baby to Read*. Polanski didn't lose a wife; he lost his family.

He fiercely denied that he had been paid by the magazine to allow them access; perhaps he felt this was closure. But if that were the case, then why bring along America's most popular magazine to such an invasion of privacy?

He told his *Rosemary's Baby* star Mia Farrow that the only living thing he found at the house when he returned was the "little stray kitten that Sharon had adopted." He continued, "The kitten was running around in all that blood in the house."

And shortly afterwards, Polanski was to bitterly recall that a few weeks after the killings he received a bill from landlord Rudi Altobelli. His friend, the agent, the humanitarian, was demanding a big chunk of money—well over $1,500 dollars from the director for compensation— for damage to the house. Altobelli determined that Polanski should shoulder the responsibility of replacing the blood-stained carpets plus the cleaning and replacement of damaged draperies. And the painting of the blood-daubed walls and doors.

Hollywood can indeed be a cruel place, although in fairness to Altobelli, the agent became infuriated by gossip column reports claiming Polanski was paid handsomely for his magazine interview.

DAYS AFTER HIS GHOULISH tour of Cielo Drive, Polanski was singing like a canary. He had agreed to take a lie detector test, so a friend dropped him off at police headquarters in downtown Los Angeles where he was to be given the polygraph by Lieutenant Earl Deemer. Despite his obvious nervousness, he knew he had nothing sinister to hide, and his mood was a little more upbeat. After a friendly opening gambit with Deemer ("Mind if I call you Roman? My name is Earl"), he seemed to relax, so much so that, in listening to the tape, it appears he was only too happy to lay it all out for his interrogator.

The detective, after all, was a perfect stranger and could even be considered an antagonist. Yet Roman was ready, willing, and able to tell his side of the story while throwing a friend or two under the bus. And realizing he was to be attached to a "truth machine," he was extremely forthcoming about his life with Sharon and his opinion of Sebring. Neither was he reluctant to spell out his own shortcomings, which were not only jaw-dropping but outright insensitive at times.

Under questioning from Deemer, Polanski talked about how he first met Sharon and as he did so, the dialogue turned into more of a confessional than a law enforcement interrogation.

"I first met Sharon four years ago at some kind of party," he said. "Marty Ransohoff—a terrible Hollywood producer, the guy who makes *Beverly Hillbillies* and all kinds of shit. But he seduced me with his talk about art, and I contracted with him to do this film, a spoof on vampires. And I met Sharon at the party. She was doing another film for him (*Eye of the Devil* opposite Deborah Kerr, David Niven, for British director J. Lee Thompson) in London at the time…in London alone. And Ransohoff said, 'Wait until you see our leading lady, Sharon Tate.'"

Polanski, who admitted he was a notorious womanizer, said he wasn't immediately smitten or impressed by Sharon when they first met, but then took her out.

"At that time I was really swinging. All I was interested in was to fuck a girl and move on," Polanski admitted. "I went through a very bad marriage, you know. Years before. Not bad, it was beautiful, but my wife (Polish actress Barbara Kwiatkowska-Lass) dumped me. I was feeling gray because I didn't have success with women. I just like fucking around. I was a swinger, ha?"

He continued: "So I met her a couple of more times. I knew she was with Jay. Ransohoff wanted me to use her in the film, and I made tests with her," Polanski said. I later learned that Polanski had been unimpressed with Sharon, and point blank told Ransohoff he didn't want her in his vampire movie. His reason? "Because she couldn't act her way out of a paper bag." But then he made a deal with Ransohoff. He would take Tate, but only if he could also star in the picture he had agreed to direct.

"Deal," said Ransohoff.

Their romance got off to a rocky start, he told the detective.

"She was being difficult, wanting to go out, not wanting to go out," Polanski said. "So I said 'Fuck you' and hung up. Probably that was the beginning of everything, you know."

"You sweet-talked her?" Deemer asked, clearly being playfully sarcastic.

"Right. She got intrigued by me. And I really played it cool. And then I started seeing that she liked me. I remember I spent a night—I lost a key—and I spent a night in her house in the same bed. And I knew there was no question of making love with her. That's the type of girl she was."

They went on film location some two or three months later. He recalled, "I asked her, 'Would you like to make love with me?' and she said very sweetly, 'Yes,' and then, for the first time, I was somewhat touched by her. And we started sleeping regularly together. And she was so sweet and so lovely that I didn't believe it. I'd had bad experiences and I didn't believe that people like that existed...but she was beautiful, without this phoniness. She was fantastic. She loved me. I was living in a different house. I didn't want her to come to my house unless she was serious. And she would say, 'I won't swallow you; I want to be with you, etc.' And I said, 'You know how I am; I screw around.' And she said, 'I don't want to change you.' She was ready to do everything just to be with me. She was a fucking angel. She was a unique character who I'll never meet again in my life."

By then, Polanski had turned the lie detector test with Deemer into something akin to a full-fledged shrink session. He was using this opportunity—bizarre as the setting was—to unload, to get it all off his chest.

He became more critical when the conversation turned to Sebring, Tate's old boyfriend and one-time fiancé. Polanski told the detective that he had quickly warmed to Sebring.

He said that when they first met in a London restaurant, he felt very uneasy. "Jay came over to our table, he kissed Sharon's hand, and said, 'I just wanted to meet you. Then he said, 'I dig you...I dig you, man.' He seemed happy to see Sharon happy."

There was naturally some discomfort as their relationship grew because he said Sharon's ex-fiancé liked to hang around the house.

"He was a sweet person," Polanski admitted. "I started liking him." All well and good on the surface, but he still had some reservations about Sebring.

"Oh, I knew of his hangups. He liked to whip tie girls," Polanski said. "Sharon told me about it. He tied her up once to the bed. And she told me about it. And was making fun of him...to her it was funny, but sad."

He delivered the next line, almost matter-of-factly, as though this was the usual boy-next-door kind of romancing, something benignly lifted from the Alex Comfort pages of the *Joy of Sex* manual.

Polanski said Sebring liked to hang around at their house and linger far past the point of comfort. "Sharon would resent his staying too long because he was always the last to leave. I'm sure in the beginning of our relationship there was still his love for Sharon, but I think that largely disappeared. I'm quite sure."

While Deemer may have been intrigued—even entertained—by Polanski's sexual directness, he was still looking for a motive for the killings because the cops had not entirely ruled Polanski out as a suspect. So he asked Polanski whether he thought Sharon and Sebring's relationship might have been reignited as a result of his long absences. The not so gentle subtext was that Polanski might have become furious because Sebring was again sleeping with his wife, and he might have turned into a jealous husband seeking to wreak personal revenge.

"So there's no indication that Sharon went back to Sebring at any time?" Deemer gently probed.

"Not a chance," snapped Polanski. "I'm the bad one. I always screw around. That was Sharon's big hang-up. But Sharon was absolutely not interested in Jay."

Deemer pushed further and asked if Sharon had any other men in her life.

"No. There was not a chance of any other man getting close to Sharon," said Polanski, who must have wanted to beat his chest as he delivered the line.

After this long preamble they took a break and Deemer once again hooked Polanski up to the lie detector, and instructed him to confine his answers to a simple yes and no.

"It's important for you to remain quiet. I know you talk a lot with your hands," Deemer said. "You're emotional...you're an actor type person so it's going to be difficult for you. But when the pressure is on I want you to remain quiet. When it's off you can talk and even wave your arms. Within reason."

With those new ground rules established, the questions became more pointed.

Q: *Did you have anything to do with taking the life of Voytek and others?*

A: *No.*

Q: *Do you feel any responsibility for the death of Voytek and the others?*

A: *Yes, I feel responsible...that I wasn't there. That is all.*

Deemer asked him for his theories on who may have been the target for the killings and why.

Polanski replied: *I've thought about everything. I thought the target could be myself.*

Q: *Why?*

A: *I mean it could be some kind of jealousy or plot or something. It couldn't be Sharon directly. If Sharon were the target, it would mean that I was the target. It could be Jay was the target. It could be Voytek. It could also be sheer folly, someone just decided to commit a crime.*

Deemer asked if Polanski knew why Sebring might have been the target.

A: *Some money thing, maybe. I've heard a lot about this drug thing, drug deliveries. It's difficult for me to believe.*

Police later discovered that on the night of the killings there had indeed been a big delivery of narcotics to Cielo Drive, ordered and paid for by Frykowski and Sebring. Investigators tracked down the reputed dealer, Joel J. Rostau, who supposedly delivered a large quantity of cocaine and mescaline to Sebring and Frykowski. He was later interrogated by police and cleared of any involvement in the murders. In May 1970 Rostau's body was found stuffed in the trunk of a rented 1970 Cadillac at JFK Airport. His skull had been fractured.

Continuing, Polanski threw a few jabs at Sebring and said while his image was that of a "rather prosperous man," there had been some whispers that he owed a lot of people a great deal of money, including $5,400 to his dentist. Polanski said, "The indication to me is that he must have been in serious financial trouble, despite the appearances he gave."

The line of questioning gave Polanski the chance to test out some of his own theories on Deemer.

"The whole crime seems so illogical," he said. "If I'm looking for a motive, I'd look for something which doesn't fit your habitual standard with which you use to work as police—something much more far out."

Polanski told the detective he had received hate mail following the release of *Rosemary's Baby* and observed, "It could be some type of witchcraft, you know? A maniac or something. This execution, this tragedy, indicates to me it must be some kind of nut, you know. I wouldn't be surprised if I were the target. In spite of all this drug thing— the narcotics—I think the police like to jump too hastily on this type of lead."

Deemer asked Polanski if Sharon was into drugs, and his reaction was strange but truthful.

"She did take LSD before we met. Many times. When it was legal," Polanski said, laughing. He said near the end of 1965 they took it together. It was his third trip and her fifteenth or sixteenth, he recalled.

"It had looked like we were going to make love in the middle of that night, but we didn't," Polanski said. "And it turned into something horrible. I was saying everything's all right and she was screaming. I was scared to death. She flipped out. In the morning she said, 'I told you I shouldn't have taken it, this is the end of it.' That was the end for me and for her."

But it wasn't the last nightmare for either of them.

THE BIG BREAK

"Virginia Graham and Ronnie Howard broke the case. We got a call from Sybil Brand, and they said that Susan Atkins had been talking to these two inmates. Another detective and I went there... Atkins had laid out the whole story. She knew everything—the position of the bodies, the kinds of stab wounds, the way the rope was thrown over the rafters. We tape-recorded everything. We got what we wanted. She wrapped it all up for us."

—Los Angeles homicide detective Sgt. Michael J. McGann to Steve Oney, *Los Angeles* magazine, 2009

Monday, December 1, 1969, at 11:00 a.m. was a cool and overcast Southern California morning. I was half-listening to Los Angeles's all-news radio station, KFWB 98—"Give us twenty-two minutes, and we'll give you the world"—when they breathlessly interrupted regular programming with a news bulletin.

There was "an important break" in the Sharon Tate murder case. That's all they said. I called the *London Daily Express* foreign desk where it was 7:00 p.m., and told them what I had heard on the radio. "Sounds like they may have finally cracked the Tate case," I told John Moger, the night foreign editor. "It could be a big one." Moger said he would make preparations for late copy. He assured me that I had at least five hours to file a story if it was to make the front page of the *Express's* first edition. "Sounds like this is what we've been waiting for," I told Moger, but not saying much more.

Minutes later, LA's City News Service sent out an urgent memo to its clients in Southern California, announcing there would be a press conference at Parker Center, at 2:00 p.m. that day. It had been a hectic morning at police central, and Los Angeles Police Chief Edward Davis, who was to be the guest speaker at a midtown service club lunch, quickly canceled and rushed to the conference room on the sixth floor of the black-windowed police headquarters. There, he met with department heads, including Lt. Robert Helder, heading the Tate probe, and Deputy Police Chief Robert Houghton, and was swiftly briefed. He smiled as he left the conference room. "Make sure you get a press release out on this. You'll need copies galore," he told inspector Peter Hagan, who was in charge of press information. Helder informed the chief he would also alert Roman Polanski and Tate's father, Colonel Paul Tate, about the conference.

Trying to get a jump on the opposition, I called Arthur Schreiber, general manager of KFWB, who had become a good friend since we met as traveling companions covering the Beatles' first American tour in 1964. I wanted to see if he had an inside track from his police sources. "I think they've finally got the killers," Schreiber said. "Our guy on the police beat says this is not another crappy police PR maneuver."

Then he told me that in early November, an anonymous caller had asked Herb Humphries, one of his station's top reporters: "Have you looked into the Hinman case?"

"Who's speaking?" Humphries asked.

"Never mind," said the male voice, "I'm calling about the Sharon Tate murders. Did you know 'Political Piggy' was scrawled in blood at Hinman's place in Topanga Canyon?"

Humphries told the caller he was familiar with the name Hinman because there had been a murder trial that played out in a Santa Monica courtroom just a few weeks earlier, although he wasn't familiar with all the details. "Anyway, we were always getting all sorts of crackpot tips that never panned out," he said skeptically.

"Remember the words they wrote on the front door of the Tate house," the caller repeated before hanging up.

I was later to discover that the same man, using the same strategy, had made similar calls to the *Los Angeles Times* newsroom and to KNXT, the local CBS television affiliate. On that occasion, the caller had insisted on being put through to Jerry Dunphy, the high-profile anchorman of the popular nightly program, "Big News." A newsroom editor had dealt with him. Years later sheriff's deputy Preston Guillory, who was one of the more than 100 officers who raided the Spahn Ranch in mid August 1969 to break up a suspected car theft ring, said in a 2011 interview with the Truthontatelabianca podcast that he had called the radio station because he was suspicious after all files on the raid vanished from the sheriff's office and he suspected some kind of cover-up. Guillory said he was fired from the sheriff's office for contacting the media without permission. "The whole thing was fishy," Guillory said. Ironically, he later went to work as an investigator for Manson's lawyer Irving Kanarek.

I phoned Dan Cooke in the LAPD public affairs office, with whom I had developed a good relationship following my coverage of the Robert Kennedy assassination in June 1968. But he gave nothing away. "Have you made arrests?" I asked, still hoping to get a leg up. And desperately looking for maybe a European angle, I asked: "Is Scotland Yard or Interpol involved? Is there a Polish connection?"

"Sorry," Cooke said. "Get here before 2:00; I can't tell you anything now." Stressing that I needed to be there at the appointed time was more than a clue that they had something big, possibly an arrest.

I got to Parker Center with ten minutes to spare, monitoring other news radio stations. They all were breathlessly speculating that suspects were already in custody. And there was genuine relief that morning because it seemed that, at long last, the cops might finally have solved the most sensational murder in the city's recent history, and the threat that bloodthirsty killers were still running loose might be over.

Police Chief Davis, who had been in the job for just a few months, dapperly attired in a dark, banker's business suit and tie, carefully negotiated around yards of TV cord and cameras, climbed the four steps onto a stage in the jam-packed auditorium, and sat down at a desk table. This time he was playing it safe. Two years later, during a rash of plane hijackings, he was to earn the nickname "Crazy Ed" for publicly suggesting swift justice for the perpetrators. "Hang 'em at the airport," he thundered. "I recommend we have a portable gallows, and after we have the death penalty back in, we conduct a rapid trial for a hijacker out there, and hang him with due process...out there at the airport."

Now, with the eyes of the world and more than one hundred journalists from around the world standing silent, Davis fussed about with a sheaf of papers in front of him and then, making sure the front line of TV cameras were ready to roll, began slowly reading in a steady monotone. Except for the whir of TV cameras, there was complete silence.

He started by saying that after almost 9,000 hours of investigation, the LAPD was happy to announce that the case had been solved. "Today warrants have been issued for the arrests of three individuals in connection with the murders of Sharon Tate, Abigail Folger, er... Frykowski, Steven Parent, and Thomas John Sebring," he read. "These murders occurred on August 9 at 10050 Cielo Drive, West Los Angeles." He fiddled with his black-framed glasses, quickly adjusted them, and continued: "These persons were involved in the murder deaths of Rosemary LaBianca and Leno LaBianca, president of Gateway Markets, of 3301 Waverly Drive, Hollywood. This homicide took place a day later on August 10th, 1969."

We were totally gobsmacked. Helmut Voss, West Coast bureau chief for Springer Corp., a German newspaper and magazine chain, whispered to me, in his heavy German accent, "It is not then copycat murders?" Police, of course, had stressed all along that the murders were not linked, and they reckoned the LaBianca murders were most likely the work of "copycats."

Davis then named the suspects who he claimed were part of a "hippie" group: Charles D. Watson, 24, of Copeville, Texas, now in custody in McKinney, Texas; Patricia Krenwinkel, 21, of Los Angeles (although Chief Davis repeatedly referred to her as "Kernwinkel"); and "Linda Louise Kasabian, 19, also of Los Angeles." Neither Kasabian nor Krenwinkel were in police custody, he said. As he spoke, Dan Cooke began handing out copies of Davis's statement along with mugshots of Watson and Krenwinkel from a previous arrest. More arrests would follow, the chief said, noting that the grand jury was likely to hand down further indictments against "four or five others," without naming them.

Davis, also for the first time, publicly suggested that "there may be some connection" between the "hippie" group and the stabbing and torture murder of musician Gary Hinman in his Topanga Canyon home four months earlier. That case had received little media coverage compared to the Tate murders. Robert "Cupid" Beausoleil, a handsome twenty-two-year-old sometime soft-core porn actor, musician, and self-described ladies' man, the son of a milkman from Santa Barbara, had just faced a trial in the beachside Santa Monica courthouse for that murder, but the case had received little media coverage as it involved an unknown music teacher in what appeared at first to be a routine drug-deal-gone-wrong death. Hinman was incorrectly described in some reports as the leader of a group of hippies.

Chief Davis made some routine observations, which seemed somewhat self-serving given the sometimes inept way investigators had stumbled around for four months without coming to any conclusions. First, he thanked other law-enforcement agencies for "their magnificent cooperation" in working with the Los Angeles police, specifically naming the Los Angeles Sheriff's office. Actually, the long probe had been marked by the lack of cooperation between local agencies. And then he praised the media for tenaciously keeping the public informed while at the same time balancing their coverage so as not to unduly alarm the public. It was total BS, of course, considering some of the initial outrageous stories. But this was not the day to bring up petty grievances. It was kumbaya time—Los Angeles cops were finally getting their long overdue day in the sun, and they were basking in the rays.

As soon as Davis finished, the questions came fast and furious. The chief responded cautiously, repeating, "This development of information from the two separate investigations led detectives to the conclusion that the crimes in both cases were committed by the same group of people." He said legal restrictions prevented him from offering more details, but he did reveal, without elaborating, that the suspects apparently had visited the Tate home before the murders, when it was leased to a different party. But he did not provide any more details except to note that the phone wires had been cut to the house on the night of the killings, adding, "It had all the earmarks of premeditation."

Even with several suspects identified, the chief stressed they still had no motive. Even harder to believe, he noted, was the fact that, "None of the suspects knew any of their victims." It was a stunning revelation, and those of us who had followed the case daily were poleaxed by that news. All those early wild stories were total fiction.

"Where do the suspects live?" Reuters' Bruce Russell shouted out in his heavy Australian accent. Davis paused: "They appeared to live together in a commune at the same address—the Spahn Movie Ranch. It could have had religious connotations, but it depends on your frame of reference. Then they moved to near the Death Valley Monument in Inyo County."

In a statement handed to me at the press conference, LAPD pinpointed for the very first time that it was on October 15 they first became aware of a link between the murder of Gary Hinman and the Tate-LaBianca killings.

They provided no further details, but when I asked around I learned that the cops began to piece it together after receiving reports of a missing seventeen-year-old girl named Kathryn "Kitty" Lutesinger. Her frantic mother insisted her runaway daughter had become pregnant following a relationship with a Robert Beausoleil, who was already in jail and facing charges of murdering Hinman. There was no sign of the missing teenager, but on October 20, H. L. "Buck" Gibbons, a deputy district attorney in Inyo County, spotted the name of the missing girl while looking through the long list of those who had been arrested at the Barker Ranch near Death Valley and were being held in the local jail for car theft and damaging government property.

Gibbons spoke to Lutesinger and she talked nonstop about what she had been told really happened at the Hinman murder house. Gibbons immediately called the LA Sheriff's investigators—Sergeants Charles Guenther and Paul I. Whiteley—who were both involved in the Hinman case. They raced 200 miles up to Independence to interview the five-months-pregnant, scared, and very confused Lutesinger. She identified the woman who was at Hinman's house with her boyfriend Beausoleil as Sadie Mae Glutz (Susan Atkins), who just happened to be residing in a neighboring cell at the Inyo jailhouse. Atkins was taken back to Los Angeles and charged as an accessory to the Hinman murder, and placed in a prison dorm at the Sybil Brand Institute where her cellmates were Veronica Howard and Virginia Graham.

BY THE TIME the front pages of the day's *Los Angeles Herald Examiner* and *Los Angeles Times* hit the streets, 17 million residents of Los Angeles County breathed a collective sigh of relief. "Police believe the victims on the two different locations were killed both to 'punish' them for their affluent lifestyle and to 'liberate' them from it," theorized the *Los Angeles*

Times. And for the first time, in the *Times'* story there was mention of another suspect described as the leader of this band of hippies who lived at the Spahn Ranch. His name was Charles Manson. But where was he?

I quickly discovered that he was already incarcerated 200 miles north of LA in the small town of Independence. In fact, he had been in police custody since October 12, and this was the second time in the past few months that Manson had been arrested by police.

The first time had been when Manson and his acolytes were released a mere forty-eight hours after being rounded up in an early morning raid at the Spahn Ranch in August 1969—just a week after the Tate murders. They were suspected of running a stolen-car racket. The Sheriff's elite squad had expected to be confronted by a heavily armed private army of young gangsters protected by a vicious band of motorcycle hoodlums known as "Satans Slaves" toting 50-caliber machine guns who "cultivated marijuana in booby-trapped fields." There were also reports that the bikers were swapping drugs for sex with under-age girls at the ranch. "We hit them from all angles at five in the morning," recalled Deputy James Harris, who photographed the raid. "One guy pulled a gun but surrendered when we stuck a rifle up his nose. They all stank like sewers, even the four babies who were handed over to child welfare. Manson was dragged out from under a building and handcuffed."

They confiscated assorted stolen cars and a cache of weapons. Prosecutors took one look at the paperwork—two dozen suspects would prove to be a nightmare if taken to court—and decided that it was just too complex to sort out who had stolen what, when, and where. And after all, they had retrieved most of the stolen vehicles. No harm, no foul.

It was a huge stroke of luck for Manson that investigators never linked him to any homicides. Taking it as a warning, he quickly made the decision to abandon the Spahn Ranch and led his clan to the Barker Ranch, on the edge of Death Valley National Park in the northeast Mojave Desert. He knew of Barker because it was close to Myers Ranch, owned by Barbara Myers, the grandmother of Manson Family member Catherine Gillies, and he had visited the Myers Ranch for a short time in 1968.

Charlie calls the cops 'beasts.' He told me he would take great pride in trying to kill as many as he can if they come for him. If they can come to get him with helicopters, or bring in the Marines or the National Guard, he will personally charge right into them with his knife swinging…this was before he had the two guns, including a shotgun. And all the women have been programmed to do exactly as he does…and they all have knives.
　　　　　　　　—Paul Crockett, gold prospector, Death Valley,
　　　　　　　　1969 police interview

For Manson's chronology which took him from the wild, wide-open spaces of the Barker Ranch to a cell in Independence, California, we turn to James Pursell, a rangy thirty-six-year-old California Highway Patrol officer with a military buzz cut who was assigned to Death Valley. In 2009, Pursell talked to writer Steve Oney about his momentous encounter with the Manson Family, in the spectacular backwater of the thinly populated national park. Pursell said local rangers were upset because their protectorate was being mutilated. All sorts of vehicles, particularly dune buggies, were scarring the picturesque pathways. Hoping to dissuade them from that practice, the park service took a large earthmoving machine to the western edge of the valley, removed the earth scars, and used the earthmover as a barrier to block the intruders from despoiling the main road.

The intruders, of course, were Manson and his followers, and Charlie was not amused. So he set fire to the earthmover. Not a wise move. A blatant case of destroying government property and a deliberate poke in the eye of the rangers who not only were pissed off by the burned-out earth mover but were sworn to protect the landscape. So they decided to roust out these malevolent offenders. Pursell and a buddy, ranger Dick Powell, headed out into the hinterland and were driving down the Goler Wash area when they ran into an old army truck driven by gold prospector Paul Crockett, who was accompanied by a teenager identifying himself as Brooks Poston. Both men had become disenchanted with life with Manson and his Family and had decided to leave the Spahn Ranch to prospect for gold.

And they were ready to dish the dirt on Charlie and the girls.

They confirmed that the leader of the group responsible for cutting up the roadways was staying at Barker Ranch in Death Valley. They described him as a strange man who put on a robe and told them he was Jesus Christ. Pursell listened intently as they elaborated: There were a large number of females there, said Crockett and Poston, and they had orgies and used drugs. And during the night, the group traveled the valleys in dune buggies as if they were re-creating the days of Rommel (World War II Nazi General Erwin Rommel) and the Afrika Korps.

Crockett wasn't reticent about telling the cops what he thought of Manson and warned them that if they came for him there would be a fight to death before he allowed himself to be taken into custody. "I would suggest if there's any way to take him…all at once…would be the only possible way to get this man…because he's insane in my mind," he told police. "He told me he doesn't care what he does, how he does, or where he does it."

Crockett said Manson had warned him, "If you become a police snitch, you'll be more afraid of me than you will of the law."

Manson may have watched too many gangster movies (or maybe Mr. Crockett had), because according to him, there was no way Manson would be taken alive if the cops came for him.

But in reality, the facts leading to Manson's apprehension were not nearly so dramatic or derring-do. In fact, it was not just anticlimactic, it was practically straight out of a comedy.

After their conversation, the CHP officer and the park ranger began their search for the intruders. "I went to the right, and Dick to the left," Pursell told writer Steve Oney. "Then I'm suddenly within a mass of young females, only a few males. Some are nude, some are dressed, and everything in-between. They were trying to hide behind sage bushes, but you can't hide too well behind a sage bush. I could see further up the draw what looked like a dry camp. Dick took off running, and he disappeared. I said, 'Come on out!' I gathered them all together. Then there was this young girl, kind of the spokesperson. Dick comes huffing and puffing back. He had been chasing a male subject. I ask her, 'Who are you? Where are you from?' And she said, buck-naked, 'We're a scout troop from San Francisco. Would you and the ranger like to be our leader?'" The girl would turn out to be Lynette Fromme. Pursell elaborated on what happened next.

"We saw a couple of vehicles. One was a rail dune buggy covered by a purple nylon parachute, the other a Toyota Land Cruiser covered by a tarp. Each had a gun scabbard holding a rifle. We got the VIN numbers. The vehicles came back stolen."

The next day, October 10, 1969, with Pursell leading the troops, police raided the Barker and nearby Myers ranches. "The local sheriff thought we were a bunch of fools, running around out there chasing a bunch of hippies. And, at first, that's what we thought—we had a bunch of hippies running a stolen car ring," said Pursell.

They netted ten women and three men. Among those arrested were Susan Atkins, Patricia Krenwinkel, Leslie Van Houten, Lynette Fromme, Catherine Share, Sandra Good, and Steve Grogan. Officers discovered more dune buggies and evidence tying the group to the burning of the park-service earthmover. "We piled all the stuff in a wash so we wouldn't forget to pick it up on the way out, which is exactly what we did. On October 12, Powell and I and another ranger went back to get it. On the way in, we saw a Chevrolet truck loaded with 55-gallon drums of gasoline. We figured more people were there, so we called for backup. I sat on a knoll overlooking Barker Ranch while the rangers went to the other side. It was beginning to get dusk, so I decided we'd better make a move. I went to the back door and shoved it open. There was a group of people. I announced who I was and ordered them to put their hands on their heads. I ordered them out.

"Then I entered the house. It was totally dark. On the table was a candle in a glass mug. With the mug in one hand and my Smith & Wesson .357 Magnum in the other, I went into a tiny bathroom. No one was there. But as I lowered my candle to a little cabinet beneath the sink, I saw long hair hanging out of the door. All of a sudden fingers began wiggling and the door began to open and this figure emerged. I said, 'If you make one false move, I'll blow your head off.' So this figure slowly uncoils himself and in a very friendly voice says, 'Hi.' I asked who he was, and he identified himself as Charles Manson. He was as polite as he could be. Over the years I've had a lot of people, including a judge, ask, 'Why didn't you just shoot him?' But I always answer, 'How can you shoot a guy whose first word to you is 'Hi'? "We rode down Goler Wash in a pickup. The girls we arrested began whispering and giggling. Charlie just stared at the backs of their heads the way a parent does with unruly kids. The girls felt it. They turned around and all of a sudden were silent. Charlie told us that his group was out there looking for a place to hide because there was an impending race war. He told us that the blacks were going to win. He told us that because we were number one, cops, and number two, white, we should stop right there, let them loose, and flee for our lives. That, of course, didn't happen."

STRANGELY, AT POLICE CHIEF DAVIS'S press conference, neither the names of Charles Manson nor Susan Atkins were uttered. We didn't know it at the time, but Atkins was about to sing to a Los Angeles Grand Jury—and implicate Manson. In fact, although no one investigating the Tate and La Bianca cases noticed, the first public reference to the Manson

Family in connection with any crime more serious than car theft had been made just a week earlier, on Monday, November 24. On that day, Danny DeCarlo, a member of the Straight Satans, a Venice motorcycle gang, was called as a key witness in Gary Hinman's murder trial which was well underway. Under cross-examination from Deputy District Attorney Ronald Ross, DeCarlo publicly made the first direct link between the Spahn Ranch, the Hinman killing, and Charles Manson.

DeCarlo painstakingly detailed a conversation he'd had with Hinman murder suspect Robert Beausoleil in which he said the defendant gave him the gruesome details of the torture and eventual murder of Hinman. DeCarlo said Beausoleil was living at the Spahn Ranch and had gone with two girls to Hinman's house to collect some money owed him after Hinman sold him drugs that he claimed were bad. DeCarlo said Beausoleil told him he'd pulled a gun and demanded that Hinman turn over $20,000 he was supposed to have. "Bobby said he hit him with a gun, punched him around a little bit."

"Get out," the defiant Hinman screamed at him.

"So he (Beausoleil) called up a guy named Charlie back at the Spahn Ranch."

As DeCarlo testified, "Bobby said Charlie came over, cut off Hinman's ear, and then left." Hinman lay bleeding and wounded for days, guarded by the girls.

Deputy DA Ross asked, "Did he (Beausoleil) say anything about what the place looked like when he got back there?"

DeCarlo replied, "Other than he could hear the maggots eating away on Gary and how the house stunk pretty bad."

Moments later, Beausoleil's defense lawyer, Leon M. Salter, in an effort to diminish the devastating testimony against his client and to remind the court that DeCarlo was testifying only under the promise that police would drop drug-smuggling charges he was facing, changed the subject. He asked: "This person 'Charlie' that you referred to in your testimony, were you aware of this person Charlie's full name?"

De Carlo stated, "Charles Manson."

The name rang absolutely no bells because the Hinman trial was playing out in a small satellite courtroom of Los Angeles County, and only the local *Santa Monica Evening Outlook* newspaper had been covering it on a day-to-day basis.

Despite the overwhelming testimony against Beausoleil, the jury was hung, forcing Judge John Shea to declare a mistrial. During the trial, evidence was presented that not just Beausoleil but others, who lived on a movie ranch in Los Angeles, were involved in the brutal murder.

In early 1970, Beausoleil was re-tried with Deputy District Attorney Burton Katz heading the prosecution in a downtown Los Angeles court-room. In an ironic juxtaposition, as the jury was deliberating Beausoleil's fate, in an adjoining courtroom Beausoleil's soulmates—Charles Manson and Susan Atkins—were being arraigned for the murder of Sharon Tate. This time Beausoleil was convicted after Family member Mary Brunner was given immunity in return for testifying for the prosecution.

LATE ON THE EVENING of December 2, just a day after Police Chief Davis had made his bombshell announcement naming the three suspects in the Tate-LaBianca murders, my London office called again. They said Reuters was reporting that Charles Manson, the mysterious ringleader of the band suspected of murdering Tate and the others, was going to appear in court. But not in Los Angeles. He was to be arraigned in Inyo County, California, on charges of car theft and damaging government property. They wanted me to get to the courthouse in Independence and cover the arraignment, but more important, land the first exclusive interview with this man Manson.

I called Van Nuys Airport and booked a private four-seater plane to fly me up to Independence at 7:00 a.m. the next morning, so I would arrive in time for the court hearing. An hour or so later, I got a call from reporter Steve Dunleavy, who worked for a chain of Rupert Murdoch papers in Australia and was based in New York. He offered to kick in part of the plane charter fee to help me defray costs if I would take him along.

I agreed. Just as we were landing in Inyo County, Dunleavy asked if I had written an updated story about the news conference and its aftermath, and if so, could he take a quick look at it? I showed him a copy of the story I had filed to London. The moment we landed, Steve hurried off to the nearest phone booth and I heard him dictating—word for word—my story to his editor in Sydney!

Manson was being arraigned in the picturesque Inyo County Courthouse, virtually within spitting distance of the notorious Manzanar concentration camp where the US government had interned thousands of American-born Japanese during World War II. Straight out of a Hollywood movie, the place reminded me of the Gregory Peck classic, *To Kill a Mockingbird*. The courthouse was a historic and imposing white-pillared edifice, within walking distance of the main drag, offering an old-fashioned drugstore, turn-of-the-century shopfronts, and old Americana architecture. I checked to make sure Manson's case was on the docket, and I did a double-take. The car thief and now alleged murder suspect I had come to see up close and personal, was listed on the court records as: "Charles Milles Manson, a.k.a. Jesus Christ." That was quite an alias.

By then, a small cadre of TV cameras and press photographers were milling outside the courthouse. I quickly rushed in to claim a seat in the fast-filling second-floor courtroom. The place was packed. In the first row behind Manson sat devotee Lynette Fromme, in a crisp white blouse, looking like a prim schoolteacher who might have been in charge of the group of social studies students from the local Owens Valley high school who packed the back rows and were thrilled to witness this drama played out on their home turf. Fromme, arrested with Manson at the Barker Ranch in October 1969, had been released after the US attorney, responsible for prosecuting National Park violations, decided it wasn't worth bringing the "barefoot hippie" to trial.

As I sat down, my imagination went into overdrive. What did I expect this heinous monster to look like? Would he have horns on his head? Would he flash me the evil eye or try to hypnotize me? When he finally shuffled in, all eyes were on him—and he knew it. At thirty-five, he was small, barely over five feet tall, a stooped and scrawny troll sporting a luxuriant Prince Valiant mop of long brown hair, bottomed off by a wild, unruly black beard. He was almost buried in an oversized blue denim prison jumpsuit two sizes too big for him, his chest hair sprouting from the open collar. A chain was looped around his waist and linked to his handcuffs. He was flanked by two local deputies. They parked him in a chair next to his court-appointed public defender, Fred Schaefer, a serious-faced boyish man in a well-worn dark business suit and skinny tie, who shoved a yellow pad and pencil in front of him. Manson picked it up and started doodling on the sheet. Then he flashed a piercing smile at a young woman sitting in the front row, who was maybe in her late teens and holding a baby. He smiled again as he gazed around and saw it was standing-room only. This man clearly loved a crowd and being center stage.

Testimony was brief. One witness said her new blue dune buggy was stolen and that she later recognized it repainted red in a used-car lot. Another claimed she saw the defendant driving stolen vehicles near the desert commune. The district attorney's presentation was cursory, attempting to briefly show that there was probable cause to remand Manson for trial on the charges of receiving stolen property. Meanwhile, Manson doodled on the sheet in front of him. He had obviously impressed local sheriff's deputy Merrill Curtis, who got to know him during his several weeks of incarceration and had seen him interact with the other young men and women who were facing similar charges and were also occupying cells in Inyo County. Having to unexpectedly house almost two dozen suspects for more than six weeks had become a big strain on his small jail. He described Manson as a "model" prisoner. He should be; he'd been in and out of jail since he was fifteen years old. "He seems to be very intelligent and well-read with a good vocabulary. He is cooperative and talkative to a point...

but careful not to implicate himself in anything…There was little doubt who was their boss," said the jail deputy. "He gives them orders and they obey him."

The public defender pled not guilty on behalf of his client.

After the arraignment, the still-shackled Manson was returned to the custody of his jailers, but not for long. He was about to leave his cramped Independence cell for roomier accommodation in Los Angeles. The district attorney down south had pressing need of Manson's attendance and much to discuss with him. Meanwhile, I approached a man who had earlier introduced himself to me as Manson's friend ("We knew each other at Terminal Island," he said without elaborating) and said he was concerned about his pal's well-being. I told him that I would like to do an interview with the man of the hour. "Let me talk to Charlie," he said. "Wow, you've come all the way from England just for this?" The man clearly did not know what was at stake here or what his friend was truly facing in Los Angeles. And yes, I would have come all the way from England "just for this" had I not lived in Los Angeles.

He came back ten minutes later. "Charlie wants $300 for an interview," he said. "He's got legal bills and other expenses."

I wasn't prepared for financial negotiations, and I countered, "Our newspaper has a policy of not paying for interviews, particularly to someone who is facing serious criminal charges. But let me check with my office."

I called the London office, and they agreed: "We don't pay accused murderers for their story." When I look back today it was probably a wise decision. Having the first interview with Charles Manson would have made a terrific exclusive, but I was later to see that he was a big talker, and there is no doubt whatsoever he would have tried to do his snow job on me, using the kind of flim-flam that became his trademark.

I shook hands with Manson's "agent" and got a ride back to the tiny airport, where Dunleavy was waiting. We flew back to the smog, discussing the impression that Manson had created. Dunleavy said he would have paid for an interview, and that the guy looked more like a homeless hippie vagrant than an accused mass murderer.

There was still more work to be done, and my next step was pretty obvious: Find out what was behind this Manson thrall. Who was he? Why would he be involved in these murder sprees? What's it all about, Charlie? But first, I had to check out this Spahn Ranch to figure out why Manson seemed to have all these young women under his spell. And back at Van Nuys Airport, I discovered things had been moving quickly. Los Angeles police Inspector Peter Hagan reported that a Los Angeles grand jury had handed down further indictments, which named Manson and Susan Atkins as major suspects. Linda Kasabian, he said, had been arrested that very day in Concord, New Hampshire, and was booked as a fugitive from justice. Police declined to reveal the circumstances of the arrest, noting only, "She was pregnant." State troopers, Hagan said, had been hunting through hippie colonies in the Taos area of north-central New Mexico trying to track her down.

Krenwinkel had pulled a hat over her head as police approached but had been arrested the same day in Mobile, Alabama, on a warrant almost identical to Kasabian's. Her attorney was adamant: "She knows absolutely nothing about the cases and will fight extradition to Los Angeles." For some reason, at this time Charles Watson was charged only with the death of the caretaker's friend, Steven Parent. He had been arrested the previous Sunday near his home by Tom Montgomery, the local sheriff in McKinney, Texas, who just happened to be his cousin. The loyal officer had put in a phone call to Watson, asking if he would pop into police headquarters when he had a moment to spare. As it turned out, Mr. Watson did not come quietly.

And the cops knew exactly where the leader of the pack was. Within twenty-four hours of his arraignment, a team of detectives was speeding to Inyo County to escort Charles Manson back to Los Angeles to face the music.

SPAHN RANCH: DOWN ON THE RANGE

"They were actually wonderful people. They were artists and musicians, they were singers and they had wonderful personalities. Each and every one of them. They never quarreled and never caused any trouble. They did everything we asked them to do. They did the dishes, the cooking, and they took care of our cowboy clothes. They did the washing and little chores all around the ranch. They even helped with the horses."

—Spahn Ranch manager Ruby Pearl, 1970 NBC interview

On Wednesday, December 3, just twelve hours after getting back to Los Angeles from Inyo County and witnessing the charade of seeing Charles Manson arraigned—merely as a car thief—I raced off again, this time to the nether reaches of Los Angeles's San Fernando Valley, to see what I could dig up about Manson's life on the Spahn Ranch.

Topanga Canyon begins at the Pacific Ocean, at Highway 1 between Santa Monica and Malibu, with inviting beaches, surf, funky cafes, and the landmark corner Malibu Feed Bin, providing supplies for local horse ranches and farms. Then it begins its long, winding way, high into the Santa Monica Mountains, with hairpin bends, past a handful of trendy cafes like the Inn of the Seventh Ray, which was once the private residence of evangelist Aimee Semple McPherson. The lower canyon had become the preferred hangout in the Sixties for the trippy, hippie crowd—flower children and emerging musicians, including Chris Hillman, at the start of his career with The Byrds, and Neil Young, who had set up house close to actor Dennis Hopper, within shouting distance of assorted members of the Eagles. It was commonplace to see a barefooted Linda Ronstadt clasping a guitar and hitchhiking to the beach, long before fame and California Governor Jerry Brown came her way. Jim Morrison, lead singer of The Doors, was inspired to write "Roadhouse Blues" after stopping off at the local Topanga Corral coffee house. It was also the home of a music teacher named Gary Hinman, who opened his house to Charles Manson and his scruffy harem, and paid for his generosity with his life.

Abruptly, the greenery and rustic nature of the canyon begins to change at the peak of the Canyon. And as you move downhill into the San Fernando Valley, away from the cooling ocean breezes, the funk disappears, and the highway dramatically changes personality. The weather also changes from cool to desert hot, and the canyon décor goes to mostly concrete, offering a line of blue-collar-affordable houses and mobile-home parks, interspersed with the standard urban sprawl of shopping centers, fast-food restaurants, and banks. Passing the community known as Chatsworth, you keep going to almost the end, then take a sharp left turn onto Santa Susana Pass Road—once a busy two-lane highway that became a ghost road when the State of California cut a new path through the nearby mountains and opened a four-lane freeway system to ease the booming Simi Valley-Los Angeles commute. A couple miles along the road, you take a bend and the road comes to a sudden end, spilling onto a dirt parking lot overrun with weeds. A rickety sign, looking as though it could collapse at any time, is attached to metal stanchions. It announces "Spahn's Movie Ranch."

At first, I thought I'd taken a wrong turn because the place appeared to be doubling as a wrecking yard for abandoned cars. I pulled into a parking spot alongside a flotsam and jetsam of odd vehicles, several of whose windshields were covered with thick layers of dust and parked willy-nilly, facing different directions. A couple of ancient pickup trucks sat next to an old-fashioned Western wagon with one wheel missing. A couple of decrepit mobile homes that looked as though they were fit only for the rubbish dump sat beside a couple of hitching posts. It was a desolate and forlorn-looking place, with no sign of life. Only the buzzing of lots of flies and the strong smell of horse manure suggested that living things might be near.

I had visited several *real* Western movie sets—some in Mexico and some in Hollywood, on the back lots of Universal and Paramount studios—but this didn't resemble any movie set I'd ever seen. This was the neglected dirt street of a true ghost town. I cautiously walked past a row of empty and dilapidated wooden buildings looking for signs of life. A couple of mangy dogs eyed me suspiciously and then resumed sniffing in the dirt. A dune buggy with no wheels sat outside a wooden building next to a half-painted Volkswagen Beetle bearing a sign that read: "Horse Rentals Hourly Rates." In the middle of the road, a rusting trailer looked ready for the nearest dump. Spahn's Movie Ranch, long past its glory days as the number-one location for Hollywood Westerns, was on life support.

A dairy farmer from Pennsylvania, George Spahn, bought the 494-acre spread from the silent screen cowboy star William S. Hart in 1948, using the proceeds from the sale of his smaller North Hollywood ranch. Along the way, he was joined by his sometime partner and companion, Ruby Pearl. Straight out of a B-movie—a small-town girl with big ambitions—she had been Al Capone's favorite barmaid back at Minneapolis's Lindy's Night Club. Figuring she had bigger fish to fry, she moved west and married twice, first to an engineer, then a wrestler named Michael Molinaro. She became a dancer in Hollywood, then switched to dog trainer and circus performer. Her main claim to fame was as the owner of a famous performing dog known as Tinker Toy, who for fifteen years was the Shirley Temple of the canine entertainment world. Even at her peak, Ruby took second billing.

Spahn took a shine to the perky redhead, and when he relocated from North Hollywood into the Valley hinterland, she accompanied him in a relationship that was to last twenty years. In the process, he left his old life behind, including his wife, Martha, and their eleven children—all named after George's favorite horses. He knew all about the movie business, following a short stint as a cowboy actor and then as a supplier of horses and Western props to the studios. He did his best to spread the word that his new abode at the deep end of Topanga was the perfect spot for location-seeking producers.

He did nicely in the beginning. In the late forties and fifties, if you were shooting a Western there was only one place to go—deep into the Spahn's wide-open spaces. The "Western town" was nestled next to a hill of giant boulders and dirt, the terrain covered with cactus and eucalyptus trees. There were picturesque streams, rock-strewn canyons and secret caves, lots of greenery, trees, stubby cactus, with deer, foxes, bobcats, the occasional mountain lion, and rattlesnakes galore. Horse trails wound through the tree-strewn undergrowth, right to the very top of the Santa Susana Mountains. There was no back door into the ranch; just one way in, one way out, giving the place a special kind of privacy, not easily accessible to outsiders.

And they did come running: Tom Mix, Johnny Mack Brown, Hoot Gibson, Wallace Beery, the Lone Ranger, the Cisco Kid, and Roy Rogers riding his faithful steed, Trigger. A coach in the carriage house was used by Grace Kelly for scenes in *High Noon*—one of the greatest Westerns of them all. *Duel in the Sun* was shot there, as were episodes of the long-running TV series *Bonanza*.

It was still cool as I walked down the dirt street with its row of wooden shacks, looking like a desolation alley. The stench of horse manure followed me as I walked past the Longhorn Saloon (it really was the longest building on the street), the Rock City Café, the jail (whose bars were made of wood), a barbershop ("haircuts fifteen cents"), and finally the carriage house, and that was it. If a strong desert wind whipped through, the whole place would be blown away. I saw not a soul, so I turned back to the Longhorn, when suddenly two young women seemingly in their teens, barefooted and sporting shorts and baggy T-shirts, burst out onto the street. I introduced myself as a newspaper writer there to report a story. One said her name was Squeaky, the other Gypsy—their legal names were Lynette Fromme and Catherine Share.

Squeaky did all the talking. She said the ranch was her temporary home. I asked if she was familiar with Charles Manson and the accusations of murder leveled against him. She looked pained, as if she had suddenly smelled a foul odor. "All we were doing out here and in the desert is playin'," she said in an aw-shucks kind of flat voice.

"What kind of man is Mr. Manson?" I asked.

"He's a very good person," she said. "He's got a lot of peace. He'd take off over the mountains and just wander around. We don't want to bother nobody. We don't want to steal from nobody. All we want to do is get away from the city."

I asked where I could find Mr. Spahn. Silently, Squeaky took me by the arm and escorted me down the street to a tiny, falling-down shack perched precariously on a foundation of cracking concrete. We walked into the room, and after stepping out of the sunshine into the gloom, my eyes took a few moments to adjust to the light. There were flies buzzing around a bowl of decaying fruit sitting on the top of an oil heater, and the overpowering smell of stale food wafted from a small kitchen area. On the wall were some crude paintings of a man in a Stetson hat. A large leather horse saddle sat on a well-worn couch in one corner, and there were half-burned, unlit candles on every shelf. An elderly man sat in a rocking chair. "This man has come to see you from England," Squeaky told him. A big black mixed-breed German Shepherd lolled at his feet.

This then was George Spahn. Although it was barely 9:00 a.m., and the ranch's dress code I assumed would surely be dirty, worn-in blue jeans and T-shirts, Spahn was formally attired: black cowboy boots, a jacket and tie, and a tan Stetson hat. One hand clasped a walking stick as if he were about to jump to his feet any second. His trendy, wraparound sunglasses didn't quite go with the rest of the outfit. He apologized for not getting up. "My eyes are real bad," he said. Then he introduced me to his attractive, middle-aged, red-haired companion, Ruby Pearl. She was, he told me, the ranch manager, although judging by the abandoned furniture at one corner, the rusting fridge nestled alongside a beat-up car, not to mention the rest of the ranch's main street—she didn't seem to be doing a very effective job.

Spahn was amiable and friendly, speaking in a soft drawl, Pearl continually interrupting to elaborate or correct him. He said they definitely did not like the notoriety of the past few days, particularly the stuff about the murder of that movie star. Business had dropped precipitously already, he complained. "All that Charlie stuff ain't good," he said. "He's an okay guy. All that bad stuff they're saying about him is crazy. Some mistake. He's no killer."

They emphasized their complete astonishment at the news of the past days, as well as charges that had been leveled at Manson and the girls who lived at his place. They were obviously trying their darnedest to distance themselves. Later I was told that old Spahn was terrified of Manson and afraid to say a bad word about him. He knew first-hand that within seconds, Manson could turn from a smiling, benevolent fellow into a raving lunatic. One day a few weeks earlier, Manson had come charging into Spahn's shack, furious because the old man had telephoned the local sheriff to report that, "Those darn motorcyclists are making life hell for us…they race around with those dune buggies all night long keeping me and my neighbors awake. And scaring my horses."

He and Pearl said when they complained to the bikers, the Manson girls went berserk and screamed, "Shut up, you whore, you pig you. We're coming to shoot you and burn your house down." And the next day Manson showed up. He cursed George for calling the cops. Manson often claimed that Spahn was just feigning his blindness. So to test him, he pulled out his sharp Bowie knife, waved it under the ranch owner's throat to try to make him blink. "You're a liar and a cheat," he told Spahn. But the old man didn't react to the blade. Two of the girls were with him, and Charlie whispered to them, "Undress—walk in front of him." They did. Spahn never blinked. Manson quickly sheathed the knife, hugged Spahn, and said, "You know I love you, George." And left. Two Sheriff's deputies showed up the next day, spoke to a few ranch residents, but took no action.

Now, in the wake of the murder arrests, Pearl told me they were upset because folks were already calling to cancel their weekend horse rentals. In a good month they could take in maybe $1,000. "All that stuff," said Spahn, "is hurting us real bad." He told me that to earn extra income, he now had to resort to sending some of his wranglers to nearby ranches to pick up dead horses and bury them. However, he admitted, there was a time when he viewed Charles Manson as something of a savior.

By 1968, Spahn's fortunes had taken a definite turn for the worst. He was now seriously in debt. Studios had discovered that they could shoot American Westerns in Mexico or even in Spain at a fraction of the cost and without worrying about union rates or overtime. Italy had also become a favored movie nation and a mecca for what had become known as "Spaghetti Westerns." As for the cowboy alleys, it was easier and cheaper just to build them in their very own film-factory backyard.

What income was left came from the odd TV commercial or low-budget biker flick. And that meant having to make deals at giveaway, rock-bottom prices. The last real movie to shoot at the ranch was in 1964—a cheapie horror/sci-fi flick called *The Creeping Terror*, about a slug-like monster that had escaped from a space ship and was terrorizing a small town. The creature made its home in a muddy pond, which the director conveniently found in the heart of the Spahn Ranch. "One of our wranglers who saw it said it was the worst film he had ever seen," said

Spahn. "Even the monster looked cheap and terrible—a real joke." But he told me: "I'm not complaining. Beggars can't be choosers. By the way," he suddenly said, "can I get paid for this interview if you sell it around? We've got plenty of bills to pay." I said I would talk to my editor and let him know. That seemed to satisfy him.

So Spahn is left, barely able to pay his property taxes and struggling with his monthly utility bills, and then one day early in 1969, Manson and his followers blow into town. No horse-drawn wagon, just a bus painted black. And its cargo turned out to be a diverse assortment of hippie types—mostly young women. Manson persuaded Spahn to let them stay for just a week or two. Or more. Their handshake agreement Spahn told me, was simple: No rent, they would provide their own bedding, and in return, the hippie band would help take care of the sprawling property and all of Spahn's needs. Fromme was assigned to be Spahn's "eyes" and de facto wife, cooking, doing his laundry, and servicing his libido when required. Years later, she was to offer a revisionist version of that sex-trade element of their relationship. "It was never sexual," she said in a TV interview. "He was like a grandfather to me."

Spahn agreed to Manson's terms, which also suited Pearl, who was fed up toiling seven days a week and working until 11:00 at night, trying to keep the ranch afloat. She agreed to stick around, although she said she needed to escape. She would no longer live on the premises. Every night she left the ranch for her own home, returning daily to manage the property and make sure the bills were paid.

After the Manson clan moved in, she complained bitterly that the electricity bills had gone through the roof. "They must be running some kind of car-repair business with all those dune buggies. The wranglers say they're burning electricity all day and night," she told Spahn. But the old man had become an easy mark for any sob story. He had allowed an array of other riffraff characters to move onto the ranch—sometimes for a week, sometimes longer. None of them paid him a penny in rent. Indeed, the occupancy rate fluctuated. Manson's crowd started at around a dozen and at times swelled to thirty or more, not including an assortment of work-for-stay guests who did not need the Manson blessing to move onto the ranch.

One of them was Donald "Shorty" Shea. He endeared himself to Spahn because he too had been an animal trainer, worked part-time as a stuntman, and dreamed of becoming an actor. He helped keep the horses groomed for their weekend paying riders. But Shea and Manson did not get along. In fact, Manson went into a fit of rage when he learned Shea had married a stripper from Vegas who was black. Shea tried to warn Spahn about Manson, telling the old man that the Family was running a stolen-car and chop shop in several of the old barns. And when the Los Angeles Sheriff's office raided the Spahn ranch and arrested Manson and his acolytes on suspicion of stealing cars in mid-August of 1969, Manson fingered Shorty as the police snitch, and was probably right. Not long after the aborted raid, Shea mysteriously vanished.

Another work-for-stay character was Danny DeCarlo, a Canadian-born former member of the Coast Guard, who was treasurer of the Venice motorcycle gang known as the Straight Satans. He was an expert on guns, and so Manson invited him to live at the ranch. He could help himself to any girl he fancied in return for protecting Manson and the ranch from drug dealers and others who might want to do harm. There was also Panamanian immigrant John Leo Flynn, known to everyone simply as "Juan." He was handy at fixing cars and was happy to toil long hours as Manson turned stolen cars into dune buggies. As a reward for his endeavors, he was allowed to take his sexual pick of the Manson women.

Octogenarian Spahn told me that the only way he was able to pay his bills was by renting out his horses—many of them mangy and infirm—to mostly weekend day-trippers who paid $2.50 an hour to get their brief taste of nature. The riders were unbothered by the decaying movie facades. They rode and trod the strange and winding paths that led to a cool, trickling stream, up the steep hillsides, through groves of oaks, with their gnarled roots reaching into dry riverbeds, into the chaparral covered hills, then higher and higher still to the rim of the rocks. And from this wilderness up high, they looked back at their smog shrouded city. One of the weekend regulars was a youngster named Bryan Cranston. The Oscar nominee and multiple Emmy winner vividly recalled that, once, while sitting on a tired old horse, he came across a small, wiry, bearded, charismatic man with dark, piercing eyes, who was strumming a guitar and singing to an audience of half-naked young women and assorted ragged toddlers.

Spahn and Pearl struggled on, never really knowing how many people were availing themselves of their hospitality. From time to time, Spahn said Manson would give him a huge chunk of cash—once, several thousand dollars—when he needed to pay an urgent property-tax bill. On another occasion, it was an old car that Manson claimed had been given to him—along with its pink slip. He gave it to Spahn, although the old rancher couldn't drive.

Barely a year later, in September 1970, Spahn's troubles grew worse. A vicious brush fire, fanned by wild and hot Santa Ana winds, swept through the ranch, completely destroying the Western street and all the facades—along with all the detritus of the Manson Family. Although Spahn and his skeleton crew of helpers managed to lead fifty-seven horses to safety, three burned to death.

When I asked Spahn and Pearl if I could meet some of the girls who lived with Manson, Fromme suddenly re-appeared from the shadows, where she had been quietly listening to our conversation. I thanked Spahn, shook his hand, and Fromme escorted me maybe some hundred yards into the back of the Longhorn Saloon. I noticed that the large community room in the back of the saloon was quite bright because the back wall consisted entirely of floor-to-ceiling windows, many of them cracked, looking out on green trees and huge boulders. This back room seemed to be a communal bedroom with numerous battered, tatty, and slightly odorous bare mattresses scattered around on the floor, like something you might find at a kid's camp. Clothes were piled in small heaps in corners of the room. It was overly warm because a heater in the middle of the room was blasting out hot air. It smelled like rot.

In the midst of this, several girls were washing each other's hair with water from a bucket, and then braiding it. I was surprised when suddenly some of the girls started singing, something unrecognizable to me. I thought this might have been some kind of odd welcoming ritual performed for all visitors. It certainly could have been a scene straight out of *Snow White and the Seven Dwarfs*—although no one there looked a likely stand-in for Snow White. It was definitely not the chorus, "Hi Ho, Hi Ho; it's off to work we go." Everyone was greatly impressed that I was from a London newspaper, but I didn't go to great lengths to explain that I lived twenty-five miles away in Studio City—that I hadn't really trekked 6,000 miles to talk to them. At this stage, there was no point in divesting them of their illusions.

Moments later, Squeaky and Gypsy ushered two young men into the dormitory. They looked like high-school students. One introduced himself as Paul Watkins, the other as Brooks Poston. And for the next few days they had me spellbound as they coolly recounted a story that blew my mind.

Spahn Ranch, 1969.

LIFE, SEX, AND DEATH
WITH CHARLIE

"I was this 17-year-old hippie acting out my social tendencies and there was this little guy in Topanga Canyon…and I guess you could say I became addicted to him. He was talented, animated. and seemed shamelessly uninhibited. He was a trip.

"These young people were the cream of the crop. You had homecoming queens, valedictorians, Tex Watson had the high hurdles records in McKinney Texas. I was student body president. You are looking at overachievers, most likely kids… with a strong social conscience. Not a bunch of bad boys and girls."

—Paul Watkins, interview with Maureen Reagan,
CNN, 1983

I wasn't sure what to expect that first time I met Paul Watkins and Brooks Poston. As far as I knew, they were both still devout members of Manson's Family and perhaps even involved in some kind of criminal activity. Their leader was in jail, facing the most hideous charges imaginable; a conviction could send him and others involved in the murders to the San Quentin gas chamber. Would I, a member of the press, be perceived as the enemy? Perhaps even a "piggie"? Much to my surprise, there was no need for concern. Watkins especially was charming and welcoming and, upon later reflection, probably grateful that he had met an independent outsider to whom he could finally unburden himself. He said they had given no other interviews.

At nineteen, Watkins was clean-cut, with an open, Young Hollywood Leading Man kind of face. He had a pageboy haircut and a pencil-thin mustache, resembling a young Clark Gable. Poston, a year older, was tall and angular with long, silky blond hair, a pointy nose and chin. He had the freshly scrubbed face of a shy choirboy. Watkins suggested we move to a quieter space—a shady spot outside the saloon. It also happened to be out of eyesight and earshot of Fromme, Sandra Good, and the handful of leftover girls still living at the ranch who were not implicated in the murders and were hovering, hoping to catch some of our conversation. He obviously didn't want to be perceived as badmouthing their leader.

We sat down; I switched on my tape recorder. Watkins did virtually all the talking—and, boy, did he talk. Chapter and verse about life with Manson—and what a strange tale it was. I grew increasingly astounded, not really sure that what I was hearing bore a resemblance to any kind of truth or reality. I kept thinking that I was being conned by these two young men who were maybe coming down from a bad trip. Either that, or they were suffering from a serious case of bats in their belfries.

As Watkins told it, there was more to Manson than anyone could ever imagine. He said he was intrigued by him from the moment he set eyes on him. It was in spring 1968, and he was a self-described "fugitive flower child," wandering aimlessly. Watkins was born in Oxnard, California, in January 1950 but as a child moved with his oil worker father to Sidon, Lebanon, and then to Beaumont, Texas, and then back to the middle-class suburbs of Thousand Oaks, about forty miles from Beverly Hills. An early passion for Bible study had been replaced by a passion for music, which led to a somewhat destructive passion for marijuana—and then more heavy chemical stimulants. "I was a seventeen-year-old hippie…acting out my anti-social tendencies," he said. "One day I went to this house in Topanga to buy some good weed. There was this little guy who was in charge, a skinny fellow with ten girls. It flashed through my mind: 'Wow. One guy! What's he doing with ten good-looking chicks? Impressive. That's where the action has got to be.' We talked, and hit it off right away. I was immediately fascinated by him. We were both into music. He was talented and animated and seemed shamelessly uninhibited. Whatever trip he was on, I wanted to be part of it. On that first day, Charlie seemed totally open. No inhibitions. 'Girls are here to be fucked and are put on this earth to do what we want,' he told me. I got addicted to him."

How had he become such a chick magnet? "Charlie didn't bullshit. Right away he said he'd spent most of his life behind bars. When he finally got out, he said he started riding around town, and he went to Haight-Ashbury and met a lot of flower children. He started meeting girls and found out that girls were real easy there, real easy to get next to, and he said he just started getting more girls and more girls together." Watkins thought, *Easy peasy. Nice work if you can get it.*

Manson, of course, was no fool. He wanted to build his harem, and he quickly realized that the good-looking kid from Texas—if he was controlled and handled in the right manner—could be a valuable asset. And Watkins was a willing consort. "I was in from that very minute," he recalled. "From that day onwards, I turned my whole life over to Charlie—my body, my mind, and everything else that goes along with it." With no official ceremony, Watkins joined the Manson inner circle, and it wasn't long before he got down to business. "I need a new love," Manson told Watkins, who he nicknamed "Little Paul"—ironic, considering Manson was barely over five feet tall, a fraction taller than his new-found buddy.

Watkins tackled his new assignment with a passion. "I'd drive out to the Sunset Strip, hang around. You could spot the runaways and the lost souls. I'd chat to one or two at a time and tell them about Charlie. About living this great life, a paradise, out at this wilderness—a real ranch. 'No obligations—no commitments. Take a look. Leave if you want to, and I'll drive you back.' Sometimes when I'd be driving, I'd stop and pick up hitchhikers if they looked halfway decent." Then came a stunning statement: "Charlie even suggested I enroll in the local Hollywood High School where there were lots of candidates. He even gave me fake ID. It was my job to pull them in. Charlie might have done it, but he was too old. I was still a kid. But once I had snagged them, Charlie did the rest to clinch the deal."

Once the girls were snared, the fun began, said Watkins. "Charlie has this technique. I brought them to the ranch, and he was always there to greet us. He'd take them into another room and give them the Charlie treatment. It never took long. If the girl was plain, he'd tell her how beautiful she was. Within an hour, he had their clothes off and was sleeping with them, screwing them, or getting them to suck his cock. Even the shy ones. They'd do whatever he wanted. And whatever they were told to do. I was impressed because in half an hour, they were like his slaves. Eventually, everyone wanted to satisfy Charlie."

And satisfy in every way, including food foraging, which they had down to a fine art. "Bartering, they called it," Watkins said. "They'd cozy up to the supermarket box boys, even the managers, and offer them sex for food. It worked this way: The guys screwed them for free, and the young men, in exchange, would carefully stack throwaway food in cardboard cartons at the back of the building instead of tossing it in the garbage cans. It saved them diving into the dumpsters and having to sort through the rotting food and the salvageable stuff." The girls became skilled at sexual bartering, often exchanging favors with storeowners. In return for a quick bang, they received fresh bread and cakes.

Then there were the orgies, masterfully manipulated by Manson. Part sex, part indoctrination, part hypnosis—often helped along with liberal doses of drugs handed out like candy. "He'd never say, 'Look into my eyes' or any of that stuff," said Watkins. "He kept repeating, like a mantra, 'Nothing can be done without your cooperation—you must want this yourself. Or he would parrot, 'There ain't no crime, there ain't no sin—nothing means nothing…I am you, you are me, we are us. There's no such thing as death.'"

And close to hand were Manson's baggies filled with drugs. "We used a huge mixture of drugs—no one kept a record. All the psychedelics, pharmaceuticals, psilocybin (better known as magic mushrooms), mescaline, a small amount of belladonna, hashish, marijuana, and opium, and, on a few occasions, peyote. I became quite an expert on cooking up the belladonna. I learned to do it on an Indian reservation in Arizona." Watkins said he enjoyed the drugs and reckoned he'd taken some 150-200 acid trips alone. As for Manson, the orgy choreographer, he often went without. "He was the ringmaster, and you'd better do what he says, otherwise he turned vicious—particularly with the girls," Watkins said. "I saw him punch them in the face, or drag them screaming by the hair if they hesitated, even for a second, to follow his orders. He ruled over them with equal doses of fear and love. Sometimes he was a violent beast—and the next minute he was gentle and soft, cuddling and comforting them like a baby."

There were frightening times when Manson played what he referred to as his "dying games," Watkins said. "He didn't ever warn you when he was going mad or was into a game. We had a room at the back of the saloon when it was orgy time. The mattresses were scattered, and the girls had pinned bits of velvet and colored hangings on the walls. I had been with Charlie for about a month. We was sitting around on acid, and I was getting kind of in a 'feeling really weird' mood—getting really stoned, and Charlie was telling me to die. He was just saying, 'Die… just die.' And I didn't just die. Suddenly he jumped me. He threw me on the floor, and he leapt on me. No one moved—everyone just watched, transfixed. He started choking me, his hands around my neck. Suddenly I couldn't breathe, and Charlie coolly said, 'I'm going to kill you.'"

Watkins took a deep breath. "I knew that the more I struggled, the more Charlie would squeeze my throat. He had this crazy thing about not being afraid to die. And I thought he was going to kill me. So I had to go limp, and when I did, Charlie released my throat. I thought he was just going to flat kill me. He let me go the very instant I ceased to fear him. I knew Charlie used his double-speak mantra with everybody who was new to the Family. He'd say again and again, 'If you are willing to die, then you don't have to die.' So in my mind I looked at it as I was being tested, that if I was going to fear death, that he would have gone ahead and killed me. I still firmly believe that today, because he was sincere in his eyes, and he was sincere in the way he was going about doing it. So when I relaxed, he let me go. Then, in a second, he became a different person. He burst into peals of laughter, pulled me back onto my feet, and said, 'Are you ready to go with the girls and make love?'"

While he realized he was being used, Watkins said he was so under Manson's thumb that he obeyed his orders, no matter what. He said once they went to a meeting at the World Knowledge Faith Love Fountain of the World, a new cult headquartered five miles away in Box Canyon. That cult, too, boasted about their all-powerful, all-seeing leader, a fellow named Krishna Venta, who had been born Francis Herman Pencovic in San Francisco, and liked to run around the premises dressed as Jesus with a crown of thorns. When Manson put in his appearance, it began to shape up as a pious smackdown. "They was all talking about their guru and how great he was," recalled Watkins. "Charlie was going to demonstrate how great *he* was. They told us how their guru had hung on the cross up there for three days, so Charlie told me to go hang up there for a week. So I got up and walked out the door and started figuring how I was going to get up on that thing. And then he came out and told me not to do it. He'd proved his point."

WATKINS' COMPATRIOT Brooks Poston, a small-town boy from the Texas panhandle town of Borger, who was quieter and shyer than Watkins, said he had his own "dying" story to tell. He'd met Manson at a party in

1968 at the Sunset Boulevard home of Beach Boy Dennis Wilson. The drummer had been sucked into the Manson circle shortly after giving a ride to two of his girls who were hitchhiking on Sunset Boulevard. They titillated Wilson by raving on and on about this extraordinary guru who had a wonderful voice and wrote music. Wilson said he wanted to meet the guy, and when he did, he immediately fell under his spell. He invited Manson to stay with him at his house. The next day, Manson moved in—lock, stock, and girls. Wilson took full advantage of Manson's largesse, Poston said, having his way with the young women, who were at his beck and call.

Poston happened to be at Wilson's house when Manson walked in. "The room came to a standstill when he entered and walked right up to Dean Moorehouse sitting on a couch. He kneeled down and gently kissed his feet. Then he asked Dean, 'Are you ready to die?' When he nodded, Charlie replied, 'You can live forever.' I think that was the first time I saw Charlie playing the part of Jesus Christ," Poston recalled.

Of course, Poston didn't know the back story. Moorehouse, a sometime Protestant church pastor, had first met Manson in 1967 when Mary Brunner, the San Francisco librarian who Manson began living with soon after he left jail, and Fromme were hitchhiking in the San Jose area. Intrigued by the threesome, the forty-seven-year-old Moorehouse invited the trio home to dinner, introducing them to his wife, Audrey, and his sixteen-year-old daughter Ruth Ann. The two men hit it off over talk of religion and the Bible. Moorehouse invited Manson and the girls to stay for dinner. They all got along so well that the guests were invited to stay overnight. Big mistake.

Not long after—much to Moorehouse's chagrin—his daughter (after a quickie marriage that lasted all of one day in a vain effort to prove her emancipation) ran off to join the Manson family. He reported his daughter as a runaway and vowed revenge. But when they met again, Poston said, Manson introduced Dean to LSD and other drugs, and the irate dad was sufficiently pacified to not only drop the complaint but dramatically change his lifestyle. When Manson and his girls moved into Dennis Wilson's Sunset Boulevard estate, Moorehouse became Wilson's gardener, and took up residence in the drummer's guesthouse—along with his assistant—Brooks Poston.

Watkins said Poston also fell head first for the Manson death-game chicanery. "Charlie would say that a lot of times a person would have an ego death, but they wouldn't physically die," he said. "So to prove his point, one night in the area of the saloon which Charlie turned into a club, Charlie told him, 'Die,' so Brooks laid down on the couch and really tried to die. He lay there for three days without moving, without getting up. No food. Nothing. No water. And whatever bodily functions just occurred." Finally, when he had seen enough, Manson told Poston to be reborn, and the frail Poston barely managed to walk out of the room.

Even the philosophical but pragmatic gold prospector, Paul Crockett, who never became a full-time Family member, once found himself at the center of a Manson fealty test. Crockett, who had fully embraced mysticism and the self-help movement, said he saw how the Devil operated first-hand when the Manson family moved to Death Valley in late 1969. "Charlie was really pissed at me because I wouldn't bend to his will whenever he wanted me to," Crockett told Watkins. "So one night, without warning, he pulled his knife and came at me, stuck the blade at my throat, 'This is sharp enough to bone a pig,' he said, and then he calmed down, put the knife away and said, 'Let's get some food.'"

It was late afternoon, and Watkins still wasn't finished. In the midst of recounting the graphic and remarkable history of his life and times with Manson, he took pains to point out that he no longer lived at the Spahn Ranch. In May 1969, he and Poston had turned their backs on the man they once worshiped. They moved to the remote Barker Ranch and, with the aid and support of Paul Crockett, they began a new life filing mining claims and digging for gold. It was only by pure chance that they were at Spahn on the day I first visited. They claimed they had driven down from Death Valley to buy supplies, were intrigued by what was going down in the wake of the murders, and sought to get a firsthand look at what was happening on their old turf. For me, it turned out to be an amazing stroke of good fortune. If I had had to rely on the words of Fromme, Good, Brunner, or any of the others, I would most likely have left empty-handed, for the girls who stuck around remained fiercely loyal to Manson and their "sisters" in jail. Undoubtedly they would have tried to feed me the usual pap that they were to deliver, for years to come, about Manson and his twisted mission: to eradicate hypocrisy, save the trees, and make the world a better place for his like-minded, brain-addled followers.

As for the nights of the murders, Watkins and Poston were in the clear. They were hundreds of miles away in Death Valley. But from everything they had told me so far, it was clear they had once been deeply embedded in the Manson culture. And they also truly once believed he was their Messiah. How could they possibly have swallowed such wholesale baloney?

Though different in temperament, there were some clear similarities. Both were self-described country hicks who hadn't even celebrated their twenty-first birthdays, innocents abroad when they stumbled upon Manson, the crafty survivor who made manipulation his forte. Both were young, and both shared similar dreams with Manson. They, too, wanted to break into the music business. Watkins played the flute, Poston the guitar—in fact, they were later to form their own music group, Desert Sun. They had come to Los Angeles with unfulfilled dreams, and here he was, their very own flesh-and-blood genie. And he had connections, able to bring these goggle-eyed hayseeds front and center for the latest rock happenings.

He waved his magic wand, and before you could say "Beach Boys," Little Paul and Skinny Brooks were hanging out with the royalty of the music biz. *Isn't that Mike Love from the Beach Boys over there in the corner talking to Cass Elliot and John and Michelle Phillips of the Mamas and the Papas? Who's that good-looking chick? Dean Martin's daughter, Deana.*

There's crazy Phil Kaufman; he hangs out with the Stones. Another blood brother of Charlie. They met in the slammer. And isn't that Terry Melcher, son of movie star Doris Day and producer of The Byrds' mega-hit "Turn! Turn! Turn!"? He's gonna give Charlie a big, fat recording contract. Plus, all the pricey drugs you could ever want—and willing, ready and able young women prepared to satisfy any sexual peccadillo you desire. It couldn't get any better, could it? You'd have to keep pinching yourself to make sure you weren't in a dream.

Hobnobbing with the rich and famous impressed the two young men. But they had also seen the dark side. And it scared them. They'd had long phone calls with Paul Crockett up in Death Valley, who had seen the Manson machine firsthand—and much of what he saw, he didn't like. Bluntly he told them: "You're part of a cult. You need to get out. And fast."

So in May 1969, they both split, heading to Death Valley. Watkins was later to put it into perspective. Before he had fled to the Barker Ranch, his role had been that of Manson's unchallenged second-in-command, vowing to do his every bidding. He was Charlie's go-to guy. His leaving created a big vacancy. And into the breach stepped Charles "Tex" Watson—ready, willing, and able to prove himself by following Manson's every command. Whatever it took.

After hours of listening—and somewhat in a state of shock and disbelief—I left Spahn, promising to return the next day. I needed to consult with my London editor and try to make sense of what I had just heard. But one other piece of information I had been given that day stuck in my mind. I vowed to take it up the next morning. Watkins and Poston were impressed with my overseas connections and relished the attention I was giving them.

They told me that Manson could predict the future. And what he saw was not very nice. A revolution was coming—any day now—and it would be bad. Really bad. Blacks in America rising up to slaughter whites. It would be a new kind of Holocaust. Everyone would be wiped out, except for Manson and his followers. Before the blood began to flow, he would escape. He had even picked out a place in the California desert near Death Valley. He knew it was there because it had been described in the Bible. He knew exactly where, chapter and verse. They would all escape in a caravan of dune buggies, which were being built and readied on the Spahn Ranch. And they would all live happily ever after, relying on water from an underground spring.

Manson had surefire confirmation of the coming apocalypse, and Watkins and Poston insisted it was true. There *was* proof. The warning was clearly spelled out in meticulous detail for Manson, and Manson alone, in the lyrics of a double album that had been released the previous year. An album commonly known as *The White Album*, by a group of singers from Liverpool, England—the Beatles.

Unaware that John Lennon was living in Los Angeles at the time of the trial, defense lawyers did not subpoena him to testify. Lennon called Manson "a fookin' wanker."

THE BEATLES MADE ME DO IT

"As far as lining up someone for some kind of 'Helter Skelter' trip, you know, that's the District Attorney's motive. That's the only thing he could find for a motive to throw on top of all that confusion he had. There was no such thing in my mind as 'Helter Skelter.' 'Helter Skelter' was a song ... it was a nightclub."
—Charles Manson, parole hearing, 1992

"Before 'Helter Skelter' came along, all Charlie cared about was orgies."
—Paul Watkins, 1969

Day 2 of my session with Watkins and Poston took place again in the shadows of the decaying ranch. My foreign editor in London woke me at 5:00 a.m. and said, "Get everything. Get as much as you can."

So I showed up at 7:00 a.m. and waited as Paul and Brooks kicked off their blankets and sleepily climbed to their feet in the same clothes they had worn the day before. "Can we go over some of the facts from yesterday?" I asked. I wanted to hear more about Armageddon, as prophesied in the *White Album*.

There were two great influences that Manson cited, Watkins carefully explained. One was the New Testament's Book of Revelation—crazy visions and fiery images, which my Irish father-in-law insisted must have been written by a mad monk who had imbibed too much wine and strong cheese in the wee small hours of the morning. "Revelations was Manson's holy grail," Watkins said. Manson, he told me, mixed and matched The Book and the Beatles, emerging with a powerful stew of carefully tailored fact and grossly exaggerated fiction. Nightly, after dinner in the Longhorn, he dished up a dessert of his unmitigated mishmash. Revelation, he preached, referred to "four angels" who were more than just angels. He alone knew who they really were—John, Paul, George, and Ringo. He had refined the legend and had it down pat. The parallels and connections, he insisted, were so obvious. Was it not written in Revelation that they arrived wearing "breastplates of fire"?

"And they had hair as the hair of women, and their teeth were as teeth of lions. And they had breastplates, as it were breastplates of iron."

Breastplates. That meant electric guitars, of course. And, "The faces of men...but with the hair of women." A perfect description of the Fab Four. Further, Revelations tells of a hellish, bottomless pit opening up in the world, and a plague of anthropomorphic locusts with long hair coming to torture the unfaithful until an angel blows a trumpet to God. Locusts with long hair? Another clear reference to the Beetles—or Beatles—who also arrived with fire and brimstone. And there were powerful Beatles lyrics in songs like "Blackbird," "Piggies," "Revolution 1," "Revolution 9," and especially "Helter Skelter," which clearly warned, "I'm coming down fast."

And what about that song "Sexy Sadie"? Any dummy could see that was written for the Family's very own Susan "Sexy Sadie" Atkins.

"Charlie said another song, 'Rocky Raccoon,' referred to black people, and then there was the Lennon composition 'Happiness Is a Warm Gun,' clearly showing that the Beatles knew it was all about acquiring firearms for the coming revolution," Watkins told me. "Charlie was quite clear. 'Helter Skelter' was the clarion call warning that the revolution was to begin." It would, he insisted, erupt in violence, pitting blacks against whites and resulting in the kind of bloodshed the world had never seen. Time and again Manson repeated it: "Listen to those songs, sing along, learn those words, and all will become perfectly clear."

I listened intently to their elaborate fable, barely able to keep my mouth shut. I bit my tongue and knew this wasn't the place or the time to offer any kind of rebuttal, even though I was dying to question the veracity of what I was hearing. But here I was, a nowhere man in nowhere land, on the edge of Los Angeles in a falling-down mess of a movie ranch, as two young strangers tried to convince me that the biggest names in rock 'n' roll had been sending secret messages to a nobody like Charles Manson about launching a racial war. And Paul Watkins and Brooks Poston, like the rest, blindly concurred, agreeing that disaster was at hand because the Beatles had said so.

I came to know the Beatles pretty well in August 1964 when I toured America with them, reporting on their thirty-one US concerts (and hijinks) for my London newspaper. And while they could behave in a Bolshie, rebellious, even juvenile way—particularly John Lennon, who often functioned in a world of his own—there was no way on earth that he (or they) had penned songs with lyrics that could in any way be construed as alerting some crafty ex-con in California that it was time to prepare for a race war in America.

Some years later I was to talk to John Lennon and Paul McCartney about this aberration. They were appalled and outraged by the very idea that their songs had been manipulated and co-opted by a mass murderer.

"What did Charlie really mean about 'helter-skelter'?" I asked Watkins and Poston.

"He ran around repeatedly telling us, 'Helter-skelter' is coming…it's coming…coming down fast," said Watkins. "He played that album fifty or sixty times, day and night. What he meant was 'helter-skelter' would lead to some atrocious murders—that some of the spades from Watts would come up into the Bel-Air and Beverly Hills district and just really wipe some people out, and cut little boys up and make parents watch.

Charlie didn't like the black man and he wanted to see him turn against his white brother in a race war. Then Whitey would go into the black ghetto and kill indiscriminately, shooting blacks like crazy, but all they would shoot would be the garbage collector and Uncle Toms and all the ones that were with Whitey in the first place. There would be retaliations, counterattacks, vigilantes, and barricades, followed by wholesale blood baths. And the black Muslims would know he was coming and come and slit everyone's throat. 'Helter-skelter' was coming down."

Watkins said the Beatles were in on the plot because Manson told them that following the carnage, they would abandon their luxurious homes in England and meet up with Manson and his band, and they would all head for the safety of a secret promised land. So convinced was he by all this that, according to Watkins, Manson claimed he had placed long distance calls to England. Even sent telegrams. Of course, he was unable to connect with the four musicians. Or if they did ever receive those messages, they were instantly deep sixed in Apple Records' bottomless pit known as "crazy fan mail."

Manson, he said, was quite specific about his great escape to Death Valley. The dune buggies were ready and waiting, and they had been stocking supplies for weeks. "Charlie used to walk around in the desert and say, 'See, there's places where water would come up to the top of the ground, and then it would go down and there wouldn't be no more water, and then it would come up again and go down again. He would look at that and say, 'There has got to be a hole somewhere, somewhere here, a big old lake.' And it just really got far out, that there was a hole underneath there somewhere where you could drive a speedboat across it, a big underground city. Then we started from the 'Revolution 9' song on the Beatles album, which was interpreted by Charlie as really meant to be Revelation 9 in the New Testament, which talks about a bottomless pit—a place where there's no sun or moon."

Manson had it all planned out, according to Watkins: "He said there would be a city of gold but no life...only a tree there that bears twelve different kinds of fruit that changed every month. And we interpreted it to mean that Charlie knew about this hole in Death Valley." He went on and on, introducing the twelve tribes of Israel—although Manson, Watkins said, considered Jews to be not far behind the blacks on his shit list. In the desert, Manson promised they would multiply, "And as we are making the music and drawing all the young love to the desert, the Family will increase in ranks to 144,000.

"And Charlie said when the Whites had all perished, all that would be left was he and his Family, and their followers. And when it was all over, Charlie would come out of the hole and clear up the mess…like he always had. Blackie then would come to Charlie and say, 'You know, I did my thing, I killed them all and, you know, I am tired of killing now. It is all over.' And Charlie would scratch his fuzzy head and kick him in the butt and tell him to go pick the cotton and go be a good nigger, and he would live happily ever after."

"What was the breaking point? What led you to abandon the man you thought was your true Messiah?" I asked.

"I began to get rather disgusted and disheartened with what was going on at the ranch because it got to be a revolution-type scene where everyone was talking about the revolution, and we were collecting guns and building dune buggies and things like that," Watkins told me. "So I ran out to the hideout we had in in Death Valley and met Paul Crockett, who started talking some sense to me. He didn't lecture me but just asked me questions to reassess my thinking. Questions like, 'Do you really believe all that crap?' Paul was telling us that Charlie was a big fraud and we should get out. I quit using marijuana and all the other drugs…and began to think more clearly."

"The motive for these murders originated, ladies and gentlemen, in the warped, twisted mind of Charles Manson. The motive for these murders was bizarre, perhaps even more bizarre than the murders themselves: briefly, the evidence will show Manson's fanatical obsession with helter-skelter, a term that he borrowed from the English musical record group the Beatles."

—Vincent Bugliosi at trial of Charles "Tex" Watson, 1971

IN OCTOBER 1973, I sat by a swimming pool in Bel Air with John Lennon, while a pretty young woman named May Pang served us cocktails. Brandy Alexanders for John, less-exotic beer and wine for me and photographer Cyril Maitland, who was with me to do a story on John for the *London Daily Express*. Lennon was staying in a one-story Spanish-style house right opposite Hotel Bel-Air that belonged to record producer Lou Adler.

Lennon had come to LA to promote *Mind Games*, his latest solo album. He hoped to kick-start a career that had been flagging, mainly due to his experimentation with politics in the previous year's *Sometime in New York City*. The double album had landed with a dull thud—critically reviled and, worse still, ignored, which the former Beatle could not stand. He was also in the midst of his well-publicized "lost weekend" (so named by Lennon himself), which lasted some eighteen months—long sessions of relentless boozing and drugging with singer Harry Nilsson, sandwiched between pill-fueled forays into the recording studio under the wacky supervision of producer Phil Spector. Nilsson and Lennon had become party animals, perennials at local nightclubs, palling around with the likes of Olympic partiers Keith Moon, Alice Cooper, and Mickey Dolenz.

He ended up in the news quite a bit during this period, and it wasn't because of his musical achievements. On one such night, totally inebriated, he got into fisticuffs with Ken Fritz, manager of The Smothers

Brothers, who were performing at the Troubadour nightclub. Fritz had tried in vain to curb their stage-side enthusiasm, which was disrupting his clients' performance. As a result, he found himself in combat with Lennon and his wasted minstrel pal. Peace was restored only when the pair was unceremoniously ejected from the premises amidst a storm of foul insults hurled by the drunken Lennon.

Lennon's wife, Yoko Ono, was in New York; Pang, who worked for the Lennons, had been delegated to keep an eye on—and share accommodations with—her oft wayward boss in what we later learned was a concubine-like arrangement devised by Ono to help salvage their tottering marriage. In retrospect, the strategy of providing another woman to share hearth and home with your husband with a view to repairing a marriage seemed a strangely off-kilter way of doing things. But that was Mrs. Lennon. And perhaps she was looking for some social distractions of her own, which she may have received courtesy of a sought-after session guitarist named David Spinozza. The possible breakup of John and Yoko would have been a big story, but Lennon did not want to go there; I should have realized that he was probably having a bit of fun with me, because he pointedly kept introducing Pang to me as "my secretary."

Over our afternoon drinks, I asked Lennon what he thought of this looney tunes character named Charles Manson, who had claimed that the lyrics on a half-dozen songs from the Beatles had been in actuality a stream of secret messages warning of the coming Armageddon from John, Paul, George, and Ringo, directed for the appreciation of Manson, with double-entendre lyrics that carried special meaning *only* to Manson. He looked at me as if I were an alien invader.

He'd been asked that question before and seemed reluctant to deal with it again. When your life is music, to have your music bastardized in that deformed way was quite appalling to him and his cohorts. I knew Lennon from the Beatles' first American tour in 1964 and, sensing that he didn't want to go there, I explained how bizarre it had been for me to sit in an American courtroom for almost a year as the Beatles were being accused of some kind of incitement to murder. He was uncharacteristically quiet for a few moments; then he responded: "Stark. Raving. Bonkers," he said. "Manson is a fookin' wanker—a dwarf. A psycho. Every crazy known to man calls, writes, or screams to us about what they think our songs are about. And usually it's 101 percent shit because there's always someone putting us under their twisted, mad-scientist microscope. Then out pops their own lunacy. Manson came up with messages in our songs that never ever existed."

That theme of interpretive incompetence, he said, had constantly dogged him and the Beatles from Day 1. "Manson was just an extreme version of the people who came up with the 'Paul is dead' thing or who figured out that the initials to 'Lucy in the Sky with Diamonds' were LSD and jumped to the conclusion that the song was about taking acid. But this was lots of bodies. World War III. When 'Hey Jude' first came out, a music writer for the *London Daily Express* wrote a story insisting that Paul had written the song just for her. [Paul actually wrote it for John's son Julian, who was getting over his parents' divorce.] So people listen to a song, chew on it, and then regurgitate it. And when they do it comes out as a terrible mess. We had all sorts of contortionists, acrobats, and clowns climbing out of the woodwork. I always said this: What has slashing people to death got to do with 'Helter Skelter'? Bugger all, if you ask me." Later, he was to add: "Why didn't that moron listen to the words of our song 'Revolution'? It clearly states my position on violence: *'When you talk about destruction, you can count me* **out!***'*

Ironically, while the Manson trial and the "Beatles Made Me Do It" motive was unfolding on the front pages of newspapers around the world, Lennon and Ono were actually living in Los Angeles, taking therapy with *Primal Scream* psychotherapist, Dr. Arthur Janov. They kept their heads below the radar as they were chauffeured from their rented Bel Air house to Janov's clinic a few miles away on Santa Monica Boulevard. They were snuck quietly through a back door into a giant nursery filled with cribs, stuffed toys, and security blankets as they re-experienced their births while being observed behind a gigantic one-way window. (The sessions were responsible for the couple's emotionally cleansing and raw album *John Lennon/Plastic Ono Band* later that year.)

I have little doubt that if any of the defense team, particularly Manson's irascible defense lawyer Irving Kanarek, had known that one of the most famous Beatles was in their neighborhood, they would have tried their utmost to subpoena Lennon as a witness for the defense. Had that happened, there is no doubt Lennon as a witness would have shot holes in the prosecution's absurdist *White Album* motive. The other Beatles, all in the United Kingdom, were equally incensed about Manson's manipulative use of their lyrics and fired back in 1995's *The Beatles Anthology* TV series.

McCartney was particularly tormented by how his "Helter Skelter" was twisted out of all recognition: "Then it got over to America, the land of interpretive people. And as a DJ would later 'interpret' the fact that I had no shoes on the *Abbey Road* cover, Charles Manson interpreted that 'Helter Skelter' was something to do with the Four Horseman of the Apocalypse," Paul said. "I still don't know what all that stuff is: it's from the Bible, *Revelations*—I haven't read it so I wouldn't know.

"But he interpreted the whole thing—that we were the four horsemen, 'Helter Skelter' the song—and he arrived at having to go out and kill everyone. It was frightening because you don't write songs for those reasons. Maybe some heavy-metal groups do nowadays, but we certainly never did."

McCartney in the Beatles *Anthology* said even their musical pal Bob Dylan got the lyrics to one of their biggest hits all wrong when he first introduced the Beatles to a high grade of marijuana in New York in 1964. Dylan said he assumed that they were old hands at rolling and smoking their own joints; otherwise, why would they sing "I get high, I get high, I get high" on their 1963 hit "I Want to Hold Your Hand."

Lennon quickly set him straight. The lyrics are, "When I touch you, I can't hide. I can't hide."

Returning to "Helter Skelter," McCartney added: "So there had been some funny little misinterpretations, but they were all harmless and just a bit of a laugh…But after all those little interpretations there was finally this horrific interpretation of it all. It all went wrong at that point, but it was nothing to do with us. What can you do?"

Ringo Starr also weighed in: "It was upsetting…I knew Roman and Sharon, and, God, it was a rough time. It stopped everyone in their tracks because suddenly all this violence came out in the midst of all this love and peace and psychedelia. It was pretty miserable, actually, and everyone got really insecure—not just us, not just the rockers, but everyone in LA felt, 'Oh God, it can happen to anybody.' Thank God they caught the bugger."

Added George Harrison. "Everyone was getting on the Beatles bandwagon. The police and the promoters and the Lord Mayors—and murderers too. The Beatles were topical, and they were the main thing that was written about in the world, so everybody attached themselves to us, whether it was our fault or not. It was upsetting to be associated with something so sleazy as Charles Manson."

IN JULY 1970, I sat in a packed courtroom with the world watching. I was completely stunned as Deputy District Attorney Vincent Bugliosi trotted out his amazing motive in his opening statement. Frankly, I thought Bugliosi might have swallowed a few tabs of acid himself. He said: "To Charles Manson, 'helter-skelter,' which, incidentally, was the title of one of the Beatles' songs, meant the black man rising up against the white man and destroying the entire white race. That is, with the exception of Charles Manson and his family, who intended to escape from helter-skelter by going through the desert and living in the bottomless pit, the place that Manson derived from Revelations 9, a chapter in the last Book of the New Testament, from which Manson told his family he found further support for his philosophy on life. The evidence will show that Manson's principal motive for these seven murders was to ignite helter-skelter and start the black-white war by making it look like black people had committed these murders."

And to support this astonishing opening statement, the prosecution called upon a parade of disenchanted Manson acolytes no longer under his witchy spell, as well as others—like music agent Gregg Jakobson, who was helping Manson get a recording contract with Terry Melcher. Jakobson told the court that he had met Manson and conferred with him some twenty to thirty times, where they discussed the "Helter Skelter" premise. Jakobson testified at some length in the August 1971 trial of Charles Watson.

Deputy DA Stephen Kay: *Did Mr. Manson ever discuss with you the recording group known as the Beatles?*

Jakobson: *Yes.*

Q: *Did he ever discuss their relationship to helter-skelter?*

A: *Yes.*

Q: *What did he say?*

A: *They were trying to give the message to those people who would listen that helter-skelter was coming. To prepare, look out.*

Q: *Did the Beatles have a song called "Helter Skelter"?*

A: *Yes.*

Q: *And what did Charlie say about this song, "Helter Skelter"?*

A: *It was the message. That was the message to the people.*

Q: *Do you think the Beatles were talking to him through their music?*

A: *Yes.*

Q: *Now, I show you Exhibit 266, a double-white Beatles album. Do you recognize this album?*

A: *Yes.*

Q: *Was that played out on the Spahn Ranch very often?*

A: *Yes.*

Q: *Now, are you familiar with some of the songs in the album?*

A: *Yes.*

Q: *And what songs would you say in this album were played the most out at the Spahn Ranch while you were there?*

A: *"Blackbird," "Helter Skelter," "Piggies," the most.*

Q: *Now, in the song "Blackbird," I show you here Exhibit 267, appears to be the lyrics of the song in this Beatles album?*

A: *Right.*

Q: *On the song "Blackbird," did Mr. Manson tell you what he felt the title "Blackbird" meant; what that was referring to?*

A: *It represented the black men.*

Q: *Did he ever use the term as it is in this song, "Blackbird singing in the dead of night, take these broken wings and learn to fly, all your life you were only waiting for this moment to arise"? Did Mr. Manson use the term "arise," or "rise," in talking about helter-skelter?*

A: *Yeah, he used to quote that whole verse, I mean, just verbatim, just the way it was.*

Q: *Did he ever say in relation to helter-skelter that the black man was going to rise up?*

A: *He would, like I said, he quoted right from there to prove his point that the black man was going to rise up. And this was a prophecy of the arising.*

Q: *Would it be a fair statement to say that Mr. Manson treated the lyrics of the songs in this Beatles album like scripture?*

A: *Oh, yes, it was his scripture.*

Q: *Now, in the song "Piggies," did Mr. Manson tell you what was meant by the word "piggies" or "pig"?*

A: *Yeah, it represented the Establishment.*

Q: *And what race was the Establishment?*

A: *Well, white, definitely the white middle-class businessman.*

Q: *Did Mr. Manson ever tell you what was meant in the lyrics of the song "Piggies," when it says, "In their eyes there's something lacking, what they need is a damn good whacking""*

A: *Here again, this was to be taken as the truth, and also as a prophecy of the coming truth.*

Q: *In other words . . .*

A: *. . . future.*

Q: *. . . that the Establishment, that the people in the Establishment needed a damn good whacking?*

A: *Yes.*

Q: *Did he ever say anything about, "Everywhere there's lot of piggies living piggy lives, you can see them out for dining with their piggy wives, clutching forks and knives to eat their bacon"?*

A: *Yeah, he knew the words.*

Q: *Would he quote the words?*

A: *By memory, and he would quote the words whenever there was a reason to or whenever they would fall into conversation.*

Q: *Did Mr. Manson have a great dislike for the Establishment?*

A: *I suppose you could say that. . . yeah, it was another world to him, not his.*

Q: *What about the members of the Manson Family, did they feel generally the same way about the Establishment?*

A: *Well, that's hard to answer, in the sense that they rarely voiced any opinions other than Charlie's.*

Q: *Did Mr. Manson compose a lot of his own songs?*

A: *Yes.*

Q: *Did he ever have a song which had the words helter-skelter in their lyrics?*

A: *I seem to remember that he borrowed the line from…*

Q: *"Helter Skelter?"*

A: *Right.*

Q: *From the Beatles?*

A: *Every once in a while in his songs he would take a whole verse or a line from somebody else's song, if he really liked it, or turn it around.*

While writing this book, I got the chance to ask Stephen Kay a key question I'd been waiting to ask for years. Did he think that Bugliosi had lost his mind in going for the "Helter Skelter" motive? Was it as ridiculous as it sounded for Bugliosi to take this route in seeking to convict Manson and the girls—and later "Tex" Watson? Kay, who was Bugliosi's second chair after lead lawyer Aaron Stovitz was fired from the case for talking to the media, insisted he never worried that Bugliosi was going way out on a limb.

"I bought into it," he said. "I thought it was *the* motive, with lots of corroboration. You just had to listen to the Beatles' lyrics, and it just went along with what they [the convicted killers] did. Writing in blood on walls and refrigerators, and in the Tate and then the LaBianca house. I knew these were a bunch of crazy people. What they liked to do most was sit around at the Spahn Ranch on LSD, listening again and again to *The White Album*. They would all have input to what they heard. It wasn't just Manson, it was all of them. They believed the Beatles were saying it, telling them what to do. They believed it along with the locusts, Revelations, the Bottomless Pit, and Armageddon. And they believed the Beatles were sending messages to black people to rise up on their own. And Manson believed that, too. And when they didn't rise up, Manson told them, 'The only things that Blackie knows what to do is when we show them. So we have to show them how to do it.' And so on August 8, he said, 'Now is the time for helter-skelter.'

"And they went out and did it all…and left their calling cards in blood. Rise. Helter Skelter…messages like that. Yes, it may have sounded far-fetched, but two different juries didn't think so. First, we convicted Manson and the girls. Then we went back for a replay and 'Tex' Watson bit the dust as well."

Others in the Manson Family would eventually bite the dust and get judicial sand kicked in their faces, as well.

Some might even call that karma.

President Richard Nixon's August 1970 "Manson is Guilty" quote almost derailed the murder trial.

PART III

THE TRIAL

August 1970 and Richard Nixon's premature comments made headlines around the world.

THE CRAZIEST LEGAL SHOW ON EARTH

"I have covered almost 50 of the most famous trials in American history, and without a doubt the Tate-LaBianca trial was the weirdest, wildest, and craziest experience I have ever witnessed."
—Bill Lignante, ABC TV courtroom artist

"This is just another LA murder case. Five years from now, nobody will remember it."
—Deputy DA Aaron Stovitz, July 1970

How do I aptly describe the Trial of the Century, also known as The People vs. Charles Manson, Susan Atkins, Patricia Krenwinkel, and Leslie Van Houten?

It began on July 24, 1970—barely one year after the killings shook America—in front of a jury of seven men and five women. The average age of the jurors was forty-five, ranging from a man in his late twenties to a seventy-four-year-old retiree. They included a retired deputy sheriff, an airline secretary, a drama critic, a security guard, and a mortician—not quite the kind of crowd that could be in any way be deemed "a jury of the defendants' peers." Then again, I doubt the Manson Family had many peers.

I had covered the 1969 trial of Sirhan Sirhan, who was convicted of killing Sen. Robert F. Kennedy in the kitchen of the Ambassador Hotel on the night he won the California Democratic primary. I thought *three months* was an endurance race—this would end up being three times as long, and one of the most outrageous trials I have ever witnessed. Indeed, it was a bad Fellini movie on acid: part theater of the absurd and part Monty Python's Flying Circus without the humor. The four defendants faced the death penalty if convicted, and so comedy had no place there; but, Manson was a classic clown, a natural performer who quickly realized that now he could achieve the notoriety and fame that eluded him as a songwriter. He made the conscious decision to do whatever he could to muck up the proceedings, masterfully doing just that with his maniacal machinations.

By the time the trial actually got underway in the Hall of Justice in downtown Los Angeles on a warm morning in late July 1970, under the gavel of Judge Charles Older—a no-nonsense, former World War II Flying Tigers pilot and Korean War veteran, who had been appointed to the bench by Governor Ronald Reagan—there had been some seismic changes in the defense lawyer lineup. To start with, Manson's pleas to represent himself were all turned down, and so, in what some described as a "revenge up yours!" move, he chose the quirky Irving Kanarek to be his mouthpiece. And Kanarek lived up to his reputation as a spoiler with the deserved reputation as the most obfuscating legal gun in town.

On June 10, 1970, before the trial got underway, my first book *Five to Die*, about Manson and his followers, was published, much to the irritation of the defense team. I was sitting in the court when Irving Kanarek came marching into the courtroom, waved my book in front of Judge Malcolm Lucas, who was ruling on pre-trial motions, and demanded that the case be moved to San Francisco because his client could now not get a fair trial.

Manson abruptly turned his back on the judge, who told Kanarek, "Instruct your client to face the proper direction."

Instead Manson yelled, "The court has showed no respect for me…I have no part in these proceedings."

Kanarek kept going and argued vehemently that the book, "created a climate of opinion in which Manson cannot get a fair trial."

The judge paused in mid-argument, took the book from Kanarek, thumbed quickly through it, and declared, "It's the usual scurrilous piece."

And he promptly denied the motion for a change of venue. And so it would go: a nine-month marathon of unpredictable and outrageous behavior, playing out daily in the jammed Department 104, on the eighth floor of the Hall of Justice, an edifice resembling a giant mausoleum. Justice was its business, though what I saw served up each day could hardly have been described as that. On the sidewalk in front of the courthouse, members of the Manson Family who had not been locked up held a nonstop vigil, sleeping in vans parked on the street so they could both visit Manson and greet the daily throng of spectators, journalists, and TV cameras. Each day, as they stood outside, pledging allegiance to Manson "and to the Family for which it stands," an insane daily melange of legal deeds and misdeeds by a cast of stranger-than-fiction characters was to play out in those hallowed halls inside. Cameras were banned from the room, so the only recorded history was in the form of illustrations captured by courtroom TV station sketch artists, including Bill Robles for CBS and Bill Lignante for ABC.

The elephant not in the room when opening arguments began was the invisible Charles "Tex" Watson—the twenty-five-year-old from the small Texas town of Farmersville who had been battling extradition to California. But, with the defendants' lawyers claiming their right to a "speedy trial," the DA's office had to go ahead without him. So, much to the surprise of nearly everyone, they proceeded without the gang's main "executioner" putting in an appearance. He, of course, would have his own day in court later.

Spectators lined up at 6:00 a.m. for the bragging rights of claiming a seat at the number-one judicial show in America, maybe even sitting within spitting-distance of Sharon Tate's father, Col. Paul Tate, who fumed silently as the perpetrators put on their crazy act. The crowd attracted a list of other distinguished spectators, including author and screenwriter Joan Didion, who'd befriended Linda Kasabian—the prosecution's star witness—and, at one time, planned to write a book about her life. Supposedly, the acclaimed writer went to I. Magnin's in Beverly Hills to pick out appropriate attire—they settled on a peasant dress—she felt Kasabian should wear when she delivered her crucial testimony. Didion's brother-in-law, Dominick Dunne, who later became a chronicler of true-crime stories, also made an appearance, along with an assortment of other writers and celebrities—actor Sal Mineo who was later stabbed to death in February 1976, Dennis Hopper, scribe Curt Gentry who had ghostwritten the bestseller *Operation Overflight* for downed U2 pilot Francis Gary Powers. We later discovered that publisher W.W. Norton was already eyeing the trial—and, indeed, Gentry was to share authorship credit with Vincent Bugliosi for his 1974 *Helter Skelter* book, which is considered the best-selling crime book of all time. The unpredictability of the show would become a big source of fascination: Manson arriving on the very first day with a do-it-yourself X carved into his forehead. It was a coordinated, behind-the-bars effort with Atkins, Van Houten, and Krenwinkel, no less; the girls marching into court dressed to the nines in clothing more suitable for a county fair dance or an audition for a local talent contest, rather than a court of law; and the Manson cheering section down on the sidewalk mimicking the antics going on in the courthouse.

As the days turned into weeks and the weeks into months, each day I thought surely nothing could or would top the previous one. I was wrong. Whatever Manson did, the three girls in court mimicked. When Manson screamed, they screamed. When he turned his back on Judge Older, they followed in puppet-like fashion. They parroted his every disruption until they eventually were forced to watch their own trial from a separate room.

Manson ranted, raved, and railed at Older, at his lawyers, at America, at the injustices of the penal system. He threatened the lawyers, the witnesses and anyone he happened to dislike at any particular moment. One day, when his lawyer, Irving Kanarek, decided not to cross-examine a witness, Manson demanded that he be allowed to do it, but Older quickly cut him off. Manson, as though fired out of cannon, suddenly lunged at Older wielding a sharp-pointed pencil. "Someone should cut your head off," he screamed. The bailiff tackled Manson before he could reach the judge, and he was dragged out of the court and forced to watch the rest of the day's testimony on a monitor in a holding cell—the same cell that, ironically, had been occupied the previous year by Sirhan Sirhan. From that point forward, Older carried a pistol under his black robes. Judge, jury, and executioner indeed.

Bill Robles, courtroom artist, captures Manson's attack on Judge Older.

Less than a month into the trial, President Richard Nixon, in a speech to law-enforcement officials in Denver, declared that Manson was guilty of murder. The next afternoon, Manson pulled the front page of the *Los Angeles Times* from a pile of documents on the lawyers' table and waved it in front of the jury. Jurors, of course, were sequestered for the entire trial in a nearby hotel and were not supposed to read about the trial or watch TV. The blaring headline read, "Manson Guilty, Nixon Declares." Again, he was withdrawn from the court while the jury was quickly removed from the courtroom and the lawyers screamed for a mistrial. It turns out Manson had been slipped the newspaper only moments before, not by Kanarek but by Atkins' lawyer Daye Shinn. Older was pissed and sentenced Shinn to two weekends in jail. In a somewhat comedic twist, Shinn later bitterly complained that his wife, who didn't speak a word of English, had given him holy hell when he was released. She didn't believe he was in jail and thought he was using the judge's sentence to conceal an affair. In 1992, Shinn was disbarred from the California State Bar for misappropriating client funds in another case.

Manson flashed front page headline to the jury in this
Bill Robles courtroom illustration done at the time.

Deputy DA Stephen Kay got a fierce baptism by fire in the Tate-LaBianca trial.

Even though the prosecution had all the ducks (and witnesses) in a row, they would later, somewhat embarrassingly, admit that it was only by pure luck that they were able to come up with a couple of key pieces of evidence to buttress their case.

Embarrassment Number 1: The bloody clothing used by the Tate killers had been retrieved, but not by detectives, who were literally beating the bushes for telltale evidence. After Atkins' confession was published in early December detailing how the killers left the Cielo house and then dumped their bloody clothing down a canyon, KABC television news reporter Al Wiman followed a hunch. Using basic logic and a timing scenario, he and a film crew drove from the Tate House up Benedict Canyon in the direction of the killers' obvious escape route back to the Spahn Ranch, looking for what might be the most convenient spot to dump their blood-soaked clothing. Lo and behold, maybe a mile and a half from Cielo, at the very first spot where it was possible to pull off the roadway onto the dirt, he stopped and looked down into the canyon. There it was—a pile of bloodstained clothing. He called police, and watched as they sheepishly removed the bounty with cameras rolling.

Embarrassment Number 2: Eleven-year-old Steven Weiss was playing in his back garden in Sherman Oaks on September 1, 1969, when he came upon a .22 caliber Colt Buntline revolver. "I brought it to my dad by picking it up by the tip of the barrel because I wanted to preserve the fingerprints," the sixth-grader coolly said. An avid fan of cop shows like *Dragnet,* he said, "I was careful not to touch the rest of the gun." Unfortunately, the police officer called to the home by the boy's father, Bernard Weiss, wasn't as careful. According to Weiss, he "touched it with both hands all over the gun. Then he emptied the gun of two live cartridges and seven shell casings, fingering them all." But police ineptitude didn't end there. They were still looking high and low for the Tate weapon. Finally, as details of the murder became public—a full three and a half months after his young son found the gun in the garden—a light bulb went off in Weiss's head. He called the police and politely suggested that the gun they were looking for might already be in their hands. "We said they already had this gun, and we thought it might be connected with the murder," said Bernard Weiss. Indeed, the weapon had been forgotten and stored in a locker in the Van Nuys police station. Tests matched the gun with bullets found at the scene. It apparently had been tossed over an embankment into the family's yard, about a mile and a half from where the clothing was found.

An interesting footnote: Atkins' Sybil Brand cellmate, Veronica Howard, and youngster Steven Weiss shared the $25,000 reward money put up by actors Warren Beatty, Peter Sellers, and Yul Brynner.

Now, let me take you behind the curtain and into the frenetic world of fact, fiction, and happenstance, as the unbelievable events that led to the craziest show on earth, starring Charles Manson in twin roles— accused killer and ringmaster—unfolded.

Manson girls at the trial.
Illustration by Bill Robles.

THE VICTIMS

10050 Cielo Drive
Murdered August 9,1969

Sharon Tate

Abigail Folger

Wojciech Frykowski

Jay Sebring

Steven Parent

Leno LaBianca
Murdered August 10, 1969

Rosemary LaBianca
Murdered August 10, 1969

Gary Hinman
Murdered July 26, 1969

Donald "Shorty" Shea
Murdered August 26, 1969

On August 16, 1969, LA Sheriff's Department arrested Manson and 25 others at the Spahn Ranch on suspicion of car theft but did not link them to the Tate-LaBianca murders which took place a week earlier. In the pre-dawn raid they were all handcuffed and carted off to jail. Then released two days later because of clerical errors.

Manson Family members quietly sit in a circle after August 1969 arrests.

Only Manson gave arresting sheriff's deputies a hard time following a pre-dawn raid at the Spahn Ranch.

Manson facedown—watched by Family members.

Manson carted off to jail August 1969—but released two days later.

THE DEFENDANTS

Charles Manson—police arrest mugshot, 1968

Charles "Tex" Watson

Susan Atkins

Leslie Van Houten

Patricia Krenwinkel

THE PROSECUTION

Each day, Deputy DA Vincent Bugliosi meets the press during the trial.

Left to right: Deputy DA Stephen Kay and Deputy DA Donald Musich face a mountain of trial transcripts.

THE DEFENSE

Left to right: Daye Shinn, Irving Kanarek, Paul Fitzgerald, and Ronald Hughes mount a disunited defense for Manson and his acolytes.

Happy-faced Susan Atkins, arrested in Inyo County, California, October 1969 for car theft and damage to government property.

SADIE SINGS—OFF KEY

Vincent Bugliosi: *Did Tex tell you why he and you three girls were going to Terry Melcher's former residence?*

Susan Atkins: *To get all of their money and to kill whoever was there.*

—Atkins in testimony to LA Grand Jury

The confessions of Susan Denise Atkins played out in three acts and ran intermittently from October to December 1969. Each time the performance was given to a very select audience. To clarify the chain of events, here's the timeline of the strange set of circumstances that led to Charles Manson's favorite love, blowing the whistle.

Act 1: Played out in dribs and drabs over two weeks in the women's dormitory at Sybil Brand Institute, where Atkins, under the stage name of "Sadie Mae Glutz" (or "Crazy Sadie," as she had also become known among fellow inmates), performed to an astonished audience of two: Veronica Howard and Virginia Graham.

Act 2: Unfolded around December 5, 1969, in the well-appointed Beverly Hills office of Atkins' attorney, Richard Caballero, as she blabbed into a tape recorder nonstop for several hours. The transcription made its way into the hands of an enterprising photojournalist named Lawrence Schiller, who enlisted the aid of a couple of *Los Angeles Times* writers. They turned it into a sensational "confessions of a killer" yarn, which was plastered on the front pages of newspapers from Los Angeles to London, where Britain's mass circulation Sunday newspaper *The News of the World*, nicknamed "The Barmaid's Bible" because of its sensational content, coughed up $40,000 for the Atkins story. It later became a quickie book titled *The Killing of Sharon Tate*.

Act 3: The first two acts could be considered out-of-town "tryouts," but this third act was "The Biggie," with Atkins on stage for another select audience: fourteen women and seven men comprising the Los Angeles Grand Jury. She did not disappoint. Polished and prepped, and accompanied by Caballero, who was not allowed to be present in the actual jury chamber room, she held the crowd breathless. Carefully costumed for the occasion by Caballero's wife, Atkins was looking uncharacteristically prim and proper in a rose-colored velveteen dress with puff sleeves in a miniskirt length. But she was not fully rehearsed—try as they might, even her lawyers realized that they couldn't control her drug-ravaged brain when it came to cataloguing those two grim nights in August.

She kept her lip buttoned as she marched past some 100 press and TV people toward the inner sanctum of the grand jury hearing room. And she seemed to be enjoying her moment in the sun, although she was later to note somewhat dramatically, "I must remind you that this whole experience seems like it happened a thousand years ago. I feel I have lived a thousand lifetimes since then." Once inside, in an emotionless, little-girl voice, she proceeded to tell her version of the "Night of the Long Knives." It was detailed. It was horrendous. And it was totally self-serving. Even in her muddled mind, she knew that it was critical for her to be convincing, that she had to make them believe that poor little "Cinderella Susan" had been swept up in a series of horrifying events that she had no control over. She had been rescued from the Devil, and now, freshly scrubbed and smelling good, she was about to take her first step on the road to redemption.

There was no doubt, Caballero told her, that the district attorney would use her decisive testimony to get indictments to bring Manson and the other girls to trial. Sure, she could be accused of being a snitch, but wasn't that better than being charged with the cold-blooded murder of seven people and wind up sniffing cyanide in the San Quentin gas chamber? By opening her heart and telling the truth, he was pretty confident that some deal could be made, even though it might result in time behind bars—and she would have to repeat her story in open court in front of Manson and the rest of the gang. Failing that, he was ready to push hard for the obvious insanity defense. Almost four months to the day of the killings, she sang as best she could.

Life really began, she said, only after she met Manson in San Francisco. Before that, it was an awful, middle-class home with no respect from alcoholic parents who fought all the time, hated each other, and hated her and her siblings. When she was just fifteen, her world was turned further upside down by the death of her mother. An unending search for love and emotion with an assortment of men who wanted her only for her body. She was insecure and even attempted suicide. Then, in 1968, the poor little not-so-rich girl set eyes on a dark troubadour in a drug-dealer's house on Lime Street. He sang "The Shadow of Your Smile" and she was smitten. It was fate. He was the man of her dreams, her lover, and she happily shared him with an assortment of young maidens he picked up in the streets of the city or hitchhiking on the highways of California. And merrily they traveled in a big bus, until they alighted at an old movie ranch on the edge of Los Angeles. All her troubles seemed so far away as Manson preached his sermon of helter-skelter, which she, "Squeaky" Fromme, "Gypsy" Share, Mary Brunner, "Tex" Watson, "Little Paul" Watkins, Clem Grogan, and every Tom, Dick, and Harry in the clan believed was the signal that a race war would explode.

Those of us who gathered outside the chambers knew nothing of what was spilling out of Atkins' mouth. Police officialdom had given out only paltry details just a few days earlier. But I had already become aware of Manson's scarcely credible helter-skelter philosophy, having heard it spelled out a few days earlier by Watkins and Brooks Poston.

"We called ourselves the Family, a Family like no other Family," she rhapsodized. "It was love in the group, complete love. We never despised anybody. We never hated anybody. We took in anybody that wanted to come in that was willing to give up everything they had for us. We all gave up each other's wants for each other." Furthermore, their beloved leader was brutally honest, she said: "He told us, 'I have tricked all of you. I have tricked you into doing what I want you to, and I am using you and you are all aware of that now and it is like I have got a bunch of slaves around me.' And he often called us his sheep." The twenty-one members of the Grand Jury sat transfixed by what they were hearing.

Atkins' ties to her newly adopted family had grown even stronger on October 7, 1968, when she gave birth to her baby, a boy they named Zezozose Zadfrack Glutz, although the child's name was to be spelled in various incarnations over the years. No maternity ward for her—Manson and the girls skillfully helped in the delivery while Atkins herself declined to identify the father—or could not pinpoint who it might have been based on her massive uses of assorted drugs and her many sexual encounters. "We all made love with each other, got over our inhibitions and inadequate feelings, and became very uninhibited," she said. "We used to dance all the time. Then we'd all gather at night and sit down and start singing, and Charlie would always play the guitar and we'd always sing songs and he used to make up the songs—songs that I have never heard before or words that I have never heard before put together in such beautiful manners. Some were happy, some were very...left me with an open head, left me just sitting there like I was dead."

Clearly infatuated, she continued, "Manson is the only man that I have ever met—on the face of this earth—the only man that I ever met that is a complete man. He will not take any backtalk from a woman. He will not let a woman talk him into doing anything. He is a man. He has more love to give to the world than anybody I have ever met. He would give himself completely, completely to anybody." Asked if she thought he was evil, she replied: "In your standards of evil, looking at him through your eyes, I would say, 'Yes.' Looking at him through my eyes, he is as good as he is evil, he is as evil as he is good. You could not judge the man."

Finally, after describing her Paradise Found experience, the topic of murder came up. Under questioning from Deputy DA Vincent Bugliosi, she revealed that on the night of August 8, 1969, they changed into black clothing at Spahn Ranch. Linda Kasabian, a newcomer to the group who had been welcomed into the fold barely a month before, was the assigned driver because she was the only one who had a valid driver's license. She was joined by Watson and Patricia Krenwinkel. They managed to squeeze into a 1959 four-door Ford that didn't have a back seat and belonged to a ranch foreman named John Swartz, Jr. "Johnny frequently let us use his car," Atkins said blithely in the kind of voice that suggested that this mission also bore Johnny's stamp of approval. Ironically, that same car was to fall in Los Angeles County Sheriffs' hands a week after the murders, on August 16, when the ranch was raided and everybody was arrested on suspicion of car theft. But the clue was missed when all charges were dropped for lack of evidence.

Atkins was nonchalant and even boastful, describing the events of that night. All jurors' eyes never left Atkins. "We sort of got lost on the way," she said. "I think we took a wrong turn and ended up somewhere on Mulholland." With few lights, it was dark; but, eventually the edgy and speed-fueled Watson directed Kasabian to the Cielo Drive cul-de-sac house. She said she came barefooted because she had sores on her feet and it was too painful to wear shoes. There was a rope in the back of the car, as well as a set of bolt cutters. "Tex had a gun. I had a knife. Linda had a knife. Katie (Krenwinkel) had a knife, and to my best knowledge, I believe Tex also had a knife. "

Bugliosi asked what they discussed in the car. "Tex told us that we were going to a house up on the hill that used to belong to Terry Melcher, and the only reason why we were going to that house was because Tex knew the outline of the house," she said. "Tex did all of the talking."

"It didn't make any difference who was there, you were told to kill them; is that correct?"

"Yes."

She said that after Watson cut the Cielo house's phone wires, "I was told to go over first; so I threw my changes of clothes over the fence and held the knife between my teeth and climbed over and got my pants caught on part of the fence and had to kind of boost myself up and lift from where I was caught off of the fence and fell into bushes on the other side. I was followed by the other three."

They had started moving toward the main house, when they saw the lights of a car coming towards them. It was Steven Parent's two-door Rambler MPX. Watson ordered them to lie down and keep quiet. Then she heard a man's voice pleading: "Please don't hurt me, I won't say anything."

Susan said, "I heard a gunshot, and I heard another gunshot and another one and another one. Four gunshots. Then we walked towards the house."

When she and Watson walked into the house and confronted Folger and Frykowski, who were together in one room, she said the couple barely expressed surprise—assuming they might be latecomers to the party.

Atkins' grand jury testimony about the Tate murders was a radical rewrite from what she had told her Sybil Brand cellmates. Here, the picture she painted was that, while she participated in the carnage that followed, Watson was the instigator—the real villain of the piece—and she was a half-hearted assassin, filled with second thoughts about wielding her knife. This, obviously, was the result of being heavily prepped by her lawyer. She was not denying that she had invaded the Cielo house, but her best strategy, most likely suggested by her lawyers, was to adopt the

"I was just following orders" line of defense. It was Watson—still fighting furiously in Texas to avoid extradition to California—who ordered her to kill Frykowsi. Instead she ended up wrestling with him, while the terrified Frykowski responded by pulling her hair.

"And then it was a fight for my life as well as him fighting for his life," she explained. Hair hurting, poor Ms. Atkins was only able to save herself by stabbing him repeatedly. And it was Watson who stabbed Folger, she said, firmly rejecting any blame whatsoever.

When it came to disposing of Jay Sebring, Atkins said Watson was also responsible for the lethal finishing touches. But when it came to the murder of the pregnant Tate, playing the blame game was not so easy. She said it was Watson who ordered her to kill the actress, but she hesitated. Jurors tensed in horror. "While she was begging for her life she said, 'Let me go. All I want to do is have my baby.' I looked at her and said, 'Woman, I have no mercy for you'…and I knew that I was talking to myself…not to her." Again, she insisted that Watson ordered her to finish Tate off. She claimed she couldn't do it and tried to create a diversion. When Watson saw her hesitate, she recalled, he delivered the final coup de grâce. "I saw Tex stab her in the heart area around the chest," she said.

It was a radically different story she was telling the grand jury. To her cellmates, weeks earlier, she bragged and claimed all the credit, saying, "I just kept stabbing her until she stopped screaming." Tate was stabbed sixteen times.

When Atkins' testimony ended, the jurors sat in a cold, silent shock. After deliberating for just twenty minutes, they handed down seven murder indictments against, Manson, Watson, Linda Kasabian, and Patricia Krenwinkel. Leslie Van Houten was indicted on two counts of murder and one of conspiracy to commit murder in the deaths of Leno and Rosemary LaBianca.

Atkins was relishing her star status in the courtroom. Even the DA had become her friend—well, sort of. He was treating her like a VIP. She had been getting long breaks from jail, being chauffeured around town by lawyers and cops who hung onto her every word as they perused the Tate murder house and drove around the streets near Cielo Drive to see if she could pinpoint exactly where she and her cohorts had dumped their bloody clothing after the massacre. But which Atkins version was to be believed? The version she delivered to the grand jury or the ghoulish recitations she had given to cellmates Howard and Graham?

In short time, Atkins began having second thoughts about her testimony. Her lawyer had received only the assurance that the death penalty might be taken off the table if she testified in the trial. And according to Vincent Bugliosi's book *Helter Skelter*, she had written to a friend in Michigan declaring, "You rember [sic] the Sharon Tate murder and the LaBianca murder? Well, because of my big mouth to a cellmate, they just indicted me and five other people."

Early in 1970, while I was first working on the story, I obtained a copy of another of Atkins' handwritten letters—an apology of sorts—sent to Howard via the jail's underground delivery system. It was a more accurate reflection of her confused state of mind after she learned that the stories she spun for Howard and Graham had been passed onto the "piggy cops." She was somewhat conciliatory in one four-page letter:

> *I can see your side of this clearly. Nor am I mad at you. I am hurt in a way only I understand. I blame no one but myself for ever saying anything. My attorney is going to go on instanity [sic]. Yes, I wanted the world to know "M." It sure looks like they do now. There was a so-called motive behind all this. It was to instill fear into the pigs and to bring on judgment day which is here now for all.*

She continues somewhat incoherently:

In the first place there are no strangers to me or "M." In the word kill, the only thing that dies is the ego. All ego must die anyway, it is written. Yes, it could have been your house, it could have been my father's house also. In killing someone phically [sic] you are only releasing the soul. Life has no boundaries and death is only an illusion. If you can believe in the second coming of Christ 'M' is he who has come to save. Insanity is reality and not caring. When you truly love you do not care about anyone or anything you just love. "M" does not care, I know this to be truth. Maybe this will help you understand, I am not going to fight this. I will let my attorney do that. I am going to save my soul, the body my soul is housed in can be destroyed for all I care. To live forever is all I want, and I really don't care about that.

Strangely, she also took the time to clarify details about the murders:

I did not admit to being in the second house (LaBianca) because I was not in the second house. I went before the grand jury because my attorney said your [Howard's] testimony was enough to convict me and all the others. He also said it was my only chance to save myself. Then, I was out to save myself I have gone through some changes since then I am ceasing to be inside rather than seeming to be. I have been going through changes about feeling guilty about testifying and all that has happened. I am also content here. My attorney gives me money. He just deposited $20 on my account. As I write to you, I feel more ease inside. When I first heard you were the informer, I wanted to slit your throat. I snapped that I was the real informer and it was my throat I wanted to cut. Well, thats [sic] all over with now as I let the past die away from my mind. You know it will all turn out okay in the end anyway. 'M' or no 'M,' Sadie or no Sadie. Love will still run forever. I am giving up me to become that love a little more every day. Changes, Changes.

Only Love if forever changing. Cease to exist just come and say you love me. As I say I love you or should say I love Me (my love) in you.

It was a bizarre rant. And the idea of confessing once again to the person who ratted her out to the authorities defied all logic. Atkins must have been a glutton for punishment or, as was more likely the case, simply demented.

Much later—in yet another court appearance—she testified in a fruitless effort to justify her actions; her delivery was in a cold and spiteful manner. All pretense had vanished by then. "I didn't relate to Sharon Tate as being anything but a store mannequin," she said. "She sounded like an IBM machine. She kept begging and pleading and begging and pleading, and I got sick of listening to it. So I stabbed her."

At the conclusion of the grand jury hearing, the DA's two top prosecutors, Bugliosi and chief trial lawyer Aaron Stovitz, were faced with a thorny dilemma: Was Atkins a credible witness? And how would the testimony of this obviously damaged young woman—who was flaky, erratic, and verging, it seemed, on the edge of a nervous breakdown— play out in front of a jury of her so-called peers? Her evidence would be the cornerstone of what would be one of the biggest trials in Los Angeles history.

Meanwhile, standing in the wings, and so far only a supporting player but more than willing to step into the starring role, was twenty-one-year-old Linda Kasabian. She was a shy, fresh-faced young mother from a small town in Maine who looked like a high-school cheerleader.

Exit: Atkins

Enter: Kasabian.

And enter: The *real* truth.

LITTLE HIPPIE GIRL

"On the hot summer night of August 8, 1969, Charles Manson, sent out from the fires of hell in the Spahn Ranch three heartless, bloodthirsty robots, and unfortunately for him...one human being, the little hippie girl...Linda Kasabian."
—Deputy District Attorney Vincent Bugliosi,
January 1971

When the unreliable braggart, Susan Atkins, once again fell under the spell of the incarcerated Charles Manson and declined to testify against him, the prosecution spent a few nail-biting days fretting that their entire case might collapse.

Atkins was a loose cannon with equally loose lips. (They didn't call her "Crazy Sadie" for nothing.) But worse, even if she had not reneged, the fact that she was back in Manson's control meant that she would be a useless and unreliable witness, and probably would have tried her utmost to distance her sacred leader from the actual killings. Years later, deep into her "found God" and revisionist period, Atkins claimed that in December 1969 she recanted only because she feared the wrath of Manson and knew that as revenge for ratting him out, he would have ordered Family members still devoted to him, to kill her. Or worse... bump off her innocent young baby.

In late December 1969, not long after her grand jury testimony, and after her stunning confession was published in the *Los Angeles Times* (much to the chagrin of her lawyer, Richard Caballero), Atkins began almost daily communication with Patricia Krenwinkel and Leslie Van Houten, as well as with Manson. All were in lockup. And furthermore, Atkins, whose lawyer was seeking some kind of "deal" in exchange for her testimony, had other big problems. In addition to Sharon Tate, Atkins was also facing first-degree murder charges in another not-so-high-profile murder case—the July 1969 torture death of musician Gary Hinman.

But strangely, once the shock of Atkins' "about turn" wore off, common sense kicked in and her predictable behavior did not seem so devastating. Overnight, Linda Kasabian, "the little hippie girl," who was the Manson Family's newest member, became the district attorney's crucial relief hitter, and savior. And Charles Manson's willing Judas. Lawyers in the district attorney's office quickly realized that Kasabian would not be as severely tainted as Atkins. Sure, she drove the "getaway car" and that would—in most cases—make her as culpable as the rest of the killers.

Still, Kasabian seemed a better "star witness" bet. Preliminary interviews indicated that while she went to the Sharon Tate house armed with a knife, she did not kill anyone. And even better for the prosecution, she never stepped inside the Tate house. Even Atkins, in her voluminous and gory grand jury confessional, never fingered Kasabian for anything more serious than chauffeuring them all to Cielo Drive.

The then twenty-year old Kasabian, prodded by her lawyer, Gary Fleischman, willingly stepped up to fill the Atkins void.

Fleischman, who was crafting his defense with the help of his friend and colleague Ronald L.M. Goldman, confronted the district attorney at a secret meeting and played their ace card: "You can't make a deal with someone (Atkins) who has blood on their hands. It is politically stupid and a prosecutorial blunder."

Fleischman battled for the best deal for his client. "They first offered second degree murder. I said no. They offered voluntary manslaughter.

I said no. I wanted immunity." Fleischman added another layer to the "deal" history when he told Steve Oney at *Los Angeles* magazine in 2009:

"Linda (Kasabian) had seen them committing mayhem at the Tate house. She had driven the killers to the LaBianca residence, but she hadn't done anything. Still, she was technically guilty of first-degree murder. I told her that a deal was the only way out. She initially didn't want to do that. These were her soulmates, no matter what they'd done. But I told her, 'You're broke, you're pregnant, and you were there. You must become a prosecution witness.'

"One day Aaron Stovitz, head of the trial division, called me. He said, 'I want to talk to you.' I said, 'I'm going to get my hair cut at the barbershop at the Beverly Wilshire Hotel. Come on over.' So he drives out, and he makes me an offer. A very strange confluence of events had occurred. They needed Linda Kasabian and she needed them.

"Stovitz, who at the time was running the case as the district attorney's chief trial lawyer and who was Bugliosi's boss, told me a few years later, 'Our backs were up against the wall and so I told Evelle Younger (district attorney), J. Miller Leavy (head of the trials division), and Joe Busch (Leavy's boss): 'We've got to go with Linda; she's nowhere near as brainwashed as Susan.'"

Kasabian got herself a priceless ticket to ride.

LINDA DARLENE KASABIAN, née Drouin, looked like a candidate for a milk commercial with her pale, creamy New England pallor, innocent, wide, green eyes, hair in ponytails, and an adorable cleft chin. But she was no Snow White. Her looks were exceedingly deceptive—the teenager with the girl-next-door appeal was a very troubled young woman.

Born in the small town of Biddeford, Maine, Linda grew up in the tiny New Hampshire riverside community of Milford, which is an easy forty-mile drive to Boston. Her relationship with her mother,

Joyce, ran hot and cold. Her father, Rosaire Drouin, a French-Canadian construction worker, abandoned the family and left for Florida when Linda was still a child. Things got worse for Kasabian when her mother remarried; she never got along with her stepfather, as she witnessed their constant fighting.

The teenager, described by pals at Milford High as a shy, starry-eyed romantic, made the school's freshman basketball team. But, battling weight problems, she dropped out of high school after her sophomore year, and in August 1965 married her high school sweetheart, Robert Moses Peaslee, Jr. The sweet turned sour pretty quickly. He was a bit of a wild boy who, a month before their wedding, crashed his car, which resulted in his fiancée sustaining a serious head wound and being rushed by ambulance to a hospital where she received several stitches. Friends said Peaslee was drunk, and he was later convicted of driving while intoxicated.

Their marriage was a disaster from the get-go; it lasted barely six months. Ironically, it was Peaslee who filed for divorce, claiming Linda's behavior "seriously endangered my physical and mental health." No one was quite sure what that meant even though their quickie marriage was the topic of much gossip in Milford.

Kasabian's troubles continued. She moved to Boston at the age of seventeen and was arrested when police raided the house (a commune) she shared with a bunch of friends and confiscated $20,000 worth of LSD and pot—an immense haul for those days. Kasabian was charged with being present where narcotics were used; but, because she was underage, she got off virtually scot free and was returned to the custody of her mother.

Soon after her divorce, Kasabian began a relationship with another Robert. Bob Kasabian was a young hippie who did not win the approval of Linda's mother, Joyce Byrd. He lived in a filthy house where no one did the dishes, she bitterly told the *Boston Globe* in 1970. His communal home was Boston's American Psychedelic Circus, which was just one of dozens of communes cropping up in big cities around the country. Despite her mother's objections, Linda began secretly dating Kasabian, and when he decided to move to the West Coast, she went with him.

They were married in Los Angeles in September 1967. That relationship faltered, according to Linda's mother. But that did not stop them from procreating.

In March 1968, the couple welcomed their first child, daughter Tanya, who was born in Los Angeles. The Kasabians were looking for "God and maybe a new life," and who knows what else. Their marriage was tempestuous at best. Several times they separated and then kissed and made up.

After one split, she moved back to the East Coast while her husband remained in Southern California. In May 1969, he called and begged her to fly to Southern California so they could reconcile. Linda and baby joined him. But, once again, Kasabian left her in the lurch.

"You could never believe what he said," complained Linda's mother. "Bob told her if they patched it up, they would travel to South America or Mexico or some exotic place. Linda would go for the line every time, would fly to California only to be told that Bob had changed his mind. It was an emotional crusher. Linda felt thoroughly rejected."

In Southern California, she aimlessly caroused around as her husband kept changing the family's goal posts. Linda's often catatonic state of limbo was exacerbated by her passion for imbibing assorted drugs, including, according to her mother, excessive amounts of diet pills and speed. LSD was her drug of choice as she chased her own private rainbow and mostly depended upon the kindness of strangers to fuel her drug habits.

By the summer of 1969, Mrs. Kasabian was an emotional wreck. Back in New Hampshire she was arrested for a minor offense—driving without a license. Although her relationship with her husband was very shaky, in June 1969, she once again returned to Los Angeles to join him. He was living with no visible means of support in a Topanga Canyon trailer owned by a well-to-do hippie pal named Charles Melton. Melton, labeled "Blackbeard Charlie" by his pal Paul Watkins, had big plans. He was going to sail around the world and the Kasabians were welcome to join him. It sounded idyllic, but sailing off into the sunset was not a priority for Linda and her baby girl.

Bob Kasabian also ditched that idea, and then disappeared to some new commune in New Mexico. Linda discovered she was pregnant again. She felt abandoned and feverishly began to look around for something to fill her void and somewhere to live.

Alone, struggling with a young child, and too embarrassed to run home to Mommy yet again, she felt adrift, isolated, and desperately unhappy. Much later she was to confess, "I went through a lot of drugs and alcohol and confusion."

She decided to stick it out in Los Angeles—a disastrous decision on her part.

On July 4, 1969, two months after she had been persuaded to return to Southern California, only to be dumped by her spouse, Kasabian met a friendly young woman with jet black hair, exotic eyes, and a gentle nature. Catherine Share, a college dropout, told Kasabian to call her "Gypsy." She was a mature twenty-six-year-old and seemed like manna from heaven to the confused Linda. Gypsy showed up at Melton's trailer with the handsome Paul Watkins.

In Gypsy, Linda found a shoulder to cry on; within minutes, the sympathetic Share became Kasabian's angel of mercy, offering to make everything better. It was the perfect storm for the troubled Kasabian. Gypsy spoke glowingly and passionately of her own family paradise, how they all lived together on a movie ranch not far away, where they sang and danced all day. She rhapsodized about their leader and "father," whom everyone worshipped. He was a gentle soul who played music all day and had taught her the real meaning of life. Everyone worshipped him.

And she invited Kasabian to bring baby Tanya to "meet Charlie" and see for herself.

It was a godsend, thought Kasabian—a serendipitous chance to find true happiness and shake off those shackles that came with an irresponsible husband who was deaf to her needs. It surely was the answer to her unspoken prayer. The answer to everything she ever yearned for.

Enter Charles Manson. Kasabian was instantly bewitched.

Manson quickly sweet-talked her with his usual pseudo-religious hippie "shtick." She was stunned when he put a label on her own father-figure angst, which was, of course, the line that seemed to work so effectively with nearly all the troubled young waifs and strays who crossed his path.

In one of her many court appearances, Kasabian explained how she instantly succumbed:

Q: *What conversation did you have with Mr. Manson while you were making love?*

A: *He told me I had a father hang-up.*

Q: *Did this impress you when he said you had a father hang-up?*

A: *Very much so.*

Q: *Why?*

A: *Because nobody ever said that to me, and I did have a father hang-up. I hated my stepfather.*

MANSON VIEWED HER as yet another typically screwed-up young woman whom he could exploit, just as he had done with all the other lost souls who thought they had found paradise in the heat, flies, and piles of horse shit at Spahn Ranch. And like the rest, Kasabian was more than easy pickings.

Within a day of arriving, she had become a true believer, having sex with Manson in a secret cave deep inside the ranch. She cooed, "Charlie can see inside me."

She was fresh meat for Manson and his like-minded drones. And Kasabian—as was the routine—fell meekly into place when Manson commanded her to have sex with anyone who fancied bedding the naïve newcomer.

Her immersion into the Family lifestyle was instantaneous. She said she felt totally at home in her strange but welcoming new milieu where pills and assorted drugs were freely distributed to anyone who so desired them. She had developed a taste for stimulants. This, she agreed, was what a real family should be like. It included going out with the other girls on garbage runs to forage for food tossed into supermarket dumpsters and providing sex to any men the Pied Piper of Spahn decreed she should sleep with. She swallowed whole his Helter Skelter scenario and the fanciful exodus—escaping the pillaging, raping, and inevitable race riots as Blackie killed Whitey.

In just one month, Kasabian fully absorbed and embraced Manson's quickie, whole deep-fried philosophy of a race war. She was a fast learner. And she accepted the whole enchilada—even that Charlie was Jesus Christ. She said she knew it, even though he never told her that.

Kasabian was also inducted into Manson's hall of crime by agreeing to steal $5,000 from her Topanga Canyon host, Melton. She then meekly turned the proceeds over to the Family. Creepy Crawlies was another "fun" game she enjoyed. It involved dressing in all-black outfits, going out to random homes in the Los Angeles area late at night when residents were asleep. The trick was to break in, steal money or souvenirs, odds and ends, but nothing big. But the real cheeky fun was re-arranging the furniture and imagining how homeowners, upon waking in the morning, would react to the havoc that had been wrought. What fun that was!

Kasabian even allowed Manson to separate her from her daughter Tanya; she willingly handed over her child to the Spahn nursery cooperative. Their raison d'être for taking child away from mother made absolute sense to her: "So we can kill her ego that you have put in her."

But barely a month later, Kasabian was to discover that she had joined a nest of vipers. Her brave new world was to be turned upside down. She was to witness a series of events that she would never forget and forever regret.

The high school dropout was to become an eyewitness, and participant of sorts, in one of the worst massacres of the twentieth century.

On the night of August 8, 1969, six weeks after she joined the Charles Manson Family at the Spahn Ranch, her nightmare started.

"I was standing out front at the very end of the porch closest to George Spahn's house, and Charlie came up to me and pulled me off the porch," she recalled. "He told me to get a change of clothing, a knife, and my driver's license. 'It's time for Helter Skelter.'"

She climbed into the driver's seat. "We got about to the middle of the driveway, Charlie called us and told us to stop, and he came to the car to my side of the window, stuck his head in, and told us to leave a sign. 'You girls know what I mean, something witchy.' And that was it." And although she didn't realize it, the "little hippie girl" was being sent out on a mission of death.

RECRUITING KASABIAN as the star witness for the prosecution was a big stroke of luck for deputy district attorney Vincent Bugliosi, who later admitted: "Without Linda it would have been extremely difficult to convict."

And in his best-selling book *Helter Skelter*, he wrote, "I'd preferred Linda, sight unseen. She hadn't killed anyone and therefore would be far more acceptable to a jury than the bloodthirsty Atkins."

Indeed. Her eyewitness account of what she saw that night at Cielo Drive was to have a powerful impact on the jury. While she didn't see all the killings, the Kasabian version was more like an account of someone who had been able to watch just the trailer of a horror film.

There were fragments and flashes of things she saw without ever seeing a complete scene played out from start to finish. At Cielo Drive, she heard four gunshots as Watson executed the caretaker's friend, Steven Parent, just as he was about to drive away from the house.

She heard blood-curdling screams. And then watched quick snapshots of gore. She never went inside the house, but vivid images played out in front of her.

"There was a man (Frykowski) just coming out of the door and he had blood all over his face and he was standing by a post, and we looked into each other's eyes for a minute, and I said, 'Oh, God, I am so sorry. Please make it stop.' But then he just fell to the ground into the bushes."

Then, knife-wielding Watson repeatedly stabbed Frykowski and bashed him so hard with the gun that the handle fell off. And then another snapshot just like the shower scene in Alfred Hitchcock's *Psycho*.

Patricia Krenwinkel, knife held high, chased the screaming Abigail Folger across the lawn.

Then numbness and nothing as Watson ordered Kasabian to return to the car.

Kasabian remembered a conversation she had with Susan Atkins and Patricia Krenwinkel before they drove back to the Spahn Ranch, as they tossed knives out of the window and dumped their blood-soaked clothing into the nearest ravine and then drove around looking for a garden hose to wash off the blood:

Q: *What did they say?*

A: *They complained about their heads, that the people were pulling their hair, and that their heads hurt. And Sadie even came out and said that when she was struggling with a big man, that he hit her in the head. And also Katie complained of her hand…that it hurt.*

Q: *Did she say why her hand hurt?*

A: *She said when she stabbed, that there were bones in the way, and she couldn't get the knife through all the way, and that it took too much energy or whatever…I don't know her exact words, but it hurt her hand.*

KASABIAN SAID that the next night, Manson ordered her and other Family members including Watson, Van Houten, Krenwinkel, Atkins, and Steve "Clem" Grogan to get in the car. For an hour or so they randomly drove around Los Angeles neighborhoods. Once, they stopped at a house and Manson looked in the window, then returned saying, "Let's drive on—there's children in that house." Then they stopped at a house in the Los Feliz area of Los Angeles, a few doors away from the home of Manson's friend Harold True, where he and family members had frequently partied. He parked the car and told them to wait. "I'll show you how to do it properly this time."

He went into the house and came out several minutes later. He ordered Watson, Krenwinkel, and Van Houten to go into the house. "You know what to do," he told them. Then he told them to hitchhike back to the Spahn Ranch.

But Manson was not ready to return to the ranch. With Atkins and Grogan along as spectators in the back seat, he told Kasabian to drive to Venice Beach where he suddenly turned nasty and, out of the blue, ordered her to kill a Lebanese actor acquaintance of hers named Saladin Nader.

Nader's offense? He had once picked up Kasabian and Sandra Good, who were hitchhiking, and took them both back to his fifth-floor apartment at 1101 Ocean Front Walk in Venice Beach. He had sex with Linda while Sandra took a nap on his couch. When they got back to the Spahn Ranch, they raved to Manson how nice he was. Manson took offense and labelled the actor "a piggy."

She testified that she deliberately knocked on the wrong apartment door, woke a stranger, which resulted in an aborted mission. Moments later Manson and Kasabian walked hand in hand on the beach like a courting couple out for a late night stroll with nary a trouble in the world.

A few days after the murders, the pregnant Kasabian panicked. She fled from the Spahn Ranch, leaving her eighteen-month-old daughter at the ranch. To most, that would seem cold and utterly indefensible, but Kasabian's survival instincts kicked in.

"I was terrified for my life," was how she explained abandoning the infant. "I went to get help. And, yes, I did leave my daughter. But I knew that she would be okay. I got to New Mexico, which is where my husband was, and told him the story."

Linda Kasabian, 1970

Kasabian said her husband wouldn't help, but her friend Charles Melton, known to Spahn Ranch members as "Blackbeard Charlie," did. He called the Spahn Ranch and was told everyone had been arrested—not for murder but for car theft. Linda's daughter Tanya had been sent to a foster care home.

After returning to Los Angeles and retrieving Tanya, Kasabian hitchhiked to Miami, Florida, to stay with her father. Around Thanksgiving her father bought her a Greyhound bus ticket and sent her back to her mother in Milford.

On December 2, 1969, Linda Kasabian was arrested in New Hampshire.

She did not fight extradition, and in February 1970, the immunity deal was signed by the eight-months-pregnant Kasabian.

A few days later she was ready to face the music and tell her story.

It was to be the "Little Hippie Girl's" finest hour.

THE PROSECUTION: A LEGEND IN HIS OWN MIND

"Vince Bugliosi was intense. Boy, was he intense. If I interviewed somebody and didn't get something he wanted, he re-interviewed them. But I didn't mind. He was strictly for conviction, and conviction meant proving these people guilty. He's the guy who made the case."

—Sgt. Danny Galindo, Los Angeles Homicide, to writer Steve Oney

"I have nothing but respect for Bugliosi as a lawyer, but his attitude pissed me off. He didn't solve the case. We solved the case. We brought the case to the district attorney's office in a pretty good package. He found more evidence, but that's what he's supposed to do."

—Sgt. Michael McGann, Los Angeles Police Department, to writer Steve Oney

Much has been written, debated, chewed over, and then regurgitated regarding the way Deputy District Attorney Vincent J. Bugliosi took an "unwinnable case" and emerged as legal hero, following the conviction of Charles Manson and his disciples in the killing of Sharon Tate and six others.

And as criminal history was writ large, there is little doubt that credit is where credit is due, and Mr. Bugliosi's, through his own self-described blood, sweat, and almost fiendish hard work and persistence, was fiercely instrumental in getting his convictions in a trial that dragged on for almost a year.

If Bugliosi is to be believed, he was the chosen one, handpicked to run the case almost single-handedly. At least, that's the gospel according to Vince, the kid from Hibbing, Minnesota. It makes a good story, particularly as laid out in riveting detail in *Helter Skelter*, co-authored with his ghostwriter Curt Gentry. Bugliosi's legend was refined continually throughout his lifetime. He had polished the story to a fine veneer in his later years, relating how he was plucked out of obscurity from the 400-plus-member DA's office and assigned to take the unwinnable case. (I find that statement quite amusing because Manson, if put in front of a jury, would get convicted of first-degree murder on a littering charge because he was so bat-shit crazy. No jury in their right mind would ever let a guy like that walk out of the courtroom and back into society.)

In 2009, Bugliosi told Steve Oney of *Los Angeles* magazine, "I was walking out of court when Aaron Stovitz, who was head of the trial division, grabbed me by the arm and brought me into the office of J. Miller Leavy, who was above Aaron. Two LAPD detectives were there, and I heard the name 'Tate.' They used to call it the Tate-LaBianca case before Manson showed up and upstaged the victims. I said to Aaron, 'Are we handling this?' He said, 'Yeah.'"

But the real back story about the way Bugliosi landed this high-profile assignment, which was to make him famous, is an intriguing one, and a classic example of someone who just happened to be in the right place at the right time.

There is little doubt that the homogenized version as presented by Mr. Bugliosi did not quite happen the way he said it did. Never let the facts get in the way of a good story was the way Bugliosi viewed things. Although, in the long run, it probably didn't matter how he landed this career-making role. The end justified any fabrication, and everyone likes a neatly packaged legend.

First, the background to Bugliosi's emergence as a legal superstar. The arrests were finally made, the investigations complete and, as the trial loomed, the district attorney's office realized they had a big one ahead and they needed to get their house in order.

In 1970, Evelle Younger was the district attorney and a stickler for discipline. He saw his mission as an empire builder, to turn the Los Angeles DA's office into the best in the nation—namely, the one with the highest number of convictions. He also saw the position as the perfect political stepping stone to higher office and he was good friends with Richard Nixon, Ronald Reagan, and Gerald Ford. One of J. Edgar Hoover's bright-eyed backroom boys, Younger was an early recruit to the CIA; he had a strong military background, ending up as a Brigadier General in the Air Force Reserve. As an admirer of the FBI director's dictatorial leadership, he tried to fashion the LA District Attorney's Office along similar lines and had a reputation as a strict disciplinarian.

A step or two down the chain of command came J. Miller Leavy ("Jules" to his top aides, "Mr. Leavy" to the rest), the department's trial division head deputy. Leavy was their legendary front man, their in-house "star." He brought much glory and national publicity to Los Angeles. His formidable track record included thirteen successful murder convictions and death sentences, particularly in two high-profile cases. He got a murder conviction in the 1957 trial of L. Ewing Scott, who was accused of murdering his socialite wife, Evelyn Throsby Scott. It was the first time there had been a first-degree murder conviction on purely circumstantial evidence, because the body of Scott's wife was never found. (Thirty years later when he was old and frail, the ninety-year-old Scott admitted to a journalist that he hit his wife over the head with a hard rubber mallet, stuffed her body in the trunk of his car, and buried her on the outskirts of Las Vegas. A year later he died.)

And it was Leavy who finally lived to see the man he prosecuted, the notorious "Red Light Bandit," Caryl Chessman, executed in the San Quentin gas chamber in 1960, after Chessman spent twelve years on Death Row for robbery, kidnapping, and rape. Chessman was the first modern American executed for a non-lethal kidnapping. Leavy got Chessman convicted under the Federal Kidnapping Act, commonly known as the "Little Lindbergh Law," which was later repealed. But not soon enough for Chessman.

As the DA's ace prosecutor, Leavy was expected to once again step up to handle the high-profile Manson case. It was right up his alley and he loved putting away career criminals like Manson.

Leavy, who was small but built like a piece of granite, always appeared in court sporting a tweed jacket. Donald Goldsobel, who worked in the district attorney's office at the time, told me Leavy was tenacious, with a devastating reputation for getting convictions in big murder cases.

"When he invited you to his office, you accepted. Jules proudly displayed a framed photo in his office of the mobster Mickey Cohen standing out in front of the Hall of Justice, wearing a watch and key chain. Jules had successfully prosecuted Mickey."

He continued: "He was the boss, like the department's poppa...he took care of the coffee room, watched everybody, and knew what was going on in the office. Every year, casinos in Gardena sent him cases of whiskey and what was left, after the office Christmas parties, went into his liquor cabinet. And so, after work he liked to entertain the troops with the booze."

New Yorker Aaron Stovitz, at forty-five, was his deputy, his chosen one, and, after seventeen years in the office, was the department's senior trial lawyer. In 1980 I interviewed Stovitz, and his version of how Bugliosi landed the job in the Manson trial somewhat differed from Bugliosi's account. Go figure. And while Stovitz's story of Bugliosi's appointment to the case may reek somewhat of sour grapes, perhaps even jealousy, his version was supported by others who knew how things happened in 1970.

Here's what Stovitz told me in Ventura, California, long after he had retired from the DA's office and was working part-time for Ventura County District Attorney Michael Bradbury:

"When we got the Sharon Tate case, I assumed Jules would take the first chair, but right away, he said he didn't want it. He said he was too old, and after forty years on the job was looking forward to retirement. In fact, he did indeed retire in 1972.

"'I'll be honest with you, Aaron,' Jules said. 'This is going to be a long and arduous trial and I don't have the energy for it anymore. I want you to take it.'

"About a week later, we were sitting in his office drinking whiskey. It had become something of a ritual—the top-level guys in the office would show up in his office to drink, chitchat, and talk shop.

"That particular evening Vince stuck his head in the door and was invited to join us. He was one of the new young bucks and he was riding high, cock of the walk, because earlier in the day he'd just got a conviction in a trial involving gang shootings in the San Fernando Valley. And he couldn't stop boasting about his success.

"Jules listened intently and then said, 'Aaron, if you've got no one lined up for the second chair, how about taking Bugliosi?'"

That was about how much thought and energy went into making the decision.

And thus, a star was born, and the thirty-five-year-old Bugliosi found himself handling the biggest case in Los Angeles history.

Whichever story you choose to believe, no one doubts that Bugliosi mounted a phenomenal case and put in the hours required to get the job done.

Even though some who worked in the office were either impressed or turned off by Bugliosi's style, the opportunity was not undeserved. And, by style I'm specifically referring to the fact that Bugliosi had developed the reputation as being a pompous ass, unabashedly pushing his me-first attitude within the ranks of the DA's office. Talented and hardworking, yes, but humility was not in his genetic makeup.

Deputy DA Donald Goldsobel, whose office was steps from Bugliosi's, recalled, "Vince picked himself. He promoted himself whenever he had the opportunity. Don't get me wrong. He was a good, hard-working guy. But he was about as arrogant as anybody can be. That's fine for people who were talented. But I can tell you this: Aaron was twice the lawyer he was."

An amiable, cigar-puffing prosecutor with a strong track record, Stovitz was happy to take the brash young colleague, whom he realized had the energy to do much of the legwork, under his wing. While Stovitz said he knew the Tate case was big, it was Bugliosi who kept insisting, "This is the trial of the century." Prescient on Bugliosi's part, to be sure, or maybe this was just his way of building himself up for the heavyweight fight that awaited him in the courtroom.

Despite Bugliosi's self-aggrandizing version of being the one who made sure the crucial Linda Kasabian immunity deal fell into place, it was Stovitz who actually worked out the minute and crucial details of the arrangement with Kasabian's lawyer, Gary Fleischman. Ed Sanders, author of *The Family*, who was writing a column for the *Los Angeles Free Press* (also known as "The Freep"), said he overheard Stovitz admitting, "Everyone will walk if Linda doesn't testify for us."

But Aaron Stovitz was soon to shoot himself in the foot—a wound that would prove fatal to his high-riding career.

While he was amiable and bright, and a terrific court litigator, his big problem was that he was too talkative. Because of the nature of this case and the media interest in its upcoming trial, he couldn't keep his mouth shut. He too began to revel in the fact that he was being bombarded daily with calls from TV, radio, and print outlets seeking his opinion. Never a day passed without a TV camera crew invading his office for a pretrial interview. He realized that the media appetite for this case was unquenchable and that they just couldn't get enough. And that led to his downfall.

One day he proudly showed a fellow lawyer a story about himself that ran in the *Los Angeles Times*. "He adored it when the paper described him a 'part Columbo...with a dash of Perry Mason,'" Goldsobel recalled.

The reporter pegged him correctly because that was the kind of guy Aaron Stovitz was. For more than six months he ran the operation as they amassed evidence and re-interviewed dozens of key witnesses who would be the cornerstone of their case.

On June 25, 1970, one month before the "trial of the century" was to begin, *Rolling Stone* magazine published a massive 30,000-word story, titled, "Charles Manson: The Incredible Story of the Most Dangerous Man Alive—a chilling, deeply investigative look into the terrifying Manson family."

The story was penned by a couple of the magazine's heavyweights— *Rolling Stone*'s founding editors, David Dalton and their Pulitzer-prize winner, David Felton. It included a jailhouse interview with Manson, which was surprisingly sympathetic toward the accused killer, enabling him to pontificate endlessly and build his legend as he honed his (take your pick)...crazy/angry/docile prophet performance for the reporters. In the piece, he came across as a...(take your pick again)... peace-loving/likeable/harmless/idealistic/loner whose mantra was love, and whose only major sin was to upset the American Federation of Musicians, Los Angeles Local 47, who had gone out of their way to distance themselves from the wannabe songwriter. The article noted that Manson had become part of what might be described as "the hippie movement," the darling of several underground newspapers who were offering "Free Manson" stickers and touting him as their misunderstood, rebel hero, with stories declaring: "Manson: Man of the Year." One underground newspaper even had Manson penning a regular column, which was meticulously hand-delivered to their office by one of his girls.

The magazine reporters got a personal tour of the Spahn ranch led by the leftover Manson girls, but their conversation left the reader with a clear vision of the young women, who finally ended up in a spirited

212 | MANSON EXPOSED

squabble over how much money they could squeeze out of those who wanted to interview and film them.

But the real kicker to the *Rolling Stone* story came in the body of the article. It quoted its major source, identified only by the pseudonym of "Porfiry"—an obvious literary reference to Petrovich Porfiry, the detective in Dostoyevsky's classic novel *Crime and Punishment*. Porfiry was described as "trim, dark haired, maybe in his early forties, he looks not like a cop but a no-nonsense college dean." Then the giveaway line: "California suntanned—New York tough talker."

Everyone in the building, even those working in the DA's cafeteria, instantly knew the true identity of Porfiry. It wasn't a difficult guess. Stovitz, of course, was one of a tiny handful of lawyers who had access to the treasure trove of mostly confidential prosecutorial evidence and he, as Porfiry, read chunks of that evidence to Messrs. Dalton and Felton, who must have thought they had struck gold. He even showed them bloody Cielo Drive evidence photos, which he then gave them to run alongside page after page of their marathon reportage.

While eating lunch in his office, Porfiry, who seemed to relish rambling on at great length about the prosecution's testimony, provided them with the most graphic details about the case, which were to be the backbone of the upcoming trial. Little was held back.

And then, much to the delight of the writers, who taped the interview, he went on to outline the case against Manson…even offering a suggestion: the backstory as to why Manson had sent out his killers.

It was all there—the murder of musician Gary Hinman; the trial of Manson family member Bobby Beausoleil, which ended in a hung jury and implicated Manson as the real instigator of the Hinman killing.

Then to the heart of the Cielo and Waverly Drive killings, which offered a fascinating, alternate reason or theory as to why Sharon Tate and the others might have been killed.

Porfiry declared, "Now, this is only a supposition on my part, I don't have any proof to support it…Manson said to himself, 'How am I going to help my friend Beausoleil out? By showing that the actual murderer of Hinman is still at large.

"'Go out to the house on Cielo Drive' (to Watson and the girls), and commit robbery and kill anyone that you see there.'

"And he instructed them to leave 'Political Piggies' in blood at the murder scene so that investigators would blame someone else for the killings. And in his demented reasoning, Beausoleil—who was facing murder charges and was in jail at the time of the Tate and LaBianca murders—would not be blamed for the Hinman killings."

And there were lots more tidbits as Porfiry waxed on endlessly into the *Rolling Stone* reporters' tape recorder.

As soon as the story broke, Younger summoned Stovitz into his inner sanctum and gave him hell. He said everyone was outraged. Judge William Keene issued a gag order on December 10, 1969, and now the defense lawyers were screaming bloody murder. Judge Keene cited Stovitz for contempt after the defense lawyers claimed that any jury pool would be forever tainted by his stupid blabbing, and the defendants could never get a fair trial. Even Stovitz's fellow deputies were amazed by their colleague's indiscretions.

Stovitz tried vainly to defend himself. He lamely declared, "I was just giving them deep background—I didn't expect them to quote me verbatim."

And indeed, there is little doubt that the writers did the dirty on him. A transcript of the opening gambit of their interview clearly shows that Stovitz, whose naïvete was astounding, considering his vast experience in dealing with the media, tried to lay down some ground rules, but was fully aware of the consequences of what might happen if he was quoted.

He said, "I'll answer all your questions if you give me one definite promise: don't quote me. And that you realize that I believe that this court order, that the judge has issued, was made to protect the defendants so they can get a fair trial."

Obviously failing to see the terrible irony, he continued, "If all law enforcement officers made responsible comments, then there would be no necessity for a gag order. But some police officers go shooting off their mouths, and ah, they use their, ah, gun recklessly, they certainly use their words recklessly, and ah, the defendant may not get a fair trial. So the judge issued a gag order. Unfortunately, that curtails us from telling you what the evidence is gonna be. 'Cause this is a direct violation of the court order."

His plea to the writers fell on deaf ears. Or maybe they kept their word. After all, surely it was "Porfiry" talking and not Stovitz!

In an article published in *Politico* in December 2017, Felton wrote: "We promised not to use Stovitz's name in our article (which we didn't) and we promised to turn off the tape recorder if he wanted to speak off the record. He never asked that. Maybe he thought we were from some inconsequential hippie rag, or maybe he just loved telling the story." Probably both.

Younger issued a final warning to Stovitz: "Keep your mouth shut—otherwise you're gone."

Alas, his warnings went unheeded.

On September 4, 1970, six weeks into the trial, Stovitz was formally kicked off the case.

The trial had resumed, but immediately recessed for the day. Susan Atkins was not able to appear in court, which meant the trial had come to a standstill. She said she was ill, suffering from stomach cramps. Stovitz thought she was malingering after a doctor who examined her said her only problem was that she was constipated and refused to take a laxative. So, as far as Stovitz was concerned, it was just another defense dodge to drag things out.

That day, after we recessed early and left the courtroom, we trooped into the hallway with no story to write. We asked Stovitz what he thought of Atkins' no-show. He smiled, and then delivered a line that he was to forever regret.

"It was a performance worthy of Sarah Bernhardt," he wisecracked.

With no fresh news that day, the wire services ran with his comment. Jack V. Fox from United Press International, Linda Deutsch from the Associated Press, and Bruce Russell, the West Coast Bureau Chief for Reuters all immediately filed new story leads using that quote.

It made front page of *Los Angeles Herald Examiner*. It was obvious that it was a throwaway line, but it was a killer quote. The point, as anyone worth their literary showbiz salt would have realized, was a lame joke. Bernhardt, the great French-born stage actress had been dead fifty years. And anyway, it was true as everyone knew. Atkins, not the most trustworthy young woman, was most certainly playing sick.

Evelle Younger was not amused.

The by-the-book district attorney summoned Stovitz to his office and removed him from the case. The quipster was toast. He was also distraught. He had invested long and grueling work hours and weeks prepping, interviewing key witnesses for trial for nine intensive months. Now, overnight, he had become a has-been. Younger's office offered some half-arsed, cockamamie explanation, saying Stovitz was needed elsewhere to handle other interoffice duties. But of course, nobody was fooled. Stovitz was banished to the District Attorney's equivalent of Siberia, and it was cold as hell.

His abrupt departure left a big vacancy. We were well into the trial and the prosecution's big gun was gone. Only the defense rejoiced.

Stovitz's assistant, Vincent Bugliosi—lean and thinning of hair, a tennis scholarship recipient, graduate of the University of Miami who had received his law degree from the UCLA School of Law—stepped in to the spotlight. Bugliosi, who had spent only five years in the DA's office but had established a reputation as being a hard-driving workaholic, suddenly found himself the prosecution's kingpin. His mission: to convict a wild, unpredictable man who everyone agreed never actually killed any of the victims.

He jumped into the job with frenzy, passion, and a touch of the triumphant "I told you so."

Into Bugliosi's chair stepped Stephen Kay, at twenty-seven, a self-admitted "raw around the edges" lawyer three years out of the University of California's prestigious Berkeley School of Law, who had only joined the DA's office in January 1968 and needed to do a massive amount of catching up.

Everyone agreed that now Aaron Stovitz was gone it wasn't going get any easier.

And Vincent Bugliosi (not "Bug-liosi"—the g is silent—he constantly corrected TV, print, and radio reporters) was to show the world what he was made of, as he declared war on Manson and his gang, as well as the media covering the trial.

The "Bug" was about to do some smashing of his own.

DEFENDING THE DAMNED: PART ONE

"Mr. Kanarek, you seem to have some sort of physical infirmity or mental disability that causes you to interrupt and disrupt testimony. No matter how many times I warn you, you seem to do it repeatedly, again and again and again ... You are trying to disrupt the testimony of this witness. It is perfectly clear. Now, I have gone as far as I am going to go with you."

—Judge Charles Older

Irving Kanarek, the spoiler of a defense lawyer, was handpicked by Charles Manson to mount his daffy defense. Earlier the judge—ignoring the stampede of lawyers who wanted to become Manson's legal protector—had appointed Charles Hollopeter, a respected Pasadena lawyer, to mount his defense. But Hollopeter didn't last long. No sooner had he taken the first obvious step and requested a psychiatric report for his client than his tenure was doomed. It was not what his client wanted, and so Hollopeter got the push after less than two weeks. Briefly, into the breach stepped freshman lawyer Ronald Hughes, who had never in his brief career, handled a court case before. Manson knew Hughes was still wet behind his legal ears. They had met when Hughes was brought to the Spahn Ranch by a friend, and as soon as he heard Manson had been arrested he came running. Manson recruited him for free, using him first as a legal errand boy.

Manson thought he could manipulate Hughes and realized his limitations. And it was Hughes who first dropped the name Kanarek in Manson's ear. Leading up to the trial Manson was in a constant state of fury.

Judge William Keene (the first of two judges appointed to the case) ruled that he could no longer represent himself because his knowledge of basic trial procedure was seriously lacking and that Manson was incompetent to represent himself and would have to have a real lawyer. Manson did not take kindly to the use of the word *incompetent*.

"Okay," said Manson, "give me (Supreme Court) Justice William O. Douglas."

"No sir," said Judge Keene.

"Okay," said Manson, "if you won't let me be my own man and use my own voice, I'll turn this trial into a circus. If I have to have a lawyer, I'll get the worst there is."

Enter Mr. Kanarek, who, to his credit, did address that "worst there is" point. It was, in fact, meant as a compliment, he pointed out. It simply meant that other lawyers shuddered in their shoes when they realized they were going to have to confront him in court. For them, battling Kanarek was a worst case scenario because everyone knew Mr. Kanarek was a tiger in court.

Whichever way "worst" was interpreted, Kanarek quickly lived up to his reputation as "The Van Nuys Bulldog," as well as "King of the Filibusters." His verbose, rambling arguments tested even the most even-handed jurist. One story had it that a Los Angeles judge became so stressed out after dealing with Kanarek's obfuscations that he had a heart attack.

Kanarek, born in 1920, was a squat, barrel-chested, grim-faced man, with a mop of dark, thinning hair tinged with gray. He looked like a pocket-sized Norman Mailer. He was fifty at the time of the trial, but looked ten years older. He seemed to wear the same crumpled suit every day, which looked as though he had slept in it. He probably had. Several lawyers confirmed that when they showed up early on many mornings, they often saw Kanarek still sleeping in his car in the parking lot.

Preston Guilleroy, a former Sheriff's deputy who later became Kanarek's private investigator, said Irving often slept on the table in the witness room and drafted his motions at dinner tables in local restaurants.

The story I was told was that Kanarek, a former chemical engineer and inventor who worked on America's Nike missile program, turned to law in his mid-thirties after graduating from Loyola Law School in 1957. He took up the new profession after becoming incensed over the fact that his ex-wife was awarded a huge chunk of money he had earned from chemical patents, leaving him to scramble to make ends meet. After that, he vowed to become an attorney, "to treat them the way they treated me."

One former high-profile client was Jimmy Lee Smith, who had been convicted of killing a police officer in 1963 in what became known as "The Onion Field" murder. In court, Smith became so infuriated with the tedious way Kanarek was handling his case that he got into near fisticuffs with his lawyer, and then threw a chair at him and refused to speak to him. Everyone in the tight-knit Southern California legal community had a ridiculous Irving story. Deputy District Attorney Burton Katz, who led the prosecution's team in their successful efforts to convict Manson family member Robert Beausoleil for the murder of musician Gary Hinman, once recalled that Kanarek had vehemently objected to a prosecution witness stating his own name. His reasoning: "Because having first heard his name from his mother, the statement was 'hearsay.'"

Kanarek was so long-winded that judges shuddered when they learned he was to appear before them. His supporters—and there were only a handful at most—said his technique was deliberate and done to confuse juries and opposition lawyers.

Brevity was not part of his style. On the first day of the Tate trial he objected to Bugliosi's opening statement over 100 times. All objections were overruled. During the trial I seldom saw him smile. His closing summation on behalf of Manson ran for over a week. However, he did give the press corps much to chuckle over. He insisted on referring to the murder victims as "having passed away," and described the two murder scenes as "the places of repose."

When drug dealer Bernard Crowe—whose nickname was "Lotsapoppa" because he was a rather large gentleman—was called to testify about the time Manson shot him in the stomach and left him for dead in an incident that had nothing to do with the Tate-LaBianca murders, Kanarek, with a straight face, dragged out the cross examination for nearly an hour. "How," he inquired, "would the witness like to be addressed. Mr. Crowe? Mr. Lotsa? Mr. Poppa or Mr. Lotsapoppa?" It was one of the rare times during the trial that Kanarek's offbeat sense of humor came into play.

He knew how to aggravate Vincent Bugliosi, often referring to him as "Mr. Bug-liosi," instead of the preferred silent "G" pronunciation.

During the trial, Stephen Kay recalled being asked by his boss, Evelle Younger, to introduce the lawyers in the case to the Spanish ambassador to the United States, who had been an interested observer in the courtroom.

At the recess, Kay took the diplomat around in the hallway but when he tried to introduce him to Kanarek, the lawyer turned away and yelled, "Who gives a shit?"

Kanarek's negative energy sucked up most of the oxygen in the courtroom so that by the end of the ten-month trial, most of us were left gasping for breath.

During the trial, Ken Clayman, who worked in the nearby Los Angeles Public Defender's office, became friendly with Kanarek and saw a more likeable side.

"Once you got to know him he was a real character and a loveable guy," Clayman said. "He just wasn't a very good lawyer, particularly with judges. They all wanted to be rid of him."

During trial lunch breaks, Clayman said Kanarek would frequently hang out in the Public Defender's lunchroom. "He would ask us for ideas of what he might do in the trial. Strangely, he didn't have a huge ego and was remarkably sanguine about his role in this high-profile case. He had no illusions; he just wanted to make it hard for them. So he threw out every *fakakta* crazy idea in the book."

One time Clayman hitched a lift from Kanarek in downtown LA.

"The trunk of his beaten up Dodge Charger was overflowing with sports coats, wrinkled pants, and crumpled shirts mixed up with dozens of legal files," Clayman said. "He kept a stack of gas receipts on the dashboard of his car. From time to time, after I became the Public Defender in Ventura and he had a case in Ventura, he'd show up with a stack of paper motions and ask to use our Xerox machine. I had to decline."

Kanarek created constant bedlam, trying, in his unique way, to persuade the jury that because Manson was never at the Tate house, he should be acquitted—notwithstanding the fact that in California, conspiracy to murder and felony murder does not require the defendant to be present when someone is murdered.

In the long-running drama that masqueraded as a murder trial, most of Bugliosi's and Kay's energy was devoted to putting a harness on Kanarek's bull-in-a-china-shop technique, and reminding the jury not to lose sight of the fact that they were there for a murder trial.

LEADING UP TO the trial, as I watched lawyers come and go with alarming alacrity, no one realized that, incredibly, Manson was manipulating it all from his jail cell—including who would represent whom.

While he had recruited Kanarek to be his on-record lawyer, Manson decided that the loyal Ronald Hughes might be just the guy to represent Van Houten. And to hell with the fact that, despite his enthusiasm for the cause, he had zero experience. Fealty was high on Manson's shopping list.

Days after he was brought to Los Angeles from Inyo County,

Manson instructed the girls who were free that they could gain easy access to visit him if he listed them as members of his defense team. Hughes made it happen. And even *after* Hughes was formally appointed as a lawyer for Van Houten, Manson used the willing new lawyer as his personal messenger, gofer, and paralegal. Hughes, so excited to be in on the action, probably never realized he was being played by Manson. And even if he did, then what the hell: he was in the big leagues.

Ron, a likeable, energetic, prematurely balding, 250-pound lawyer of Falstaffian proportions, approached the trial with great enthusiasm, like a high-school kid who had stumbled into an *Animal House* frat party. For him it was on-the-job training. Besides having had no trial experience whatsoever, he was also penniless. He had an old car that constantly broke down. One day he showed up late for the trial and told the angry judge that he had been pulled over by a California Highway Patrol officer who noticed his vehicle was belching smoke. The officer took one look at his rusting clunker and deemed it was unfit to be driven on the highway. The car was towed away.

Hughes was not being paid by Van Houten, and consequently he lived hand-to-mouth. For weeks afterwards, until he could afford to get another set of wheels, I, along with other journalists covering the trial, gave him rides back to his abode in West Los Angeles when the trial recessed. I say "abode" because he lived in a garage at the back of a friend's house. In one corner sat his version of a bed—a large mattress on the concrete floor, covered by a tacky blanket. In the other corner was his desk, piled three feet high with transcripts and an assortment of legal documents. The garage had no heat. Nailed on the wall over the desk, next to a rusting file cabinet, was a framed California Bar Association certificate. Hughes proudly admitted he had just passed the bar—on his fourth try. The garage was depressing, to say the least. There were no windows, just holes cut in the roof covered by see-through plastic, which he said were perfect skylights.

"I can lay on my bed and count the stars," he told me. His office phone never rang off the hook with clients looking for legal advice because he didn't have a phone. It had been disconnected because he couldn't afford to pay his bill.

Hughes, with his unkempt beard, looked like a hippie and was rather proud of his appearance. He said as soon as he met Manson he had been lured to enjoy some of the delights of Family life at the Spahn Ranch after lending his legal skills to sorting out Manson's wannabe recording career. Hughes liked Manson and they became—as Hughes put it—"soul brothers."

Ron made no secret of the fact that he had availed himself of Manson's pharmacy and liked to drop acid with Charlie and the girls, but insisted that was long before the murders. Listening to him rave on about the accused murderer, I thought that partaking of Manson's poisoned fruit was not quite the credential a lawyer looking for work might want to put on his curriculum vitae.

Before he became a lawyer, he'd had a stint in the Army during the Korean War. After that, he managed a rock group called United States Government, which gave him the credentials to enthusiastically support Manson's talents as a songwriter and singer.

The moment Hughes was officially linked with Van Houten, he proved he could also follow orders. And quickly. He requested that Manson be allowed to defend himself, which at first glance would seem to be the provenance of Kanarek and not Van Houten's lawyer. The other two motions were: forget about a Van Houten psychiatric exam— something all her previous lawyers had prioritized—and also, deep six the idea that she be tried separately.

Manson had found himself an able pawn.

Yet, despite following his puppet master, Hughes immediately became the most popular defense lawyer on the case, mainly because he loved hanging out with us reporters covering the trial. Free drinks every night, and solely for the pleasure of Ron's company. Nice fringe benefits.

Still, he also brought a certain naïveté, unpretentious charm, and even comedy to the scene, along with no preconceived notions about the rituals and habits practiced by the courtroom media. The remarkable thing about Hughes was his swift rise to fame. He graduated from the UCLA School of Law in 1969, and then for a few months he was a gofer for the Los Angeles Public Defender's office, running odd jobs in downtown and enjoying the camaraderie of an office that specialized in handling cases for defendants who couldn't afford to hire high-priced lawyers. Then, with one spectacular leap, he suddenly vaulted from starving law-school graduate with no visible means of support to high-profile defender of Van Houten in the most celebrated murder trial in history. What's more, the TV networks, radio, and daily newspapers were clinging to his every utterance.

I'm sure Hughes thought he'd fallen into a pile of shit and come up smelling like a rose. Theo Wilson of the New York *Daily News*, regarded as the doyenne of journalistic trial reporters, always referred to him fondly as "the flower child of a defense attorney." Hughes often described himself as a pauper and reinforced that image by showing up every day in the same green suit, shirt, and tie for the first two months of the trial. Finally, one day his jacket literally fell apart at the seams. Martin Kasindorf, who was covering the trial for *Newsweek*, loaned him his own jacket so he would not have to appear before the judge in shirtsleeves.

Kasindorf happily recounted that incident for this book: "They were about to go into chambers when the judge asked poor, impoverished Ron to put a jacket on. Now, he was in shirtsleeves—a short-sleeved shirt. He looked around the courtroom and either asked for volunteers or made the appeal wordlessly. His eyes met mine and I volunteered my checked sport jacket. He thanked me, put it on, and wore it into chambers. The effect was hilarious. I am a skinny little guy and Hughes was big and fat. The sleeves of my jacket came down to barely his elbows. I'm sure there were quiet guffaws in the courtroom over how it looked. When Ron came out of the in-chambers conference, I got my jacket back."

Soon after, several of us suggested starting a fund to help buy the hippie lawyer a new outfit, but somehow he scrambled through and came up with enough money to purchase a couple of suits ($5 apiece) at a Hollywood studio auction. One, a double-breasted gray outfit, he proudly informed us had been worn by Spencer Tracy in the 1960 legal drama *Inherit the Wind*. And to prove it he showed off a label sewn inside. Maybe it was true because it looked a little tight on his big frame and was very short on the sleeves. He also bought two togas from *Ben-Hur*, but thankfully never showed up in court wearing them. That wardrobe change might have even upstaged ol' Charlie, a tough act to follow in his buckskin and coat of many colors. When Judge Older cited Hughes for contempt for yelling at Bugliosi, he offered him the choice: a $75 fine or a night in jail. Hughes chose jail. "I'm a pauper," he explained as he prepared to spend the night behind bars, where a free breakfast awaited him before he showed up for court the next day.

In this topsy-turvy trial, the defendants did confer with their own lawyers from time to time, but certainly not with the prosecutors. However, Stephen Kay remembers that over a three-day period, he got fairly friendly with Hughes, and during recesses he found himself in a peculiar debate with Van Houten. The topic: Is the death penalty a deterrent?

"Ron listened quietly as we argued," Kay told me. "Van Houten was no dummy. She had a high IQ that was in the top five percent in the country and could hold her own in any debate. But even I felt our conversation bordered on the absurd. Here I was, trying my darndest to send this woman, who most of the world considered was a real looney tune, to the gas chamber. All the while, Ron sat there smiling like a proud father admiring his daughter's rhetoric."

His ineptitude showed too often. When he cross-examined star witness Linda Kasabian, he seemed to go wildly off track and kept asking a series of irrelevant questions about her smoking habits and then her passion for yoga. The prosecution successfully objected to two dozen of his questions until Hughes got the message. After he finished with

Kasabian, at the completion of almost eighteen days in the witness box, he turned theatrically to the judge, and in a booming voice, declared, "Your honor, I suggest that the jury now be allowed to cross-examine this witness."

His understanding of how the media worked was also severely tested. In her 1996 memoir *Headline Justice*, veteran reporter Theo Wilson tells an amusing story about dealing with the neophyte lawyer after Nixon's throwaway line declaring Manson guilty.

"I was in the press room when my city editor called and said, 'We must have the defense's reaction immediately.' It was lunchtime, and the only lawyer around was Ron Hughes. I told him what Nixon had said."

Wilson recalled the conversation, starting with her plea to Hughes:

"I need a comment."

"Well, fuck the President," said Hughes.

"I can't send that." Wilson put Hughes on the phone with the city editor. "Fuck him," repeated Hughes.

"We can't use that," the editor said. Wilson sat Hughes down, and with the phone in her hand said, "Okay, Ron, how about if you say, 'We demand a mistrial and that you are upset that the President, a lawyer, would violate the defendant's rights and call him guilty while still on trial'?"

"Yeah," said Hughes. "Let's say that, but…fuck him also."

IN NOVEMBER 1970, as the defense rested its case and the trial was recessed for ten days, Hughes went on a weekend camping trip. The break was supposedly to clear his head and sample the natural waters of Sespe Hot Springs in Ventura County and prepare his closing arguments. But he never returned. His unexplained disappearance was the shocking talking point in court for the next few weeks. There were rumors that he had been bumped off, although no one came up with a strong motive as to why. To this day there are those who insist that Hughes was killed because he had incurred Manson's wrath. In support of that theory, Kay told me that he vividly remembered Hughes announcing to his colleagues and the defendants that during the break he was heading to the great Ventura hinterland. Somehow, in the wilderness, he hoped to find the peace and inspiration to write his closing argument.

Kay wasn't so sure.

"Manson resented the fact that Ron—like his predecessors—at one time suggested that Van Houten be tried separately," he recalled. "I remember this very clearly, just as if it happened yesterday. Charlie pointed across the counsel table at Hughes, and with that icy stare of his, he said, 'I don't want to ever see you in this courtroom again.'"

Bugliosi later claimed that Sandra Good had told a documentary filmmaker, in a segment that got little exposure when it first came out, that the Manson Family was responsible for thirty-five or forty murders, and that the death of Hughes was the first of those "retaliatory killings."

Hughes was accompanied on his camping trip by two teenagers, James Forsher and Lauren Elder. They drove together in Elder's Volkswagen and said they dropped the lawyer off near a river with no clear plans for a return journey. They were not considered suspects. Shortly afterwards, three young men reported to police that they had seen Hughes, who was hard to miss, in the Ventura back-country. They were given lie-detector tests, but no criminal action was ever taken, and no sightings of Hughes were reported after that. Police in helicopters scoured the area a dozen times. On March 29, 1971, on the same day the jury returned death-penalty decisions on all defendants—and four months after Hughes vanished—two fishermen discovered a body floating down a creek. The corpse was so badly decomposed that the only way they were able to identify Hughes was through his dental records.

Much later I spoke to Michael Bradbury, the former Ventura County District Attorney, who was familiar with the case. "It was not murder," Bradbury insisted. "Our investigators examined it closely and decided that Mr. Hughes had been caught in a terrible rainstorm. He was probably under the influence of drugs and, being such a large man and not very physically agile, most likely was swept away by the creek's onrushing waters during a flash flood." An autopsy determined, "death by natural causes," and as far as the local cops were concerned: case closed. AP reporter Linda Deutsch said that the mysterious disappearance of Hughes played into Bugliosi's 'Manson death squad' theories.

"Vince even accused Mary and I of causing Hughes's death! He summoned us to his grim little office and said because we had given negative information about Ron to *Time* magazine, Ron became so distressed he went out and killed himself by throwing himself into a mudslide! Vince threatened to expose us for that."

But that did not stop the gossiping back in the Hall of Justice. It wasn't every day that an attorney involved in a sensational murder trial disappeared just like that. Had Manson and Hughes fallen out? Did the Manson women, for reasons we didn't know, bump him off? During the trial Hughes had begun to hedge on the question about his relationship with Manson, telling us one day in the hallway, "My relationship with Charlie is still friendly. He's a weird dude, but we've always seen eye to eye...on most things."

Those close to the case agreed that Hughes' sudden disappearance was too much of a coincidence because strange things happened to people who crossed Charles Manson. During the trial, five members of the Family were indicted for trying to kill Barbara Hoyt, an eighteen-year-old former member who had agreed to open up for the prosecution. The pretty, dark-haired Hoyt told police that members of the Family, including Squeaky, Gypsy, and Clem Grogan, had persuaded her to go to Hawaii on an all-expense-paid holiday so she could avoid testifying. They even purchased a couple of tickets with stolen credit cards and designated that she be accompanied by nineteen-year-old Family member Ruth Ann "Ouisch" Moorehouse. She was the daughter of Manson pal and one-time pastor Dean Moorehouse, who had turned his very young daughter over to Manson as a sort of peace offering.

As Hoyt later described it, she and Moorehouse checked in under assumed names and lived for a few days at the Hilton Hawaiian Village Hotel. They were worried that the LAPD might have put out a nationwide warrant for Hoyt. Abruptly, Moorehouse announced she would have to return to California, but Hoyt could stay. At the Honolulu Airport, Moorehouse suggested Hoyt should have something to eat. She returned a few moments later with a hamburger. Moorehouse watched her eat it, then jumped on her flight back to LA. Hoyt took a bus back to the hotel, but en route she suddenly felt woozy, began to freak out, and panicked. She jumped off the bus and ran screaming into the street where she finally collapsed. An ambulance rushed her to the psychiatric ward of a nearby hospital. Toxicological reports later deemed that her illness was caused by the hamburger, which had been heavily laced with a lethal ten tabs of LSD.

She finally recovered and was able to testify, which she did with vigor and to great effect.

"Yeah, they tried to kill me," Hoyt declared as she left the grand jury room. However, police dropped the attempted murder charges and settled for convictions of five Family members for conspiracy to prevent a witness from testifying. They were slapped with a puny ninety-day prison sentence.

Another Manson victim who survived a deadly attack was Paul Watkins; once Manson's right-hand man, he had also become a key prosecution witness. In March 1970, Watkins had a spat with three of the Manson women who called him a "Judas" for giving up dirt on Manson—information Manson's attorney obtained through a motion of discovery. Watkins was sleeping in a camper when he suddenly woke surrounded by smoke and flame. Blinded and choking, he managed to get out. Investigators could not determine the cause of the blaze. Watkins, who was treated for third-degree burns, said it could have come from a candle or a marijuana cigarette. However, a Family member later claimed to have set the fire as a lesson not to cross Manson.

Linda Kasabian's lawyer, Gary Fleischman, said he knew firsthand that death threats were not simply the result of an overactive paranoid imagination. Not only were members of the DA's staff threatened—and given round-the-clock protection as a result—but Fleischman feared that he, too, would be a target. Manson was fully capable of ordering a hit on the man that he knew had engineered Kasabian's devastating testimony.

"It freaked us all out when Ronald Hughes got killed. How many times do you hear of a defense lawyer getting killed in the middle of a case?" Fleischman told *Los Angeles* magazine's Steve Oney. "I was living in a two-story apartment in Beverly Hills, and I had a couple of these kids—Linda's husband, Bob, and a guy named Charlie Melton—sleeping on my doorstep. Bob and Charlie were really just warm bodies. They were just eating my food and smoking my dope. But they lived with me for several months. I wanted someone there if Squeaky Fromme tried to sneak in and slit my throat."

Other Family members—even those not facing murder charges—were considered major threats. Five members of the Manson Family were arrested in 1971 after a shootout at an LA-area gun store. They had broken into the shop in a vain effort to amass weapons that they said would be used to break Manson out of prison. The shootout happened as police responded to a silent alarm, unleashing shotgun blasts into the getaway van. When the shooting ended, three members of the Family—"Gypsy" Share, Mary Brunner, and Joseph Jones—were wounded trying to escape in a white Ford van. Three others were also arrested. The bizarre motive for stealing the weaponry: so they could free Manson while he was facing charges in the murder of Gary Hinman and stuntman Donald Shea. All were convicted and given stiff, ten-to-twenty-year prison sentences. And maybe, if the guys could wangle it, they could once again enjoy a reunion singalong with Charlie in adjoining cell blocks.

DEFENDING THE DAMNED: PART TWO

Despite Kanarek's run-amuck strategy, there were other lawyers in the courtroom who, happy or not, found themselves aligned with the quirky counselor in a genuine effort to get their clients acquitted.

Marvin Part had a quick walk-on role as Leslie Van Houten's second lawyer in mid-December 1969. Van Houten was just nineteen when she was implicated in the murder of the LaBiancas. Part, bright, competent, had worked for the district attorney, was now in private practice. He advised Van Houten that she should be tried separately. It made sense, he said. She was only involved in the LaBianca murders and had nothing whatsoever to do with the carnage that took place at Sharon Tate's house one night earlier. With all the girls lumped together, Part said he worried that the jurors might also blame Van Houten for *both* nights of murder.

Van Houten had been arrested in Inyo County along with most of the Manson followers, and was originally booked under one of her fake names: Leslie Sangster. Her background mirrored many of the other stories of aimless young women who had been lured into the cult by Manson's jailhouse gibberish. Part later told me he had listened with utter astonishment and growing horror to the tape recordings of his client being interrogated by homicide detectives.

"I knew right away this girl has no will of her own," Part said. "She's insane in a way that is almost science fiction."

His immediate strategy, he said, was a no-brainer: not just to separate his client from the rest of the defendants, but to go for some kind of diminished capacity as well. Her madness was all there on the tape. At an early pretrial hearing, he begged the judge to listen to his client's interview because surely the jurist would realize that the teenager was completely nuts. But Van Houten reported back to cellmate Susan Atkins: "My lawyer wants me to have a separate trial." Atkins immediately got the word to Manson. Forty-eight hours later, Part was gone.

Still, he was able to take a few good-natured swipes at the domineering Manson.

In February 1970, he and a bunch of local lawyers, members of the Los Angeles Bar Association, wrote and staged a show called *Oh! Calcourta!*, a spoof of the 1969 hit musical *Oh! Calcutta!* They performed it at the association's annual dinner and dance at the Century Plaza Hotel in Los Angeles on Valentine's Day 1970.

Their sketches, performed by several well-known local lawyers, caused much controversy. One song with new lyrics that caught the audience's attention was called "Defendant Manson." It was sung to the *West Side Story* song, "Gee, Officer Krupke." Another lawyer in a black Manson-esque fright wig warbled, "Lawyers Are Standing on My Head." Then the amateur thespians finished up with a chorus that declared, "Always remember, folks…the family that slays together, stays together." Unfortunately, Judge William B. Keene, who was the case's presiding judge at the time, was seated in the front row. Two months later Manson—without stating a reason—filed an affidavit of prejudice against Keene, who quickly departed, making way for Judge Older.

With Part gone, the newest candidate to lobby to represent Van Houten was Ira Reiner, another legal luminary who worked for a private law firm and made a big push to get appointed to the case as soon as his predecessor left. The dapper, ambitious Reiner, who had once represented the Screen Actors Guild, said he had already consulted "about eight times" with Manson, who agreed he would be the perfect advocate to argue Van Houten's case. Reiner never thoroughly explained why it had been necessary to meet with Manson, and no one questioned him about it either. Early news reports described Reiner as "a friend of Manson," although, frankly, I scoffed at that suggestion because I couldn't quite see Reiner and his wife, who later became a judge, as the kind of people who would be breaking bread with Manson at, say, Chasen's—a chic Hollywood hangout and one of their favorite local restaurants.

Reiner said he wanted to show his dedication to his clients and his passion for legal combat, so he planned to get his hands dirty with a little field research. A few days later, the Reiners traveled to the Spahn Ranch to see what an alleged hotbed of homicide looked like. After a guided tour by Squeaky, Gypsy, et al, he reported: "The kids are really pleasant. It's really quite nice there once you get over the smells and the junk and the rubbish."

He did not conceal the fact that he realized that being part of the high-profile trial would further his career. And he was right. He was later elected the city's district attorney, a position he held from 1984 to 1992. He also had ambitions to run for governor of California, but those plans collapsed after he led the city's expensive six-year investigation into the highly publicized McMartin Preschool scandal in which the school administrator, a number of her staff, and family members were accused of running a child molestation ring. After a lengthy investigation, all charges were dropped in 1990 due to a lack of evidence. Another failure under his aegis was his office's inability to get a conviction in the high profile March 1991 Rodney King police beating case. In April 1992 in the aftermath of the police officers' acquittal, rioting broke out in Los Angeles, leaving 63 dead and 2,373 injured. There was enough egg on the face of Reiner to make omelets, and his chances for higher office dissipated.

Years later I met him at a dinner party at the home of British actor

Michael York where he admitted that he'd taken the Van Houten case for the publicity. But he insisted he wasn't upset about being replaced.

"I wasn't being paid a penny, and I thought the trial would last about two or three months," he said. "I was in private practice and every day working on the case was costing me dearly."

THE DISAPPEARANCE of Ronald Hughes threw the trial into total disarray. Judge Older faced a big dilemma: Would he declare a complete mistrial or just a mistrial in the case of the lawyer-less Van Houten? Or would he take the easy way out and make the pragmatic decision to find a substitute who could represent the defendant in a competent and efficient manner despite the obvious handicaps? A new lawyer would have to swiftly pick up the pieces after more than half a year of testimony, countless witnesses, and thousands of pages of transcripts. It was not a scenario any lawyer would relish.

Older consulted with Paul Fitzgerald, Patricia Krenwinkel's lawyer, and decided to get Van Houten a new attorney. She screamed that she didn't want one. The trial was entering its last lap, closing arguments were up next, and this was a crucial moment. Into the breach stepped Maxwell Keith, a solid lawyer from Pasadena, who dressed like a banker in his Ivy League suits and who had an excellent reputation among his colleagues. He would be faced with the unenviable task of being an effective surrogate at such short notice. Yet he agreed to be dropped into the front lines of a case that was convoluted and complex. His first chore was gargantuan: read and absorb several months of testimony. It meant burning the midnight oil and required him to wade through some 118,000 pages of transcripts in double-quick time.

His appointment didn't please Manson, who asked the court to dismiss *all* the attorneys, noting, "They aren't our lawyers; they won't listen to us." And then in another contrarian statement, he said he wanted the girls to represent themselves, demanding that the case be reopened so they could put on a defense, claiming they had twenty-one witnesses lined up to testify for the defense. His requests were denied.

The plus for Van Houten was that Keith owed no allegiance whatsoever to the doctrine of "one for all and all for one"—that "one" being Charles Manson. All he was obligated to do was to represent Van Houten to the best of his ability. And thus, in his substitute capacity, he came to the game with no baggage. He delivered a powerful closing argument for his client. He was succinct and precise, and most reporters covering the trial agreed it was the best of the defendants' closing arguments. Despite his huge handicap, he turned out to be one of the most able counselors in the trial—although judging by the caliber of some of his colleagues that might not be such a marvelous compliment.

Keith also had an ace-in-the-hand that he didn't have to play right away. After the jury handed down guilty verdicts on all defendants on January 25, 1971, Keith felt that because he came so late to the party, he had not done as competent a job as his client deserved. So he fell on his legal sword. He testified that because of the time constraints placed on him, he was unable to mount an adequate defense. The ploy worked. An appellate court threw out Van Houten's conviction. In 1976, she was granted a new trial on the grounds that she was denied proper legal representation after Hughes had disappeared right before closing arguments. The retrial in 1977 ended in a hung jury. Released on bail, she was re-tried in 1978 and convicted of the first-degree murders of Leno and Rosemary LaBianca and conspiracy in connection with the Tate murders. She was sentenced to life in prison, where she remains to this day.

"Paul (Fitzgerald) felt Patricia Krenwinkel's role in the events was as a victim of brainwashing by Charles Manson. He felt a tremendous responsibility to keep defending her."
—Los Angeles Attorney Jill Abramson

DAYE SHINN was yet another defense lawyer with scant criminal experience who ended up representing the petulant and unreliable hysteric, Susan Atkins. Shinn, at least, was one of the few lawyers who got some money up front—part of the $45,000 earned by Atkins when she peddled her confession story to a bunch of international newspapers in December 1969. He got in on the action by first approaching Manson as a potential client, then landing Atkins by default after her first lawyer, Richard Caballero, was fired because he wanted to plead insanity for his client.

When he came on, Shinn was told by Manson to ignore that line of defense—and that none of the girls was to even consider the idea of chickening out by playing the "I'm crazy" card. (What's even crazier was the fact that Atkins was still writing former cellmate Ronnie Howard long letters after Howard had ratted her out to the cops.)

Shinn had worked as a used-car salesman to put himself through law school. Of Korean extraction, he still spoke in a broken English accent that at times made his arguments somewhat difficult to follow. His legal experience was mostly in the field of immigration, where he was often hired to obtain green cards and documentation for his wealthy clients' Mexican maids. He supplemented this immigration work with a handful of personal-injury claims, but had never before handled anything as big as a major capital crime. He muddled along, saying very little—although he was cited for handing Manson the *Los Angeles Times* front page that read, "Manson Guilty, Nixon Says." For that indiscretion, he was sent off to spend time in the clink.

His jail experiences brought some welcome levity to the court. Shinn reported back to the judge that the accommodations were not at all to his liking.

"I was in a cell with a kidnapper and a robber, and I couldn't sleep in such a strange place," he said. Another time when he was cited for contempt, he complained to the judge that he had to do "guard duty" while in jail. "I had to sleep in an upper bunk that was about two feet wide, and I had to be on guard—so I wouldn't fall out." And, of course, he claimed that his wife—number six—called him a liar and told him she thought his tales of being locked up by the judge was merely a cover story to hide an extramarital affair. Judge Older wasn't pleased, and his face showed it.

Like most of the defense lawyers, Shinn operated on the whims of Manson. He frequently brought milkshakes into the courtroom—not for Atkins, but for Manson. To say his criminal defense skills were extremely limited is a considerable understatement. Bugliosi was later to note that one of his cross examinations was an *amicus curiae* for the prosecution, so bad it helped the Bug's team. In Shinn's closing arguments, he tried in vain to damage the credibility of Graham and Howard.

"How can you believe them?" he asked the jury. "They each have fifteen aliases—while none of you on the jury has more than eight."

Jurors were not amused.

WHILE SOME MEMBERS of Manson's legal eagles were untested and inexperienced, with nary a clue about how to handle clients who faced death, Paul Fitzgerald was exactly the opposite—a shining beacon of legalistic know-how with a long track record of staying the course, even with an unpredictable client. With a formidable reputation as a powerhouse in the Los Angeles Public Defender's office, his ego and skills allowed him to mostly avoid Manson's manipulation and maintain a certain degree of sanity. It was not an easy balancing act, particularly as he had to keep his sanity alongside not just inexperienced teammates but also Kanarek, the loose cannon.

"I don't have the rest of my life to spend here," he angrily interrupted Kanarek in the full throes of one his circuitous rants.

Fitzgerald came to the trial with an impressive track record, with only one client out of twenty-one murder cases being shipped to Death Row—quite an achievement in the underappreciated, underfunded public defender's office. He was an expert in his field and wrote training manuals for other lawyers. He had a long, lean face, a much-broken nose—a souvenir of his days as a Golden Gloves amateur boxer—and shadow-ringed, hollow eyes that gave the impression that he had spent too many sleepless nights. Or that he'd been elbow-bending after a long night at the local bar.

Ironically, his first introduction to the sinkhole he now found himself in had been to meet Manson. He had one conference with Manson in his public-defender capacity, but was immediately dismissed when Manson raged on about representing himself. But he was bitten by the Manson bug and desperately wanted to stay on in any capacity. His office said he couldn't represent anyone else in the case because it would be a conflict of interest, as the office had represented one of the suspects in the Gary Hinman murder case; so he promptly resigned, turning his back on his $26,000-a-year salary and a nice pension, swapping it for a client who couldn't pay.

He thought joining the defense team as a private attorney would be a thrill ride. And with the publicity, it could lead to big-buck offers from private law firms. He was enamored with the celebrity side of the law, and several years later he became friends with the writer John Gregory Dunne, who put much of Fitzgerald in his bestselling 1982 novel *Dutch Shea, Jr.*

"For Paul, the law was deadly serious business," Dunne once told me. "He had some of the greatest stories I've ever heard because he defended some of the worst people in the world...and he made no apologies for it."

So Fitzgerald ended up as the lawyer for twenty-three-year-old Patricia "Katie" Krenwinkel. "Her story was very tragic," he told friends. "A middle-class, normal, nice girl who, through the use of drugs and basic brainwashing, turned into a killer and accessory to murder."

And to him, as the most polished and experienced of defenders, fell the unenviable and virtually impossible task of trying to coordinate the anything-goes defense team into some semblance of common sense and unity. Long after the trial ended, I met him at a lawyer conference in Los Angeles where he was the principal speaker: "As lawyers, I mean, what could we do? We were out of control. At some point we were along just for the ride."

Out of court, Fitzgerald was also an amiable saloon bar companion and always keen to analyze what we journalists thought had gone right or wrong after a shambolic day in court. So we frequently hung out together at the end of the day and listened to the learned lawyer as he chatted—off the record, of course—about his odious clients. He admitted he was familiar with the effects of acid as he, too, had frequently imbibed. He said that long ago he realized that while acid might have enhanced the mind, it could also maim the brain. Early on, over drinks at the Redwood Bar and Grill, just round the corner from the Hall of Justice, he conceded that he firmly believed his young client, along with the other girls, did what they were accused of doing because they were all zonked out on the daily doses of LSD that Manson doled out.

The Manson girls in court, and those who parked themselves each day on the sidewalk, also liked Fitzgerald's no-nonsense Irish charm, his lived-in face, and his joy of conversation, which he liked to refer to by using the Gaelic word *craic*. It meant dialogue, fun, and music, and had nothing whatsoever to do with the "crack"—the cocaine version. The girls embroidered his suit jackets with "witchy designs" to ward off evil. High praise, indeed, for it was an honor they had only bestowed on one other man.

The savvy Irishman became the team's lead lawyer because, unlike Kanarek, he could communicate on the same level as Bugliosi and Kay. Still, it was an uphill battle, and he struggled, sometimes fruitlessly, to keep the chaotic situation under control. There was always Manson's behavior, over which he had absolutely no control. And, as he was officially representing Krenwinkel, Manson's "united" dictum did not sit well with him. He realized that no matter how good a job he did, it was most likely that all the defendants would go down with the ship if convicted. If a jury produced guilty verdicts on three defendants, there was no way his client would escape.

On top of it all, Fitzgerald had bills to pay. He had two young children and no weekly paycheck. With no steady salary on the horizon for heaven knows how long, he was living on his savings and he began to worry about maintaining his lifestyle. I think he reckoned he might be able to claw back some of the money he was losing with a book; and certainly, he felt it would up his profile and lead to clients who actually paid. Still, he took the risk. The ladies loved him. One female reporter fell madly in love with him during the trial, but he was already taken. A regular in the spectator section was his current companion, Erica Gavin, a beautiful actress who started out as a stripper and moved on to play the title role in 1968's X-rated, soft-core porn film *Vixen*, then graduating to small roles in mainstream pictures.

When soft-core porn film director Russ Meyer was hired by big-gun studio 20th Century-Fox to direct 1970's *Beyond the Valley of the Dolls*, Gavin got a part in the picture. There was more than a touch of irony there, with Sharon Tate being one of the stars of the original *Valley of the Dolls*.

For me, the erudite Fitzgerald was the best inside source for information. And the most fun. He even told me that he had planned to subpoena John Lennon to testify for the defense about the "Helter Skelter" lyrics. I knew that was a mission impossible, but I didn't tell him so. There was no way Lennon or McCartney would allow themselves to be called as witnesses for such a spurious, fishing expedition of a reason. And I decided not to tell him that it wasn't Lennon who actually wrote the lyrics, but McCartney. Be that as it may, the idea—as far-fetched as it would have been—of getting any Beatle into court would have been sheer catnip for the defense team.

Fitzgerald also knew how to play the media. Sandi Gibbons, the City News Service reporter who later went to work as a press officer for the Los Angeles DA, was stunned when she received a handwritten birthday card from Van Houten handed to her by Fitzgerald. Was it a rather lame effort to curry favor with the reporter? Whatever the answer, Gibbons, to this day, keeps the card in her scrapbook.

Kenneth Clayman, who worked in the Los Angeles Public Defender's office with Fitzgerald, told me the lawyer had a brilliant mind and knew how to use it.

"He could have made millions," he said. "He did go into private practice, but he also got into drugs, alcohol, and ran off the rails a little bit."

In fact, Fitzgerald went on to represent Krenwinkel and Van Houten at parole hearings—all of them unsuccessful. He became a much sought-after legal lecturer. When he died from a heart attack in 2001 at the age of sixty-four, his old murder trial legal partner, Irving Kanarek, showed up at his funeral looking wan, lost, and very thin. Surprisingly, Kanarek didn't have much to say.

Now that was a first!

Press Party Frolics

Standing in back row Vincent Bugliosi (far left) puts in a rare appearance at a "Come Dressed as Your Favorite Manson Family Member," press party.

Bugliosi came as himself. The lawyers and reporters who showed up in this 1970 picture taken at the downtown LA Hilton hotel are:

Bugliosi, deputy DA Burton Katz, John Kendall (LA Times), Myrna Oliver and Bill Farr (LA Herald Examiner), John Goodman (KNX radio) and his wife Donna, Jerry Laird (KNX radio.)

Front row: author George Bishop, Chuck Boyd (CBS,) Mary Neiswender, (Long Beach Press Telegram,) Ron Hughes, (Van Houten's defense lawyer,) Linda Deutsch (AP) and Sandi Gibbons (City News Service.)

MEET THE PRESS

"People say I'm an extremely opinionated person. If opinionated means that when I think I'm right I try to shove it down everyone's throat, they're correct. As for arrogant, I'm arrogant and I'm kind of caustic. The great majority of people I deal with are hopelessly incompetent, so there's an air of superiority about me."
—Vince Bugliosi, *Playboy*

For nearly a year, I trotted along and took my front-row seat at the trial. It was unlike any I have ever covered, and it provided wildly unpredictable, bizarre behavior by the defendants and another group of people who, like me, were writing and reporting on the trial. I am talking about those ladies and gentlemen of the Fourth Estate—the press, the supposedly unbiased third wheel in this legal circus, who had no official role other than to report on what was being played out daily. We were simply present as unbiased onlookers, to efficiently, accurately, and effectively record what took place in front of judge and jury as well as outside the courtroom.

But in this particular case, with Bugliosi using every trick in the book to send "the diabolical dictator and his mindless but bloodthirsty zombies" to the gas chamber, some members of the press forgot their role as silent watchers and became inextricably entwined—sometimes in the most alarming and unimaginable fashions. Allow me to chronicle some of the many ways they impinged upon events surrounding the trial from the very beginning, often with chilling side effects.

To start with, when stories of the murder first broke in early August 1969, headline writers had a field day. The victims were no mere ordinary souls but high-profile personalities; and as a result, early accounts produced a slew of largely irresponsible suppositions, citing everything from drug orgies to black magic and voodoo as being responsible for the carnage.

Even the stately *Life* magazine, a month after the Cielo massacre, gave grieving widower Roman Polanski a chance to provide a fully illustrated guided tour of the blood-stained house. And in December, when the LAPD named the suspects, before you could say Tate-LaBianca, the confession of Susan Atkins—based on an interview she had given to her lawyers—was spread-eagled all over the front page of the *Los Angeles Times*. The paper paid $5,000—big money back then—to entrepreneurial photojournalist Larry Schiller, for permission to run the story.

Fast-forward to a month before the eagerly awaited trial was to begin; an issue of *Rolling Stone* carried a nearly book-sized 30,000-word story about Manson titled "The Most Incredible Story of the Most Dangerous Man Alive." That article eventually led to career changes for two individuals—namely Stovitz and Bugliosi. For Stovitz, it was the precursor to the death knell of his role as the district attorney's chief trial prosecutor; for Bugliosi, it was the opportunity of a lifetime.

But the press wasn't finished stirring the pot. On October 9, 1970, William Farr, a reporter for the *Los Angeles Herald Examiner*, reported that authorities knew that the chief architect of the Tate-La Bianca killings had also compiled a celebrity death list. The story headlined, "Liz, Sinatra on Slay List—Tate Witness" was splashed on the front page. Leaked from grand jury testimony of Susan Atkins' Sybil Brand cellmates, it made for pretty sensational and gory reading, spelling out in great detail the fate that awaited the celebrities. Among the revelations: Elizabeth Taylor's famous violet eyes were to be removed and mailed to her ex-husband Richard Burton. Castration was to be his fate. Ol' Blue Eyes Frank Sinatra was to be skinned alive while hanging from a meat hook. Welsh heartthrob Tom Jones was to have his throat cut while engaged in sexual intercourse with Susan Atkins—at knifepoint, if necessary. And Steve McQueen was cited as well, though the exact manner of his liquidation was not spelled out by Atkins; she did tell Graham that she felt the superstar was getting "too politically inclined," which went "against her grain." Whatever that meant.

Farr received the information in transcripts surreptitiously passed to him by one of two lawyers. And no one knew which one of the two it was. Suspicion pointed to Bugliosi or Daye Shinn. When the judge asked Farr to reveal his source, he refused, citing California's shield law that safeguards the right of journalists to protect their sources. Not surprising, the prosecution pointed the finger at the defense, which in turn blamed the prosecution. The case dragged on, and eventually Farr paid for his exclusive by serving forty-six days in jail. Bugliosi and Shinn were indicted by a Grand Jury, but eventually a judge dismissed the case against the two.

Bugliosi claimed he was not happy with Farr, but he reserved special ire for Mary Neiswender, a veteran police-beat writer who was covering the trial for the *Long Beach Press-Telegram*. Neiswender had become the envy of the press corps for one reason and one reason only—throughout the trial she had acquired unbelievable access to Manson. (She later wrote about it in her 2012 memoir, *Assassins…Serial Killers…Corrupt Cops—Chasing the News in a Skirt and High Heels.*)

Week after week throughout the trial, there appeared under Neiswender's byline exclusive interviews with Manson. When I spoke to her in 2019, she recalled her one-on-one talks with the man at the heart of the murder. She was the only reporter to have access to him while the trial was playing out. Other trial reporters—jealous of her unfettered access—reckoned that once again Manson had gained control over a woman and was feeding her only what he felt would benefit him.

"I thought Charlie hated women," she told me. "So why did he choose me? How did it happen? I maneuvered a way to get a phone call to him through a lowlife Mob friend who had worked for the Teamsters Union in Long Beach Harbor and who had met him in the prison law library—Charlie was planning to go proper and be his own lawyer." She said her longshoreman pal called her on the phone while in the library, and "then he handed the phone to Charlie, who, he told me, had slithered under a table. We started talking. I had Charlie all to myself." She insisted she was never his propaganda machine, though he likely had some Machiavellian reason for talking with her. Perhaps for "media relations."

"I tried to keep him away from the rest of the press," she said. "All the major network big names in the TV news divisions as well as newspapers and magazines had written asking for interviews. He asked me, 'Do you think I should do this one, or that one?' And I would say, 'Oh, hell no, Charlie.' I kept the whole press away from him. I said, 'Tom Brokaw is going to put you in a pressure cooker...and you don't need that.' I knew he was insecure, and I used his insecurity against him. I guess that was a switch for someone like Charlie." But along the way, she insisted, "I wasn't about to give my soul away. And I never did."

She began to visit him regularly in prison. "Charlie set it up so I was listed as a 'friend' with no police record. And as Manson didn't have many friends without a police record, I was home and dry." Later on, she said, when her stories became more trial oriented and upset those in the district attorney's office, he suggested she change her designation from "friend" to "witness."

It was an uphill battle, Neiswender recalled. "I had to fight first with his jailers and later with the judges to make that 'witness' designation stick. They knew I wasn't a witness, but it was just a way around the system."

The "witness" said she got to know him very well. "We never shook hands or anything like that. Charlie was clever, street-wise, and charismatic. He knew how to get around people. Despite stories to the contrary, Charlie couldn't stop a clock with his eyes or make you shrivel up and die, although he tried." But she never ever underestimated him, or ever forgot who he was and what he did. She said that frequently, when Manson telephoned her, if she wasn't in the office, her editors would automatically put his calls through to her home in Rolling Hills. Her children came to answer the phone and yell, "Hey, Mom…it's Charlie." She insisted he didn't have her home phone number, "But he did know where I lived because a few months later three Manson Family members unexpectedly dropped by, told my young son who was in the house alone that they had been sent by Charlie, and then asked him for a box of matches. I was furious and I called Charlie and said, 'You sonafabitch.' He promised me it would never happen again." When he couldn't reach her on the phone, he'd send her handwritten notes. "His handwriting was middle-school, but his vocabulary was that of a college graduate. Don't forget—he had a doctorate in street smarts and manipulation."

In a strange way, those calls and letters brought her closer to Manson, she said. "Most of the time, Charlie made a lot of sense. He said, 'Here are twelve lyin' jurors who all say they never heard of me or Sharon Tate or the murders—you believe that? They've made up their mind. I'm the one they're going to send to the gas chamber; with my long hair I'm a perfect scapegoat.'"

He carefully massaged the scapegoat scenario, repeatedly stressing that not only didn't he murder anyone, he didn't force kids into dope— just the opposite. "If they let me go," he told her, "I'm still trouble because I could turn into a monster. They've given me the weapon of fear. Everyone's afraid of me." During those *tête-à-têtes*, she said, "I noticed how carefully he would watch my face to see how far he could push. When he felt he had pushed the line, he would break into his little-kid smile."

During the trial, Neiswender wrote a series of "exclusive" stories based on her interviews. "Manson's Conscience Clear" was one; another, titled "Forces that Shaped Manson," focused on his unhappy childhood and his prostitute mother's abandonment of him. The stories had changed from her earlier ones, which had headlines that screamed, "Wolf Gang Pack of Thrill Killers." She was later to observe, "One-on-one, he was okay, but in court he was a totally different guy—a performer."

While the rest of us in the press corps were being regularly scooped by Neiswender, Bugliosi was absolutely furious about Manson using a reporter as his private conduit. "Vince despised me—he hated me until he died," she told me. "It had started when I first got onto the case and did stories on the judges and the attorneys—anyone who could help me. I had already made friends with the judge. It's the way I operate, and it worked for me. I wrote a story about Vince. And then Aaron [Stovitz]. I called Vince a 'near genius.' It was a very flattering story. But my big mistake was when I described him as the 'balding prosecutor.' It was like a bomb went off."

Later, Neiswender recalled that he summoned her and Linda Deutsch of the Associated Press, who was getting her very first taste of big trial coverage and at first assumed the lunacy she was witnessing was normal procedure, into his office. "He lived in that office the entire trial, and he said, 'If you don't straighten out and do what I say, I will release an article I've written for *Life* magazine.' I didn't know what that meant, but what upset me more was his foul language. He was treating me like a naughty child. He kept accusing me of being anti-cop. What with that and his swearing, I'd had it. 'You jackass, I've got the words "cop lover" tattooed on my ass,' I screamed at him. From then on, we never even said hello for the rest of the trial. Whenever he saw me coming he would cut off the conversation. I didn't need him—I was on good terms with Aaron. He was easy to get along with—he even came to our press parties, which we held at what we called 'trial central': room 905 at the Hilton Hotel where reporter Theo Wilson based herself."

One evening during the trial, Neiswender remembered that Bugliosi surprised everyone by showing up at a media party where guests were instructed to, 'come dressed as your favorite Manson Family member.' Several reporters came as Linda Kasabian or Mary Brunner with crosses painted on their foreheads. A crudely written sign posted on the wall at the party read, "I'm the devil…here to do the devil's work," which was the phrase Watson purportedly delivered shortly after arriving at the Cielo Drive house.

"Vince didn't stay long," recalled Neiswender, "Ron Hughes stayed until the end."

Realizing that getting too close to the press was a slippery slope, Bugliosi opted mostly to keep his distance, although other reporters frequently heard from him indirectly when their editors called them with a reprimand from the chief prosecutor. He religiously monitored the local papers and his personal clips. His sister meticulously clipped every article that mentioned her famous brother, and she would alert him of any negative press. If he was displeased, as he often was, he would call the journalist's editor to harangue or complain about the coverage. On one occasion, Theo Wilson and Sandi Gibbons, the reporter for the local City News Service, were confronted by Bugliosi. "Vince apologized— sort of," recalled Gibbons. "He said when he called a female reporter 'a cocksucker' he was referring only to Neiswender. 'I didn't mean you girls,' he said."

A day later, a newspaper colleague, so aggrieved by Bugliosi's language, complained to DA Joe Busch, noting that Neiswender was a good Catholic mother of two, who was outraged at such foul language. Busch ordered Bugliosi to publicly apologize, recalled Linda Deutsch. "Vince bit his tongue and said something like, 'Mary you know I've been under a lot of stress.' It was all about Vince." Another time Deutsch and Gibbons were amazed when the smiling prosecutor waxed on endlessly about how happy he was with their coverage. The two women reported back to gathered media: "Pope Vincent the Last has just blessed us."

But mostly we saw the dark, serious, and severe side to Bugliosi, although I know he worked hard to impress the press. "Vince had one technique he always used with the press," his deputy Stephen Kay recalled. "He didn't care what the press asked him because when he left the court every night, he walked over to where the cameras were. He ignored their questions but delivered just one sound bite. He told me he had learned the sound bite by heart the night before, having practiced it in front of a mirror. At the time I thought, 'Why waste your time practicing a sound bite?'"

Kay, who had completely the opposite attitude with the press, later told me that Bugliosi disliked women reporters more than their male counterparts. He lumped them all under the derogatory label of "sob sisters," and complained bitterly that the reporters wrote sympathetic stories about the Manson girls who camped out in front of the Hall of Justice.

"One time, I was kind of crouched down to talk inside the railing and the lady reporters were sitting in the front row. Vince turned to me and said, 'Don't ever let me catch you kneeling to those whores again.'" And on one occasion in court, Bugliosi almost got into fisticuffs with Susan Atkins. She was being dragged out of the court for repeatedly interrupting the proceedings and made a sudden grab for Bugliosi's papers. He reacted by grabbing the documents with one hand and swinging at her with the other. He missed.

My own experience with him was a strange one. We were pleasant to each other during the trial, although I knew he was resentful of the media. In 1976 he ran for district attorney opposite incumbent John Van De Kamp, who, much to Bugliosi's chagrin, had been appointed to the job after Joe Busch died. That year I had written a long profile on Bugliosi for *Los Angeles* magazine. It was relatively pro Van De Kamp, the rich and efficient, but dull white-bread candidate compared to the flashy, live-wire, shoot-from-the-hip Bugliosi in his three-piece Brooks Brothers suits, still riding high on his Manson triumph. Van De Kamp's team was doing as much as it could to jazz up his image and put a little pep in the step of the man who had been given the job after Busch's death. Everyone knew Bugliosi's name, yet he was still the outsider—a bit of a wild card. My magazine piece chronicled two incidents in his life: I labeled them "The Milkman Case" and "The Cardwell Affair."

Leading the anti-Bugliosi charge was George Denny, an affable Beverly Hills lawyer who insisted he, too, was a serious candidate for the office, but really wasn't.

Denny was more a hatchet man and distraction, who wanted to take Bugliosi down; he continually insisted that Bugliosi was "unfit for office." I later learned that Denny might have had a hidden agenda. He was Irving Kanarek's personal lawyer and good friend; although, having watched Kanarek in action, I couldn't see how he endeared himself to too many of his colleagues. Denny was apparently also somewhat aggrieved after hearing how Bugliosi had treated opposing counsel in court, and particularly after those covering the trial gleefully reported that Bugliosi once publicly described Kanarek as "The Toscanini of Tedium"—a devastatingly accurate phrase that you just knew Vincent had pondered long and hard to create. Denny's version of the milkman story was this: Bugliosi had used the power of the DA's office to hound his former milkman, one Herbert Wiesel, because he suspected that Wiesel had fathered Bugliosi's son! Wiesel sued Bugliosi for slander, and the case was settled out of court. Denny represented the milkman and told me at the time: "Bugliosi came to my office and handed me $12,000 in $100 bills as part of the settlement and later delivered an additional $500. Denny said part of the liquidated damages clause stated that anyone revealing the total amount of the settlement publicly could be penalized to the tune of $15,000. Nonetheless, he announced the terms of the settlement at a press conference, openly inviting Bugliosi to bring damages. Bugliosi's version of the story was that at the time he believed the milkman had stolen $300 from his home, so he quite legitimately used the DA's investigators to try to confirm the fact.

The other black eye that was inflicted on Bugliosi occurred in June 1973. A Santa Monica divorcee, Virginia Cardwell, claimed that she was having an affair with Bugliosi. She further asserted that he gave her $448 to have an abortion, and when he found out she had not had the abortion, he exploded and violently attacked her. She reported the attack to Santa Monica Police, but later withdrew her complaint, telling police she had hired Bugliosi to obtain her tardy alimony payments and that her injuries had been caused by her small son wielding a baseball bat. Again, there was an out-of-court settlement, noted Denny, in which Bugliosi paid Cardwell. All along, Bugliosi claimed his relationship with Cardwell was strictly lawyer-client.

"It's not that Bugliosi is not a good lawyer, or a hardworking and skilled trial lawyer, but to me one of the most terrifying things you can conjure up in government is a prosecutor who misuses his power," said Denny. "That's why I took him on before. There are many talented people who have a flaw in their character. His flaw happens to be a massive ego and an inability to tell the truth, as I've experienced it in these two cases. With those credentials a person ought not to become District Attorney."

Bugliosi, who invited me to his home to meet his wife Gail (they had two young children, Wendy and Vince Jr.) and rebut all allegations, told me: "I'm not going to dignify those charges by a comment. If I did these things, my wife of twenty years would not be living with me."

Bugliosi relished the idea of painting himself as the rebel and the outsider, in direct contrast to the establishment Van De Kamp. He suggested I talk to a couple of high-profile supporters—his tennis pals, actor Robert Conrad and comedian Bill Cosby, with whom he regularly played at Hugh Hefner's Holmby Hills Playboy mansion. His campaign also had the support of the DA's veteran prosecutor J. Miller Leavy, who had approved him being brought aboard for the Manson trial. "Vince may come across tough and aloof," said his campaign manager Harvey Englander, "but a few TV spots will show him as a warm, nice guy—a fellow who cares much about his wife and family and wants to make your home as safe as his."

At several political rallies I attended, Bugliosi was introduced to wild applause as "the man who got Manson." Ironically, when the race was in full throttle, I spoke to Stephen Kay, who said he was supporting Van De Kamp. Bugliosi lost. Not long afterwards, I met him at a conference of TV critics in Beverly Hills, where Vince was a panelist with George DiCenzo, who played Bugliosi in NBC's 1976 miniseries based on *Helter Skelter*. ("Every day Vince came to the set, takes me aside and tells me how I should play him," DiCenzo laughed.)

On the film set Vince and I shook hands. "Do you still hate me?" he asked.

The answer was no, of course I didn't hate him. But I must confess to thinking that his sad question clearly showed that for all his bluster and ego, deep down inside he still had a mile-long streak of insecurity, and that, until his dying day, he would never be able to shake it off, despite his phenomenal success in court and acclaim as an author.

GIRL PULLS GUN ON FORD

The President flees for his life from the Manson clan assassin

They met— then her pistol would not fire

Ford runs off with Security men after the attempt

Ivar Davis LOS ANGELES Friday

A WOMAN disciple of convicted killer Charles Manson pulled a gun on President Ford today as he shook hands with her in a crowded street.

The President grimaced and ran for his life as a Secret Service agent pounced on the slender, red-haired woman and snatched the gun away.

The assassination attempt came as Presidents Ford mingled with a large crowd of well-wishers outside his hotel in Sacramento, California.

Secret Service agent Larry Buendorf pounced on the girl, injured his finger when he jammed it into the breech of the gun to prevent it being fired.

As she was grabbed and handcuffed the woman, Lynette Fromme, 26, shouted : "It didn't go off. It didn't go off."

Later she was charged with attempting to murder the President.

Mr. Ford said after the incident : "I saw a hand coming up between several others in the front row and obviously there was a gun in that hand."

He added : "Let me add with great emphasis, this incident under no circumstances will lessen my accessibility to the American people. I won't hide from one fool to another."

Carved

President Ford's Press secretary Ron Nessen confirmed the woman was loaded and said : "The President was aware of the gun, but was not hit in any way."

Miss Fromme has been one of the most faithful followers of Charles Manson, who was convicted two years ago in the murder of actress Tate and the others.

Ford : 'I saw a hand —there was a gun in that hand'

"It didn't go off" screams Lynette Fromme after police grabbed pistol

Fell

Other guards grapple to get handcuffs on Lynette . . . the Manson fanatic

Our bomb fear...

By Paul Hopkins

Vital 20 minutes at the Hilton

'Evil girl' spotted

By Patrick Clancy

Lynette Fromme finally gets her moment of "glory" in September 1975.

PART IV

COLLATERAL DAMAGE

"Squeaky" Fromme makes the headlines

SQUEAKY AND ALL

No one really knows how many innocent people have been executed at the behest of Charles Manson. The list of those who died in 1969, from the Gary Hinman killing in late July through the night of August 10 with the LaBiancas, has been chronicled in meticulous detail for over half a century, but it is more than likely that many others lost their lives after being targeted by Manson or those infected by his deadly toxicity. Law-enforcement officials have placed that number as high as possibly thirty-five. Hardly anyone who clashed or came into conflict with the Family escaped unscathed.

During the trial, threats of bodily injury or death were ever-present. The trial judge carried a concealed weapon in court. The key prosecutors, warned about being targeted for harm, received twenty-four-hour police protection. Even the murder trial jurors were given extra heavy protection.

I got a taste of that vitriol on July 24, 1970, when I spotted Fromme on the street outside the Hall of Justice in downtown Los Angeles. It was a few days before my thirty-second birthday—a broiling LA summer's day with the temperature inching up to the high 80s. Lyn "Squeaky" Fromme (who insisted her surname was pronounced Fro-mee) sat cross-legged on a street corner outside the County Hall of Justice, where the trial was being held. And she was ready, willing, and able to offer her mangled thoughts to anyone who would listen. And listen and record they did—the local TV networks knew they could always rely on Squeaky for a sound bite to fill that "News-at-11" slot.

On Day One of the trial, Fromme was accompanied by three other deluded female companions (Mary Brunner, "Gypsy" Share, and Sandra Good) as they continued their strange vigil. Squeaky wore her standard shorts, flip-flops, and peasant blouse, looking like any high-school girl hanging around the mall. As her reputation grew, she would develop delusions of theater, dramatically donning a flowing red cape—a latter-day Little Red Riding Hood proclaiming her love and devotion to Manson.

In the brutal morning sun, her pale, porcelain, freckle-faced features made her look waif-like, frail, and almost malnutrition-sickly. And she was so very thin. She was not yet as infamous as her more despicable compatriots on trial inside the courthouse—Susan Atkins, Patricia Krenwinkel, and Leslie Van Houten—but that was to change five years later when she would grace the cover of *Time* magazine as "The Girl Who Almost Killed Gerald Ford."

On September 5, 1975, as the thirty-eighth president of the United States walked through Sacramento Capital Park to meet the state's new governor, Jerry Brown, he reached to shake hands with the girl in the red cloak; instead of a greeting, he found himself staring into the barrel of a .45 pistol. Before Fromme could get off a shot, she was tackled by Larry Buendorf, Ford's vigilant Secret Service protector. He grabbed the pistol—which she had concealed by strapping it to her leg under her ankle-length dress—and ferociously wrestled it from her hand. The ninety-five-pound, would-be assassin was pushed against a tree, handcuffed, and then carted off to jail to earn her ignominious place in history.

"To me, (Ford's) life didn't mean more than the redwoods," she declared. Later she jovially chatted about the "incident" with totally inappropriate affect—as if describing a mishap at a picnic in the park.

Back on that hot July 1970 day in downtown Los Angeles, this time her role was much simpler: that of worshipper. She had shaved her head and carved a crude and still bloody cross on her forehead in homage to her "life soul" leader.

We first met seven months earlier at the Spahn Ranch when she and other Family members boasted with passion about the fanciful tales of their heroic and much misunderstood leader. She greeted me with a friendly wave.

"Hi, Ivor," she sang in her flat, emotionless voice. And then, in a plaintive, little girl voice asked me if I knew what it felt like to have a sharp knife slipped down my throat. It was a hideous threat I never forgot. I deliberately did not react but walked past her and the other girls who also waved at me as though greeting an old friend.

But I ran to the nearest phone inside the courthouse. Knowing what I knew about the Manson Family's propensity for violence, I quickly called my wife, Sally, and urged her to pack a suitcase, gather our three-month-old daughter, Rebecca, and move out of our San Fernando Valley home. For the next month, they stayed with friends in a safe LA suburb. Only I knew where she was. And I sweated it out every day she was away.

It wasn't just hype or ballyhoo or me being extra cautious; everyone in the orbit of Charles Manson took those threats seriously. So did I.

Left to right: Susan Atkins, Patricia Krenwinkel, and Leslie Van Houten laughed all the way to guilty verdicts.

THE GIRLS: DOUBLE TROUBLE

"It was clear to me after our first interview that this girl had no will of her own. She was totally delusional...insane in a way that is almost science fiction."

—Marvin Part, Leslie Van Houten's lawyer, January 1970

"The seven random murders of strangers was [sic] *so shocking and bizarre as to leave the world incredulous. Can a person like this (Krenwinkel) ever walk the streets again?"*

—Patricia Krenwinkel parole hearing. Aug 1982

For almost fifty years, Leslie Louise Van Houten (prisoner W-I3378) and Patricia Dianne Krenwinkel (prisoner W-08314) have paraded numerous times, and with relentless regularity, in front of a California Parole Board in pursuit of their freedom.

Both women are convicted killers: Krenwinkel had taken part in two nights of murders, while Van Houten participated only in the murders of Leno and Rosemary LaBianca on the second day of the killing spree.

The two were sentenced to die in the San Quentin gas chamber after the showcase trial that began in July 1970 and ended almost a year later. But when the death penalty was abolished by the California Supreme

Court in the People v. Anderson ruling in April 1972, their sentences were changed to life in prison with the possibility of parole. A year after the April 1972 ruling, the death penalty was reinstated in California, but that did not apply to all the defendants in this case, and they would not return to Death Row.

They were spared their lives, and yet they have consistently complained about the inhumanity of spending their natural life behind bars.

So, who exactly were these young savages: nineteen-year-old Leslie Van Houten, and her partner in crime, twenty-one-year-old Patricia Krenwinkel? And what led these expendable girls who—without so much as a whimper or protest—silently set out on a journey that would destroy not only their own lives (becoming collateral damage in their own hideous way), but, worse still, they would eliminate seven innocent people from the face of the earth.

Van Houten

Leslie Van Houten's route to what turned out to be a lifetime in jail was much more circuitous and byzantine than that of her codefendants.

In 1976, a California appellate court overturned her 1971 conviction and ordered her to be retried. That was in large part because of Ronald Hughes' disappearance. His body was discovered four months later in a remote wash in Sespe Hot Springs, California. Some members of the Manson Family, as well as Deputy District Attorney Vincent Bugliosi, claimed Hughes' death was no accident and that other Family members had actually bumped him off. Though the autopsy ruled out foul play, to this day, many still believe it was homicide.

The appellate court decreed that Van Houten's substitute lawyer, Maxwell Keith, had not been given sufficient time to mount a full defense because he came so very late to the game. Keith, strangely enough, was the one who passionately pursued this course, questioning his own

Johnny-come-lately competence. He went on to defend Van Houten in a second trial, which ended in a split jury verdict with the judge declaring a mistrial. Before the third trial began, Van Houten was released on $200,000 bail—the funds pulled together by a bunch of family friends. In 1977 while out on bail for some six months, she stayed under the radar working as a legal secretary while she lived with a friend. In an odd note to a case where the bizarre was often the ordinary, while on bail, Van Houten wangled an invitation to the Oscars with a female friend. John Waters, the counterculture film director, or "champion of the trash into art aesthetic" as one scribe described him, revealed that the elegantly attired accused murderess attended the Academy Awards unrecognized. Waters became a friend and vocal parole supporter for Van Houten. In a series of articles he wrote in 2009, he was deeply sympathetic to her plight after bonding with her on frequent jail visits.

"Leslie is a good friend and someone who has taken full responsibility for the terrible crime she participated in," he wrote.

Every year on Oscar morning he visits her in prison. "Then I go from prison to Elton John's post-Oscar party. Had she not encountered Manson she could have ended up making movies with us instead of running with the killer dune-buggy crowd."

Of course, Waters had a history of kinship with women behind bars. After she was released from prison, he became friendly with the San Francisco heiress Patricia Hearst who was convicted of bank robbery in 1976; upon her release from prison, she went on to costar in several of his movies.

And in yet another strange twist, Van Houten asked Krenwinkel, her prison mate, to testify for her in the third trial. Krenwinkel refused. Doing that, she felt, would be traitorous to Manson, whose photograph still hung in her prison cell.

Van Houten's third trial ended in conviction on two counts for the murder of the LaBiancas and one count of conspiracy. She was sentenced to seven years to life in prison.

Since then, every single parole hearing outcome has been the same. Deputy District Attorney Stephen Kay, Vincent Bugliosi's second chair in the first Manson trial of 1970, appears before the Board to argue vehemently to keep Van Houten and the rest of the Manson family incarcerated. However, more recently, Van Houten found sympathy with the board.

But thrice the sitting California governor denied her parole. First it was Arnold Schwarzenegger, then liberal Governor Jerry Brown, followed by Gavin Newsom in 2019. Brown declared as he had consistently ruled whenever other Manson Family members came up for parole, "Van Houten has failed to adequately explain to the panel how a model teenager from a privileged Southern California family, who had once been a homecoming princess, could have turned into a ruthless killer by age nineteen."

How, indeed, did the homecoming princess who grew up in Monrovia—a white, middle-class suburb of Los Angeles—end up being part of the Manson killing machine?

Van Houten was born August 23, 1949, in Altadena, a small town on the edge of Pasadena, California. The family then moved ten miles east to the growing suburban community of Monrovia. Back then, if you asked anyone in Southern California where Monrovia was, they might have guessed it was somewhere near Lithuania, Latvia, Transylvania, or any of those countries that end with "ia."

In the 1960s, Monrovia was a pretty anonymous town nestled in the foothills of the San Gabriel Mountains, known only to some as the home of Pulitzer Prize-winning writer Upton Sinclair. Just down the road sits the famous Santa Anita racetrack, long home to some of America's top thoroughbreds; farther west is the Pasadena Rose Bowl. Many families escaping the booming suburbia of Los Angeles found that Monrovia offered affordable houses, which, although small, sat on bigger parcels of land. Van Houten grew up in the pleasant but humdrum community that was often shrouded by a dense and visible layer of smog during the summer, being trapped in the Los Angeles Basin by the surrounding San Gabriel Mountains.

In the early 1960s I worked as a police reporter on the *San Gabriel Valley Daily Tribune* and Monrovia was my beat. The town was dullsville when it came to crime. Only an occasional burglary or drunk driver broke the monotony and resulted in the attention of officers from the tiny local police department.

In 1970, when I first wrote about the suspects in the story, which was captivating the nation, I noted that Van Houten's history closely paralleled that of Charles "Tex" Watson in its mundane normality, except that she, unlike Watson, came from a broken home.

From the outside looking in, Van Houten appeared to live contentedly with her teacher mother, Jane, in a pleasant, safe, tree-lined working-class neighborhood. In the early sixties the small tract homes, comfortable but not lavish, sold for $18,000, with a backyard pool thrown in for the money. The pools were popular when the summer temperatures in Monrovia edged into the high eighties and low nineties. Neighbors said the family was popular in town.

Tony Strauss, now a top California lawyer, grew up across the street from Van Houten. He and his wife Michelle both graduated from Monrovia High two years after Leslie and remember her as, "very much the pretty girl next door type."

"Monrovia had an *Our Town* innocence to it," said Strauss. "Everybody knew everybody else and we'd hang out at Stueve's Ice Cream Parlor or Shakey's Pizza or watch movies at the Crest Theatre or one of the two drive-ins in town. Courting couples favored Gold Hill or Monrovia Canyon. For excitement we'd cruise down Colorado Boulevard in Pasadena on a Saturday night or take a special outing to Grauman's Chinese Theater on Hollywood Boulevard or for a big-screen movie at the Cinerama Dome on Sunset."

Van Houten became terribly distraught by her parents' split when she was fourteen years old. She, her older brother, Paul, and their two younger siblings, Elizabeth and David (Korea-born children who were adopted by the Van Houtens), remained in Monrovia with their mother.

After the separation, her father Paul moved to Palos Verdes, an upscale Southern California beach community where ironically Paul and Doris Tate once lived.

One balmy evening in August 1966, an excited Leslie Van Houten and a pal drove into downtown Los Angeles after snaring a couple of tickets to see a new British pop group perform live in concert at Dodger Stadium. Van Houten said she screamed along with 45,000 others packed into the baseball venue the moment the Beatles ran on stage. She was not to know, of course, that the Beatles, or at least their music, was to feature so prominently in her future.

IN LATE 1969, Leslie Van Houten put Monrovia on the map in a not-so appealing manner. When the story of her arrest first broke, I wrote that she was a high school kid who had turned a bad corner, and that her story mirrored that of Watson and Patricia Krenwinkel, along with scores of disenchanted teenagers who had become hooked on the booming drug culture. To most who knew her, Van Houten was remembered only as a typical teenage girl with a fresh-faced smile posing in 1963 for pictures with five other lovely freshman princesses at Monrovia High. To outsiders, she was the perfect student and a good archer. Off campus, she was a member in good standing of Monrovia's Job's Daughters—the youth affiliate of the Masons. She sang in the church choir and was active in youth religious groups. But behind that smile, she was deeply troubled, even though friends never realized the smile masked an unhappy teenager. Two years after her parents broke up, sixteen-year-old Van Houten was already seriously into drugs, especially heavily into acid. She was to admit later she worked hard to put on a happy front.

"I could still live with going to school and living within the structure of society. But the more I dropped acid, the harder it was to relate to different people," she explained in a 1977 interview with Barbara Walters.

Friends never noticed her deterioration. But her secret drug use was taking its toll. In the last two years of high school, she withdrew from all the groups in which she had once been active. She no longer danced, although it had been an early passion and she began to embrace the growing hippie movement, speaking out publicly against the Vietnam War.

Life at home had become intolerable. At seventeen she became pregnant—after a fling with a fellow high school student—and her mother made her get an abortion. What was even worse was that Leslie had the abortion at home—and the fetus was buried in the family's backyard, said one of her lawyers, Rich Pfeiffer, in a 2019 REELZ network documentary. After graduating from Monrovia High in 1968, she talked about moving to Hollywood and becoming active in the anti-Vietnam War movement. Instead, she moved to a commune in Northern California and fell in and out of love a few times. It was in Haight Ashbury that she met Catherine "Gypsy" Share, a like-minded rebel and the two bonded instantly.

Share's life was a drama straight out of a World War II Hollywood movie—born in Paris in 1942, her childhood was riddled with tragedy. Both of her paternal grandparents died in concentration camps, and her maternal grandmother died in an Eastern European ghetto.

Her father, a Hungarian violinist, and her German-born mother were members of the French resistance during World War II. Both committed suicide when she was two years old rather than being taken prisoner by the invading Nazis. Prior to her parents' suicide, her father made life-saving arrangements through the French underground resistance movement for his daughter to be adopted by a French woman, who then married an American. They ultimately left France and made their way to Hollywood, California, where life for Share was happy and secure—that is, until tragedy struck yet again. After being diagnosed with cancer, her adoptive mother took her own life. Share's own life seemed to unravel; she felt that her adoptive stepfather, who had remarried, rejected her. She was just sixteen years old when she found herself out in the cold again and looking for a new family.

AT THE TIME Van Houten met Share in San Francisco, she also met her charismatic boyfriend, the handsome would-be musician/actor Bobby Beausoleil—the oldest of five children in a working-class Catholic family. His father, Charles Beausoleil, was a Santa Barbara milk-truck driver who also worked as a clerk in a local liquor store to help put bread on the table for his growing family. At Santa Barbara High (where he never graduated because he got into trouble for a burglary and was punished by a stint in reform school), Beausoleil quickly earned the nickname "Cupid" because of his popularity with women, as well as the fact that he had, as a sixteen-year-old, played a walk-on role as Cupid in the 1967 documentary *Mondo Hollywood*. The film, which featured a darker and quirkier side to Hollywood ("Outshocks any Mondo Picture Ever Made!!! Hollywood Laid Bare!" read the posters), also contained snippets of archival film footage that featured Britain's Princess Margaret and her then husband Antony Armstrong-Jones and assorted filmland icons like Jayne Mansfield and Sonny and Cher, as well as a brief scene introducing an up- and-coming stylist to the stars named Jay Sebring. Beausoleil's other claim to early movie fame was to be picked by director Kenneth Anger, not only as a young protégé, but to play the devil in the 1967 movie *Lucifer Rising*. Anger had also offered the devil role to Mick Jagger, who declined, although Jagger's then girlfriend, Marianne Faithful, appears in the picture. When the movie was eventually released in 1972, Beausoleil was still in it. By then he was in prison but was still able to compose music for the film.

Although Beausoleil was still in a relationship with another woman, Share and he became romantically involved after starring together in the 1969 soft-core porn Western movie *The Ramrodder*, which had been mostly shot on location at the Spahn Ranch. Van Houten moved into the couple's San Francisco apartment and ended up sharing bed and board with Beausoleil. When they all moved back to Southern California in early 1969, Share, Beausoleil, and Van Houten hooked up with a musician named Manson, who invited them to join his traveling entourage.

It took only a matter of days for the gullible nineteen-year-old Van Houten to become an instant convert to the lifestyle according to Manson.

In mid-1969, she vanished from her family's radar and no one heard a whisper about her until early December of that year. Her former high school buddies were stunned when a mugshot of their one-time pal and dreamer made the front page of local papers and key newspapers across the country. But this time she was identified as a member of the notorious Manson Family, and as a key figure implicated in a shocking orgy of killing.

Decades after the murders, Van Houten disavowed Manson and was able to talk with some clarity about how she ended up spending her life behind bars. "As I started to go to school, I never felt I fitted in, I never had that sense of belonging—and I was watching my family fall apart—and coming closer to a sister that was on the road to her own destruction. When my father left, I seemed to want more living out of life than what was expected of young girls at that time: drugs, sex, breaking away from the norm. I was desperately seeking someone.

"I was eighteen or nineteen...I dropped out of college, I started losing contact with friends. I went to live with my sister. I started to drink, using hashish and marijuana—whatever my sister had around. I thought there had to be more. I was looking for a way out, had never developed a sense of who I was or...I wanted to please. I wanted for the first time to feel safe, feel like someone was going to care for me. I had never felt like that. And in giving up and moving on with Manson, I was basically just throwing away the rest of my life."

"I didn't 'sleep with the devil,' I slept with an ex-con who had an extensive record of pimping and abusing women. But at the time I didn't know that."

She described life at the Spahn Ranch to her friend John Waters. "The place was set up and run the same way as a stable of hookers, although none of us realized it at the time."

Waters, campaigning for forgiveness and freedom for Van Houten, wrote passionately of her redemption efforts.

"Leslie and I have shared good times and bad times…and, yes, Leslie does have good times. She's taught illiterate women to read in prison classes, she's stitched a portion of the AIDS quilt, made bedding for the homeless, recorded books on tape for the blind. She has clerked for the administrators, the nurses, the associate warden, the head of education, the kitchen, and the priest. And it's not that she jumps from job to job—rules restrict inmates from working longer than two years in the same position. She can be lighthearted, too. She even sang 'Santa Baby' at the prison Christmas show one year. But it all came to naught."

At one of her countless parole hearings in the early eighties, she was asked to assess Manson: "I feel he's a very pitiful and pathetic human being, and I'm very sorry that people still continued to give him attention. If he were ignored, he would just die or fade away."

Years after her conviction, I attended a private dinner with Marvin Part, one lawyer assigned to defend Van Houten. Our host (and mutual friend) was Beverly Hills lawyer Bernard Patrusky, who was at UCLA School of Law with Part and told me Marvin was now dying to talk. And he was, talking freely about how he fought unsuccessfully to separate his then client from being tried with the others. But most important, he was frustrated at not getting her to the nearest psychiatrist.

After his first interview with her, he came away stunned by what he heard and decided to interview her a second time, and this time he taped her crazy rantings so he had everything on record.

"I'll never forget her words. She said she believed Charlie was Jesus Christ. She worshipped and loved him deeply. And she said she truly believed some of the Beatles' songs were warnings and messages to Charlie about a race riot and blood running in the streets of America. And she just mimicked the whole insane Manson propaganda. The Family would all escape to an underground city in the desert, although she wasn't quite sure where this underground city was. She said Charlie's girls were chattel and whenever he told her to have sex—with men or women—she blindly obeyed. She said she took acid trips every day. I couldn't believe what I was hearing. In my lifetime in law, I had never come across anything quite as unbelievable as what this young woman was telling me. And she was smiling and recounting it all so mundanely.

"It was so clear to me that Leslie was as nutty as a fruitcake. I would have been in grave neglect of my duty if I didn't give the judge my opinion." Nutty as a fruitcake or not, within hours of asking for a psychiatric report, Marvin Part was shown the door. His strategy to save his client's life ended.

"Leslie was quite apologetic," he remembered. "When I visited her in jail the next day she was so innocent and so stupid, and she said, 'Charlie says I have to get another lawyer,'" And with that, Marvin Part instantly became just another inconsequential part—a mere footnote—in the history of Charles Manson.

"When we slept together, when we made love, all I remember is just crying and crying to this man...he said, 'Oh you are so beautiful.' I just couldn't believe that. I just started crying."
—Patricia Krenwinkel, 2017 *New York Times*
TV documentary, *My Life After Manson*

Patricia Krenwinkel

When I think back to 1970 and a year covering the Sharon Tate trial, I have a hard time coming up with a vivid picture of Patricia Krenwinkel.

Sure, she, Susan Atkins, and Leslie Van Houten made an impression as an unholy trio, marching into court, smiling and sometimes singing, decked out in wildly colorful ankle-length satin dresses or, alternately, with floppy, blue jail-issue denims. Those flamboyant dresses, some of which were pilfered by other Manson women from Sunset Boulevard stores or local thrift shops, were tailored with ornate embellishments by the girls at the Spahn Ranch and delivered to the jailhouse with some regularity.

I later discovered that their bespoke tailoring included bonuses that jail officials never knew about. Into the hems of those heavy garments, the Spahn girls sewed tabs of LSD, which might have explained much of the trio's wildly irrational courtroom behavior.

The three carefully coiffed their hair in a way that drew attention to the swastikas carved into their foreheads. They sang and generally misbehaved and deliberately shattered the traditional courtroom decorum.

They never seemed to take the charges against them very seriously. In fact, I clearly got the impression that, to them, the whole legal exercise was treated as a charade—an attitude that later bit them hard in their asses.

The problem was, of course, that most of our attention was fixated on the unpredictable antics of the ringmaster—the Madman Manson. The girls were definitely the Three Stooges, who were prepared to step out of line and behave badly, which they did whenever their ringmaster cracked his verbal whip.

Krenwinkel and Van Houten, along with Susan Atkins, seldom uttered a word unless Manson ordered them to. They were simply ciphers, sidekicks to Manson. The Tweedledums and Tweedledees of the courtroom. Sometimes they acted silly, sometimes obnoxious, hyperactive, and even cunning. Robots with no personalities whatsoever, unless they were ordered to have personalities. It was obvious from the outset that Manson was their puppet master obsessively pulling their strings. Watching this all unfold, I lost count of the times when one of them was addressed by the judge or a lawyer and they turned silently to Manson for his approval. He was no fool, although playing it that way in the long run probably did not work to his benefit because the jury could clearly see the female codefendants were still tightly under his control. And that image fit nicely into the district attorney's scenario: Manson should be found guilty because he was in total command and whatever he decreed, however absurd and ridiculous his demands, they would obey. And thus, this was the picture I saw played out every single court day.

Observing their daily antics, it appeared that Susan Atkins was dangerous and totally unpredictable. Leslie Van Houten was the real Beauty to Manson's Beast, while Katie Krenwinkel—to put it bluntly, the homely one—was nowhere near as bold as the other two and a lot grimmer.

Unprepossessing or not, and still deeply in Manson's thrall, Krenwinkel, like Atkins, had carried out the slaughter on two nights with relish. At Cielo Drive, Krenwinkel, like a character from a cheap horror movie wielding a knife, showed no mercy: She chased Folger onto the lawn, pinned her to the ground and stabbed her repeatedly even as she pleaded, "Stop, I'm already dead." Folger was so brutally carved up and had lost so much blood that investigators at first thought her white nightgown was red.

The next night, Krenwinkel's savagery continued. She stabbed Rosemary LaBianca while she pleaded for the life of her husband. And when he was dead, she planted a carving fork in his stomach. She wrote "Healter Skelter" on the fridge and "Death to Pigs" on the wall with the LaBiancas' blood.

"I stabbed her, and I kept stabbing her," she was to confess. And when asked how it felt, she replied, "Nothing, I mean, what is there to describe? It was just there, and it was right."

At the end of the second night of carnage, Krenwinkel and Watson raided the LaBianca fridge and helped themselves to some chocolate milk and cheese. And Watson jumped in the shower to wash the blood off and raided Leno LaBianca's wardrobe for a change of clothes!

Then the killers calmly walked down the drive and hitchhiked back to the Spahn Ranch.

PATRICIA DIANNE KRENWINKEL was born in December 1947, and like many of the girls who were mesmerized by Manson, she grew up in a comfortable middle-class home. Her neighborhood was the Los Angeles suburb of Inglewood, a community in the shadow of the then rapidly burgeoning Los Angeles International Airport. Her mother Dorothy was a doyenne of the local social scene, working tirelessly for socially correct and respectable causes: March of Dimes, The World Church Women's Council, and Campfire Girls.

Widowed in 1943, she was left with a daughter, Charlene. The following year she married insurance agent Joseph Krenwinkel, and four years later Patricia was born.

Even as a young woman, Krenwinkel (her parents called her Pat) hated herself. She was fourteen years old and fighting ballooning weight. Her worried mother took her to a doctor who prescribed an assortment of drugs such as Benzedrine and Dexamyl—a form of amphetamine given by doctors in that period to treat a wide-ranging list of problems, including depression, obesity, addiction, and narcolepsy. Her friends from that era recall the fragile young woman being totally devastated when, at a school dance, her partner remarked as he led her off the dance floor, "For a fat girl, you don't sweat much."

Krenwinkel went on crash diets, which resulted in her precipitously shrinking from size fourteen to size eight in just weeks. But "Slenderella" young Pat discovered that diet-drug side effects led to wild moods and irrationality. To overcome her low self-esteem, she piled on the makeup and dyed her hair bright red.

What she didn't realize at the time was that she was also suffering from a hormonal imbalance, which produced too much testosterone. She experienced physical affects—excessive hair growth all over her body as well as changes in her voice. These noticeable changes often made her the target of jokes among high school friends and, later, Family members as well.

She got along well with her half-sister, Charlene, who was seven years older. However, she was constantly irritated by her parents nagging at her to conform, as they tried to mold her into something she was never comfortable being. They pushed her into Campfire Girls and attending the Bible school where her mother taught. From the outside, she appeared to be living the idyllic childhood, surrounded by a menagerie of pets; a dog, hamsters, goldfish, and canaries. She was also an active member of the local wildlife society.

But deep down inside she knew it was all a front. She began to rebel. She attended two local high schools, sampling along the way all manner of drugs. Yet, despite the happy veneer, she despised herself.

The divorce of her parents when she was seventeen exacerbated her unhappiness. Krenwinkel and her mother moved back to Dorothy's hometown of Mobile, Alabama. There, Patricia enrolled in the private Spring Hill Jesuit College, and even talked about becoming a nun. But she dropped out after only one semester. Missing the hang-loose Southern California lifestyle, in 1967, she flew from Mobile to Los Angeles and moved into a cheap apartment with her half-sister Charlene in Manhattan Beach.

She took a job as a file clerk but was bored. After work one day she visited her sister's friend who offered her marijuana and introduced her to an amiable man who was staying there. He pulled out his guitar and sang as the adoring young women looked on. She was instantly charmed by this minstrel.

On September 12, 1967, she left her job without warning, not even bothering to pick up her final paycheck. She abandoned her car in a beachside parking lot and hitched a ride on a black bus heading for a destination she knew not where. To her father, Joseph, she cryptically wrote, "I've left to find myself."

On and off over the next few weeks, Krenwinkel's father received numerous calls from his daughter, but she was tight-lipped about what she was doing. Each time they spoke, she asked him for cash. He refused, offering instead to send her a one-way airline ticket to Alabama. Patricia hung up on him.

The next contact Joseph Krenwinkel had with his wayward daughter was in mid-November 1968. He sat across a wooden table in police headquarters in Independence, California, where the shocked Krenwinkel was informed that his daughter was being held on suspicion of being involved in the murder of a spiritualist and author named Karl Stubbs who lived in Olancha, some twenty miles from Lone Pine. The eighty-two-year-old Stubbs was found lying in a pool of blood outside his home. He claimed he had been ferociously beaten by a group of "hippie types"—specifically, two young men and two young women. He was rushed to Lone Pine Hospital where he died.

There were no eyewitnesses to the attack, so, consequently, local police were forced to release her into the custody of her father. On the long drive back to Southern California he angrily demanded: "What the hell is this all about?" Krenwinkel gave him the silent treatment. Her father gave his daughter a one-way ticket to Alabama.

A year later his ex-wife called him in hysterics. Their daughter had been arrested again, but this time the charges were much more serious.

FOR CHARLES MANSON, Patricia Krenwinkel—desperate for any display of affection or attention—was easy pickings.

In her version of the story, Krenwinkel said she and Manson went to her half-sister's apartment in Manhattan Beach and he immediately took her to bed and made passionate love to her. She said she felt truly adored. He flattered her by telling her all the things she so desperately wanted to hear. She was spellbound by his words as well as his sexual prowess. When he told her that she was the most beautiful woman he had ever met, she sobbed with joy.

The young woman, who had grown up feeling rejected and ugly, said this was the first time in her life that she felt totally accepted by a man.

Years later, at the benign-sounding California Institution for Women in Corona, California (located barely an hour from Los Angeles and where she and Van Houten and briefly Susan Atkins had become model prisoners), Krenwinkel, with the advantage of hindsight and decades behind bars, was able to offer a passionate and articulate assessment on how and why she succumbed so easily.

"It all comes from wanting to be loved. The saddest part is my definition of love was totally skewed. My life is a very convoluted story. In the beginning it was just me and him (Manson)—and I thought I was in love—I accepted everything I was told, and I gave up every little bit of me to that man who demanded every little bit of me. It started only as one woman with one man that turned into one of the most disastrous, most horrendous, most abominable situations. We all followed because we didn't know how to stop a monster. At twenty-three, I ended up on Death Row and away from him. In a cell twenty-three hours a day. I was going to have to make the decision of my life—everything I had ever believed…I would now have to be fully responsible for the damage, the wreckage, and the horror."

And for her entire adult life, Patricia Krenwinkel tried without success to overcome that damage, wreckage, and horror.

Sadly, well into her seventies, she's still trying.

Polanski in Paris 1994.

ROMAN POLANSKI:
A WANTED MAN

"In their rush to assess what had happened, some of the mainstream press brought the nature of Roman Polanski's movies into the nature of the crime and held the movies responsible. Roman was a total innocent. Neither his life nor his movies had anything to do with this. But because he'd made Repulsion *and* Rosemary's Baby, *he was made to seem responsible."*

—Warren Beatty, to Steve Oney,
Los Angeles magazine, July 2009

Roman Polanski was no stranger to controversy. Peter Bart, the former editor-in-chief of *Variety*, came to know the director when, earlier in his career, Bart had gone to work for Paramount boss Robert Evans. He worked on two of Polanski's films, *Rosemary's Baby* and *Chinatown*, and noted that the director had a propensity for landing in hot water. "Roman was a brilliant man, the best-read, most-cultured director I have ever met in my life," Bart recalled years after he left the studio. "But in those days, people who were close to Roman tended to die. He was always at the edge of the flame."

"It was very personal to me and to Bob Evans," Bart remembered in a piece he wrote for the showbiz online magazine *Deadline*. "A year earlier we'd persuaded Polanski to come to Hollywood to direct *Rosemary's Baby*, which he'd now completed. We were mindful of his troubled past—a survivor of both Nazi and Russian terrorism—but Polanski now seemed cheerfully upbeat as he left for London for a brief post-production meeting. His bride, Sharon, who was pregnant, had told him she would invite a few friends for dinner in his absence."

In March 1977, eight years after the murder of his wife and friends, the forty-three-year-old Polanski found himself in deep trouble. Facing Superior Court Judge Laurence Rittenband at the Santa Monica courthouse, he was charged with five sexual offenses involving thirteen-year-old budding actress and model Samantha Gailey, whose stage mother, TV actress Susan Gailey, was pushing her toward a celebrity career. Polanski, in his rented Mercedes convertible, had taken the young girl to the Beverly Hills home of his friend, actress Jacqueline Bisset. Polanski said he was doing a fashion-magazine shoot for a French publication, *Vogue Homme*, which was not linked to the American *Vogue*. The theme of his unusual photo essay reportedly was "The Sexualism of Teenage Girls." But because the light was fading, he decided he needed a new location, so they drove to the Mulholland Drive hilltop home of his *Chinatown* pal Jack Nicholson. No one bothered to ask why an A-league Hollywood director with an international reputation felt it necessary to seek freelance work as a magazine photographer.

Some Polanski friends knew that he liked very young women, but they later wondered why a thirteen-year-old model would participate in a photo shoot without an adult chaperone. Samantha's mother, who was a working actress with some success, had green-lighted the shoot and the young girl was later to say that it was Polanski who had insisted that her mother's presence might inhibit his junior-high-school model. Susan Gailey said she thought a layout with the famous director would benefit her daughter's acting ambitions. Much later, in her own 2013 memoir, *The Girl*, which was penned under her married name, Samantha Geimer, the young woman denied that her mother had pimped her out to Polanski in pursuit of fame. In her book, she admitted she was both attracted and repelled by the diminutive Polish-French director. "Mostly I was thinking, 'Eww, there's this guy who's like—my size and sort of looks like a ferret,'" she wrote. "But he's super powerful and he wants to photograph me…Me!'" In her grand jury testimony, young Gailey recalled that Polanski shot some topless pictures of her and then asked if she was on the pill. "We did photos with me drinking champagne," she recalled. "He was friendly, and then right toward the end it got a little scary and I realized—you know—he had some other intentions, and then I knew I was not where I should be. I just didn't quite know how to get myself out of there."

The charges were serious. They included sodomy, lewd and lascivious act upon a child under fourteen, and providing alcohol and drugs to the young girl. Initially, Polanski claimed Gailey was much more sophisticated than her years—a pretty flimsy defense, as was his statement that even though she was underage, she'd already had sex with her boyfriend. And the grand jury testimony, released after the case was closed, was pretty damning, reflecting that Polanski plied her with champagne and part of a Quaalude (which he said had been prescribed for him by his doctor for jet lag). Then he began performing oral, vaginal, and anal intercourse on her, despite her demands that he "keep away." Gailey testified that she realized what Polanski's intentions were when he directed her to remove her underwear and climb into a Jacuzzi. After he took photos of her in the bath, he stripped off his clothing and joined her in the water. So much for the façade of a photo shoot.

He pled not guilty, but then in August 1977, the prosecution and defense made a plea deal—or so everyone thought. Realizing that he would face a long prison sentence for the charge if he went to trial and was convicted, the director pled guilty to a lesser charge of engaging in unlawful sexual intercourse with the girl, in exchange for dropping the major offenses. Additionally, by avoiding trial, he had a better chance of not facing deportation on the grounds of moral turpitude.

I covered the case in the Santa Monica courthouse. At the deal hearing, the straight-arrow deputy DA Roger Gunson posed a question to Polanski: "Do you understand it is possible that you could be placed on probation, with or without being required to serve up to one year in county jail?" Polanski, dapperly dressed in a double-breasted suit and tie, seemed very contrite. He replied simply, "Yes." He said he clearly understood that it was entirely up to the judge to decide on jail or probation and to determine whether to order him deported. He knew deportation would destroy his Hollywood career. The judge made it clear that it was within his purview to change his mind about sentencing and probation, "in light of further consideration of the matter." Rittenband left the final decision until the completion of Polanski's ninety-day prison evaluation.

Polanski was sent to state prison in Chino for a series of tests that Rittenband said would help the court reach a fair and just decision. Polanski agreed to undergo "a mentally disordered sex offender examination," which required him to have a full psychiatric evaluation at Chino by Dr. Alvin E. Davis (working for the defense) and Dr. Ronald Markman (representing the prosecution). Strongly supporting this course of action was the girl's family lawyer, Lawrence Silver, who urged the judge to avoid "putting her through a harrowing trial." In a letter to the judge, Silver wrote: "Whatever harm has come to her as a victim would be exacerbated in the extreme if this case went to trial. This is not the place for a recovering young girl."

Polanski's examination was completed in just forty-two days, and prison officials advised the judge that test results showed his sentence should not include additional incarceration. Polanski was released on his own recognizance to await the final decision. Meanwhile, his legal team had lined up an impressive list of famous names—people who sent letters to the probation department in support of Polanski's no-more-jail-time plea. Among them were friends, including *Rosemary's Baby* star Mia Farrow and Paramount's Bob Evans, among others, all of whom testified to Polanski's sterling character, and stressed his dark past life and emotional traumas.

Farrow declared that she had received aid and comfort from Polanski and Tate "when my own life was on shaky ground." And long-time Polish friend Gene Gutowski—who produced Polanski films, including the earlier *Repulsion* (1965) and, much later, *The Pianist* (2002), which was to bring the exiled Polanski his first Best Director Oscar—complained about the sensational press coverage his friend had received. "There is, in fact, very little that is dark or sinister about Roman; he has remained amazingly normal and well-adjusted and generous to a fault," Gutowski said. "He is a loyal and kind friend and completely trusting, possibly excessively so. As a result, he has been used from time to time by young and ambitious females who felt that being seen with Roman in public… would lead to their advancement or gain them publicity. Unfortunately, this sometimes also resulted in an aura of notoriety being attached to Roman."

But perhaps the most sympathetic of all reports came from psychiatrist Davis at Chino. He declared that Polanski was not mentally ill or disordered and was not a sexual deviant or a pedophile. "He is of superior intelligence, has good judgment and strong moral and ethical values, and has normal remorse and regret for his consequences," Dr. Davis said. "Although not attempting to bid for sympathy, defendant has told his life story that ranges from the terror of his childhood in the Krakow ghetto, the deportation of his parents to concentration camps, and subsequent death of the mother at Auschwitz. The defendant's hiding from the Nazis during the war years, the rejection from state schools because of his religious heritage, to the horrors of the murder of his wife and unborn child at the hands of the Manson gang. The defendant has not only survived, he has prevailed, surmounting the uncounted adversities. He has risen to the heights of his chosen profession and has become one of the leading creative forces of the past two decades."

Davis was on a real jag, as he—deviating somewhat and switching from psychiatrist to instant movie historian, and apropos of nothing in particular—added: "Possibly not since Renaissance Italy has there been such a gathering of creative minds in one locale as there has been in Los Angeles County during the past half century. The motion picture industry has proved a magnet to many: World War II and the lowering of the Iron Curtain have provided an additional influx of the great artists of our time." Phew!

He suggested that Polanski undergo some kind of therapy, "not for a sexual problem but for unresolved depression." And he added a warning that locking Polanski up again would not work, noting: "An unusual degree of stress and hardship would result from incarceration."

Back in the Santa Monica courthouse, Judge Rittenband, very much a PR-conscious fellow, whose whole modus vivendi was wrapped up in his fame as a "celebrity judge," relished his high-profile judicial notoriety.

When I covered the court beat for the *Santa Monica Evening Outlook*, the perennial bachelor Rittenband was considered quite a character. He was either loved or hated by lawyers who appeared in front of him. One lawyer called him "a gouty old bully;" another, a "no-bullshit guy who rules with an iron rod." He had handled other celebrity cases: the divorce of Elvis and Priscilla Presley; the child custody battle between Marlon Brando and his wife, the fiery Indian-American actress, Anna Kashfi; and a paternity suit filed against Cary Grant. Those who knew him at the private Hillcrest Country Club said he liked to boast to his cronies about his famous cases—even while they were unfolding. The judge was not impressed with the probation report. "Whitewash," he declared in private. And he suggested he was having second thoughts about the final disposition of Polanski's sentence. It included the suggestion of at least an additional forty-eight days added to the original 100 days he had earlier decreed for Polanski's Chino examination.

What further had incensed the judge was a photo snapped by European paparazzo Istvan Bajzat, which was prominently featured in the *Evening Outlook*, as well as in newspapers around the world. It showed the boyish Polanski, cigar in one hand, arm around a beautiful 15-year-old girl, believed to be German actress and model Nastassja Kinski, in a

Munich beer hall where they were celebrating Oktoberfest, giant steins of beer set in front of them. After being told by Polanski that he had been hired to direct a big budget movie, *Hurricane*, and that the livelihoods of scores of employees on the shoot had become his responsibility, the judge had granted Polanski permission to travel abroad before sentencing. But there was nothing about a party time in his instructions.

The judge summoned Wally Burke, who covered the court beat for the *Santa Monica Evening Outlook* and was one of Rittenband's main conduits to the media, into his chambers. Burke told me, "He was hopping mad. He waved the newspaper photo under my nose and angrily declared, 'We're gonna put this little Polish cocksucker away for the rest of his life.'" No one disagreed that Polanski had demonstrated an extreme lack of good judgment. It seemed he had not altered his wayward habits. Adding fuel to the fire, he flaunted his behavior with the underage Kinski, daughter of actor Klaus Kinski. Two years later, he hired her to star in his 1979 movie *Tess*—a film that was dedicated to the memory of Sharon Tate.

The judge ordered Polanski to return to California. It was obvious that tea and sympathy might not be Rittenband's choice offering at final sentencing. Chino inmate number B88742Z returned to California from his Munich jaunt, then made a life-changing decision. He swiftly packed a bag and hopped a British Airways flight from Los Angeles to London—then on to Paris, where he knew the government had no extradition agreement with the US. He justified his abrupt departure by claiming that Rittenband had reneged on his agreement during talks with his own lawyer and the deputy district attorney, and now was ready to send Polanski back to prison. So he fled.

I FLEW TO PARIS in late 1994 to meet with Polanski, still a fugitive from the United States. I was on assignment for *Los Angeles* magazine to talk about his latest directorial effort, the film *Death and the Maiden*, based on the play by Argentinian-Chilean novelist Ariel Dorfman, starring Sigourney Weaver and Ben Kingsley. The film deals with torture, brainwashing, and possible false memory. But the subtext of my transatlantic trip was quite clear: his powerful friends and lawyers in Hollywood wanted to put a full court press on Judge Rittenband in his case. They hoped I would paint Polanski in a positive light that would somehow change the anti-Polanski climate, which worsened after he fled. It was a gamble, but they reckoned an upbeat story in Los Angeles might result in barriers to his return to America being lifted. Roman the Fugitive would be welcomed back into the bosom of Hollywood and crowned Roman the Forgiven, opening the door to Roman the Redeemed. Or something along those lines.

I wasn't fool enough to believe that Polanski would beg for some kind of forgiveness in our interview. He had already stated his version; he ran because they done him wrong, and he believed Rittenband planned to do the dirty on him. Returning to Los Angeles with no new deal in place would result in prison suicide. The idea of incarceration was abhorrent to him. It was common knowledge that sexual predators—particularly those who exploited underage girls or children—faced brutal treatment from fellow inmates. What Polanski's people told me was that, under the guise of promoting his new movie, the director would not hold back, and no subject was off limits. He was willing to unburden himself in something akin to genuine mea culpa. It seemed a stretch, but I was up for it.

The fact was that Polanski desperately wanted to return to Hollywood and pick up the pieces of his shattered career. Things were not going as well as he had hoped since he went on the lam. His $40 million 1986 production of *Pirates* flopped big time, returning only $6 million worldwide. Two years later, *Frantic*, a Harrison Ford-fueled Hitchcockian homage, also disappointed at the box office. And *Bitter Moon*, also released earlier that year, a masochistic black comedy starring Peter Coyote and Polanski's new actress wife, Emmanuelle Seigner, also took a nosedive. Steven Spielberg reportedly had talked to him in the early nineties about doing *Schindler's List*, but he turned it down, feeling it was too close to his own personal story. As a result, he had been forced to take on acting roles in low-budget films such as *A Pure Formality* opposite Gerard Depardieu. In the movie, directed by Giuseppe Tornatore, Polanski plays a police detective trying to solve a murder.

Our lunch date was set for 1:00 p.m., but shortly before noon he called very apologetically. "I'm sorry, there's been some confusion," he said. "Can we meet right away? I must leave by 2:15 at the very latest. I must take my daughter to preschool."

Ah, propaganda already, my cynical journalistic brain thought. *Here's Roman now in his most current role—a devoted dad doing fatherly duties.* At that time he had a two-year-old daughter, Morgane, from his marriage to Emmanuelle Seigner. We met at his favorite restaurant on Avenue Montaigne, a few doors from the fashionable Nina Ricci and Christian Dior shops, where the maître d' fussed much too much when my journalist wife, Sally, and I said we were meeting Polanski. He quickly led us to a discreet corner table where the director was already seated.

I was intrigued to examine the Polish terror-cum-cinematic genius up close. He was relatively relaxed in a setting he was comfortable with—one he perceived he could control. Here was the movie legend my old *London Daily Express* photographer, Harry Benson, had once amusingly described as "the original five-foot Pole you wouldn't want to touch anyone with." He wore blue jeans, a two-button, white T-shirt under a black linen blazer, and high-heeled cowboy boots. Still boyish, his brown, shoulder-length hairstyle was slightly flecked with touches of gray. He was sixty-one but looked twenty years younger. He again apologized for the last-minute change in our appointment, beckoned the hovering waiter over to the table, and ordered single glasses of red wine for each of us. Then he ordered escargots for a starter. When we politely declined the appetizer, he declared, "Did you know a snail has the largest penis of all living creatures…proportionate to its size?"

Having never studied the sex life or anatomy of a snail, and assuming that this opening gambit was part of the famous Polanski sense of humor, we ordered roasted chicken and pommes frites and began the interview. He talked easily while shucking—if that's what you call extricating dead, garlic-saturated snails from their shells. And he got straight to the point. He much preferred making films in Hollywood…period! It was a somewhat brave thing for him to say, and I sensed it was sort of a test balloon. He knew that I knew his flagging career was desperately in need of some kind of resurrection. "Yes, I know it would be entirely different if I were living in the United States and had direct contact and went to the lunches and parties," he said. "This [Paris] is a great disadvantage because, if you are there [in Hollywood], you can tap into film financing much more easily. But there are things we have to live with."

He was referring to his past, so I felt it was an invitation to revisit it. I mentioned I was at his 1969 press conference, just a few days after he had returned to Beverly Hills from Europe. It was at the Beverly Wilshire Hotel, and he had faced an accusatory media. In almost emotionless, accented English he angrily spoke: "I thought they wanted to crucify me." He said that most journalists at that hostile conference were insinuating that he was in some way responsible for the Cielo Drive carnage. "My problems didn't begin in 1977 [with the underage Samantha Gailey]. They began with the Manson murders. The victims were blamed as if they'd killed themselves in some sort of orgy of sex and drugs, rituals and black magic. I think in America they felt a kind of guilt because of what had happened to me in their country. I was a good person who had become a monster." Polanski needed no prompting; he was off and running. "Sharon smoked grass, but that was it. And she stopped when she was pregnant. Suddenly they turned her into a witch—a depraved drug addict."

I asked if he was actually as "out of it" as he appeared when I saw him at the first press conference in August 1969, following the murders.

"I was unbalanced at the time—a real emotional wreck. And confused. I just assumed that someone that knew us, someone in my own circle of friends, killed Sharon. I had no idea whatsoever that it had nothing to do with them…For a long period before they found the culprits, they were clearly blaming the victims for their own deaths. And they pointed the finger at me, for somehow being involved in it. The absurdity of it was so odious, so warped, so horrible. Until then I had wonderful relationships with the press."

He was devastated, he said, by all the stories that ran in newspapers and magazines. "All of it somehow mixed up with supernatural, with the devil. They demanded of me: 'Why do you make so many films about the devil?'" He said he had completely lost his drive for making movies. "After Sharon's death, everything seemed so futile. Nothing made sense. Nothing," he said. "I had difficulty finding anything worthwhile. What kind of project would make sense that I could give up a year or two of my life and still feel it was worth it?"

All well and good, but now I wanted to know his take on that ill-fated photo shoot where he plied a young girl, barely a teenager, with drugs and alcohol and then sodomized her.

He was not in a redemptive mood; rather, he seemed to be justifying his foolish actions. "I was about to make a series of photographs of young girls of that age, for a French magazine," he said. "I found it quite an interesting enterprise, because I like girls of that age, and girls of that age like me. And it just went too far."

Saying he went too far wasn't exactly the admission that everyone wanted, but it was a good start. I wanted to know how he would explain it all to his children. "Always with the truth. I won't lie to my daughter—not even about Santa Claus. I never will." I asked what he would tell his daughter about his having sex with a thirteen-year old. "Only the truth—and that is not what you are saying," he challenged me.

He portrayed himself as a changed man, an artist in exile, a husband and father—and still actively working. "I am not a masochist. Here in Paris, I am respected and happy. I have a family, and protecting them at this stage of my life is the most important thing. I don't want to subject them to the tabloids. Here in France, we have very strict laws regarding privacy. Even the paparazzi respect privacy. But I miss LA—mainly going into the hills to visit friends who lived sometimes in a little shack somewhere with a tire hanging from a tree as a swing. Wonderful. There's a tremendous amount of terrific people, kind and generous. You won't find people like that here. I miss people there very much, and I miss the delicatessen Nate 'n Al. And life is so comfortable there. So easy."

"Then you do want to go back to Hollywood?" I asked. He paused. "I don't know how I could go back there because I have such tragic memories of that place that every time I'd go back there I was in some state of shock. So now, it would be suddenly greater."

With lunch finished, Polanski posed for a few pictures in the street, then rushed off to pick up his daughter, fairly sanguine about his fugitive plight. He knew strings were still being pulled in California to help pave the way for the prodigal's return. Only it has not yet worked out the way he hoped. Still, years after our Parisian lunch, the campaign to get all charges against Polanski dropped is an ongoing one—so far, without success. But not for want of trying.

He hit the headlines again in September 2009 when—at the behest of US authorities—he was arrested in Switzerland after going to the Zurich Film Festival to collect a Lifetime Achievement Award. After a protracted legal battle, he won his latest campaign to avoid extradition and returned to his family in Paris. In 2018, I spoke to his Los Angeles lawyer, Harland Braun, who has been trying, without success, to get all charges dismissed because of what he calls "prosecutorial and judicial misconduct." "It's well-documented," Braun told me. "Roman is the victim of a lying judge. Roger Gunson, a very honest deputy DA, confirms that Roman would have definitely gone back to prison." Over the past few years, he told me, several attempts to straighten things out, "which have included secret emails between another judge [Rittenband died in 1998 at age 88], along with affidavits from all concerned, have not been successful. Roman had already done ten and a half months of jail time and house arrest. Now, all other judges in this political climate are simply afraid to touch this case."

In recent years, even his victim, Samantha Gailey Geimer, publicly pleaded to authorities to forgive and forget. "I have forgiven Polanski and moved on," she said, though she may have moved on because she received a settlement from Polanski in 1993 that is reckoned to be in the region of $200,000. Years later, she made a strange statement to the media about the rape.

"I was not as traumatized as everybody thought I should have been," she said. "You don't have to fall apart to show that what happened to you was wrong."

Still Polanski, now in his eighties, with grown children, knows his legal headaches continue. And the fact is, unless a US court rules otherwise, if he should dare to set foot in America, he will be arrested.

Dennis Wilson

DENNIS WILSON: BEACHED

"Sometimes the Wizard frightens me. The Wizard is Charlie Manson, who is a friend of mine who thinks he is God and the devil. He sings, plays, and writes poetry, and he may be another artist for Brother Records."

—Dennis Wilson to Britain's *Rave* magazine, Spring 1969.

"I don't talk about Manson. I think he's a sick fuck. I think of Roman and all those wonderful people who had a beautiful family and they fucking had their tits cut off."

—Dennis Wilson (Beach Boys drummer), 1976.

Beach Boys drummer Dennis Wilson's strange "love affair" with Charles Manson was fast and furious. Even grotesque at times.

The ignominious 1968-69 chapter in Wilson's frantic and oft-wasted life lasted less than a year before it suddenly burned out with reprimands and death threats. And a lifetime of fear for Wilson.

While it most likely did not accelerate Wilson's train wreck of a life, which came to a tragic end in December 1983 when the thirty-nine-year-old rock star drowned in the still waters of the Marina Del Rey channel in Southern California, his death provided yet another tragic chapter in Manson's tawdry life, with Wilson joining the list of innocent victims (or maybe not so innocent in Wilson's case) who could legitimately be added to Manson's ever-increasing catalogue of collateral damage casualties.

However, it started out as every red-blooded, heterosexual American's wildest sexual fantasy. In December 1968, Wilson, the Beach Boys' resident wild man, gave an interview to David Griffiths, a writer for the London-based pop weekly, the *Record Mirror*.

Wilson was in a retrospective mood. He talked about the Beach Boys quitting the tour circuit for the recording studio, and their ongoing battles with drugs as they pursued even more hits to follow up on big sellers like "I Get Around," "Sloop John B," and "California Girls," as they tried to reinforce their niche in the record business as genuine California surfin' guys.

In the *Record Mirror* interview, Wilson was simply oozing with delight at the enviable predicament he had found himself in.

"I live with seventeen girls," was the eye-grabbing story headline, which sounded like Wilson had found his very own twentieth century harem. Obviously, he was enjoying the reputation that went with the image of a blond, handsome young rock star, who, besides being rich and famous, was also capable of satisfying over one dozen females. A bit like those oil-rich Arab princelings who can pick a new concubine for every day of the week.

Wilson was twenty-four years old and part of the hugely successful family pop group whose surfing music in the Sixties had swept across California, and had proven appeal to vinyl buyers from Liverpool to Lapland. The band—Dennis and his brothers, songwriter and bassist Brian and lead guitarist Carl, along with their cousin Mike Love as singer, and friend Al Jardine also on guitar—had established themselves as clean-cut, sun-bronzed young gods, surrounding themselves with bikini-clad chicks who hung onto their every musical utterance. But, if truth were told, only Dennis lived up to that carefully crafted surfer image. The closest the others came to a surfboard was to use them as props on assorted photo shoots.

In reality, the Wilson brothers were not at all like their carefree, surfin' music-created images. Dennis was the good-looking blond Adonis—a sex symbol, but maybe the most dysfunctional of them all with his uncontrollable passion for drink, drugs (including heroin), and sex, along with his multiple marriages (five in all) and divorces. He got lots of competition from his elder brother Brian on the crazy meter. At their peak, Brian suffered from a fear of flying, which put something of a crimp on his touring. Brian was already well into his own disturbed mind "trip," which resulted in him sitting in a sandbox he installed inside his home, in a near catatonic state when he wasn't indulging in drugs.

With fame and everything good, bad, and ugly that came with it, Dennis continued his pursuit of who knew what. Truth, nirvana, the meaning of life, aided and abetted by the best illicit drugs money could buy. And money could buy a whole heap of chemicals—not to mention an endless river of alcohol to wash down all those pills.

Booze and drugs, of course, was not unusual as the seasons of sex and rock and roll took their toll on stars who overdosed. The Sixties and Seventies were chockablock with tales chronicling the abrupt demise of pop idols: Jim Morrison, Janis Joplin, Jimi Hendrix, Keith Moon, Elvis, Gram Parsons, Brian Jones, and Sid Vicious.

"Dennis was the essence, the spirit of the Beach Boys," was the way Fred Vail, a business associate of the Beach Boys, once described it. "We used to think of him as the Steve McQueen or James Dean of the group."

Vail noted that while Dennis was charismatic onstage during live performances, when it came to studio recordings, he was a second-class citizen. That happened when the group's fifth hit single, "Little Deuce Coupe," was released in 1963 and Dennis had been replaced by session drummer Hal Blaine.

Wilson's version of how his most recent idyllic state of affairs came to pass made intriguing reading for readers of the British rock weekly. But perhaps it should have come with a warning label.

"I live in the woods in California, near Death Valley, with seventeen girls. They're space ladies," Wilson told the *Record Mirror*, "and they'd make a great group. I'm thinking of launching them as the Family Gems," he kidded.

So how did his enviable and odd state of affairs come to pass?

"The way I met them (the women) was strange," said Wilson, who was spending much of the time in an alcoholic and chemical haze. "I went up into the mountains with my houseboy to take an LSD trip. We met two girls hitch-hiking (near Malibu, according to legend); one of them was pregnant. We gave them a lift, and a purse was left in the car. About a month later, near Malibu, I saw the pregnant girl again, only this time she'd had her baby. I was overjoyed for her, and it was through her that I met all the girls."

On that second encounter, he thought the young women's names were Patricia Krenwinkel and Ella Jo Bailey—nicknamed "Katie" and "Yeller"—although it is possible that he confused things. Neither Krenwinkel nor Bailey actually were pregnant or gave birth. However, another Manson acolyte, Mary Brunner, who had first met Manson in San Francisco, delivered a baby boy in April 1968 around the time Wilson picked up the women. The father of Brunner's child was listed as Charles Manson and the infant named Valentine Michael Manson, nicknamed "Pooh Bear." So it is possible that the two women hitchhiking the second time might have been looking after Pooh Bear as doctrine among Manson women was that new babies were to be raised by everyone, not solely the birth mother.

Wilson then raved to his passengers about his recent spiritual re-awakening triggered by his appreciation of the rock world's latest religious passion—the works of the Maharishi Mahesh Yogi, founder of the trendy Transcendental Meditation movement. Wilson was not the only rock star who latched onto the Maharishi. He also caught the eyes of not only the Beach Boys, but the Beatles, and in particular George Harrison.

In February 1968 Beach Boy Mike Love hied off to Rishikesh in

Northern India to study with the Maharishi. He was joined by all the Beatles, some with wives and girlfriends, folk singer Donovan, and twenty-three-year-old Mia Farrow, who had come with her younger sister Prudence.

Love and Dennis were both beguiled by the words of the fifty-year-old Maharishi and became instant disciples.

They persuaded other group members to take it further. In May 1968 the Beach Boys began a US concert tour introducing a unique special act. The program opened with the spotlight on the tiny, heavily bearded Hindu preacher, who delivered a long lecture in his trademark squeaky voice to the youthful audiences touting the benefits of meditation.

Then he was followed by the Beach Boys, introducing music from their new *Friends* album with a repertoire of songs strongly influenced by the spiritual and mellow Transcendental Meditation philosophy.

Not surprising, the Maharishi was an instant flop on the pop concert circuit. Twenty-nine concerts were booked—mostly for college audiences—but because of lax ticket sales, the tour was canceled after just three performances. Cancellations cost the Beach Boys $250,000, with one rock critic describing the odd pairing as, "one of the most bizarre entertainments of the era." Wilson, much taken with the Maharishi, said the guru told him, "Live your life to the fullest," and so Dennis couldn't wait to proselytize anyone who crossed his path, including his young female hitchhikers.

"I told them about our involvement with the Maharishi and they told me they too had a guru, a guy named Charlie who'd recently come out of jail after twelve years. His mother was a hooker, his father was a gangster, and he'd drifted into crime."

Wilson was also intrigued by his young passengers.

As the conversation grew more animated, the young women accepted his invitation to see his house on Sunset Boulevard. Dennis, ever the gracious host, dropped them off at his palatial pad, an old hunting lodge he was leasing on the famous boulevard.

"Take a swim and hang out," he said. "I'm off to the recording studio. Make yourself at home. I'll be back soon."

He did eventually return, but not until three in the morning.

Vincent Bugliosi later wrote in his book that while Wilson was reluctant to talk to him about Manson and was greatly relieved that he was never called as a witness in the trial, he did gleefully tell the prosecutor what happened in the wee small hours of the morning when he arrived back at his house after the recording session.

"The door opened and he was greeted by a small, skinny guy with a beard and dark piercing eyes. He had never seen him before," wrote Bugliosi.

"Startled at first, he said, 'Are you going to hurt me?'"

"The man smiled. 'Do I look like I'm going to hurt you, brother?'"

And then, much to the drummer's astonishment, the skinny guy kneeled down in front of Wilson and gently kissed his feet.

It was an old routine that Manson had used many times to great effect, particularly to disarm anyone who might pose a threat to him.

Wilson realized immediately that this was their guru Charlie, the one the girls had told him about. Wilson was even more impressed because, as he entered his own house, he saw that the tiny man in the buckskin jacket and jeans was surrounded by half a dozen pretty girls in various stages of undress.

"Mi casa es su casa," Wilson said, ogling the girls. "Let's party."

Manson knew he had struck gold, for this was definitely the start of a beautiful friendship. At least for the time being.

Wilson was immediately taken with Manson, succumbing totally to his jiggery-pokery and crazy philosophy. They shared LSD from Manson's stash, talked music, drugs, free sex, and all sorts of deviant pseudo-philosophies.

As Wilson recalled in his London pop magazine interview, "When I met him I found he had great musical ideas. We're writing together now. He's dumb, in some ways, but I accept his approach and have learnt from him."

Manson, of course could spot suckers a mile away, and when he saw this one he realized this could be his jackpot. Wilson was a big fish…and a Beach Boy to boot!

And it didn't take a brilliant brain to realize that Wilson could be his passport to the Big Time, the opening he was looking for on the way to inevitable rock music immortality. "Come stay," said the big-hearted drummer.

The Spahn Ranch was a bit of a filthy hole, true—but it was Manson's filthy hole. Still, a rock star mansion on Sunset was the place to be. Wilson's leased house at 14400 Sunset Boulevard was an historic landmark. Built in 1923 and once inhabited by actor-humorist Will Rogers, it boasted 8,000 square feet and included a spacious guesthouse and large pool area. It was in Pacific Palisades, and just a short hop, skip, and jump westward down Sunset to the beach, where surf was always up. At first Wilson said he got only good vibrations from Charlie and his nubile, fun-loving girls.

"This is Charlie," Wilson proudly introduced Manson to all comers who showed up at his frequent parties. "Charlie is a wizard, a genius—a real gas."

"He was like a proud father showing off his favorite son," said Paul Watkins, Manson's second in command, who enjoyed Wilson's hospitality along with all the perks that came with it. "We must have watched the Beatles' *Magical Mystery Tour* film maybe forty times on Dennis's big screen. On LSD it's even better."

And Wilson's party guests were a wide cross section of people—movers and shakers in the music biz who were only too happy to hobnob and be nice to Wilson's new and odd half-naked houseguests.

But, however you cut it, the relationship was mostly a one-way street. Dennis gave and they all took.

Not long after Manson swapped the Family's transient lifestyle for a degree of stability—if you could actually use that term to describe the Family's cockeyed lifestyle—he was soon able to twist the pliable Wilson around his little finger. In return he provided Wilson with assorted drugs, morning, noon and night, and willing twenty-four-hour sex partners. Strangely, while Manson and his women abused drugs daily, they rarely touched hard liquor.

Manson preyed on Wilson's weaknesses: his satyriasis, his ego, the whole "I live with seventeen women" boastful scenario. They had long debates about music, with Dennis talking Charlie up to his assorted friends who flocked to Dennis's soirees, along with the other Beach Boys, who were anxious to get a close-up look at this strange guy who had become Dennis's new guru. Wilson thought Charlie was the bee's knees, destined for the big league—the next Bob Dylan.

Another famous guest at the Wilson manse, who was also impressed by his pal's guest, was Neil Young, the Canadian-born musician who performed with Buffalo Springfield and Crosby, Stills & Nash. In his 2012 autobiography *Waging Heavy Peace*, Young wrote that he remembered Manson helping himself to Young's guitar at a Wilson party—and strumming away unprompted.

"His songs were off-the-cuff things he made up as he went along," Young writes, "and they were never the same twice in a row. Kind of like Dylan, but different because it was hard to glimpse a true message in them, but the songs were fascinating. He was quite good."

Young described Manson as "stone brilliant—a frustrated artist and real smart—but a little intense." He called Mo Ostin, at Reprise Records, and told him, "Check this guy out. He's good…but just a little out of control."

So impressed was Young with his new musical pal that he even gifted Manson with a motorcycle.

UNENDINGLY, WILSON rhapsodized about Manson. "He taught me a dance. The Inhibition. You have to imagine you're a frozen man and the ice is thawing out. Start with your fingertips, then all the rest of you, then you extend it to a feeling that the whole universe is thawing out."

And Wilson felt he was also living an Arabian night's fantasy seven days a week, and that it might end in a "'live-fast-die-young" finale. As it did.

Half-naked nymphets with odd names like "Squeaky," "Gypsy," "Sexy Sadie," and "Snake" were his for the taking. Also, hanging around was the very pretty Ruth Ann Moorehouse, nicknamed Ouisch—and at seventeen, definitely jailbait. Her creepy father Dean, an ex-pastor-turned-handyman, watched unmoved as his teenage daughter pleasured whomever Manson decreed. The father then moved into the Wilson guest house, tending the garden in exchange for free rent. Moorehouse wasn't averse to helping himself to the menu of drugs that were at his beck and call 24/7. And the women. Even Dianne Lake, who was fourteen when she was sucked into Manson's cave, went to bed with sleazebag Moorehouse. Lake was to write a memoir in 2017 in which she recounted in graphic detail her firsthand memories of the Manson/Wilson relationship.

In that Alice-in-Drug-Wonderland book, *Member of the Family*, she writes that she was frequently offered up for sex by Manson while staying at the Sunset Boulevard house.

"I don't remember having sex with Dennis, but I do remember having a good time. And we all cuddled up to Dennis to keep warm," she wrote. She says Manson often loaned the girls out, and after Wilson took her and two other Manson girls to a "family cookout" on the Colorado River, "everyone got stoned."

Then, back on Sunset Boulevard with Lyn Fromme, Nancy Pitman, and Sandra Good, "We'd drop acid at least once a week, and each night we'd play music or have group sex."

"We did our best to sidetrack the visitors (to Wilson's house) dancing, singing, often having sex with them," she wrote.

Lake contends that all those sexual sacrifices were for a good cause. "Charlie had led us to the communal Promised Land. Everything he'd asked for had come to pass. There was music, there was sex, there were drugs. We were living free of hang-ups, with no more worries about where stuff was going to come from. Our anti-materialism and practice of living in the now were working. Charlie's beliefs were being validated more and more each day. Just the fact that he'd been able to captivate someone as famous as a member of the Beach Boys was proof enough."

Manson was no fool. He knew if he served up fourteen-year-olds like Lake to those who fancied a touch of child porn, then he immediately had heavy-duty evidence that could be used to blackmail those men who had partaken of the forbidden fruit. It was a vicious and heavy-duty bargaining tool, and Manson knew lives could be destroyed if those sexual peccadillos were to be made public.

From time to time, with Wilson at the wheel of his burgundy Rolls Royce, the girls took him to supermarkets and he watched with delight as they dived in the dumpsters for abandoned food, despite the fact he could buy them anything they wanted.

Paul Watkins and Brooks Poston, who joined the Manson Family shortly after they moved in on Wilson, were also enthralled by their proximity to the rock star and their comfy accommodation at Hotel Dennis. "Life with Dennis…was fun and games, sex, trips to dumpsters in the Rolls, orgies, group sex, unlimited pot, and acid trips," recalled Watkins.

"Dennis was at Charlie's beck and call—sometimes like a puppy dog or puppet," Watkins told me. "He, like the rest of us, worshipped Charlie, although they sometimes argued because Dennis said he knew everything there was to know about music and Charlie said he also did. Charlie kept saying that music industry people were a bunch of lying lowlifes."

Paul Watkins tagged along with Charlie and some of the girls when they went to a recording session in Hollywood, which Dennis and one of his music writing pals, Gregg Jakobson, had arranged.

It wasn't Manson's first try at recording. Soon after he was paroled and had moved back to Los Angeles from San Francisco, Charlie looked up Gary Stromberg, a producer at Universal Studios whose name was given to him by Terminal Island prison inmate Phil Kaufman. In a podcast for Podbay.FM (Episode 8) several years later, Stromberg rather relishes telling the story of his offbeat encounters with Manson.

"I used to send letters to Phil in jail and dip them in acid and he would give them to his friends, including Charlie. And then Charlie wanted to get to know me. Universal had started its own record division under Russ Regan, and one day I get a call from the guard on the Studio front gate who says, 'There's a guy named Charlie Manson in a white bus whose says he's here to see you.' He comes into my office with five girls—and they're all loaded. Charlie and his merry band of gypsies start singing, the girls start to get undressed. They are as high as a kite. I call Russ and say come over and take a meeting, and see what's going on."

Stromberg then takes the barefooted Manson and the girls to Regan's office. "He's in full hippie regalia and he sits lotus-style on Regan's desk and Russ is totally intimidated. He starts to play and sing these fucking weird songs and the girls start dancing. Russ says, 'What the fuck is this?' but gives us a few hundred dollars to make a demo."

Manson and company then move to the Gold Star recording studio on Santa Monica Boulevard near Vine Street in Hollywood—a venue favored by the big recording artists of the time like Sonny and Cher, Jimi Hendrix, and the Monkees.

"They hire an engineer," recalls Stromberg, "everyone takes acid, the girls take their clothes off, and Charlies starts improvising with love songs about eating out of the garbage dump. He's singing these weird songs and Russ walks in to see how his money is being spent and wants to take control. He says, 'What about singing some blues songs? Baby, I know you've got it in you.' But the thing (recording) was terrible."

As a sop to Manson, Stromberg says he suggested Manson might like to get involved in a movie they planned to make at Universal about a black Jesus who confronts Romans—who in the movie are belligerent Southern rednecks. That project also came to naught.

Afterwards, Stromberg, who admits he enjoyed lunches and

socializing with Manson, recalls, "Then the shit really came down after the news broke about Manson's arrest. Suddenly those tapes disappear."

Regan, as the boss of the record company, with an impressive track record in the music industry that saw him sign young singers like Elton John, Barry White, and Neil Diamond, was panic stricken and terrified by the thought that his dazzling career might come crashing down if he was linked to an accused mass murderer.

And Stromberg says he too was scared because Manson once came over to his house and knew he was married to a black actress. After the arrests he said the FBI told him they had a list of people Manson intends to kill, "and your name is on that list."

Stromberg said he was so terrified he ran off and hid out in Europe for three months.

Not long after, those tapes popped up, this time in the hands of Manson's ex-jail pal Phil Kaufman, who had been released from Terminal Island. He produced a new album from those tapes in an effort to cash in on Manson's notoriety. But the album, called *Lie*, flopped.

MANSON'S RECORDING CAREER was going nowhere fast. His second recording session—this one set up by Wilson's buddy Jakobson—was also a disaster.

"The studio guys and engineers kept telling Charlie what to do, and he ignored them," recalled Paul Watkins, who went along for the second studio session. "Charlie insisted the girls sing along in some recordings. No rehearsals, kind of a seat-of-the-pants thing. By the time we left, Charlie was totally pissed off by the way they had treated him." A third time, Manson and the girls showed up at Brian Wilson's house to record an album of songs that also never saw the light of day. Wilson, hiding in his bedroom, avoided them.

Stephen Despar, a recording engineer who designed Brian Wilson's home studio, described his encounter with Manson at one recording session. "I think Brian, Carl, and Mike saw right through Charlie's shroud of self-proclaimed truism, but also realized he was just a means by which Dennis could find easy sex with many young girls, and so indulged Dennis's use of the studio as a way of staying on his pimp's good side." His version of the recording session quoted on the website called the Smiley Smile Message Board blog, went like this: "There were several late-night sessions, until I finally refused to record him further. I can handle almost any artist's idiosyncrasies, of which Charlie had many, but it was the smell of this unkempt and unwashed human that I had to sit next to at the console that I could not or rather did not wish to endure any longer," said Despar. "Finally I told him that if he wanted a successful demo recording he was going to need to settle down and listen to me. I was on his side. 'Just follow my instructions and play real good. Give me your best, and I'll give you mine.'"

Eventually there was no happy ending for Manson and the girls in Wilson's makeshift paradise. Endless reveries of unprotected group coitus had its negative side, at least for Dennis. The nasty kicker was that those who took advantage of willing sex partners quickly discovered that one insidious side effect of this sexual freedom was widespread clap.

In all the wide-eyed propaganda about the Manson Family's "Isn't this wonderful" free love doctrine of group sex—particularly at the Sunset Boulevard estate—one of the unwelcome outcomes was a severe outbreak of gonorrhea, which was to affect both men and women.

The clap was rampant.

Young Manson recruit Dianne Lake said hygiene was never a top priority. "The girls battled impetigo, crusty sores, and skin infections—not to mention the clap. Personal hygiene was somewhat lacking."

After a particularly widespread outbreak of the disease that persisted, host Wilson had to call his personal doctor for urgent appointments, and then ended up footing the bill for penicillin treatment for everyone affected. Or at least the Beach Boys did.

Nick Grillo, the Beach Boys' manager, and the accountants at the group's Brother Records office were stunned when, over a period of a couple of months, they received medical bills from Dennis Wilson's family physician chronicling massive penicillin treatments for assorted patients they had never heard of. Another large bill also raised eyebrows: dental treatment for a patient they had no knowledge of by the name of Sadie Mae Glutz.

And that wasn't all. Mr. Wilson was footing the bill for other things. His Ferrari, driven by Family member Clem Grogan, somehow collided with a moving wall. Or so "Scramblehead" (as Grogan was called) insisted. He later admitted; "I wanted to see how fast it could take a curve."

Beach Boy Mike Love, who attended several of Manson-sponsored free-for-all parties at the mansion, wrote about being offered the opportunity to shower with a couple of Manson girls. He reportedly declined. He was also concerned that his kin was being royally screwed by Manson and his followers, and not just in the carnal sense.

"Bruce Johnston and I finally drove out to Dennis's house to meet his new roommates over dinner," Love recalled. "After we'd eaten, Manson told us to come into the den where he turned on a strobe light, which revealed all of his girls lying there naked. He started passing out LSD tabs and orchestrating sex partners. I love the female form, but this was too much even for me."

Love said there was one more incident that truly upset him. In 1968, he discovered that his wife Suzanne was having an affair with his cousin Dennis. He said after they separated he was told that his ex-wife and his cousin would often go out, leaving his two young children with a new babysitter—one that Dennis had hand-picked, named Susan Atkins.

In his 2016 memoir, *Good Vibrations: My Life as a Beach Boy*, Love encapsulated the entire Dennis madcap lifestyle noting that his cousin was always guileless in the way he treated those who crossed his path, particularly when it came to allowing Manson and his girls to have the run of his spacious home and roam freely on his three acre estate. He observed that they exploited Dennis, used his charge cards, took his clothes, ate his food and drove his Mercedes which they also wrecked. And then they repaid his generosity by ransacking the house and helping themselves to just about everything that wasn't nailed down including his guitars and gold records. By the time it was all over, Love reckoned that Wilson's hospitality cost him dearly—somewhere in the range of $100,000 plus.

IN HIS DECEMBER 1968 interview with the British *Record Mirror*, the bloom, for Wilson, was still not off the rose. When asked if he still supported "those people," he replied, "No, if anything they're supporting me. I had all the rich status symbols, Rolls Royce, Ferrari, home after home. Then I woke up, gave away 50 to 60 percent of my money. Now I live in one small room, with one candle, and I'm happy finding myself."

But that was bunk. When Wilson had finally had enough, he chickened out and was unable to confront his guests and tell them to leave. Instead, he fled his mansion and moved into the home of his music company friend Gregg Jakobson. Then into a smaller house in Malibu.

Around that time, he talked about his radical downsizing to British rock writer Keith Altham: "I give everything I have away. What I am wearing and what's in that suitcase is it. I don't even have a car. I have a 1934 Dodge pickup truck which someone gave me. (Presumably the gift giver was Dennis's houseguest Charles Watson, who owned a Dodge pickup.) I could have anything I want. I just have to go out and get it. If it's worth having, it's worth giving. The smile you send out will return to you."

Dennis, however, was forced to hand over the problem of dealing with his long-running guests to his Brother Records office, and within days, Manson and the girls were legally evicted. They all eventually moved back to the familiar, comfortable squalor of the Spahn Ranch. But that wasn't the end of it.

In their free and easy music partnership, Manson had presented Wilson with a song he had written called "Cease to Exist."

Wilson said he liked it, and he left Manson with the distinct impression that it would be part of the Beach Boys' next recording. And it was.

Only Manson's "Cease to Exist" was now called "Never Learn Not to Love." It was released in December 1968 as the B-side to the group's "Bluebirds over the Mountain" single.

And even more aggravating was that the songwriter was listed only as Dennis Wilson. Manson didn't get a mention.

Wilson reckoned that Manson owed him something for his largesse, and in a way this was payback time. But Manson did not quite see it his way. In his eyes he had been double-crossed, and Wilson had purloined what was rightly his. It just fed into his whole philosophy that everyone in the record business was a crook and a liar.

"'Cheats. Con men. Selfish bastards,' was what he called them," remembered Paul Watkins. "Funny, because Charlie was just getting a taste of his own medicine."

Not long before the August 1969 murders, Manson met Wilson, handed him a bullet, and cryptically declared, "Every time you look at it, I want you to think how nice it is your kids are still safe."

Charlie got the desired effect because Wilson was truly terrified. After the murder story broke, he told *Rolling Stone*, "As long as I live I'll never talk about that."

So WHAT DO WE KNOW was going on in Manson's mind during his sojourn on Sunset?

There was little doubt that he had his own agenda and was already mapping out his showbiz career, which involved writing music and even traveling to perform with the Beach Boys. He was always careful to keep in touch with his probation officer and feed him the kind of propaganda that, through years of experience, he knew would keep the bureaucracy off his back. On one occasion, he asked his probation officer for permission to travel to Texas with the Beach Boys, claiming he was scheduled to perform with them. It sounded like an effort to impress. But shortly afterwards, he did an about-turn, informing the probation department that the Beach Boys had gone to Texas without him. It is unconfirmed, but it is quite possible that in Manson's strange mind, he reckoned that if the Beach Boys could hit the road in May 1968 with one guru from India—namely the Maharishi—it wasn't too much of a stretch to envisage that he too might get to share the stage with the Beach Boys.

An intriguing inter-office probation department letter dated December 12, 1968, sheds fascinating light on the stories Manson was spinning and the crafty way he tried to manipulate those whose job was to keep tabs on him. Like a child trying to please a parent, he spins his yarns. How much was true and how much merely a figment of his imagination is open to speculation. It shows how Manson was trying—with some success—to influence his probation officer, who swallowed his tall tales hook, line and sinker.

Dear Mr. Wahl,

We would like to review our courtesy supervision of subject and bring you up to date on his situation.

Last July 1968, Manson thought it best for everyone to move from the home of Dennis Wilson in the Pacific Palisades area, so he located himself at Spahn's Movie Ranch situated between Chatsworth and Santa Susana. At one time the ranch was used frequently as a location for Western movies, and presently it is used in stabling horses. There is a considerable number of livestock at the ranch now. We visited Manson there on 10-3-68, and found him dressed in Western clothes and performing well in his role as a cowboy. He claimed that the setting provided him with enough activity to do something worthwhile, and that he was distant enough from any negative influence.

On November 5, 1968, Manson called our office requesting that he be permitted to leave Spahn's Movie Ranch as he had an opportunity to locate himself on another ranch known as Meyers Ranch about twenty miles east of Trona, California. Manson claimed that he was getting bored at Spahn's Ranch and that Meyers Ranch would be a good change. He was anxious to continue with ranch life as a means of not taking on too much responsibility and thought in that respect it would be simple for him to stay out of trouble. Manson also claimed that Dennis Wilson was giving him advances to pay his expenses which would be deducted from any royalties due Manson when two of his songs are released on the next Beach Boys record album. We decided to allow subject to change his residence.

Subject last personally reported to our office on 12-5-68 advising that he was still staying at the Meyers Ranch and that he had to be in Los Angeles on business that date for a talk with Dennis Wilson. Subject claimed that his two songs were being released and that he had $5,000 coming from one song and that he was to make a personal settlement with Wilson on the balance due him from the other song. Subject claimed that he had also been gold prospecting in the Death Valley area, and by good fortune had discovered a vein of gold bearing ore in one of the mountains at a high altitude. Manson stated that he and two other prospectors had already filed a claim on this mine.

Subject has submitted his monthly reports to our office regularly and otherwise has kept us informed of any changes effecting [sic] him. He is courteous and polite with us, and would like to remain in our district. There have been no further negative reports about subject and it may be that subject will continue to improve in his conduct while in our district. We, therefore, would be willing to accept a transfer of supervision if you so desire.

Very truly yours,
Angus D. McEachen
Chief U.S. Probation Officer

Terry Melcher was a reluctant trial witness in 1970.

TERRY MELCHER: QUE SERA SERA

"Everybody speculated that Manson sent his minions up there to get rid of Terry because he was angry about not getting a record deal. But Terry and I talked about it later, and Terry said Manson knew he had moved because Manson or someone from his organization left a note on Terry's porch in Malibu."

—Mark Lindsay, musician and former housemate of Terry Melcher

"I like Terry. Terry is a nice, gentle person. He's a peaceful person. He doesn't lie. He's treated me right. I would consider him a friend. But I think all this madness has scared him. I think it scared him into thinking that I am somebody I am not. A lot of people think that Manson is some great monster, but the only monster Manson is what the media created. And the district attorney created"

—Charles Manson, radio interview

In November 1994, I flew to Carmel, California, to interview Doris Day. She had long ago abandoned her movie career and the Hollywood environs for the calm confines of Northern California. There, she lived in almost splendid isolation in a mountaintop house, which she shared with a score of stray dogs she had collected on local streets. The seventy-two-year-old was about to release *The Love Album*, a compilation of her old hits drawn from three Hollywood recording sessions done in 1967. The story went that the tapes of those recordings had been lost and were now miraculously rediscovered. They included evergreens like "For All We Know," "Are You Lonesome Tonight," "Life Is Just a Bowl of Cherries," and "Let Me Call You Sweetheart," all slowed down and sung with great feeling.

The album was going to be launched in England, and her longtime publicist, Linda Dozoretz, called to say that Day would be happy to grant me an interview for the London *Daily Express*—she knew she had a strong and faithful fan following in Old Blighty. Indeed, the star of *Calamity Jane* and those *Pillow Talk* romantic comedies opposite Rock Hudson—her handsome leading man, who himself had led a secret life until his dying day—was still a big name even if she had put her career in Hollywood mothballs for the hermitic life. And she was still the Unsinkable Doris Day, having survived two marriages and the recent death of her third husband and manager, Martin Melcher.

Soon after he died in 1969, Day discovered that Melcher's managerial skills had been seriously lacking. Relying on blind and ignorant faith in the so-called financial acumen of the family's longtime lawyer and financial advisor, Jerome B. Rosenthal, her fortune had disappeared. To the tune of $200 million. The family's legal team claimed that for decades, Rosenthal had made investments using the riches from Day's career without the knowledge of either Day or Melcher, as well as helping himself to fat commissions.

But she was lucky: to the rescue came her handsome twenty-seven-year-old son, Terry, her only child and the apple of her eye. He put aside his career as a record producer, and for years literally went to war to recover her funds that he claimed had been ripped off by Rosenthal. In Day's 1976 autobiography, *Doris Day: Her Own Story* written with A.E. Hotchner, Terry tells about an ugly showdown he finally had with the man he had always called, "Uncle Jerry" soon after his stepfather died and they discovered the missing millions. In her book, Day recalls her son telling her she was broke: "Mom, these past four days, I've had a showdown with Rosenthal, and the bad news is—God, I wish I didn't have to tell you—but the fact is, you don't have anything. Not a penny. The hotels are bankrupt, all the oil wells are dry, and there aren't any cattle. Nothing, Mom, and what's even worse, you have a lot of debts—like around $450,000. Most of it is taxes. They have to be paid. You may have to sell this house."

After a nearly decade-long legal battle, Melcher was able to recoup enough money to prevent his mother from having to file bankruptcy and lose her home. Finally, a California Court of Appeal upheld a $22.8 million judgment in her favor against Rosenthal, although after ten years of appeals, she finally received only a fraction of that amount—some $6 million paid to her by Rosenthal's insurance company. When Rosenthal died in 2007, she was shorted for good. The re-release of *The Love Album*, which Melcher produced, was one of the gimmicks used by her son to help get Day back on her feet. He was also in charge of the Doris Day Animal Foundation.

When my writer wife, Sally, and I landed at Monterey Airport, Melcher was there to greet us. I had first met him in 1967 at parties thrown by Derek Taylor, once the press officer and friend of the Beatles, who had moved to Hollywood from Liverpool and London. Because of his Fab Four connection, Taylor was quickly hired by The Beach Boys, The Byrds, Paul Revere and the Raiders, and other up-and-coming groups working with Melcher. A fast-rising music producer, Melcher was close to them all and was credited as cowriter, along with John Phillips, Mike Love, and Scott McKenzie, of the 1988 hit "Kokomo."

He was Doris's son from her first marriage, in 1941, to trombonist Al Jorden. As the story goes, being an abusive, womanizing man who beat up his young wife, he ordered the eighteen-year-old newbie singer, Doris Mary Ann Kappelhoff, to abort their child before they married. They split up in 1943, and three years later, she had switched musical instrument allegiance from trombone player Jorden to saxophonist George Weidler. That one lasted just three years, and she hired a new lawyer in Hollywood to handle her divorce: Jerome B. Rosenthal.

In 1951 Day married for the third time—to her agent, Martin Melcher. He legally adopted the young boy, who took the Melcher name. However, the stepfather-stepson relationship was not a smooth one. Melcher complained that the boy was a spoiled brat, and "a sissy" to boot. He felt the need to toughen him up, insisting he be sent away to a military school.

Despite his stepfather's negativity, Terry developed ambitions to perform, and he had some minor success early on, first as a singer billed as Terry Day; then, along with future Beach Boy Bruce Johnston, in the groups Bruce and Terry and, more notably, The Rip Chords ("Hey Little Cobra"). At Derek Taylor's party we talked cordially, though the main talking point at Taylor's party was its most celebrated guest: in the lobby, perched on a high-backed wicker chair, sat Brian Wilson. "Brian isn't feeling too well tonight," Taylor apologized, soft-pedaling his condition. Physically Wilson was present; mentally, I wasn't so sure. While guests mingled, he sat still and lifeless, neither talking nor reacting to the guests who approached him as though he were a prize exhibit. I can attest that he was breathing; but, for all he did, he could have been a marble Buddha statue.

On the other hand, Melcher was quite full of himself, as one might expect from the son of showbiz privilege. He was slightly arrogant, a typical California rich kid, with a sun-kissed mop of carefully coiffed blond hair and a bushy mustache. He had struck gold partly because of his musical know-how and partly because his famous mother was a big stockholder at Columbia Records, though, in all fairness to Terry, he did exceptionally well, quickly proving he had the right touch. Aside from producing the likes of The Byrds and Paul Revere, success enabled him to become the Beatles' sub-publisher for the US, Canada, and Japan. Along with Taylor, record producer Lou Adler, and John Phillips, they promoted the hugely successful June 1967 Monterey Pop Festival, a watershed moment in popular music.

On the personal front, Melcher also enjoyed a high-profile lifestyle, dating a slew of gorgeous women including Tuesday Weld, Michelle Phillips, and Candice Bergen. Another child of Hollywood, Bergen was a model and the daughter of America's most famous ventriloquist, Edgar Bergen. She, like Melcher, had grown up in the privileged confines of Beverly Hills and Manhattan, and they made a handsome couple as they set up house together in a hilltop mansion on Cielo Drive in April 1966. Despite this, Melcher was enjoying a hedonistic way of life—with a couple of close pals, including the priapic Dennis Wilson, they proudly formed an exclusive little club whose drug-fueled members aimed to bed as many groupies as possible. They called themselves the "Golden Penetrators."

The Penetrators stepped up their activities soon after Charles Manson and his female entourage moved into Wilson's house on Sunset Boulevard, where sexual fodder was free and plentiful, requiring no courtship whatsoever.

In 1994, Melcher greeted us warmly when we landed in Monterey for the short drive to Carmel and our meeting with Doris. He was oozing charm, looked a little chubbier that I remembered him, and his hair no longer was surfer blond. He knew we were there to write about his mother's new album and that the market for nostalgia in England and other parts of Europe was strong—whereas in America a re-release of Day's old songs might be greeted with ho-hum. Without prompting, he waxed enthusiastically about his brand-new Cadillac. "Just look at this," he said, pulling out into traffic for the fifteen-minute ride. "The technology is amazing. All you do is punch in any address you want, and the car will direct you how to get there." He was like a schoolboy showing off a new toy as he twiddled a few knobs, and lo and behold the car went into navigation mode, flashing directions on the dashboard screen. Our destination was the Cypress Inn, a charming Spanish-style boutique hotel owned by his mother in the middle of town. When we walked into the bar, it was filled with the usual cocktail crowd—but with one big difference. Most customers sipping martinis had dogs in their laps. Doris Day's hotel was one of the first pet-friendly hostelries, and considered the crown jewel of Carmel.

I reminded Melcher that we had met at Taylor's parties and, as we ordered a round of drinks, we exchanged small talk about our mutual friend. I told him that I had toured with the Beatles in 1964, and added that in 1970 I had also written *Five to Die*—the first book about the Manson murders in 1970 with journalist Jerry LeBlanc. I told him I was very familiar with the case and particularly his involvement in the trial. At the mere mention of Manson's name, he suddenly froze. He shuddered, and his face turned grim. Even a quarter-century later I had obviously opened an old wound. Suspiciously, he asked: "You *are* here to talk to Doris, right?"

"Of course," I said, trying to allay his concerns. "I know all about the case because I was at the trial and saw you testify. You looked pretty miserable. And I know all about your visits to the Spahn Ranch with Gregg Jakobson and a camera crew to shoot a documentary." For several long moments, he was silent. I don't think he had spoken about the case with anyone, much less a journalist, in decades. I could see his mind debating whether or not to open that door. Then he spoke. "You must swear to me that if we talk about any of that stuff now, you won't write a word about it," he said. "Your story is only about Doris and the album. Promise?" I agreed. He ordered another drink and began to talk—cagily at first—about his Manson misadventures. He sighed, "It destroyed my life...destroyed."

"Dennis [Wilson] thought Charlie was some sort of guru, that he was a genius who also wrote great music," he began. "I'd met Charlie at Dennis's house. Whenever he sang, he took the place over. We had to listen."

Then a few months later, in May 1969, Jakobson invited Melcher to go to the Spahn Ranch and listen to Manson play. "Gregg was real excited about him and kept saying how original he was. He told me there were three guitars and maybe thirty voices in great harmony. So I went. I listened. I met Manson one other time at the ranch and then returned once again not long after."

But this first "audition" stuck in his memory, because it was unlike anything he had ever seen.

"We walked into this crummy, rundown ranch, and then we scrambled over the ground, as this scrawny guy—one hand holding a guitar—clambered up on a big rock overlooking a stream," he told me. "And he sang maybe ten or fifteen songs. And it was pretty odd because from time to time the girls sitting on the dirt below him kind of joined in—disjointed harmony and amateurish. They oohed and aahed whenever he said a word. I was impressed by Charlie's strength and the obvious leadership that he had over these people. I was also impressed by their ability to survive out in the country there, camping in tents with no bathrooms or showers. A totally different hippie way of life. I'd never seen anything like that in the rock 'n' roll world."

Was he also impressed by Manson's singing? "Average," he replied. "Not impressed enough on that level as far as his musical talents to want to pursue it and make a record with him. But I knew someone who I thought might help." So, indeed, on his next visit, Melcher and Jakobson brought session guitarist Mike Deasy, who owned his own mobile recording studio. Deasy had worked with all the music greats: Elvis, Sinatra, Streisand. And he obviously enjoyed his Spahn outing a little too much; during the performance someone slipped him a tab of LSD, and he collapsed on the spot. He had to be carried back to Melcher's car and driven home.

Afterward, Melcher insisted he made no promises to Manson about a contract. "I guess I was hedging because I didn't want to rain on his parade. I told him he'd have to join the musicians' union, and he wasn't crazy to hear that. They were living in the rough, so I gave him everything

I had in my pocket. Maybe fifty bucks, which, in retrospect, probably wasn't wise. Later I heard that Charlie told the girls that the cash was a down payment on future contract riches." Certainly being seen, in plain sight, receiving cash from the big shot record producer gave the impression that he had been a hit. "I gave them the money because I felt sorry for them," Melcher told me. (At the time of our interview I did not know there had been rumors in music circles that when Melcher agreed to audition Manson, he was at the time wearing another hat: representative of Apple Records, through his connections with his friend Derek Taylor, who had gone back to London to work for the Beatles' label. But a friend of Melcher's later told me that Melcher seriously thought that Charlie might be the perfect fit for Apple!)

But what disturbed Melcher most during his so-far idyllic journey to the rustic confines of the movie ranch was a sudden and dramatic change in the beatific mood that had been carefully staged by Manson and the girls. "As we all walked back up to the parking lot level of the ranch, I saw this guy all in black sitting in a truck. He got out. He had a six-gun strapped to his waist, and I wasn't sure whether it was loaded or not. But it was scary because it looked like he was going to draw the gun. He did. And he was totally drunk. He started waving it in front of us. Charlie carefully handed his guitar to one of the girls. He went up to the guy with the gun, took it out of his hand and began savagely beating the shit out of him. The guy was bleeding profusely and fell to the ground almost unconscious. There was no conversation. Charlie retrieved his guitar, and we all moved on. I saw this gentle musician suddenly turn into a savage." When news of the August 1969 murder at his former residence broke big, Melcher said he and Bergen were like the rest of Hollywood—terrified out of their minds. "It was my old house, although we'd moved out in January 1969. Then Roman leased the place from Rudi (Altobelli). Corpses and blood in the place we once lived. Our home. And pregnant Sharon. And what was worse, no one knew who the killers were. So it was panic stations for everyone we knew. There were just rumors and gossip along with those weird stories about Roman and Jay and drugs. Everybody was running scared. It made no sense. Candy kept telling me that if we still lived there we'd be dead."

But Melcher's journey into hell really began in late November 1969. Two men in business suits with bulges in their jackets showed up at his house in Malibu. He knew instantly that they were cops—LAPD homicide detectives, in fact. And they didn't beat about the bush. "Do you know anybody who wants to kill you?" one detective asked. "I was stunned," he said. Melcher asked if this was about Tate's murder. The detectives were tight-lipped. Cryptically, they told him that arrests for the murders were imminent. "But, please, keep this to yourself." When he asked for more information he was met with polite silence. "As they were leaving, one turned to me and said simply, 'You might think about getting some guards and guns into your house.'"

He was floored. Guards and guns—what did that mean? Were the killers after him? And things only got worse. Just days after the detectives' visit, the suspects were publicly identified. Upon hearing Manson, Watson, and Atkins named, Melcher says he went into shock, followed by deep depression. "Candy called it our Kafkaesque period. I could hardly speak. I knew them. My brain was scrambled. I didn't know what to think. Only that I knew this guy and that in my gut I had known all along that he was big trouble. But I had no idea how bad."

What Melcher did not talk about was the fact that, along with the emotional traumas surrounding the murders, his two-year relationship with Bergen was also falling apart. Years later I approached the actress about discussing the period, but she declined. However, she had addressed the issue in her best-selling 1984 memoir *Knock Wood*. She writes that their relationship was already wearing thin. "My professional absences were a strain on a relationship already overloaded with tensions."

She recalls that Melcher returned from the Spahn Ranch audition and asked if she would like to accompany him when he returned to meet Manson and his girls who, he said, sat naked around their leader as they

322 | MANSON EXPOSED

all sang. "Why can't they sing dressed?" she snapped. "It was a rhetorical question: we both knew I'd hate it and they—beatific and bare-assed and peering into the hole where my soul should have been—would hate me..."

Melcher's paranoia wasn't helped by police returning to his house. They were not threatening, but on one visit they told him that several of the girls were pregnant, and they all claimed he was the father. "I got so pissed about that, I got out some pictures of girls I'd gone with and I said, 'Now look, why would I hang out with women like that...when I have this?' That made sense to them, and they backed off."

Melcher, of course, was bluffing about that because he did partake of the girls, as did his pals, including Dennis Wilson. When Susan Atkins' full confession broke on the *Los Angeles Times*' front page in mid-December, Melcher said he was bereft. He ran out and bought a double-barreled shotgun and slept with it by his bedside. "The whole thing turned people against each other. Some people were scared of me. I recognized that because that was my own mindset. I was afraid of everyone else. When I finally went to a psychiatrist, he offered no easy answer. Just this: 'Be prepared to be crazy for a while.'"

And he was. "I was like the walking dead—a zombie swallowing Valium morning noon and night, anything that would help numb my pain. I couldn't sleep because every day the cops came back. They'd show me photos of hippie-looking guys and kept asking, 'Do you know who this is?' I recognized Tex Watson right away. Only he looked much weirder in their photo. I'd met Tex at Dennis's house. Gregg and I liked Tex. He came to parties at Cielo Drive when I was overseas and Gregg was housesitting."

He said he was even more terrified when first summoned to testify in December 1969 to the Los Angeles Grand Jury about his relationship with Manson, and then again when called as a prosecution witness in the 1970 trial, even though Bugliosi carefully limited questions to Melcher's visits to the Spahn Ranch. In court, he looked a shadow of his former self, no longer the cocky record mogul—instead of bronzed, gray-faced, drawn, and looking quite ill. And I noticed he trembled, talking so softly that he was repeatedly asked to speak up into the microphone so he could be heard.

AFTER THE MURDERS, Melcher had turned down all interview requests. But in 1974 he suddenly emerged in an interview with Tom Nolan for *Rolling Stone*. He had his reason for breaking his silence. After a few years of near-reclusive living and depending on drugs for his daily survival, he was trying to pick up the pieces of his shattered life. Literally. In April 1972, he had crashed his Harley, breaking both his legs, and risking amputation of one. He spent eight months in and out of hospitals, his recovery slow and painful but helped by a new marriage to actress Melissa E. Brown. He had spent the last couple of years recording an album of his own music, called simply *Terry Melcher*. It was an eclectic, mournful odd lot that included Jackson Browne's sad song, "These Days," a duet in which he got a little help from a singer named Doris Day.

It was to be his comeback. On the album front cover he sported a neatly coiffed handlebar mustache and wore a white suit over a white turtleneck. On the back, he posed with Melissa. His backup musicians were Ry Cooder, Beach Boy Bruce Johnston, and his old Byrds pal Chris Hillman. One critic, confused by the offering, and interpreting the music as being part byproduct of Melcher's disturbed life, wrote: "It's an eccentric work that suggests he's given up on optimism but even on despair." Indeed, Melcher had put blood, sweat, and tears into the album, writing, singing, and playing piano. He hoped it would be his reentry into normalcy, and a music world he loved, after the traumas of the past.

And he decided *Rolling Stone* would be the perfect platform to aid that re-entry. So, for the first time, he talked publicly about the Manson madness, particularly about his court appearance and the ordeal he faced testifying in front of Manson and his three crazed, wild-eyed girls.

"Manson sat there smiling at me through the whole thing," he said. "The three girls, too. One of them had her skirt up, doing a little leg thing under the table. When I was finished, their lawyer, Irving Kanarek, said something like, 'We want Mr. Melcher to know that the defendants have never borne him any ill will.' And of course, I've felt wonderful ever since," he cynically added.

When Melcher died of cancer in 2004, ten years after we had talked in Carmel, friends said they were still firmly convinced that he really had been Manson's target up on Cielo. The theory had led to endless stories reinforcing that thesis. As for Melcher, he said to *Rolling Stone* that it was almost a year after the murders that he finally realized that was not the case. Manson and his gang of killers were *not* looking for him the night of the slaughter. "[Manson] had been trying to get in touch with me to play me some more music. He found out where I lived in Malibu," Terry told the magazine. "So he went to my house, but I wasn't home. He took a telescope off the sundeck to show it to my friend Jakobson so Gregg would give him my number. Manson knew where I lived.

"He knew I didn't live in Bel Air. Gregg didn't bother to tell me about that until almost a year later. The police didn't bother to tell me that. For nine months they had me thinking those people got killed because I couldn't be found. My guilt was monumental. I felt, 'Why couldn't it have been me? How much easier it would have been!'"

Even Manson himself blew the revenge motive out of the water in his own interview with *Rolling Stone* magazine in December 2013. "Yeah, it was Terry Melcher's house and he [Melcher] lied to everybody at the ranch, said he was gonna do stuff he didn't do. He got their hopes up, you dig? Terry was a spoiled brat that had seven automobiles and didn't have nothing to worry about. I'd cheated him in a card game and won a house!" (Whatever that meant.) "It was part card game, part con, all devil, heh heh. But I won it. He owed me. So, Terry Melcher was part of it. He did a lot of things that wasn't right. But no one was mad at Terry Melcher. Not really."

After dinner and drinks at our Carmel hotel, Terry seemed visibly relieved, as if unburdening himself had helped. He made me swear once again not to write anything he'd told me, particularly about his nervous breakdown. "This story you're doing is for Doris. She's gone through hell and needs a lot of support."

He lightened up considerably when I asked if we could do our interview at Day's house in the Carmel Hills. "You wouldn't want to do it there," he laughed. "The place is overrun with dogs." So the next day we met her for lunch at the Quail Lodge Country Club. Melcher did the introductions, then quickly excused himself. Our conversation stuck mostly to her music and her life. She was bouncy and upbeat and said she had no desire whatsoever to make movies again. Then she alluded indirectly to the Manson case: "We've gone through some hard times, particularly after Marty died. He ran everything, wrote the checks, and I left everything to him. My money, my movies, my life. Then we went through financial hell. I thought we were broke. Thank God Terry came in and took over. He had a lot on his plate, but he rolled up his sleeves and said, 'Mom, we can beat this.' And we did."

"And you can imagine," she added, "how upset he was after those murders at his old place? As soon as I heard, I called and said, 'There's maniacs around. Quick…leave the country. Go to France. Get away now until things calm down. We argued. He said no: his work was in LA. So what did he do? He moved to my house in Malibu."

The interview about Day was published ten days later. As promised, no mention whatsoever was made about Melcher and Manson. Or the house on Cielo Drive.

Bernard "Lotsapoppa" Crowe was shot and left for dead.

REPORTS OF HIS DEATH WERE GREATLY EXAGGERATED

Whatever's necessary to do, you do it. When somebody needs to be killed, there's no wrong. You do it. And kill whoever gets in your way."

—Lynette "Squeaky" Fromme,
1973 documentary *Manson*

While criminologists will probably pontificate into the twenty-second century in an effort to explain the mayhem of August 1969, most agree that one major incident took place in late July 1969 that, on closer examination, might be considered crucial to making some kind of sense of the events that played out less than a fortnight later on Cielo Drive. The killing of Gary Hinman was inexorably linked to what happened on those two August nights.

Within a few days of the Hinman murder, Bobby Beausoleil, a key suspect, was in custody. In a piece of criminal stupidity, Beausoleil had helped himself to the victim's car and was arrested on August 6, 1969, in San Luis Obispo after an alert officer spotted him sleeping in the back of the vehicle. A routine DMV check indicated the owner of the Fiat station wagon was Gary Hinman, recent murder victim. Police said

Beausoleil's clothes were blood-stained and a knife was found in the car's tire well. Beausoleil, who had given police a fake name, was then booked on suspicion of murder and returned to Los Angeles.

As far back as December 1969, when I first went to the very heart of darkness—the Spahn Ranch—to learn more about who Manson was and talked to Paul Watkins and Brooks Poston, two of his most devoted servants at one time, they offered this explanation: The Cielo Drive murders were carried out in a desperate effort to get Bobby Beausoleil off the hook.

"Charlie really believed that Bobby was taking the fall for him," Watkins told me half a century ago. "He wanted to get Bobby out of jail because, after all, he was the one who got Bobby into that jam in the first place. He had sent him to get the cash and stocks and bonds from Hinman, and now Bobby was rotting in jail and facing life in prison. And Charlie could sympathize about what life in prison was all about."

Watkins said Manson was also impressed because "Bobby never blew the whistle on him or anyone else involved in killing Gary. 'He's young but he's no snitch,'" Charlie told Watkins. Well, save for the fact that Beausoleil threw Susan Atkins under the bus when he was arrested, implicating her in Hinman's murder.

It did not take a giant leap in reasoning for both Watkins and Poston to surmise that Charlie probably sent Tex and the girls out to kill and to write anti-police and racist daubings like "Political Piggy" in the victims' blood on walls of the all the murder scenes, which were to be nearly identical to blood splatters found at the Hinman house. Those signature "messages" would confuse investigators into believing that a black gang was responsible for the crime.

Stupidly simplistic as that sounded, both Watkins and Poston said that Charlie felt that when detectives investigating the Tate killings saw those striking similarities at the Tate and LaBianca houses, they would rule out Beausoleil and realize the real killers were still on the loose.

If Manson's twisted and simple-minded kindergarten reasoning worked, the cops would then realize they had the wrong guy. And Bobby Beausoleil would be kicked free!

Manson's reasoning was often bizarre, to say the least. For example, after the LaBiancas were massacred, Manson ordered Linda Kasabian to take Rosemary LaBianca's wallet and credit cards and dump them in a gas station rest room in an area of Los Angeles (Sylmar) he believed (wrongly) was a black neighborhood. His warped thinking went like this: Some locals would find the wallet, use the credit cards and police would immediately assume the murder of the LaBiancas was the work of blacks.

IN THE EARLY HOURS of the morning of August 1, 1969, just days before Bobby Beausoleil was arrested on August 6 for the murder of Gary Hinman, another assault played out at an apartment on Franklin Avenue in the heart of Hollywood, next door to the famous Magic Castle and just a few blocks from the popular Grauman's Chinese Theater and the star-studded Walk of Fame. The victim was twenty-seven-year-old Bernard Crowe, a black musician-turned-drug dealer known in local dope-dealing circles as "The Crowe"—and affectionately nicknamed "Lotsapoppa." And despite Manson's repeated insistence that his own hands were clean of blood, and that he had never taken a single life, it is clearly established that in the early hours of August 1, he had cold-bloodedly and with malice aforethought, fired bullets into Crowe's body and left him for dead in his own apartment. It later was revealed that Crowe—who survived the assassination by playing dead and was rushed to the ER by friends after the shooting—had been shot by the same .22 Longhorn pistol that was used by Tex Watson at the Sharon Tate house a week later.

There have been several conflicting versions of what really happened that morning, including one penned by Watson in his 1978 memoir *Will You Die for Me?* While captivating, his colorful rendering could be construed as being totally self-serving, considering Watson wasn't even on the scene—although he was the root cause of the violence. As he told it, that summer he had resumed running his own part-time drug trafficking operation out of an apartment he shared with a girlfriend identified only by the fictitious first name of "Luella." (She later was identified as one Rosina Kroner, the girlfriend of Watson's Texas school buddy David Neale, who had provided friendship and Los Angeles housing to Watson.) No sooner had Neale been called up for military service, Watson moved in on his best pal's gal. However, he was still under the thrall of Manson, who ordered him to round up cash so they could build up the dune-buggy armada in the desert, which was to be the Family's escape route once helter-skelter broke out and the blood began to flow in the streets of America.

Watson, whose brain was more than slightly scrambled by his massive intake of assorted hallucinogens, offered to sell Lotsapoppa some good dope: 25 kilos of grass for $2,500 in cash. Crowe agreed and, after much toing and froing, gave Watson the cash, and Watson left promising faithfully to return with the contraband. "I have to come back with the stuff," he said flashing a big smile. "You got my girl." But instead of returning—and with little regard for "my girl"—he drove straight to the Spahn Ranch and turned the cash over to Manson. Crowe was furious at the blatant rip-off and angrily called the Spahn Ranch looking for "Charlie"—meaning Watson. Manson took the call, feigning ignorance about the deal. But Crowe was relentless—if he didn't get his cash back, he screamed, he would come right over to the ranch with an army of "associates" and wreak havoc. Manson reacted even more angrily. Taking along Family member Thomas James Wallerman, a former Marine Corps Vietnam veteran, known simply as "TJ the Terrible," as backup, he sped over to Crowe's Hollywood apartment.

In his memoir, Watson recounted what he had been told by TJ: "Charlie had gone to the apartment with Randy Starr's .22 Buntline revolver. TJ was supposed to shoot him [Crowe], but he froze up and just hid behind Manson. After a brief back and forth, Charlie grabbed the gun and pulled the trigger…and nothing. Twice. Just as the towering black man begins to taunt them, the gun goes off and Crowe's got a hole in his chest/stomach. Before running out, Charlie points the gun at one of the victim's friends and demands he give him his jacket. Why? Because it was buckskin and it had fringes. Okay, but then they bailed."

Various other versions had Manson trying to talk Crowe out of seeking revenge on Watson, and then, after shooting him, kneeling down and kissing the feet of the severely wounded dealer before taking his leave, much as he had kissed the feet of Dennis Wilson in 1968, upon first meeting him at his Sunset Boulevard mansion.

A few days later, Manson, believing Crowe was a member of the Black Panthers, boasted to all comers at Spahn Ranch that he had killed Lotsapoppa. Such blatant self-promotion was uncharacteristic of him because throughout his trial and later his many TV performances, he had repeatedly insisted that he had no blood on his hands. Still he reckoned that by boasting about the killing of Crowe it would show that he feared no one, not even a Black Panther, and the shooting proved that he could and would take justice into his own hands if necessary.

After the shooting, Watson returned to the Spahn Ranch and recalled that Charlie was on such a high that he couldn't stop talking about how he 'plugged the blackie.' Everyone assumed Crowe was dead particularly when the next day there was a news report that the body of a Black Panther had been dumped near UCLA.

Watson was later to write that Manson's delusions of helter-skelter moved to red alert status. He became manic, claiming that he noticed more black men than usual were renting horses at the ranch. He worried that the Black Panthers were out for revenge and decided he needed to get out of Dodge real fast. For several days Watson said he saw an uncharacteristically panic-stricken Manson running around, making sure all Family members—walkie talkies at the ready—were armed and prepared in case the Panthers stormed the place. "Helter-skelter is coming down fast," he kept repeating.

Watson said much later he learned that Bernard Crowe—who in fact never had anything to do with the Panthers—had not died. His friends had rushed him to hospital and he had stayed out of sight, fearful that if Manson found out the Big Crowe was still alive, he might come after him again.

Crowe lived his entire life with that bullet lodged near his spine. During the Tate-LaBianca trial, Crowe's lawyer contacted Bugliosi and said his client was willing to talk to police as long as he didn't incriminate himself in any way. The prosecution offered to have the bullet removed, knowing it would help them prove that the bullet in Crowe came from the same gun that was used on Cielo Drive. No thanks, said Crowe. However, he did have a walk-on role in the trial. During the penalty phase, the prosecution called him to confirm that Manson had shot him at point blank range, to emphasize to the jury that Manson was capable of being an executioner.

I well remember Lotsapoppa's trial appearance. For the first time, Manson looked stunned—the man he thought was a corpse showed up to give evidence. And then, Manson's defense lawyer Irving Kanarek embarked on a marathon cross-examination that dragged on interminably, to no apparent purpose. By the time Kanarak was finished with his cross-examination, I'm sure Lotsappopa wished he were dead.

Manson was much later to offer his own frenetic spin on what took place at Crowe's apartment on the night he "killed" the dealer. He stressed that he had severely chastised Watson for not cleaning up his own mess, especially after Crowe threatened to seek violent revenge at the ranch if he didn't get his cash back: "It was about $5,000," Manson said in a TV interview years later. "I told [Tex], don't drag your shit to me. I told them face them. [Tex] said, 'They will kill me.' So I said, 'Okay, run home to your mummy.' [Crowe] says, 'You took my money, and we are coming to burn everything down and take the ranch.' He said, 'All you white bubbas are together.' I had to get nasty with those people. He couldn't do it, so I ended up shooting the dude."

Still, whatever the true picture, Manson knew he alone had cleaned up Watson's mess. Maybe even saved his life. In his own mind, he had bumped off this Black Panther, and Watson owed him big time. Eight days later, he decided it was payback time. Watson was sent on a mission—he was to go the house on Cielo Drive on the night of August 8, 1969. And unleash holy hell.

Whistleblower Veronica "Ronnie" Howard, who died mysteriously in 1979, told police what Susan Atkins revealed about the murders while both were in jail. Some believe she paid the price with her life.

AND THEN THERE
WERE NONE

*"Me and Tex and Bruce and Charlie took him for a ride, and we
hit him on the head with some sort of big something and it stunned
him; then we took him out and away from the road and he started
saying, 'Why, Charlie, why?' and Charlie said, 'You know why,' and
he stabbed him."*

—Steve Grogan testifying at his 1971 trial for the
murder of Donald "Shorty" Shea

Although Charles Manson did not actually murder drug dealer
Bernard Crowe, there is little doubt that his fingerprints were to
be found on corpses of people who had strong links to Manson
and his servile sycophants. During the Sharon Tate trial, the prosecutors
said they believed there were others who had fallen afoul of Manson and
could be the victims on a confidential list of those the DA lumped under
the catch-all phrase of "retaliation murders." These were unexplained
deaths or killings supposedly carried out, if not directly by Manson, then
certainly with his tacit approval. Although he was incarcerated, prosecutors said he did not hesitate to make it clear to those Family members still
running free that these "traitors" were Enemies of Manson—and that was
enough to encourage his demented troops to do whatever was necessary
to eradicate those perceived foes from the face of the earth.

One of those early killings was believed to be the brash, fledgling lawyer, Ronald Hughes, representing Leslie Van Houten. There was a report that, just before Hughes went camping, Manson—annoyed by Hughes' mutinous suggestion that Van Houten be tried separately—turned to him and hissed, "I don't want to see you in this courtroom ever again."

Vincent Bugliosi and Stephen Kay both said the accidental drowning theory was ridiculous—they believed Hughes was murdered by Manson surrogates.

Following are some of the other tragic stories behind a series of unexplained and random deaths of victims linked to the Manson Family:

Donald Jerome "Shorty" Shea
Died: August 26, 1969
Age: 35

Donald Shea was a struggling Hollywood stuntman, a foreman at the Spahn Ranch, and he fell deeply—very deeply—afoul of Manson. The "Shorty" nickname was a bit of a joke: at six-foot-four and weighing in at well over 200 pounds, he resembled a heavier version of Spaghetti Western bad guy actor Lee Van Cleef. He reportedly served in the military in Korea and was medically discharged in 1951 after crushing his pelvis and hips in a parachute accident. He harbored dreams of becoming the next Clint Eastwood or Burt Reynolds, but never quite made the cut, although he did land bit roles in such forgettable films as *The Fabulous Bastard from Chicago* and the odd soft porn flick. But it didn't pay much, so from time to time he supplemented his meager income by working as a bouncer at strip clubs or as a salesman at local porn shops. He had lived at the ranch before Manson and was an adept horse wrangler; but, from the moment Manson rode into town in his black bus, the two men clashed. The hot-headed Shea was irritated by what he saw as the Family trying to take over. (He was right, of course!) And Manson believed it was Shea who had tipped off the Sheriff's office that Manson was running a stolen car ring and converting the vehicles into dune buggies. (And he was right, of course.) On August 16, 1969, more than 100 combat-ready sheriff's deputies, backed up by helicopters, launched a pre-dawn raid on the ranch, arresting Manson and his girls and carting them all off to jail.

Manson sidekick Clem Grogan, at his parole hearing in 1978, said Manson did indeed detest Shea for triggering the ranch raid. His comments perfectly capture Manson's mindset at that time. "Well, we spent three days in jail, and we were released. And we didn't get back none of our property. The pink slips were confiscated to four or five dune buggies that we couldn't get back from them; the children put into foster homes. And what it really did is made everybody really upset at this guy because I was led to believe that he was doing it to get us evicted off the ranch. And that was the only place we had to stay at the time. And it was through his actions that he caused us this trouble…there was a feeling almost of hatred toward the guy because of what he made us go through, the children and stuff. Like we had held the children in really almost the highest position. They were home-delivered and breast-fed. This was mostly the whole reason we was all together, to put the children in a good environment, free from social indoctrinations and stuff, try to raise them as natural as we could. And then to have someone come along and form a false story and have them put in foster homes, it was really a blow to the women and men that were at the place at the time."

Two additional issues turned Manson and Shea into the bitterest of enemies. One was that Shea gave Manson the hiding of his life after Manson had broken the jaw of a young lady friend. And, of course, Shea did whatever he could to help evict Manson and the girls from the Spahn Ranch. The final straw was when Shorty married Magdalene "Nikki" Fuery, a black Las Vegas stripper, and showed up with her at the ranch. Manson was an out-and-out racist, and their mixed marriage was the final turning point as far as he was concerned. On August 26, 1969, just days after the Manson family's release from jail following the Sheriff's raid at the ranch, Manson took revenge. Aided and abetted by a posse including Tex Watson, Bruce Davis, and Clem Grogan, they ambushed Shea on the ranch and dragged him into the back seat of a car. The burly Shea fought for his life but was outnumbered. They beat him over the head with an iron pipe and viciously stabbed him. The message was clear: mess with me at your own peril. Elaborate and gruesome details of the killing were deliberately circulated to send the message—including word that that the killers had beheaded the stuntman, cut his body up into a dozen pieces, and buried the remains in a number of graves all over the ranch. Family member Barbara Hoyt was so terrified that after she heard blood-curdling screams from the dying Shea, she fled to Hawaii fearing that she, too, would be killed if she remained.

Even though there was no body to prove a killing had actually taken place, the disappearance of thirty-five-year-old Shea eventually resulted in murder charges being filed against Manson, Watson, Grogan, and Davis. In the fall of 1971, after a forty-three-day trial, Grogan was sentenced to die, and the rest were given life sentences. But in December 1971, Judge James Kolts ruled that Grogan "was too stupid and too hopped up on drugs to decide anything on his own," and that it was really Manson who decided who lived or died. The death sentence was commuted to life. (Grogan, Family members said, was a bit of a simpleton and thus given the nickname "Scramblehead." That very well could have been an act, as later a video of him would prove he wasn't quite as dumb as everyone thought.)

In December 1977, Grogan agreed to help authorities locate Shea's body. He drew a map, and Sheriff's Detective Bill Gleason, who had devoted much time to investigating the murder, went along as Grogan led them to Shea's unmarked grave. Sure enough, the shovel-wielding Gleason brought the investigation full circle when the stuntman's skeletal remains were unearthed. Shea's head had not been severed; however, his left hand was missing. The coroner listed "multiple stab and chop wounds" as the cause of death. Because of his cooperation, Grogan was paroled in November 1985—the only convicted killer in the Manson clan ever to get parole.

Joseph Vance Randall, a.k.a. Randy Starr
Died: August 4, 1970
Age: 38

Also known as "Randy Starr," Joseph Randall was another larger-than-life character, living in a trailer at Spahn Ranch. It may have been a coincidence, but he died suddenly just a few weeks after the Tate-LaBianca murder trial began. In contrast to the evidence of the passing of Shea, there were no bloody footprints or eyewitnesses to lead investigators to his corpse, but he was to be a key witness for the prosecution and would have testified to an important point: that he gave the .22 caliber Buntline revolver that was used by Watson in the Tate murders to Manson in exchange for a pickup truck. Manson then passed the pistol on to Watson on the night they left the ranch for Cielo Drive.

Starr was straight out of a Coen Brothers movie: A one-armed cowboy, he had served in Korea during his 1952-54 Marine Corps service. He lost the complete use of his left arm in a tractor accident, but it didn't stop him from becoming a stuntman, his trademark specialty being a daredevil trick that saw him dragged and dropped with a rope around his neck while attached to a galloping horse. He liked to dress the part—all in black leather, a gun on his holster and strutting around the ranch for the benefit of weekend visitors who rented horses. Like Shea, he lived and worked for George Spahn and also eked out a small living as a stuntman, with odd parts in low-grade movies, like 1964's *Creeping Terror*, in which he also got an assistant director credit for persuading Spahn to allow the crew to shoot some scenes at the ranch for a deep discount. He also appeared in a couple of cheapie films released posthumously—*Machismo: 40 Graves for 40 Guns,* and a hardcore porn flick, *Hard on the Trail.*

He also had a dramatic, albeit distinctly memorable, real-life walk-on role with Manson in May 1969. Inebriated and with his six-gun strapped to his waist, he turned menacing when Manson finished his audition with Terry Melcher. As Melcher watched in shock, Manson disarmed Starr and proceeded to savagely beat him to a near pulp. The incident dissuaded Melcher from getting involved with Manson as a musician.

Questioned by Tate-LaBianca investigators, Starr was to be a key witness for the prosecution. He had already testified to the grand jury that he saw Manson with a sword in late July of 1969, shortly after the Hinman murder. Manson boasted to him, "I cut a guy's ear off with this." But shortly after his questioning, he was unexpectedly dead—an ear infection leading to meningitis, expiring at the Veterans Administration Hospital in Los Angeles. How he had suddenly fallen ill with a disease that so swiftly became fatal was never explained.

John Philip "Zero" Haught
Died: November 5, 1969
Age: 22

The murder of Shorty Shea was the subject of much gossip and innuendo after he suddenly vanished. Contrast that with the death by apparent suicide of John Haught—a death that, as with that of Randy Starr, remains shrouded in mystery. Haught, who referred to himself as "Christopher Jesus" but was called "Zero" by Family members, was born in West Virginia, grew up in Ohio, and, after serving in the Navy in Vietnam, moved to Southern California and began living with his friend Kenneth Brown near the ocean in Venice. In early 1969, he and Brown met Manson girl Cathy Gillies, and he was swiftly welcomed to the delights of the Spahn Ranch, where his skills in transforming stolen Volkswagens into dune buggies was appreciated by Manson and Watson. In October 1969, Haught was one of those arrested in the raid at Barker Ranch. After his release, he moved with other Family members to another house in Venice rented by pal Mark Ross. Ross was a handsome wannabe actor/musician whose main claim to fame was helping director Robert Hendrickson line up interviews for his 1973 *Manson* documentary.

On November 5, almost a month before the Manson Family was linked to the Tate-LaBianca killings and before the names of the murder suspects were made public, Venice police were called to a house at 28 Clubhouse Ave. There they found Haught, lying in a pool of blood on a mattress in a bedroom. One bullet hole had pierced his right temple; there was a leather gun case and a still-warm .22 caliber Iver Johnson revolver lying beside the body. In the house at the time were Bruce Davis, Catherine Gillies, and two lesser-known Manson women—Madaline Joan Cottage (aka Linda Baldwin) and Sue Bartell. Questioned separately, they all told the same story: Haught killed himself playing Russian roulette. Cottage said that she had been lying in bed next to Haught when he just happened to notice the gun in the leather case on the bed stand. She said he remarked, "Oh, here's a gun," picked it up and slipped the weapon out of its holster, saying, "It only has one bullet in it." Holding the gun in his right hand, she said he spun the cylinder, placed the gun muzzle to his right temple and pulled the trigger.

At the sound of the gunshot, the others ran into the bedroom. Haught, bleeding profusely from a hole in his head, lay on the floor in front of her. Cottage told them: "Zero has shot himself—just like in the movies." When police arrived, Davis told them that Haught had picked up the gun and shot himself—but when the weapon was dusted for prints, police found no prints belonging to either Davis or to Haught. And there were no prints on the gun's leather case, either. Moreover, the weapon was found to be fully loaded—seven live shells and one empty one, which clearly indicated that the odds had been heavily stacked against the "player." At the time, police didn't link Davis or any of the girls in the house to the Manson Family. Police ruled the death as suicide.

The next month, Sgt. Mike McGann, lead detective in the Tate case, was interviewing Leslie Van Houten at Sybil Brand Institute when he told her that Haught had died while playing Russian roulette and that Bruce Davis was also present.

Van Houten asked, *Was Bruce playing it, too?*

No, said McGann.

Zero was playing Russian roulette—all by himself? she asked.

McGann: *Kind of odd, isn't it?*

Van Houten: *Yeah, it's odd.*

It seems obvious that neither McGann nor Van Houten believed the story, although no charges were ever brought. Sometime later, a story circulated that an unknown witness had called *Los Angeles Times* reporter Jerry Cohen, an expert on the Manson case, and told him that one of the girls shot Haught, even though his death was ruled a suicide.

At the penalty phase of the Tate-LaBianca trial, Gillies again said she had seen Haught kill himself. "He walked into the next room. [Linda Baldwin] was lying on the bed. He sat down on the bed next to her, reached over, grabbed the gun and shot himself—out of the clear blue sky."

Joel Dean Pugh
Died: December 2, 1969
Age: 29

Much international scrutiny has been focused on the supposed suicide of Minnesotan Joel Pugh. His untimely death was certainly odd—it came barely twenty-four hours after Los Angeles Police Chief Edward Davis held the press conference at which he announced to the world that the four-month-old Tate and LaBianca murder cases had been solved. The names of most of the key suspects in the murders were made public, and Chief Davis revealed that they had fallen under the spell of the leader of "a travelling band of hippies." No one can confirm if Pugh ever learned of this sensational development before he died. But it was big news everywhere. My own story made front-page headlines in the

London *Daily Express*, and there were major stories as well on British television and radio stations.

At the time, Pugh had been living in the small, nondescript Talgarth Hotel in the then-unfashionable part of London's South Kensington district. He was the longtime boyfriend of Manson's most devoted follower, Sandra Good, whom he first met in 1968 in San Francisco where she was attending state college and he was working as a lab tech. She was his first love, and he was besotted with her. Their backgrounds were similar—both came from professional homes. His mother, Marjorie, was a homemaker and his father, David, was a prominent radiologist at the prestigious Mayo Clinic in Minnesota. Good was a trust-fund kid whose stockbroker father was living in San Diego and providing her with a steady $2,000 a month income. Big bucks for that era.

Pugh was a troubled young man who suffered from depression—a condition that also had afflicted his father. Still, it seemed like a match made in heaven. The bright-as-a-button, pert, and pretty Good, and Pugh, who was described by friends as "an original, if slightly off-beat character who combined his professional endeavors with a quirky sense of humor." And their romance was going swimmingly well until in March 1968 when she was taken to a house on Topanga Canyon and hooked up again with the girls she had first met in San Francisco: Mary Brunner and Lyn Fromme, who were firmly affixed to Manson. Pugh was distraught because he saw his true love drifting away to spend time with another man. "When she started hanging around with Manson, Joel was extremely embarrassed about it," Joel's brother Daniel told British writer Simon Wells, author of the 2010 book *Charles Manson: Coming Down Fast*. "He regarded Manson as a phony who was very full of himself and a sort of embarrassing character. He didn't want Sandy to have anything to do with a guy like that...sort of uncool by association. Manson was what Joel, in his own words, would have called 'a Gnarl.'"

Good, already fixated on Manson, and dallying with Bobby Beausoleil, moved permanently back to LA to stay in Dennis Wilson's house.

A year later, in September 1969, she gave birth to her son, Ivan, choosing to have the child in hospital, rather than being delivered by the Family. And she named Pugh as the father on the birth certificate— even though he told friends he had vehemently insisted she not do so. Family members later reckoned the father of the child was more likely to have been Bobby Beausoleil, who was serving time in prison for the murder of Gary Hinman at the time of the birth. Some years later, Beausoleil confirmed that he had fathered three children, including one with Good.

A month later, on October 10, 1969, the new mother, with infant at hip, was behind bars following yet another police roundup. This arrest took place at the isolated Barker Ranch. She gave her name as Mrs. Sandra Pugh.

One of the oddest anecdotes involving the new mother occurred soon after they were taken to the Inyo jailhouse. Baby Ivan had been taken by local social services, but, according to Dianne Lake, the other girls, concerned that Good's breast milk might dry up, took turns nursing at Good's breast.

According to Wells, depressed by the breakup, Pugh embarked on trips to the South American rain forests, Morocco, and Spain, courtesy of his parents, who were worried about his mental state. He finally alighted in London in late October, feeling pretty fragile and checking into a ground-floor room at a budget hotel with an unidentified "hippie" girlfriend. His companion left soon after, and Pugh stayed on for several weeks, befriending the hotel manager Joseph Falk and his seven-year-old son. Then came his sudden death—a maid had tried to get into his room to clean it, but it was locked, and in the early evening the friendly hotel manager became worried. He unlocked the door and discovered Pugh's naked body under a sheet. Pugh's throat was slashed twice, and there were cuts and bruises on his wrists and arms. There was no suicide note, only strange writings on the bathroom mirror, and police found cannabis resin in the room. It looked like a classic case of suicide with the coroner ruling that way, adding—somewhat superfluously—that the balance of his mind was disturbed.

The timing seemed oddly coincidental. Some surmised that he may have become greatly disturbed after learning that his girlfriend's bosom pals had been fingered as suspects in a mass murder. But when news of the sudden death of a person with links, tenuous or otherwise, to the Manson Family reached the Los Angeles offices of Bugliosi and Kay, they became deeply suspicious. "Strange things were happening to people in Charles Manson's circle," Kay recollected at the time, "and we wondered if Manson's deadly tentacles had stretched 6,000 miles to London. And if so, why so?"

Then there was this strange coincidence: As it turned out, Manson's partner in crime Bruce Davis—who was later implicated, charged, and convicted for the murders of Shorty Shea and Gary Hinman—had been in England around the same time as Pugh. Checks with Scotland Yard confirmed it was true—Davis had been visiting a Scientology retreat in the UK and apparently lived in London from November 1968 until April 1969. They couldn't, however, pinpoint with any certainty whether Davis was in the country at precisely the time Pugh died.

Was it such a great leap to make the murder link? Despite the concerns of the DA's office about Pugh being bumped off, author Wells, said: "I spoke with most in Joel's circle and his family, and it is clear that Joel's relationship with Sandy was defunct around the time of her defection to Charlie's mob. Similarly, Joel never met Manson or traveled to Spahn Ranch or the other places the Mansonites were based, although Sandy did attempt to hook up with him [according to his friends] to 'acquire' his surname for her child, reportedly, for Social Security reasons. Did Bruce Davis murder Joel? That is probably only really known to Bruce Davis. I wrote to Bruce for him to clarify any knowledge of Joel Pugh, or indeed his movements in the UK. He failed to respond."

346 | MANSON EXPOSED

Veronica Howard
Died: October 3, 1979
Age: 43

When I first covered the Sharon Tate murder case back in late 1969, I'd heard all about "The Informer." Except, at the time, in order to protect her true identity and for safety reasons, Veronica Howard went by the name of Shelley Nadell. I later discovered that she had a tendency to use assorted names—including Nancy Johnson, Veronica Hudson, and Veronica Whatever Surname Took Her Fancy That Week. But this time she was not concealing anything. It was a tragic footnote to her sad life: looking somewhat bedraggled, she appears on camera holding the front page of the Los Angeles *Herald Examiner* with a headline that screamed, "Shot Fired at Tate Witness."

Wearing a red dress with a plunging neckline, her red hair piled bouffant style, Howard looked a little dazed as she made her pronouncement in a brief segment of the *Manson* documentary. In monotone and sounding slightly slurry-voiced, she declared, "Ladies and gentlemen...because I, Ronnie Howard, broke the Tate and LaBianca case and prevented no telling how many more murders, I've been shot at, assaulted, harassed, beaten, threatened—and it's very likely that by the time you see this picture I may be dead." She was not exaggerating. Less than a decade later, she was just that. And again, the circumstances surrounding her death were complex and, to my knowledge, never thoroughly investigated.

Howard, of course, was no angel. At the age of seventeen, she was convicted of extortion and sent to a federal prison. After her release, she moved to Southern California, where the attractive young woman found steady employment on what was loosely called Hollywood's "party girl circuit," working as a call girl or freelancing for a Hollywood escort service. She landed back in jail in October 1969 for forging drug prescriptions to feed her habit. At Sybil Brand, she was desperately hoping to get paroled when she met Atkins, and Atkins began spilling the beans about the murders. She finally got the cops to listen to her, although she worried that she would get the reputation as a jailhouse snitch, and, following her fifteen minutes of fame, she was finally paroled.

There is no doubt whatsoever that without her crucial testimony the case might never have been resolved. She shared the $25,000 Tate reward money with the youngster who found the murder gun. But everything went downhill after that, and she later was to bitterly claim that her life had been forever ruined as a result of her revelations. She said she was fired from waitress jobs because none of her coworkers wanted a stool pigeon in their midst—although that explanation is somewhat difficult to swallow given the gravity of the killings. But, obviously, somebody out there didn't like Ronnie Howard. It was common knowledge that several deluded Manson Family members were not shy about threatening anyone who, in their crazed thinking, had done their Jesus wrong. And one night, shots were fired into her apartment, leaving bullet holes in the wall. She also claimed she was the victim of physical attacks on her way home from work. It became so bad, she lamented to a reporter, "I should have kept my mouth shut in the first place."

But a decade after her crucial testimony came a series of unexplained events that were to result in her death. On her way home from a weekend in Las Vegas, she and her husband Richard Lopez and his brother Rudy found themselves at a downtown Los Angeles bus station. It was September 21, 1979. The possibly apocryphal story went like this: They hailed a cab. The men went to retrieve their luggage, and Howard climbed into the back seat of the car. But when they returned, she and the cab were gone. Later that night, a terrified Howard called her husband to say she'd been beaten and knocked unconscious and dumped in the gutter in an industrial section of LA. The driver, she claimed, had robbed her of the $400 in cash she won in Las Vegas, as well as about $800 worth of jewelry—though she apparently had never reported the robbery. Four days later, she complained of severe headaches, dizziness, and nausea, and she was taken to Queen of Angels Hospital, where she was treated and then sent home.

On October 1, her husband found her semi-conscious in her bedroom; he was unable to rouse her. She was rushed to Cedars Sinai Hospital, where doctors discovered a subdural hematoma that they believed had been overlooked or neglected during her earlier hospital visit. She died two days later, with doctors noting she had suffered an unexplained blunt force trauma to her head that had resulted in brain-stem compression. No one was ever able to say with any certainty that her death was linked to the Tate-LaBianca case. But her untimely death has left more questions unanswered. It appears there had been no police follow-up or investigation surrounding her death on record—even though she always predicted that she might become a victim of the Family.

Laurence Merrick
Died: January 26, 1977
Age: 50

Was it pure coincidence? Six—or maybe two—degrees of separation? Merrick had teamed up with Robert Hendrickson to produce and co-direct *Manson*, the powerful, no-bullshit inside story of the Manson clan. The film ran into all sorts of legal problems, including an ownership dispute between Hendrickson and Merrick. The startling footage—plus scenes that had never before been aired publicly—was resurrected a few years ago and given a new "missing tapes" lease on life on TV around the world.

In January 1977, Merrick walked out of his acting school at Vine Street in Hollywood—the slightly pretentiously titled Merrick's Academy of Dramatic Arts, which catered to would-be actors using G.I. Bill money. Suddenly he ran screaming to his students, "Some son-of-a-bitch shot me, and I don't know why." At first his students thought he was acting, but they quickly realized that their teacher was dying in front of them. He was rushed to Hollywood Presbyterian Hospital, but it was too late. He had been shot several times in the back by a gunman described only as "a young, heavyset guy with a dark complexion" who fled the scene. Rumors at the time of the murder were rampant, suggesting that the shooting could have been linked to the notorious Manson gang and that Manson had put Merrick on his hit list because, once again, he felt he had been ripped off by showbiz types who were blatantly exploiting the Family.

In making their documentary, Merrick and Hendrickson had, over a period from Manson's arrest in late 1969 through 1973, shot more than 100 hours of interviews and footage on a 16mm camera. The footage showed the Family in a utopian setting, frolicking at the Spahn and Barker ranches, with members talking about the joys of being part of Mansonia. The film featured everyone from Manson—in jail at the time—to George Spahn to Squeaky Fromme, who appeared caressing a rifle and talking tough about Manson. Even Bugliosi sat for an interview. Some Family members participated in the belief that they would be recompensed, but no one saw a single penny—although music composed by Brooks Poston and Paul Watkins was used, as was Manson singing his song, "Cease to Exist."

What might also have exacerbated anger toward the filmmakers was the fact that Family members who were not in jail believed they would be depicted in a sympathetic light. Until they saw the movie's sensational ads and posters.

Here's how one read:

MEET ONE MAN'S FAMILY

The Terrifying Truth Behind the Tate-LaBianca Massacre

REVEALED FOR THE FIRST TIME outside the courtroom, staggering details of the most hideously bizarre murders in the annals of crime. SUPPRESSED UNTIL NOW. YOU WILL

ACTUALLY SEE each member of the Manson Family and HEAR their horrifying philosophy of sex, perversion, murder, and violence. NOT PERMITTED on TV, radio, or family newspapers! Told in their own words by the killers themselves.

When *Manson* was released, it was nominated for an Oscar, which helped soothe Manson's temper—even though it lost to *Marjoe*, a film about the swindling televangelist Marjoe Gortner.

Merrick's background was a fascinating one. A veteran of the Israeli Defense Forces, he was sent to America in 1960 by the Israeli government to promote Zionism. When he fell in love and married actress Joan Huntington, they moved to Hollywood. Before embarking on the documentary, under the banner of his own high-sounding company—Merrick International Pictures—he had directed two cheapies: *Guess What Happened to Count Dracula* and *Black Angels*, the latter a biker movie about a Highway Patrol lieutenant who wants to start a race war between black and white bikers! Merrick said he became familiar with the Manson Family while shooting his biker movie on the Paramount movie ranch, which was not far from the Spahn Ranch. He invited Family members to come watch the two-week shoot—and to scrounge food. After the documentary, the two directors split following a bitter dispute over who owned the film.

In 2007 Hendrickson, who obtained the rights to the footage, released *Inside the Manson Gang*, a reheated, hopped-up version of the old film, and he included his own voiceover narration: "Walk with Robert Hendrickson through the Gates of Hell," he intoned in a deep baritone voice. "The Tate-LaBianca massacre will seem to eclipse even the Vietnam War. This is not for the faint of heart." He also published *Death to Pigs*, a 2012 book of pictures he had taken and interviews he had conducted while making the original doc.

On June 27, 2016, a writer purporting to be Hendrickson posted this on the Manson Family blog website:

Laurence Merrick actually CREATED mucho great pain and suffering for MANY good and decent people. I KNOW, I am a witness. And IF the Court had NOT found that Merrick intended to defraud ME out of my MANSON film and "consequentially" ruled in my lawsuit FAVOR, I might have caused some drastic result in HIS disfavor.

In MY final private discussions with HIM, I realized HE was mentally ILL himself and that ANY continued association with HIM could ONLY end badly. Even HIS most trusted confident [sic] Leo Rivers finally realized that Merrick was a walking KARMA time bomb and LEFT his employee [sic].

Because Merrick KNEW so much about the REAL Hollywood scene at that time period and because HE desperately wanted Charlie Manson's POWER, there may be a good story BOOK here."

Four months after that posting, on October 1, 2016, Hendrickson died of natural causes at the age of 72.

IN THE 1977 homicide of his late partner, Merrick, detectives ran into a dead end. But then four years later the cold case suddenly came alive. Dennis Michael Mignano, a struggling rock singer and would-be actor, phoned police in his hometown of San Jose and said he wanted to tell them about a murder he had committed. He said he tried confessing to friends and even his psychiatrist, but no one believed him. He said he had gone to Hollywood for an audition with Merrick, and the teacher had cast some kind of black-magic spell on him, which later caused him severe problems. In November 1982, Mignano, who had a long history of mental problems, was found not guilty by reason of insanity and committed to a mental hospital for life. Unconfirmed reports say that he was released, after four years, into the custody of his parents, and currently lives in his late parents' old house in San Jose.

Another weird link and odd coincidence to the already violent Mignano affair: six months after Merrick was gunned down, Mignano's twenty-one-year-old sister, Michelle, who dabbled as a topless dancer, and supposedly hung out with Hells Angels, was murdered. Her bullet-riddled body was dumped in a railroad tunnel in San Jose. She was shoeless, but wore white gloves and a fur jacket! No one was ever arrested for that execution-style killing.

In an intriguing interview before his own violent demise, Merrick stressed that he was always fascinated by the Manson Family, but the key reason he got involved with the documentary was because one of his early acting students was a beautiful young actress. Her name: Sharon Tate.

10050 Cielo Drive from walkway.

10050 Cielo Drive mailbox.

The blind George Spahn allowed Manson to take over his ranch.

While Paul Watkins was Manson's chief procurer, he became disenchanted with Manson's dictatorial style and fled the Spahn Ranch before the murders.

Charles Watson was very familiar with Cielo Drive and stayed overnight when Terry Melcher was overseas.

Bobby Beausoleil convicted for the murder of Gary Hinman.

Barker Ranch in Death Valley, circa 1969, where Manson was arrested.

Winifred Chapman, housemaid who discovered the bodies at 10050 Cielo Drive.

Manson arrested October 1969 in Inyo County.

Bedroom at Barker Ranch after police raid in October 1969.

Left to right: Susan Atkins, Patricia Krenwinkel, Leslie Van Houten often marched into court in 1970 singing and smiling.

Poster found tacked to door at Spahn Ranch.

Manson Family transportation by dune buggy.

Ranch hand John Swartz's 1959 four-door Ford was used by Tate killers and is on display at the Los Angeles Police Museum.

Polanski with *Rosemary's Baby* star Mia Farrow in 1968.

Sheriff's deputies hunt for Manson at Spahn Ranch in August 1969.

PART V

JUSTICE

The verdict, January 1971: All guilty.

TEX WAS HERE

Vincent Bugliosi: "Did anything else occur that evening of August 8 that you remember?"

Charles Watson: "Charlie called me over behind the car, down at the far end of the ranch, and handed me a gun and a knife and he said for me to take the gun and the knife and to go up where Terry Melcher used to live and to kill everybody in the house, as gruesome as I could, or something to that effect."

In the days leading up to Manson's trial, much emphasis was placed on the fact that before the murders, Manson had visited the house on Cielo Drive—once for sure, probably even twice. The inference was that during these visits, he had cased the place and was thoroughly familiar with the layout, and that this, in some way, led him to direct his murdering minions there to kill all those in attendance. Manson's familiarity bred cold-blooded murder.

But the truth was, the one man who knew the detailed layout was the other Charles: Charles "Tex" Watson. It was true that Manson did have some prior knowledge of the premises, but that connection was somewhat flimsy. Less flimsy was that, months before the killings, Manson had a very brief encounter with Sharon Tate. These are the established facts of Manson's knowledge of the Cielo Drive house. Make of them what you will.

His first visit was verified by a solid witness and confirmed by Manson himself; although, to describe the occasion as a "visit" is not quite accurate. The brief story was told in court by Doris Day's music-producer son, Terry Melcher, who had lived at the Cielo address for a time and had allowed himself to become enmeshed in the deadly Manson web.

One day, in the summer of 1968, Manson sat in the back seat of Dennis Wilson's car as the drummer drove Melcher home to Cielo. Manson was in the backseat, strumming and humming and riffing on his new songs. Wilson opened the electric gates by pushing a button, and then drove up the driveway, stopping in front of the main house. Manson never got out of the car. Melcher, who had been auditioning Manson but was still not committing to a possible record deal, said goodbye, jumped out, and went into the house. Wilson drove away through the open electric gate, which automatically closed thirty seconds later. That was it.

The second Manson visit occurred on March 23, 1969, and was confirmed by two witnesses. And it was longer in duration. Months after Manson had auditioned for Melcher, he had the distinct impression that he was getting the runaround. Melcher, after a couple of visits to listen to Manson perform, waffled over a final decision, offered a slew of positive remarks about his music, and promised to return for a third visit. But on the appointed day, he was a no-show, with no explanation. Manson was hopping mad. He'd prepped everyone for Melcher's return visit and, after hanging about for more than an hour, realized he had been stood up. It was a huge embarrassment for him, and Manson's ego did not allow for that kind of snub. Unable to reach Melcher by phone, he drove to Melcher's house with plans to confront the producer and get him to make good on his promises. (Melcher later said to friends that he never promised Manson anything and that he'd done a good deed just by giving him his time.)

At Cielo Drive, Manson leaned through the railings and pushed the button to open the electric gates, which allowed him into the parking area by the main house. He got out and, as he headed toward the front door of the house on foot, Shahrokh Hatami, a friend of Polanski and Tate, appeared to block his path. Hatami knew his way around celebrities and high-profile types. As a photographer working for magazines like *Paris Match* and *Elle*, Hatami had established a career shooting beautiful women like Elizabeth Taylor, Brigitte Bardot, Julie Christie, and Ingrid Bergman, and as a photojournalist he had covered the revolution in his homeland of Iran, the Beatles' early years in Liverpool's Cavern Club, and Hollywood film sets, shooting stills on movies like *The Thomas Crown Affair* with Steve McQueen and Faye Dunaway. Frequently the women he photographed became personal friends, as did Sharon Tate. Hatami had become very protective of the vulnerable actress.

Instinctively he was suspicious because it was obvious this guy, appearing out of nowhere dressed like a homeless vagrant and smelling like one, didn't belong in a high-rent neighborhood like Benedict Canyon. "May I help you?" he asked, making sure there was no way Manson could get past him. Manson stopped in his tracks and smiled. He said he was visiting the people who lived in the main house and tossed out a few names to Hatami. None of the names meant anything to the photographer. "Why don't you check at the guest house," he said. "Mr. Altobelli lives there. He owns the house." Just then, out of the front door stepped Tate. She looked at Manson. He looked at her. They exchanged not a word, Hatami told police. Manson smiled, then slowly retraced his steps in the direction of the guest house.

Moments later, Rudi Altobelli's three dogs—two poodles and a Weimaraner—began yelping. Altobelli, who had been taking a shower, heard the noise and slipped on a robe. Somewhat annoyed by the interruption of his ablutions, he carefully opened the front door. He recognized the little man on his doorstep immediately—he was a hard man to forget. He had encountered him months earlier at a party at Dennis Wilson's house, when everyone had sat around devoutly listening to demo tapes Manson had recorded a few days earlier at fellow Beach Boy Brian Wilson's home studio.

As a top music and film agent, Altobelli had spent a lifetime dealing with ego-driven clients, and his innate bullshit detector had served him well in the shallow world of show business. He was polite but very cool toward the caller with his long stringy hair and bad odor. What also disturbed him was that he had witnessed the dictatorial way Manson had treated his women, who, at Wilson's house, jumped to attention at his every word as though he were a latter-day slave owner. Melcher, Altobelli said cautiously, had moved away [in January 1969] and, unfortunately, he didn't know where he was living. He was lying, of course—he knew that Melcher was with Candice Bergen at his mother's house in Malibu.

Manson was not so easily dismissed. Recognizing Altobelli from the Wilson party, he launched into a long-winded explanation about his urgency to talk about a record contract Melcher was negotiating for him with Columbia Records. Altobelli knew otherwise. Then Manson attempted to butter up Altobelli. Could he make an appointment with Altobelli, another day perhaps, to discuss his budding music career, as well as his role in a documentary that Melcher and his buddy, music talent scout Gregg Jakobson, had begun filming? Melcher, Manson said, told him he would have to join the musician's union, and that meant he needed an agent. Would Altobelli be interested? Altobelli knew that, while Melcher had frolicked with the Manson girls, no such record deal was in the offing. Firmly and politely, he declined to meet with Manson, explaining that he was about to leave for Europe on business the very next day and wouldn't be back for at least a year.

Thus, Manson's personal contact with Cielo Drive ended. However, while it had been brief and fairly inconsequential, another member of his family—Charles "Tex" Watson, it later turned out— knew the Cielo Drive home inside out.

Testifying in August 1971 at Watson's much-delayed murder trial in downtown Los Angeles, Melcher revealed details about Watson's knowledge of the Tate house. None of it had come out during the earlier, year-long Manson trial. The Deputy DA once again led the prosecution's case, in an exchange that went like this:

Vincent Bugliosi: *Have you ever seen Mr. Watson inside your former residence at 10050 Cielo Drive?*

Terry Melcher: *Yes.*

Bugliosi: *Approximately how many times?*

Melcher: *I can't be certain—several. Watson was a friend of Wilson and Jakobson and was often tagging around with either or both of those men, so whenever they would drop by—not 'whenever,' but often when they would drop by, he would be with them.*

Bugliosi: *Can you give us an approximate number of times that you saw Mr. Watson inside your former residence at 10050 Cielo Drive?*

Melcher: *I would say approximately six. It's a very rough, rough guess.*

Bugliosi: *Do you recall what part of your former residence Mr. Watson was in on any of these occasions?*

Melcher: *He could have been in one room, or he could have been in all the rooms; I really don't know. I wasn't keeping track.*

Bugliosi: *During what period of time was Mr. Watson at your residence?*

Melcher: *All six times would have fallen somewhere in the summer of 1968.*

Bugliosi: *To your knowledge did Mr. Watson ever stay overnight at your residence?*

Melcher: *No. Mr. Jakobson took care of my house for me for about four months while I was in Europe doing some recording.*

Bugliosi: *When was that?*

Melcher: *I left in the fall of 1968 and Watson may have stayed there then.*

Bugliosi: *You don't know?*

Melcher: *I'm not certain; it's possible.*

Melcher—who was terrified of being implicated in such a sordid case, not only because of the horrendous savagery, but because he had allowed himself to be sucked into the Manson sexual morass much deeper than he wanted anyone to know—had tried his best to distance himself from Manson and his girls. But Melcher did admit that when he gave parties—on one occasion, a buffet dinner—he was sure Watson was at the dinner table. Then, on cross-examination, he admitted that his links to the man who became Manson's chief assassin were probably much closer. Melcher even loaned his black XKE Jaguar, along with a credit card, to Watson so he could drive his pal Dean Moorehouse (the former pastor and father of Ruth Ann) to Mendocino, where Moorehouse had to appear in court on a charge of selling LSD. At his own murder trial Watson reckoned he had been to Cielo Drive at least three times.

There were others who also testified that Watson was a regular at Cielo Drive parties. As a prosecution witness, Deana Martin—who was twenty at the time—told of the night in October 1968 when a group of guests left Wilson's house and headed to Melcher's digs on Cielo. Watson was a passenger, she said, but there was no sign of Manson. One can only surmise that either he wasn't invited or Melcher made a point of leaving him out, fearing that if Manson and his bevy of women—some of whom had consorted with Melcher—were to show up, they might embarrass him with his live in companion Candice Bergen.

Martin was later to write about her links to Watson and Manson, particularly Manson, in her 2004 memoir, *Memories Are Made of This.* Manson, she recalled, tried to ingratiate himself with her by giving her a beautiful silver ring. However, she says she got negative vibes from Manson and his girls at a party at Wilson's house in the summer of 1968. They made derogatory remarks about the boyfriend she was with. Much later, after Manson was arrested, two Los Angeles detectives flew to Las Vegas, where she was performing, to interview her. "They wanted to know why Manson gave me the ring and I told them, 'I guess he thought it was a cool thing to do, seeing who my dad is.'" What she didn't say was that Manson also suggested she might like to join his family.

Later she said her father—who had starred in a movie with Sharon Tate—was furious upon learning that his daughter had socialized with Manson. Then he told her he had received "a horrible letter threatening to kill certain members of our family," which he turned over to the FBI. The issue of Watson's familiarity with Cielo Drive brings up an intriguing legal question. If Irving Kanarek, Manson's obstructionist attorney, had been aware that Watson knew the layout of the murder house inside out, might he have successfully argued that his client's culpability would have been hugely decreased because it was only Watson who was intimately familiar with the terrain? Kanarek could then have argued that Watson was therefore the real architect of the crime and bore all the blame for the killings. And not his client.

But, during that first murder trial, Watson was safely tucked away in a Texas jail and neither Kanarek nor any of the lawyers representing Atkins, Krenwinkel, or Van Houten had the slightest idea that Watson knew the lay of the land. With that knowledge, they certainly would have tried to shift the blame for the murders onto Watson's shoulders. That issue was never raised, nor did it ever come up, simply because Watson—by design of his hometown friend/lawyer—was never a co-defendant in the first trial.

Would the jury have been swayed? And would those Watson facts have cast doubt in jurors' minds, when clearly on the night of the killings, Manson stayed at the Spahn Ranch? Anything was possible in that trial. But there is one intriguing footnote to all of this speculation, offered by John Douglas—an ex-FBI agent who wrote the 1995 bestseller *Mindhunters*, detailing the life of the elite FBI squad members who spent inordinate amounts of time visiting and interviewing convicted killers. (The book was later turned into a series by Netflix.)

Douglas interviewed Manson in jail and, in his book, said, "I believe he did not plan or intend the murders of Sharon Tate and her friends—that, in fact, he lost control of the situation and his followers. That's why he went out with them the next night to the LaBianca house—to show them how to do it properly. When I asked Manson why he hadn't participated in the killings, he explained—as if we were dense—that he was on parole at the time, and he couldn't risk his freedom by violating his parole." That rings quite true. Manson often went to extraordinary lengths to provide glowing—if fanciful—progress reports to his probation officers about his life as a free man.

However, neither man—Manson or his henchman—would evade justice for long.

NO SYMPATHY FOR
THE DEVIL

"He did what Manson told him to do; he wasn't the tour director, he wasn't the leader, he didn't give the orders. He didn't plan these murders."

—Attorney Maxwell Keith, opening statement,
Charles "Tex" Watson trial, 1971

"He has little insight and feels he was captured by an evil force."
—Dr. James O. Palmer

"I was losing myself, my individual thinking, like I was becoming Charles Manson and I was becoming the girls. I remember we could look into each other's face and it would be the same face; my face would be Manson's and the girls' faces would be Manson's, and just have one face."

—Charles Watson, 1971 murder trial

Many who followed the gory details of the Tate-LaBianca murder trial were puzzled by one very odd thing. While Charles Manson and his obeisant young women had turned the trial into a preternatural proceeding, missing from all the madness and hoopla that came with the daily spectacle was the abhorrent individual who prosecutors all agreed was a true killing machine. It was he who had taken the Manson women to Cielo Drive, commanded them to wipe everyone out—and then ended up doing a lot of the dirty work himself.

The "invisible" defendant was Charles Denton Watson, known simply as "Tex" by his murderous cohorts. He was the chief hitman on that night of carnage, yet he never appeared in court with Manson, Atkins, and the rest. Where was he this whole time?

The answer was simple: Watson and his legal team successfully fought extradition to California for almost a year. As Manson performed daily in front of his jury in Los Angeles, the twenty-four-year-old Watson languished in a small but comfortable jail cell in McKinney, Texas, a twenty-mile drive from his family home in Copeville, and 1,500 miles from LA. It was a calculated strategic move on the part of his lawyer and old family friend Bill Boyd, who filed countless legal briefs to oppose extradition on an assortment of grounds. He also did not permit Los Angeles detectives to interview his client. It worked, and it kept Watson out of the heat and diminished his role in the murders.

In his McKinney cell, for the time being out of sight and out of mind, Watson listened to, ironically, Beatles records on his turntable and, on a TV provided by his parents, watched Perry Mason courtroom dramas and the nightly network coverage of the Tate-LaBianca murder trial. Such were the perks of doing time in his hometown jail. From time to time his mother, Mary Elizabeth Watson, dropped by to deliver home-cooked meals to her son, now a strict vegetarian. His daily routine included yoga exercises, following a regimen, he was later to claim, was practiced by Charles Manson. He regularly got letters from several of the Manson girls who were not in jail, and since there was no space dedicated for conferences at the jail, he met with Boyd in an upstairs room, conversing with him through a closed door as he took a hot bath!

Finally, though, Watson lost his bathing privileges, and his attorneys lost their legal battle to avoid extradition after the U.S. Supreme Court refused to hear his case. And so, on September 11, 1970, with the Manson trial well under way, he was returned to Southern California to finally face the music. Alone and represented by a whole new local defense team, led by veteran criminal defense attorney Sam Bubrick (nicknamed "Hollerin' Sam" by colleagues for his high-decibel style) and Maxwell Keith, who was no stranger to the twists and turns of the high-profile murder case. In December 1970, Keith had stepped in at the last minute to represent Leslie Van Houten after Ronald Hughes' disappearance, and now he was on the Watson team.

The defense knew it had to pull something special out of the bag. The mountain of evidence clearly pointed to the fact that Watson was the chief assassin and no jury in California, given the flood of media coverage and the loathsome nature of the crimes, could ever acquit him.

And there was another big issue that did not help Watson. By the time he came to trial in May 1971, the world already knew in graphic detail all about the killings, and, more important, the death sentences that had been handed down to Manson and the girls barely a month before. The only hope, they all agreed, was if they emphasized what to them was so obvious: sure, their client was as guilty as sin, but he had been brainwashed by the master manipulator of them all, Charles Manson. Watson was to be the first murder suspect in the history of jurisprudence to plead innocent to a terrible crime on the grounds of what could be termed the "Manchurian Candidate defense"—in his drug-altered state, he knew not what he did. He, too, in fact, was a victim, deserving of the jury's sympathy.

Watson was later to explain in his 1978 memoir that Bubrick, who had lots of experience representing clients facing the death penalty, "was convinced we could at least have the charge reduced from first to second-degree murder on the basis of a 'diminished capacity' and, if not win an acquittal, have me hospitalized." A tall order, even for six-foot-two Watson. And in pursuit of that strategy, he pled innocent to the seven murders by reason of insanity. Thus was launched the next chapter in Watson's short life: the invasion of the psychiatrists. The court ordered him to be transferred from the Los Angeles County Jail to the Atascadero State Hospital, halfway between LA and San Francisco, on California's Central Coast, which housed mentally ill convicts. There, he was put under the microscope of the crème de la crème of psychiatrists to determine whether he was truly mentally disturbed or whether, as the prosecution believed, he was faking his insanity to escape the death sentence.

It helped that since his arrest, Watson had undergone a dramatic physical change, not only in mind, but also in body. By the time he arrived from Texas, the rugged former high-school football star, who once could have been mistaken for a male model, now looked like…well, shit. He did not at all resemble the police mugshot handed out to the media when he was first named as a suspect that showed a black-bearded, wild-eyed character with a Beatles mop top and drug-glazed eyes. That photo had been taken by police shortly after he had been arrested early in 1969, after crashing his car while driving under the influence. Now his husky athletic frame was bent and stooped. The already trim 165-pounder was almost skeletal, down to 110 pounds. He was pale and wan, shrunken-looking, like a prisoner who had undergone two years of torture at the notorious Hanoi Hilton. A Los Angeles County prison doctor told the court that he was in a vegetative state and was rapidly reverting to a fetal state. He was mute and non-communicative. And because he was not eating, they kept him alive using feeding tubes. He was so incapable of taking care of himself that he had to be bathed and shaved by others. In court, he was barely able or willing to respond to questions. Watson's lawyers, of course, knew he was totally culpable of the crimes, but their goal was to do whatever was necessary to save him from death. Whether he was faking his condition was anyone's guess—but if he was, he sure was sacrificing a lot for his art.

Over the next three months, more than eight psychiatrists drove up to Atascadero to examine the forlorn and shrunken inmate, and to wonder if this insipid man could really be the same one who had boasted,

"I'm the devil, here to do the devil's work," as he set about carving up the pregnant Sharon Tate. They prodded and poked and interrogated, depending solely on Watson's own memories, and their findings were all laid out in a voluminous 103-page report that reflected the defendant's own personal narrative: that he was an impressionable kid who took a disastrous wrong turn by moving to California.

Indeed, Watson was the "typical" good small-town kid, the All-American boy next door who had grown up in a salt-of-the-earth, God-fearing, American heartland family, living in a modest whiteframe house. He was the youngest of three kids. Dad, Clarence Denton Watson, was a hardworking local businessman who ran a small store and one-pump gas station and grocery store in the one-horse town of Copeville, Texas, population 150. His "helicopter mother," Mary Elizabeth, worried herself sick about whether their church-going boy, so devoted to his parents and older siblings, would grow up to be her pride and joy. Sure, she vetted his girlfriends, but what mother didn't? And when he sneaked a beer with his dad, both father and son made sure Mom didn't find out. He was an honor student, an ace track high hurdler, a member of Future Farmers of America, whose handsome face appeared some eighteen times in the 1964 yearbook of Farmersville High School. The idyllic background presented to the army of shrinks seemed like something that could have been lifted straight off the canvas of a Norman Rockwell painting.

He pumped gas at his dad's station and developed a natural talent for fixing cars, which was to come in handy a little later at Spahn Ranch. He didn't shirk hard work. Starting at the age of fourteen, he harvested onions, toiling forty-eight hours nonstop in a local warehouse. In 1967, he even landed a job as a baggage handler for Braniff International at Dallas Love Field airport, a job that opened Watson's narrow world, providing him with discount airline tickets, which offered opportunities for the handsome young man to sow a few wild oats and hook up with assorted stewardesses on flights to Acapulco.

"God was very much part of my world," Watson recalled in a 1978 self-serving memoir, *Will You Die for Me?* (co-authored with prison chaplain Ray Hoekstra). His belief in God was unyielding. "He was The One you talked to every Sunday at the Copeville Methodist Church. He was The One who had long blond hair and beard (like no other man you ever saw) and wore a white robe and sat under palm trees with children on his knees in the Sunday-school calendars about believing in God." That was the way Watson put it.

The psychiatrists played up the whole small-town humble upbringing bit in their report. "Charles had a perfect attendance at school, was never in trouble with the law," noted Beverly Hills psychiatrist Dr. Keith Ditman. "He always tried to please his mother, a woman who was 'always on the run' doing everything for everybody. She was called 'Hot Rod Speedy Lizzie': a stern disciplinarian—often using a strap to punish him."

Then it all changed. Watson tried a stint at University of North Texas in Denton, just fifty miles from home, but he was restless. "I had no feelings [about college]," he told the doctors. "I just went along. My parents' world of church and God and rules wasn't what I wanted." So he decided to go west and put some distance between himself and his overprotective mother, who had broken up his two serious relationships with girls, according to one psychiatrist's report. "I can't tell you what to do—you're twenty-one now," she told him. In August 1967 he moved to the City of Angels which, unbeknownst to him, was to turn into his very own Sodom and Gomorrah. He hooked up with an old football team fraternity pal, Dave Neale, who introduced Watson to nightclubs and the Sunset Strip.

In the early Los Angeles days, he impressed many he met. A friend from that era recalled the first time he met Watson; he felt the guy was, "totally unreal"—a dramatic contrast to the typical, let-it-all-hang-out twenty-something LA types. "We couldn't believe him," Neale said. "He was so polite he would stand up when girls our age came into the room, and he called them all ma'am." He enrolled in California State University, Los Angeles, and moved into a shared apartment in Silver Lake, a small bedroom community barely spitting distance from the home of grocery store owner Leno LaBianca and his wife, Rosemary. Through a girlfriend, he began dealing a little dope. Then he dropped out of college and began dealing a lot more dope. He had smoked pot before, but slowly he began to sample more of the exotic stimulants making the rounds. In between, he started his own business called Love Locs, selling wigs to Beverly Hills women who were impressed by the handsome young Texan, fussing around them so attentively. But he quickly discovered that selling wigs was not as lucrative as selling drugs.

Several psychiatrists who interviewed and tested Watson at Atascadero seemed only too happy to accept at face value Watson's spoon-feeding narrative. His storybook upbringing, he repeated: the good boy from Texas who, through no fault of his own, had undergone a traumatic transformation from innocent abroad to serious druggie. Then brainwashed to kill, corrupted by a corrupt town and its decadent residents. "A naïve Texas boy without a conscience, who didn't know right from wrong," was the way he described himself to one psychologist. Poor guy, one doctor observed, faced by this den of iniquities, "He felt inadequate and insecure about himself."

Although he didn't realize it at the time, Watson's first big mistake was to pick up a good-looking blond surfer guy who was thumbing a ride home from the beach near Malibu to his home in Pacific Palisades. In late 1968 Watson was driving an eye-catching antique 1935 Dodge pickup when he pulled over for the hitchhiker, who affably recounted why he had to depend on the kindness of drivers to get a ride home. He owned a car, two in fact, he told Watson. One was a Ferrari and the other a Rolls. But he'd had some damned bad luck and wrecked both cars. He introduced himself as Dennis Wilson. Watson said the name didn't register until he said he was the drummer for The Beach Boys. Watson was greatly impressed.

They hit it off instantly, and Wilson invited him to hang out at his pad. In fact, a big party was planned for that evening. Twenty-four hours later, Watson had moved his bags into the big, spacious house on Sunset, filled to the brim with exotic houseguests. Wilson excitedly introduced him to one guy who was also staying with him. "Meet Charlie," he told Watson. "He's a musical genius." And with Charlie came a bunch of good-looking young women who lazed around the pool topless. It didn't take long for the devout, churchgoing kid from Copeville, Texas, to get with the program. Here he was, living rent free in a rock star's mansion filled with women and all the drugs one could ever wish for, along with a flood of famous and near-famous faces who came to party. There was Doris Day's son, Terry, and Dean Martin's stunning daughter, Deana. Rock legends and record producers. Wilson was generous to a fault, allowing the kid from Copeville to help himself to anything he fancied from the drummer's vast wardrobe. Overnight, they were all affectionately calling him "Tex."

Of Watson's time with Wilson, one doctor wrote: "While living with Mr. Wilson, he began smoking hashish. Once he ingested some rosewood seeds and had very frightening hallucinations. He was so out of control that he punched his fist through a door." Watson's reaction to drugs was sometimes like that. He lost all control. And yet he continued the cycle, seldom bothering to take any responsibility for his actions. "Mr. Wilson had many friends who would stop by, bringing acid and other hallucinogens," said one psychiatrist. "When Manson visited, his girls would bring baggies filled with acid. Mr. Watson, of course, followed their lead and began dropping acid."

Manson, who had survived in life by conning just about everyone who crossed his path, quickly got the measure of the gawky hick from Texas. When Watson and the rest of the Wilson freeloaders were eventually kicked out of the Sunset Boulevard pad, Watson seemed lost and strangely innocent. He admired the guy with the gentle voice and manner who ran around shepherding his flock of young lambs, and when they all left the high-rent district for the Spahn Ranch, Manson welcomed the now homeless Watson to his flock. It was just another of life's adventures for Watson and he eased into the transition just fine. Wrote his doctor: "Later on the Spahn Ranch, Mr. Watson took LSD daily. Manson would also give him speed, especially when he was working on the dune buggies. Manson would continually attract hippies to the ranch with his guitar, his music, and his girls. Invariably, they all brought drugs along with them."

Watson told the headshrinkers that at one time he had second thoughts about the Spahn Ranch lifestyle because of the excessive use of hallucinogens; so in December 1968 he abandoned Manson and moved in with his old North Texas State University pal David Neale and his actor brother whose stage name was Jay Scott, while they lived in houses in Topanga and Laurel Canyon. But three months later Watson says he was distraught when he learned that another of their school pals, Tommy Caraway, had been killed in Vietnam. Watson flew home to be a pallbearer at the funeral.

Watson, who had managed to dodge the draft because of an old football knee injury, decided to return to the Manson fold. He was warmly welcomed back by the girls, though not so much by Charlie. No one abandoned Manson—Charlie did not forget things like that. He had already replaced Watson with a new number one: Paul Watkins. Watson found himself desperately trying to get back into Charlie's good graces, and he said he would do anything Charlie wanted him to do just to prove his undying allegiance. "He [Manson] was like a magnet," Watson told one psychiatrist. "He told me that going against him was going against myself, that we're all the same mind. I became confused, and eventually Charlie put me through the change."

Watson was now building dune buggies—mostly from stolen cars—and his auto-mechanic expertise was much valued by Manson. Watson explained: "Charlie would only give us 'awareness drugs,' LSD, amphetamines, cocaine. He never gave us downers. When I worked on the dune buggies, he gave me speed." The lifestyle of Charles D. Watson, according to the gospel of Charles D. Watson fed to the doctors, went like this: "Every night Manson gave them drugs and they would gather together in song. In the morning Manson would 'compute me'—giving me a list of chores…Manson also fed them his helter-skelter philosophy: the racial war from which only the Family would survive, the beautiful people, the people with no fear."

Back under Manson's control, Watson was like putty, the doctors reported: "He succumbed to a steady diet of drugs. Acid and speed, and he also began using belladonna, the weed that grew wild on the Spahn Ranch. Mr. Watson's first experience with belladonna occurred in March 1969, when he chewed the boiled root and began having severe psychotic symptoms. He became confused, disoriented, assaultive, and hallucinated wildly." Watson told doctors his wide cocktail of drugs included, acid, mescaline, psilocybin, THC, and STP. The effect was devastating according to Watson, who told a psychiatrist, "I began talking to space people in space language."

Another time, after chewing belladonna, he went on a wild driving rampage, crashed his car, and was carted off to the county jail. Upon release from jail, and hobbling badly, he returned to the ranch, and resumed taking belladonna. According to Dr. Ira M. Frank of the UCLA Neuropsychiatric Institute, his drug intake became more intense. He mixed and consumed LSD, belladonna, methedrine, and cocaine. The mix, said Frank, took a terrible toll on him. "Perpetual distortions, illusions, and hallucinations, severe distortions of body image and body integrity and loss of sexual desire and the ability to perform," Frank noted. "He also showed a marked decrease in intellectual functions including impairment of memory, concentration, judgment, and loss of interest in intellectual pursuits."

Most striking, however, wrote the doctor: "Mr. Watson became completely submissive and relinquished what little identity he had as an individual, to the identity of the Family."

In his summation, Frank wrote: "In Manson, Mr. Watson found a powerful, omnipotent father figure, a man who was the real head of his family, a man who demanded unquestioned loyalty, obedience; a man who dominated and directed his girls in a way that Mr. Watson may have wished his own father had taken command. In addition, Manson and his family gave him a feeling of acceptance, of belonging, of being a somebody, a king upon whom beautiful girls showered their affection. This feeling of belonging came at a very high price, however, for Manson demanded the same total submissiveness from Watson that he demanded from his girls. To control them, Manson kept them in a continual state of drug-induced psychosis. Lastly, in this highly suggestible state of intoxication, Manson methodically employed a highly effective technique of progressive desensitization [through] which he carefully rehearsed the details of the murders in such a way as to disassociate their feelings from their actions."

Dr. A. R. Tweed was perhaps one of the fiercest proponents of the "not responsible for his actions" argument for Watson. "While in a highly suggestible state of intoxication he was gradually desensitized to believe that to kill was not wrong and, robot-like, he was able to carry out the wishes of his master and disassociate his feelings from the actions," Tweed wrote. "This seems borne out by the cold, detached manner in which the acts were accomplished. All this while only hearing the voice of Manson within him computing his every action. He actually believed at the time that they were really imaginary people. It was in such a drug-induced psychotic condition that the acts were carried out."

There was more of the same from Frank, who interviewed the patient more than half a dozen times in March and April 1971 and, returning to Watson's family roots, offered a plausible reason for the homicidal rage: "He was the 'ideal son' raised by a domineering mother, with an inadequate sense of self-identity—passive, dependent, and identified somewhat to a passive submissive father. He lead [sic] a life of letting others decide his role and behavior...In Manson he found a powerful father-figure who kept him in a state of drug-induced psychosis—a suggestible state of intoxication where he was desensitized to the act of murder by disassociating feelings from actions...During the murders he was in such a drug-induced psychotic state where he mechanically and without feeling had already given up everything and had become Charles Manson. They kept making love to him."

Said Watson: "I wanted them to want me."

Watson himself was later to recall: "Prosecution psychiatrists would claim I had faked much of my disintegration. But it was not true. All the little pieces just finally came unglued."

Repeated often to the doctors in great detail, his story was an appealing one. More important, the psychiatrists seemed delighted to be in on the Watson case. This was the kind of investigation that comes along only once or twice in any psychologist's professional lifetime. Watson was pure gold, and his Byzantine history, along with the notoriety of the murders, would surely make for exceptional dinner party conversation— not to mention providing enough grist for a cover story in any medical journal dealing with aberrant behavior. But would a jury buy it?

After three months at Atascadero Hospital, Watson was returned to Los Angeles for trial. Despite the use of the covey of defense psychiatrists, the jury showed no sympathy. Jurors, like the prosecution—led again by Vincent Bugliosi and Stephen Kay—were not convinced that Watson was insane when he murdered. Just plain evil. His trial, which began in August 1971, lasted only two months, compared to the almost one year devoted to Manson and the girls. Media interest and coverage was greatly diminished—lukewarm, in fact. I had covered every single day of the Manson trial, but this time my London editor felt covering day-to-day would not be worthwhile and instructed me to, "keep an eye on the case and file if anything big happens."

And that's what I did, showing up when key witnesses were due to appear, and particularly on the day that Watson testified in his own defense. I noticed that despite psychiatrists' protestations of his melted mind, Watson seemed to be fairly cagey and in control of his answers. Whenever there were tough questions, he dodged the prosecution's bullets by going the amnesiac route.

Some of the same faces who had testified the previous year, including Colonel Paul Tate, Linda Kasabian, and former family members Brooks Poston and Paul Watkins, paraded into the courtroom and repeated their testimony about life under the Manson regime. Watson, unlike Manson and the girls the year before, often looked a little dazed, even medicated, but never produced anything like the histrionics that Manson and the girls had trotted out a year before. He was always neatly attired, preppy style, in tie, slacks, and blazer. He had a Bible on the table in front of him. But this time his lawyers allowed him to testify. He did so, almost matter-of-factly, admitting his part in the killings and then dramatically demonstrating how he stabbed his victims.

"I raised my hand up and I stabbed them like that," he said as he brought his hand up and down in stabbing movements.

But he denied stabbing Sharon Tate. He was, he insisted, just a zombie, doing what Manson had ordered.

On the night of the killings he said he had taken LSD, speed, and belladonna. "I couldn't make it out," he said, when asked about his victims. "They were just blobs."

But there was no remorse: "I was doing what Charlie told me to do," he said.

How zonked out was he? He told psychiatrist Dr. Joel Fort—who was known as "the hippie doctor of Haight Ashbury and had campaigned long and hard to decriminalize marijuana—that the victims at the Cielo house were, "running around like chickens with their heads cut off."

Fort, testifying for the prosecution, was pretty clear, insisting that in his opinion Watson acted voluntarily despite his claims that he was merely a Manson robot.

What was different about evidence in the Watson trial was this: At the first trial, Linda Kasabian had testified that when they went out on the second night murder spree to the house on Waverly Drive—which happened to be just steps away from a house rented by Manson friend Harold True where Charlie and the girls often partied—it was Manson alone who first went into the LaBianca house and tied up the couple. Then he sent his mindless minions back to do the killing. At his trial Watson testified that both he and Manson went into the LaBianca house and tied up the terrified couple. Manson then returned to the parked car and sent Krenwinkel and Van Houten to join Watson and kill the LaBiancas. Manson drove off after telling the trio to hitchhike back to the ranch. That was the main discrepancy, although at both trials the jury was given the same gruesome, blow-by-blow account of how the trio murdered and mutilated the LaBiancas and carved "War" on Leno LaBianca's stomach, as well as leaving their grisly calling card: a fork in his stomach and a knife embedded in his throat.

Each time I attended the trial in the courtroom of Judge Adolph Alexander in the Hall of Justice, I noticed a sad-faced, middle-aged lady in dark glasses. She was smartly dressed with well-coiffed brown hair and sat in the front row, her eyes fixed on the defendant. He never acknowledged her and spent most of the trial blankly staring straight ahead in behavior that Bugliosi insisted was merely part of an act to reinforce his insanity plea.

Only when she testified on behalf of her son did I realize who she was. And I watched the expressionless Watson very closely. He sat, head bowed, and did not look at his mother even when she, distraught and having a hard time choking back tears, said in a soft, low whisper: "He was our pride and joy. When he finally called us on August 20, 1969, it was funny. He sounded like he was floating on a cloud. He talked about a man called Jesus who was named Manson. I didn't know what to think of him."

The next time he called, she said, he asked for money for an airline ticket home, saying, "Manson took everything he had."

Upon his return before his arrest, she recalled: "I certainly wouldn't have known him then. He laughed and slapped himself, as though he was on a cloud. I didn't know anything about dope. People in our little town don't have anything to do with dope."

And yet, despite his mother's worries, soon after the massacres and before his arrest by his cousin the local McKinney, Texas, Sheriff Tom Montgomery, Watson hadn't exactly been living the life of a penitent monk. He testified that he took trips to Mexico and Hawaii and after returning to Texas began dating and having a sexual relationship with an old girlfriend.

On October 12, 1971, the six-man, six-woman jury found twenty-five-year-old Watson guilty of seven counts of first-degree murder and one of conspiracy to commit murder. A week later, after two and a half hours of deliberation, they ruled he wasn't insane. One week later, on October 21, they sent him to San Quentin to await execution. But the devil dodged death. The death penalty was abolished in 1972.

He spent the next several decades using people to try to find his next lifeline.

THE VERDICT

"This man was not guilty of murdering my daughter. Okay? Of all the seven murders that I know of, he did not commit one of them. All right? I feel that he has taken the blame for all of them, and the ones that should be blamed for [them] is [sic] Tex Watson, and Susan Atkins, Patricia Krenwinkel, all of the girls."

—Doris Tate, mother of Sharon Tate,
Ron Reagan Show, 1991

On January 25, 1971, after more than seven months in the courthouse's Department 104—and only forty-three hours of deliberations—the jury handed down its verdict. My story ran the next morning on the front page of the London *Daily Express*: "Charles Manson and three girls he called his witches were found guilty of murder today and now face death in the gas chamber or life in jail." Despite my early qualms about the prosecution using the outlandish "The Beatles Made Me Do It" motive, the verdict came as no big surprise.

Since jury selection began on June 15, 1970, we had listened to a parade of witnesses—not to mention the over 300 exhibits painstakingly logged into the record as the prosecution laid it all out. Over 200 potential jurors were put through the *voir dire* mill over five long, drab weeks of repetitious questioning before the candidates were whittled down to a dozen and the alternates were seated. With energy to burn and neatly dressed in his, by-now-trademark sober, dark-blue, three-piece Brooks Brothers suit, crisp white shirt, and muted blue tie, Vincent Bugliosi finally stood up, and in measured and oft thunderous tones—at times sounding like an evangelical preacher—laid out his complex case. The jurors looked genuinely startled, even a little overwhelmed, as they were offered, for the first time, a truncated summary of the horrendous events that had played out on August 9 and 10 of the previous year.

To make sure we got it right, reporters covering the trial from beginning to end, who had been vetted and given reserved courtroom seats, were handed a thirteen-page opening statement—quite an unusual step in a major capital case. Bugliosi followed his script scrupulously. His co-counsel Aaron Stovitz told me some time later that he had been learning it by heart for days before. Bugliosi liked the flashy phrases, and he was barely a third into his delivery when Bruce Russell, the lanky Australian who was covering the trial for Reuters News Agency and a movie buff, turned to me and whispered, "Is he auditioning for *Inherit the Wind*?"

Bugliosi was impressive, and his overheated rhetoric made for good, quotable stuff. "What kind of diabolical, satanic mind would contemplate or conceive of these mass murders?" he asked. "The evidence will show Manson to be a megalomaniac who coupled his insatiable thirst for power with an intense obsession for violent death. The evidence will show Manson's fanatical obsession with helter-skelter—a term he got from the English recording group, the Beatles. Manson was an avid follower of the Beatles and believed that they were speaking to him through the lyrics of their songs." He quickly painted a picture of Manson as a phony: "Evidence will show defendant Manson to be a vagrant wanderer, a frustrated singer and guitarist, a pseudo philosopher, but most of all a killer who cleverly masqueraded behind the common image of a hippy, that of being peace-loving." The jurors were riveted, and scribbling furiously on legal pads—in fact, Bugliosi had urged them to take copious notes because of the complexity of the case and the diversity of witnesses he planned to call.

The first shock came moments after Bugliosi wound up his opening salvo: the defense lawyers declined to offer any opening statements. They said they would save what they had to say for their closing arguments. That night, as we gathered at the Hilton Hotel bar for cocktails and analysis, some thought it was a brilliant defense maneuver; others said it signaled total chaos in their ranks. "Insanity," reckoned veteran court reporter Theo Wilson. "The prosecution has already got the jury by the balls. This is a real defense screw-up. There's no way they can turn it around."

So, from late July until mid-November, the prosecutors painstakingly dominated the proceedings. Some eighty witnesses, ranging from the very first, Sharon Tate's father Col. Paul Tate, to Winifred Chapman—the Polanski maid who had made the grisly discovery at the Cielo Drive house—and on to a slew of homicide detectives, Thomas Noguchi (known as "the coroner to the stars" because of the numerous celebrity deaths he had handled), Terry Melcher, Veronica Howard and Virginia Graham, Susan Atkins' Sybil Brand cellmates. They all swore to tell the truth, the whole truth, and nothing but the truth in the marathon parade aimed at bolstering the prosecution's case.

But the star witness was Linda Kasabian, who was given immunity in return for her testimony. She spent seventeen straight days in the witness box, offering a first-hand account of going with the killers to the Tate house and describing in minute detail what she saw and heard when Manson accompanied them all the next day to the home of the LaBiancas. At twenty-one, she was remarkably poised, although she often burst into tears—particularly after her description of what she had witnessed at the Tate house. And she confirmed Bugliosi's helter-skelter scenario.

Manson's lawyer Irving Kanarek immediately tried to object to her testifying in the first place. "This witness is not competent," he said. "She's insane." And in his cross-examination, he tried to show what an unreliable witness she was. Yes, she imbibed LSD regularly, as well as all manner of stimulants, she admitted. Kanarek wanted to know if she remembered how exactly she behaved on trip number twenty-two, and again on her forty-fifth trip. He was trying to paint her as being a totally unreliable witness just telling a pack of lies to get immunity. But she remained amazingly serene, and his barrage seemed to have very little effect on deflating her damaging testimony. In fact, Kanarek went so hog wild in repeatedly ignoring the judge's warnings not to interrupt that he ended up spending a night in jail for contempt. He was to spend other nights locked up for contempt. Kanarek ate up seven days in his cross examination. Tempers often became overheated: even Bugliosi was fined $50 for contempt in his war of words with Kanarek. And so it went with each prosecution witness, and the defense trying vainly to punch holes in their credibility.

Veteran trial reporters were stunned once again when it came to the defense's turn to put on rebuttal witnesses. Facing a Mount Everest of damaging evidence, the defense lawyers remained unanimous: They were not calling a single witness. They were saving their best for end-of-trial summation. It later turned out that the girls wanted to tell their story—and would have unanimously testified that Manson was innocent of the killings. Van Houten's lawyer, Ronald Hughes, was outraged by the decision. "I refuse to take part in any proceeding where I am forced to push a client out of the window," he declared. That remark may have been responsible for Mr. Hughes' abrupt exit from the trial.

None of us in the press corps could believe what we were hearing. The girls wouldn't testify. And neither would Manson. Was it a brilliant and daring maneuver? Part of the debate was that the prosecution certainly hadn't proved its wild case—particularly against Manson— and by testifying, the girls could have opened themselves up to heavy cross-examination.

FROM THE VERY first time I saw Manson in person—in a tiny courtroom in Inyo County, California, in early December 1969—he was always "on." He loved strutting his stuff, no matter how unpredictable and unexpected it was, and Hollywood central casting couldn't have found a better candidate when it came to playing the villain. He was The Bogeyman incarnate—a reprobate, a deviant. In his mind, it was Charlie versus the corrupt world. That attitude continued in the Tate/LaBianca murder trial. As I filed into court week after week after week, my media colleagues and I wondered, "What will Charlie get up to next?" It was a game—until you realized the horrors of what Manson had wrought. He wrote his own wild script, and the performance was never the same.

Unlike the usual suit, shirt, and tie worn by many a defendant to suggest Mr. Ordinary Man wrongly accused, he wore blue denim, ornate medieval-style shirts, or buckskin, along with a waistcoat of many colors, elaborately designed and sewed for him by the girls still hanging out at the Spahn Ranch. He showed up with his head shaved bald, crosses carved into his forehead that shape-shifted into swastikas. We marveled at how on earth this maximum-security inmate was able to obtain implements to carry out this kind of minor surgery—apparently he'd managed to get hold of some sharp instruments in jail and indulged in a bit of self-mutilation. "I have X'd myself out of your world…your courtroom is man's game. Love is my judge," was his stated reason for this narcissistic move, according to printed notes handed out in the street to arriving media by Squeaky Fromme and the rest of the Manson outlaws. And then came another shocker: After his attorneys put on the slimmest defense possible, Manson decided he had to be heard. And the judge decided that Manson, for legal reasons, should have his say; yet he excused the jury for a preview, thus allowing Manson to take center stage. The result was a rambling, nearly one-hour-long rampage for the benefit of judge, lawyers, spectators, and the media, full of Manson homilies, outrageous personal and wacky opinions, gibberish, and double-speak. A disorganized manifesto—an unfettered policy statement—that ranged far and wide, from his own childhood to helter-skelter to life, death, and the Beatles. It had nothing whatsoever to do with the senseless slaughter of seven innocents in August 1969:

I never went to school, so I never growed up to read and write too good, so I have stayed in jail and I have stayed stupid, and I have stayed a child while I have watched your world grow up, and then I look at the things that you do and I don't understand. You eat meat, and you kill things that are better than you are, and then you say how bad, and even killers, your children are. You made your children what they are. These children that come at you with knives. They are your children. You taught them. I didn't teach them. I just tried to help them stand up.

He sermonized about his Family:

Most of the people at the ranch that you call the Family were just people that you did not want, people that were alongside the road, that their parents had kicked out, that did not want to go to Juvenile Hall. So I did the best I could and I took them up on my garbage dump and I told them this: that in love there is no wrong. I told them that anything they do for their brothers and sisters is good if they do it with a good thought...I was working at cleaning up my house, something that Nixon should have been doing. He should have been on the side of the road, picking up his children, but he wasn't. He was in the White House, sending them off to war.

He even saw himself as a political commentator, with strong anti-war sentiments:

I don't understand you, but I don't try. I don't try to judge nobody. I know that the only person I can judge is me...But I know this:

that in your hearts and your own souls, you are as much responsible for the Vietnam War as I am for killing these people…My father is the jailhouse. My father is your system—I am only what you made me. I am only a reflection of you…I have ate out of your garbage cans to stay out of jail. I have wore your second-hand clothes…I have done my best to get along in your world and now you want to kill me, and I look at you, and then I say to myself, YOU want to kill ME? Ha! I'm already dead, have been all my life. I've spent twenty-three years in tombs that you built.

Then he turned his attention to his fellow defendants in a self-serving statement:

These children were finding themselves. What they did, if they did whatever they did, is up to them. They will have to explain that to you. It's all your fear. You look for something to project it on, and you pick out a little old scroungy nobody that eats out of a garbage can, and that nobody wants, that was kicked out of the penitentiary, that has been dragged through every hellhole that you can think of, and you drag him and put him in a courtroom. You expect to break me? Impossible! You broke me years ago. You killed me years ago.

Older asked Manson if he had anything further to add to his remarks. Of course, he did:

I have killed no one. And I have ordered no one to be killed. I may have implied on several different occasions to several different people that I may have been Jesus Christ, but I haven't decided yet what I am or who I am. Some called him Christ. In prison his name was a number. Some now want a sadistic fiend, and so they see him as that. So be it. Guilty. Not guilty. They are only words. You can do anything you want with me, but you cannot touch me because I am only my love. If you put me in the penitentiary, that means nothing because you kicked me out of the last one. I didn't ask to get released. I liked it in there because I like myself.

Older suggested Manson stick to trial issues, which Manson obliged. He addressed the helter-skelter motive:

Helter-skelter means confusion, literally. It doesn't mean any war with anyone. It doesn't mean that some people are going to kill other people. Helter-skelter is confusion. Confusion is coming down around you fast. If you can't see the confusion coming down around you fast, you can call it what you wish. Is it a conspiracy that the music is telling the youth to rise up against the establishment because the establishment is rapidly destroying things? Is that a conspiracy? The music speaks to you every day, but you are too deaf, dumb, and blind to even listen to the music…It is not my conspiracy. It is not my music. I hear what it relates. It says "Rise," it says "Kill." Why blame it on me? I didn't write the music.

I do feel some responsibility. I feel a responsibility for the pollution. I feel a responsibility for the whole thing… To be honest with you, I don't recall ever saying, "Get a knife and a change of clothes and go do what Tex says." Or I don't recall saying, "Get a knife and go kill the sheriff." In fact, it makes me mad when someone kills snakes or dogs or cats or horses. I don't even like to eat meat—that is how much I am against killing. I haven't got any guilt about anything because I have never been able to see any wrong. I have always said: "Do what your love tells you, and I do what my love tells me." Is it my fault that your children do what you do? What about your children? You say there are just a few? There are many, many more coming in the same direction. They are running in the streets-and they are coming right at you!

When he finished, Older asked Manson if he wanted to repeat his statement to the jury. He surprised everyone again by firmly declining to repeat his tirade for the benefit of the jury. "I have already relieved all of the pressure that I had," he said. Then, turning to his three codefendants he added, "You don't have to testify now." And he sat down.

MANSON'S FINAL DECISION not to testify in front of the jury weighing his guilt or innocence, who would also decide on life and death, seemed at first an odd choice given his constant claims that he had been railroaded by a vengeful DA. But, upon reflection, it may have been a wise choice. It was patently obvious that if he had agreed to be a formal witness in his own defense, he would have opened himself up to cross-examination from Bugliosi, who would have loved to rip apart his half-baked beliefs. Bugliosi would have gone straight for Manson's throat. This way, the media could report on his ramblings, allowing Manson to spread his invective and get away without a confrontation. And if he took the witness stand, then inevitably so would Atkins, Krenwinkel, and Van Houten, which would have opened a veritable Pandora's box for the defense. Manson was shrewd enough to avoid that pitfall.

So, following his Manson Show, the court recessed for several days, allowing the defense to prepare its closing arguments. But when the trial resumed in late November, there was another huge shock: Van Houten's lawyer Hughes had disappeared. A short delay was called, after which Older appointed Maxwell Keith to represent Van Houten, and Bugliosi delivered his final argument. Then, after a Christmas break, the other defense lawyers came to life with their closing arguments. Keith and Krenwinkel's lawyer, Paul Fitzgerald, tried their darndest in defense of their clients. Keith, so late to the party, emphasized that Manson was the real villain of the piece and Van Houten was merely a puppet. Fitzgerald stressed that the jury should not forget that key witness, Kasabian, was a walking laboratory of mind-blowing drugs, and therefore her testimony was tainted.

Speaking for Susan Atkins, Daye Shinn took a half-hearted shot at denigrating Howard and Graham, suggesting they had concocted Atkins' confession to get swift parole. And Irving Kanarek, as expected, droned on and on about how his client was a misunderstood, peaceful man. It was excruciating, almost at a torture level, to sit through his summation as he rambled on for seven nonsensical days in a vain effort to seek mercy for a client who had deliberately turned the trial into his own unruly playground and was obviously in no way going to beg for anyone's mercy. Halfway through, Older interrupted, reminding him, "Mr. Kanarek, you are filibustering." I wasn't surprised when I heard later that after just one day of listening to Kanarek, some jurors demanded pills so they could stay awake during his marathon dirge.

Shortly before noon on January 25, I sat in my assigned courtroom seat in the second row. People stood lining the walls as the guilty-on-all-counts verdict was formally read by court clerk Gene Darrow. It was almost anticlimactic. We knew it was coming. Time seemed to stand still. *This was a movie, and not for real*, I thought. The defendants sat impassively listening as each juror was then routinely asked to confirm the verdict. Manson appeared emotionless, scratching his beard and smiling at the three girls. It *was* unreal, and for a moment I wondered if any of the women really realized what was happening and where they were. It took almost thirty minutes to read all the convictions, and when it was complete, Manson suddenly came to life. Pointing to the judge, he bellowed: "We weren't allowed to put on a defense. You won't outlive that, old man."

I rushed out to the nearest phone to dictate my story to make the paper's early first edition in London. They said it would be the front-page splash—pushing over a story about a former heavyweight boxer named Idi Amin, who had seized power in Uganda.

With the judgment phase over, the same jury proceeded to determine the penalty, as dictated by California law. And so, for another eight weeks it dragged on—though at least this time the defense attorneys made a bigger effort to persuade the jury not to give their clients death.

Finally, on February 1, witnesses for the defense were called: Patricia Krenwinkel's parents, Joseph and Dorothy, and Leslie Van Houten's mother, Jane. All emphasized the normal upbringing of their offspring before they took the corrupt path to Manson. Lynette Fromme, Sandra Good, and Catherine Share talked about the delights of being members of the Family. Even Susan Atkins testified to her normal upbringing—but then, under questioning, calmly admitted she was guilty of murder. Manson's only penalty-phase witness was his parole officer, Samuel Barrett, who didn't do much in support of Manson's cause noting that, because he had 150 or more parole clients to look after, his memory about Manson was a little fuzzy.

But it was way too little, and way too late. After another eight weeks, on March 29, the jury said all four defendants should be sent to San Quentin's death row to await execution. Unlike their victims, fate would ultimately spare them from death.

"Manson," a documentary about Charlie and his clan, was nominated for an Oscar in 1972—but didn't win.

CHARLES MANSON:
SUPERSTAR

"I've got a thousand faces, so that makes me five hundred schizophrenics. And in my life, I've played every one of those faces. Sometimes because people push me into a role, and sometimes because it's better being someone else than me."
—*Manson in His Own Words*, by Nuel Emmons

"I'm the most famous human not only that is alive but the most famous human being that ever lived—and I'm not even dead yet,"
—Charles Manson, 2019 REELZ documentary
MANSON: Final Words

"Mr. and Mrs. America, you are wrong. I am not the King of the Jews, nor am I a hippie cult leader. I am what you have made me, and the Mad Dog Devil Killer Fiend Leper is a reflection of your society. Whatever the outcome of this madness that you call a fair trial or Christian justice, you can know this: In my mind's eye, my thoughts light fires in your cities."
—Manson, after his 1971 conviction

For decades, millions of Americans' worst nightmares came true: Charles Manson regularly invaded their living rooms. For, though he never made it as a rock star, he went on to achieve a different kind of international fame—or rather infamy. He became, hands down, the best-known mass murderer in American history, constantly "refreshing" his fiendish image by appearing in the eighties and nineties with some regularity as the star attraction on countless TV news magazines, fronted by an assortment of high-profile hosts, who vied with each other to give him his fifteen minutes of fame once again. He was a hot property in primetime, no less, and if you saw him on ABC and were mesmerized, then you might catch him doing a flamboyant encore on the rival CBS or NBC. Except it was never quite the same performance. There was a new script, a new look, and new lively combat with his interrogator. An astonishing achievement considering he had been incarcerated since his arrest in Death Valley, California, since October 1969.

Performances came with a variety of poses and demeanors. He was never penitent. Never guilty. Of anything. Affable to start, practiced and pensive. For your viewing pleasure, you had your choice: Crazy Charlie, Manson the Belligerent, or Manson the Wistful, a misunderstood, medicated monster. There was also Charlie the Clown, the Jester, the Avenger, society's fall guy. The Conservationist. The evil, wild-eyed killer, an illustrated man with tattoos from ear to wrists, complete with that swastika on his forehead. It either refused to heal or, more likely, he touched it up for each appearance.

He twiddled with his long, Jesus-style brown locks—though, by the time his run on the home box had ended, his hair had turned gray. One day he was clean-shaven, the next he was heavily hirsute, stroking his beard like a college professor pondering a question. He jangled his prison chains, strutted around in a variety of costumes, from blue jeans to billowy, yellow pajama-style pants to prison-issued orange jumpsuits. His mood changed frequently, sometimes in the course of one appearance; one minute he would be laughing; the next, he was twitchy and testy, slurring his words. He tossed out obviously rehearsed lines. It was also a platform for his vitriol, if the interviewer allowed him to get away with it. And nine times out of ten, they did it because he was such great entertainment—no threat because he was locked up for life. I, along with millions worldwide, watched his performances with fascination; it was obvious he was carefully prepping for these interviews and knew what his audience craved from him.

He was remarkably sanguine with Ron Reagan, Jr., although he couldn't resist a dig about Reagan's privileged presidential heritage. "I'm not a generation of the Sixties—I'm a generation of the Thirties," Manson told him. "I played on the same ball club that your old man made movies about."

Reagan Jr. pulled out a CD of Manson singing his own songs. Sensing he could bond with Reagan, he suddenly switched, becoming the humble questioner: "Do you think I've done something bad…that I should be ashamed of?"

"I honestly don't know what you've done or haven't done, so it's not for me to judge," Reagan replied. Then, getting a little tougher and, turning the tables, he asked, "What's evil to you?"

"I'm God to my friends," Manson answered. "And the devil to my enemies."

Asked what Christ would have thought about what went on in the Sharon Tate and LaBianca houses, he said, "We all have Jesus within us."

And when Reagan asked if Watson had Jesus in mind "when he was sticking a knife and fork in Leno LaBianca," Manson's response was strange, to say the least. "Tex didn't have any choice, he was trapped in his mother's mind. He had to do what he did. He was a slave to society because that's what he was thrown into by the world he lived in…I walk the line…I keep a close watch on this heart of mine…I walk the line. I walked with Tex. But when Tex took out his knife, I said, 'Excuse me, I've got to go in the canteen and get myself an ice cream!'"

NBC's super-macho Tom Snyder and the combative Geraldo Rivera for ABC both opted for a "take-no-prisoners"-type interview. Manson responded in kind. He'd grown up handling jailhouse bullies and those prison mates determined to crush this diminutive criminal professional. To Snyder he declared, "I've been in jail all my life. I was raised here. It's the maniacs outside I can't handle. I'm playing for my life...you are working for money, mister. I haven't killed anyone."

"What about Shea?" Snyder asked, referring to Hollywood stunt-man "Shorty" Shea, who incurred Manson's wrath by marrying a black woman and tipping police off about Manson's car theft racket at the Spahn Ranch.

"What about him?" Manson retorted testily.

"What about Hinman?" Snyder replied, referring to musician Gary Hinman, who was killed by Bobby Beausoleil a few weeks before the Tate-LaBianca killings.

"I cut the dude's ear off...because of the way he treated Bobby, who was a kid. I was a Beatnik in the fifties before the hippies came along. I was in the Cook County jail in Chicago while you were playing cricket in high school."

Their dialogue was far-ranging. "I knew I wasn't going to go to the gas chamber because I'd never done anything wrong," Manson said. "You put me on *Life* magazine and had me convicted before I walked into the courtroom. But sometimes I feel I'm as scared to live...living is scary, dying is easy." And then he giggled nervously. "I've been an outlaw...ever since I was born...reform school aged ten, I learned to box and cry and learned to do all the things you learn at reform school...I escaped...and went to prison...and asked the guys in prison, and they told me all the things they knew...I was told try sincere and honesty...and I said, 'I've tried everything else...maybe I'll try sincere and honesty.'"

Manson said when he first got married at the age of twenty it was purely for sex. "I miss women [giggling again], as long as they keep their mouth shut and do what they need to do ...that's what a woman is supposed to do...I don't want them snitching on me." That seemed like an obvious reference to Susan Atkins, who first blew the whistle on Manson, and then Linda Kasabian who was the prosecution's star witness.

When Snyder asked what he would do if he ever was released from jail, Manson smiled broadly. "Get out of here…where would I go? They said I was incorrigible and not only incorrigible, but I'd never grow up. And I kinda agreed with them. I live and die by my words…I have all my life…for forty-five years in prison. My word is my bond. I broke no law. I didn't step out of line with God. I didn't step out of line with The Man."

In 1986, with Charlie Rose on assignment for the CBS program *Nightwatch*, Manson, who liked to carefully tailor his attitude to what he thought he knew about each interviewer, immediately greeted him like a fan or an old pal when they met in San Quentin. "Hey, Rose, how are you? I've been watching you on the tube," he said, brightly shaking hands with his interviewer.

Rose asked how his day had gone, noting, "The weather in San Quentin is better than the weather in Washington—I left four inches of snow."

Manson replied, "I'm kind of nervous. I've been locked up in the hole for a long time…so, for me, coming out of the cell is a whole brand new experience for me."

Rose shrugged off the feigned intimacy and got down to brass tacks. "How do you feel about those murders?"

"How do you feel about 'em?"

Ignoring the retort, Rose plunged forward: "What did you think of Sharon Tate and her unborn baby?"

"It's not in my world…I don't live in that world."

"Care?" Rose asked.

"What does that mean…care? Break my teeth out, break my ribs, kick me down a hole, and then come back and tell me about care…I don't know what care is, man."

Asked if the Tate death was murder, Manson replied: "No. No

murder in a holy war. I did not direct nobody to be killed, man." He jumps to his feet, furious, argumentative, and threatening. Then he begins to sing a Beatles song from *The White Album*: "Why don't they do it in the road...no one will be watching us." Banging on the desk, his performance gets wilder. He pumps his fist, as the watching guards on the sidelines nervously stiffen. "I am not a violent human being...I said [to the girls] if you are going to do something...leave something witchy... just as I would tell you...if you are going to do something well...do it well...have a good day."

"Did you tell them to mutilate?" Rose asks.

"If you are going to do something, do it with your soul and heart... they are responsible for their actions. I am responsible for my actions."

"What do you say to those who say, 'Charlie Manson is a psychopath'?"

"There's a whole lot of us nowadays . . ."

"Or he's schizophrenic...?"

"I can be that. Aren't we all?"

Asked where Charlie Manson came from, Manson responded: "I come from the heart of Bing Crosby...Frank Sinatra...Tom Mix... Roosevelt. I come from the hills of Kentucky, from hard times...baloney Sunday dinner. I come from Depression...I know my father...is all men. I am loved...I am love."

Another right-turn from Rose: "Do you make scorpions in jail?"

"I make little things out of string...I send them everywhere. No one pays me for them. I make all kinds of things. I am spiritually allied with the scorpions and the wolf."

He ranted about Nixon, and then Ronald Reagan being shot, and he surprised Rose by claiming he likes listening to classical music in jail. "Then I go down to LA and some district attorney wants to get rich and make a lot of money, and he dumps it on me. They took my rights, man. You don't take my rights."

OUT OF ALL of his interviews, Manson seemed most to enjoy jousting with ABC's perfectly coiffed Diane Sawyer, who had come to Corcoran State Prison in California in December 1993 to interview him for *20/20*. It turned out to be Manson's last major network TV interview, although much of that material was reworked and reshown in later documentaries about Manson. Sawyer, a superstar with the network and married to Oscar-winning director Mike Nichols, started gently once prison guards removed the chains around her subject's hands, waist, and feet. But once the niceties of Manson noting that they both had an affinity for Kansas—because he knew that she had been born in Glasgow, Kansas—Sawyer dispensed with the small talk: "Why did they kill everyone there?"

"They freaked out. Tex was stoned. Everyone was loaded."

"Is Charlie Manson crazy?"

"Whatever that means...Sure he's crazy. As mad as a hatter? What difference does that make now? Everybody is crazy." Then he trotted out the whole "woe is me" story—the unloved, throwaway kid from a broken home, all delivered with an aw-shucks country drawl. "When you get in trouble you call your mother, I ain't got no mother...to call. When you go to the bank...draw some money, pay lawyer...I ain't got no money...I can't go to no lawyer."

When the Sawyer interview ended, and before Manson was taken back to his cell, a pretty blonde production aide stepped out in front of Manson and asked if she could have a photo taken with the World's Most Dangerous Man. They posed, and while she took great pains to make sure neither of them touched, she still beamed broadly as if taking a typical holiday snap. That done, Manson turned to Sawyer as if a new important thought had just flashed into his mind—a jovial footnote perhaps, a kind of throwaway trademark line from Peter Falk as Detective Columbo in the NBC TV series—but this was delivered seriously: "One other thing, please. Everybody says I'm five-foot-two. When I was arrested I was five-foot-seven—then I went down to five-six...then five feet...By the time you all die, I will be about three feet tall."

They all laughed, and Sawyer took the bait. "How tall are you, Charlie?"

"I'm five-foot-six and three quarters."

Apparently, size did matter to Charlie.

THERE'S NO PLACE LIKE...JAIL

"I ain't never been anything but a half-assed thief who didn't know how to steal without getting caught. The only home I've ever known is one of these concrete and steel prisons."
— Charles Manson, *In His Own Words*

"You can jump up and scream, 'Guilty,' and you can say what a no-good guy I am, and what a devil, fiend, eeky-sneaky slimy devil I am. It is your reflection and you're right, because that is what I am. I am whatever you make me."
— Manson at trial

After his conviction, Charles Manson knew he would never see freedom again. "Where would I go?" was his consistent answer to anyone asking what he would do if granted parole. Not a chance in hell. And he knew it. But the reality is, if he had been executed somewhere along the way before the death penalty was abolished in early 1972, there would have been no legend. And you wouldn't be reading this.

"He doesn't mind life behind bars," noted Vincent Bugliosi, on hearing the death penalty ruling. "I said to myself, 'Charlie's beaten the rap.'"

Except for a few brief interludes, Manson's life was spent incarcerated. He may have felt during his Los Angeles sojourn that his music career was taking off and he would be "bigger than the Beatles," but his was a wasted life spent mostly behind bars with not a hint of remorse or regret. So he did the next best thing and managed to survive in a series of prison and protective housing units (PHU's), which became home to him for the rest of his life.

"A prison within a prison to provide separate housing for inmates who cannot be safely controlled in the general population" was the way the California Department of Corrections described the Manson digs.

Over the years, the California prison system transported him back and forth, and back and forth yet again, mostly in a heavily guarded bus to wherever they deemed he should go. It turned out that no warden, even in the toughest of pens, wanted to keep Charles Manson on the books. His endless games and mind-fucks labeled him trouble with a capital T. So they moved him around and around like a contagious leper.

Post his murder conviction, in April 1971, Manson tasted the special treatment given Death Row inmates at San Quentin, which was spitting distance from San Francisco Bay. He learned very quickly that his crazy, loudmouth guru act didn't fly.

According to Edward George, author of the 1999 book, *Taming the Beast: Charles Manson's Life Behind Bars*, written with crime writer Dary Matera, Manson didn't have it easy in the brutal San Quentin hell-hole. George, a former seminary student and Naval pilot, was transferred from a cushy prison job in the picturesque Sierra Nevada mountains to the cesspit of San Quentin. And it was there that he inherited the notorious prodigal son of the California prison system.

During the eight years he worked with Manson as a prison counselor, he was both charmed and repulsed by "the little motherfucker."

"Although Manson repeatedly bragged that 'there's plenty of sex in prison,' I'm sure he was in no way prepared for his fate at San Quentin," George wrote. "The small, thin, chauvinistic guru was pursued like a schoolgirl and eventually 'punked' by an extremely dangerous and aggressive Aryan Brotherhood inmate—a tough, brutal criminal who took what he wanted and made Manson his mate, forcing the once-dominant cult leader into the passive, submissive 'woman's' position of his nightmarish childhood—both literally and figuratively.

"Although he had gained an important protector, the role reversal had to grate on whatever remained of Manson's sense of personal dignity. Playing housemaid to an arrogant, abusive sexual bully while waiting to be executed had to be the worst period of his life."

Explaining Manson's ping-pong prison life, George admits he too became entranced by Manson. He noted that when the death penalty was abolished, what to do with Manson created a massive headache for the California prison authorities.

"To get rid of him, San Quentin quickly transferred him to the California Medical Facility (CMF) in Vacaville for psychiatric evaluation. Found mentally stable, he was sent to Folsom...and had to survive among vicious gangs like the Aryan Brotherhood, the Black Guerilla Family, the Mexican Mafia...Some members of these groups itched to create a name for themselves by 'offing' the world's most famous felon."

At Folsom, he was a huge headache, noted George. His girls camped outside the prison and harassed the staff. The faithful, including Lyn Fromme and Sandra Good, were not allowed to visit, although they were later able to exchange letters with him. In the early days in San Quentin there were rumors that Manson might marry Fromme, which then might have allowed her to visit him.

"Do you want to marry her?" jailer George asked. "He looks at me, and he has this crucifix on the wall in his cell and says, 'Can you imagine me coming off the cross to get married?'"

In addition, Manson, as he did when he was free and running wild in Southern California in the mid and later sixties, had instructed some of the girls to sexually service a handful of inmates in return for his protection. While the girls were not allowed to visit Manson, there was nothing to stop them—at Manson's direction—from visiting other selected inmates and in a laissez faire attitude, particularly in the outdoor

Folsom visiting areas, to provide an assortment of creative sexual treats ranging from blowjobs to other masturbatory exercises. It was a win-win situation for Manson as well as his fellow jailbirds. And Manson was not reluctant to order his girls to provide sexual services to Aryan Brotherhood members who were not behind bars, which earned him IOUs from Brotherhood inmates.

During his fluctuating and circuitous travels around the worst prisons of California, Manson was beaten up, berated, set afire. Even his precious guitar was smashed to pieces by spiteful inmates sick of his endless strumming. In 1974 while at Folsom he was viciously attacked by former Family member Kenneth Como who was a member of the jail's Aryan Brotherhood. Como had fallen in love with "Gypsy" Share and later they were briefly married. Ironically Como was serving a sentence for robbing a gun shop in Hawthorne, California, in August 1971 with Share and other family members in a crackpot scheme to get enough weapons to break Charlie out of jail. Armed guards at Folsom had to break up the fight between Manson and Como, although Manson came off much the worse for wear. But it wasn't all bad. Manson peddled autographed photos, recorded music, and welcomed the crème de la crème of TV celebrity interviewers into his guarded chambers.

Over the years, he continued his tour of the California prison system, quickly learning—as on the outside—how to work things to his benefit.

For example, when he was shipped to Vacaville prison for his frequent psychological examinations, he decided the place was more to his liking. So to extend his time there he punched a guard and was "punished" by a three-month stay, which included more examinations and the relative comfort and safety of a maximum security isolated cell. It sure beat the hell out of the accommodations and hostilities of a San Quentin or Folsom cell.

Whether it was an act or not, prison officials frequently wrote him up for a variety of offenses, noting the "deterioration of his mental condition." That signaled an excursion. So, in dizzying repetition, he was frequently shipped back to CMF at Vacaville, his prison of choice, for more sessions with the shrinks.

In 1982, James Dowding was getting his first post-doctoral experience as a forensic psychologist and encountered Manson at Vacaville. After eight sessions with Manson, he got to know him pretty well. Writing about his interviews in a 2019 article for the New Worcester Spy web magazine based in Worcester Massachusetts, he recalls: "He guarded and protected himself well through his theatric meanderings. I could always tell if he didn't like the way the inquiry was going, because he would make some veiled or more pronounced threat that essentially ended the discussion. For example, at one point he said, 'You know, I still have friends on the outside.' I simply glared back at him without a response and moved the topic to another area.

"Much of what he had to say had a certain dramatic tone and intent...a soliloquy of sorts that was a running commentary on how the world had abused and mistreated him."

In summation, Dowding observed, "In my professional opinion he never did 'wield the knife,' but essentially derived satisfaction from guiding and coercing others to fulfill his murderous impulses."

Joseph McGrath, a lifelong employee of the prison system, now retired and working as a consultant, became closely acquainted with Manson in the eighties. In a 2018 interview, McGrath told me he ended up with Manson after the warden at Corcoran Prison called to say they were sick of Manson and wanted to unload him.

Corcoran was a three-hour, 170-mile drive from Los Angeles, located in the middle of an old cotton field in Kings County, Central California, and it housed some of the most dangerous felons.

"He's involved in some drug smuggling deal, and there's one problem after another," the Corcoran warden told McGrath. "We need a break. Let me send him up to you guys and see what the shrinks say about him."

Once again Manson headed to Vacaville.

For the first time in his life, Charles Manson was provided a certain degree of stability at Vacaville. His cell was surprisingly roomy and personal, decorated with a straw hat, assorted photographs, and a cross. He had a four-foot-tall private locker, and he even managed to string his own washing line to dry out clothing as well as a bathroom-style wall bar to hang clothing and towels. There, in a supposedly safer environment, he was "royalty," considered a star, almost immediately turning his cell into a 24/7 home and office. McGrath became Manson's correctional counsellor and, despite their adversarial relationship, he paints an oddly fascinating—even affectionate—glimpse of Manson behind bars.

McGrath recalled: "In 1983, I had an office in the middle of the tiers, where the cells were. I put Charlie in a cell directly across the walkway of my office to keep my eye on him. So, from time to time, he would pop over from his cell to my office. It was like a neighborly over-the-garden-fence chat. That's how I got to know him. He told me he didn't want to get out. He'd say he'd been locked up since he was nine—since going to reform school."

McGrath didn't think he was up to taking on the real world. "Jail time was an opportunity for him to stay in the limelight and do his thing—even appear on the six o'clock news from time to time. What bemused me over the years was the amount of people that would write saying they loved him. Twenty to thirty letters a day from all over the world. I had to read and vet those letters. They would say, 'I love you. I am here for you. My children love you. You are my hero and I will do anything for you.' And they'd send him money. Mostly they came from women."

He said Manson needed special handling: "You had to stay on top of it because Charlie was always trying to pull off some scheme. Not criminal or threatening, but a few cons, so I had to stay one step ahead so we wouldn't look stupid. There are individuals in prison who try to manipulate everything that happens to them if they think it is in their best interest. They will file a grievance and get courts to litigate. Charlie was not that kind of guy—he tried to stay low profile"—however Manson would be defined low profile in California's prison system.

McGrath assigned Manson to work as a porter. Essentially, his duties were mopping, cleaning, and housekeeping. "He had a special card from me that showed what his job was. One day he was pushing his basket on rollers through an area he wasn't supposed to be in, and a guard confronted him. Then he flashed his card under the guard's nose. Of course, everyone knew who he was. He liked to push it. He was not trying to escape, but he got his kicks challenging the system. It was a cat-and-mouse game for him because he liked to show he could beat the system and get away with what he could get away with. In his cell, he listened to lots of music, and he always had money. So he managed to rig up his cell so he could play his guitar, sing, and even record his music. And somehow he would smuggle those tapes out of prison and make a lot of money."

In fact, in 1993 a company called Grey Matter Records released a 13-track album of Manson music with songs titled *Boxcar Willy and Big Bad Joe* and *Marilyn Monroe was my Childhood Shame*, which featured Manson singing to his own acoustic guitar accompaniment. It was actually recorded at Vacaville prison. In the hopes of cashing in on the more notorious "sexier" prison, it was titled *Live at San Quentin*. Anything Johnny Cash can do Charles Manson can do better! Location or not, terrible sound quality plus inmate background noises did not a hit make, although today, those recordings may be worth a few shillings in the Manson memorabilia marketplace.

At Vacaville, Manson called McGrath "Mr. Mac," and he liked to play mind games. "He had a certain crazy look in his eyes, always trying to impress you, to get you to believe he was supernatural," recalled McGrath. "In the clinical sense, I don't think he was crazy. He knew what he was doing. He may have been screwed up, but he liked to play those games, and he was good at it. He could convince you of anything, if he could get you to buy into his premise. He was masterful at that. Charismatic and fascinating. I would talk to him for hours on end about the government contaminating water, cutting down trees, and ruining our environment—and some of that is very true. Then he would carry that to the next level and turn to me and say, 'You're going along with system? So, aren't you part of the very problem they create?' He could convince people who were not very well grounded in their beliefs because he truly was a fantastic persuader. What a manipulator.

"He always returned to the same line. 'So, you think I'm the prisoner? But you are really the prisoner. Here's the thing. If you don't get up in the morning and come to work, your family doesn't eat. Right? Your family doesn't get medical care. Right? You're out of bed at four in the morning and you have to do what The Man tells you to. Otherwise you don't survive.' And then he would say, 'I've got a warm bed, I get the food. You're the slave to the system. I'm the one whose every whim is catered to!' In some ways, he was almost demonic. And spiritual. I don't want to say he had power, but there was an aspect of him that was also truly frightening."

McGrath recalled several top-level government prison officials coming to Vacaville especially to meet Manson. One day, he said, "a bigwig bureaucrat" whose title was Federal Receiver and who was involved in overseeing a new health program for inmates arrived with his secretary. McGrath ushered him in. "And there this guy stood, almost star-struck, his eyes with a mile-wide smile, as if he couldn't believe he was meeting our very own celebrity inmate. The Fed and Manson shook hands, and then Charlie turned and politely greeted his secretary. She was a neatly dressed lady in her early thirties, attractive in a civil service, buttoned-down sort of way. However, not beautiful. Charlie turned and, as he gently grasped her hand, she froze on the spot. If you could have seen the look on her face—her eyes were big, her face was a combination of scared shitless and awe, her hands shook. Charlie began complimenting her, saying what a beautiful young woman she was. Smoothly he segued into personal stories about being in prison since he was young. I knew I needed to end the conversation and escort them out. Right then. Just before they left, Charlie turned to the federal guy. 'I wanna tell you something,' he said, switching his attention to the Receiver. 'Mr. Mac—this guy here with us—is squared away. If he tells you, then his word is as good as gold. One of the best fellows I've ever met.' The government guy turned to me and with a wry smile said, 'Mac, I don't know whether to give you a pay raise or a character reference—from Charles Manson.'"

But not everyone was fascinated by Manson's company, or his gift of the gab. While mostly he tried to avoid physical altercations with other inmates, there were times when he was bashed and beaten by inmates who felt they might garner notoriety by pummeling the pipsqueak Manson. One inmate at Vacaville even tried to kill him in September 1984. McGrath's version of the story was this: The inmate was a mentally ill thirty-six-year-old prisoner named Jan Holmstrom, who was serving a ten-year sentence for the second-degree shotgun murder of his gynecologist father, Emil, in Pasadena in 1974. Holmstrom had been adopted as a baby by a wealthy Pasadena family, and without warning he turned on his adoptive father. After the murder he was diagnosed as paranoid schizophrenic.

McGrath said Manson got his kicks by tormenting Holmstrom. "He'd shout negative things at him through the walls about him being a member of the Hare Krishna sect," McGrath recalled. "And then he would make those little doll figures from threads he disassembled from sweaters and other clothes. On one he put a rope noose around the doll's neck, and then hung it over Holmstrom's cell. I guess that was the final straw." Shortly after that incident, at the end of a hobby-craft class, Holmstrom poured paint thinner into a paper cup, pretending it was water. When he got close to Manson, he threw the contents of the cup into his face, then tossed a match at Manson, setting his face alight.

"The guards heard Charlie screaming, 'My face is on fire,' and when they reached him his face was aflame," McGrath said.

He was badly injured, with second- and third-degree burns on his upper body.

"His beard saved him from worse injury," said McGrath. "They rushed him to the jail hospital where he spent three weeks recovering. He could have died. Later, when he recovered, I called him into my office and said, 'Charlie, you are not the victim—he was. You've been tormenting this guy.' We moved Charlie to protective housing at Soledad."

"God told me to kill Manson," Holmstrom blankly told prison officials. His sentence was extended for the murder attempt; but, ten years later, after he was paroled, he was in trouble again. In November 1994 he was pronounced not guilty by reason of insanity for the stabbing murder of a man inside a San Francisco Hare Krishna temple. Again, he explained, "I killed him for God."

Even in lockup, Manson managed to operate a for-profit business. "Thousands wrote him from around the world," recalled McGrath. "They didn't just write: They praised him. They sought photos, autographs, and begged to be his pen pal. Whatever it is that Manson had, he continued working his spell on women, too."

At one time, devotees Good and Fromme moved closer to his prison of residence—particularly during his stays at Corcoran—and that resulted in Manson expanding his enterprises. They included a lucrative sale of autographed photos (signatures usually faked by the girls) plus continued efforts to peddle his music. Visitors smuggled him assorted drugs and contraband concealed in body orifices that even the wildest imagination couldn't conceive of. Along the way—much to the chagrin of his guards—he collected a hacksaw, or two, or three. On one of his return visits to San Quentin, guards found a hacksaw blade in his shoe and put him into isolation. It was a deliberate strategy by Manson, who did not fancy his chances mixing with the general prison population and realized the blade would be easily found, and as punishment he would be immediately placed in safer isolation.

After decades in jail, Manson's prison rap sheet was long. He was punished for an assortment of infractions: spitting in guards' faces, verbally assaulting mostly female guards, tossing hot coffee at a prison staffer, starting fights, deliberately trying to cause a flood, and setting his own mattress ablaze. He was cited for having pot and LSD in his cell, along with a nylon rope and a catalogue offering delivery of a hot-air balloon—which suggested a remarkably novel escape plan! When cellphones came into fashion, Manson joined the tech revolution by acquiring illegal phones and using them to make phone calls to as far away as Canada, although prison officials never bothered to run down who he was calling. Laughably, his punishment for using the cellphones: the loss of ninety days "good time" credit toward parole.

He was still intent on getting his music out there, and on another occasion, using smuggled tape recorders, his raspy voice recorded, "I've seen the world spinning on fire, I've danced and sang in the devil's choir." It was a new song, smuggled out, then broadcast with much PR ballyhoo on the TV program *Inside Edition*, much to the embarrassment of the Department of Corrections.

Even though Manson was safely tucked away in prison, an incident in March 1992 caused me great personal distress. Much to my horror, I discovered that a teenage relative of mine had written to him in prison. I knew he received hundreds of letters weekly from all over the world, and at first I dismissed the fan letter as a passing aberration. The immature young woman, of course, knew about my earlier Manson book, *Five to Die*, published in 1970, and told him who she was and how she was related to me. She probably thought the connection would give her some bragging rights on campus, particularly if Manson responded. And he did. He sent her a handwritten rambling, nonsensical reply on two sides of a yellow legal pad that made virtually no sense whatsoever. "I am not a manipulator pre say [sic]...Who put you up to wrighting [sic] me. Are you related to the Davis that I know. NO LIES...people are never who they start out to be." Along with the letter came a neatly typed note from someone who signed simply, "St. George." He wrote: "I encourage you to write to Charlie. I have known Charlie for several years. He is not a 'disturbed man.' The people who did the killing carry burdens of their own making and choosing. If anything, Charlie carries their burdens."

I much later discovered that St. George appears to be George Stimson, who started a pro-Manson website and is the author of the 2014 book "*Goodbye Helter Skelter*," which labels itself as "a new look at the Tate LaBianca Murders." The cover of his book seems to have been deliberately designed to resemble the Vincent Bugliosi best seller "*Helter Skelter*," with similar red print on a black cover design. "This book will change everything you think you know about Charles Manson," claims the author.

After hearing about the letter I called Deputy DA Stephen Kay, who was a regular at dozens of parole hearings for Manson and Family members. He became a kind of unofficial gatekeeper, making sure that the gang would never be paroled. "It's pretty commonplace for troubled young women to write to Manson," he told me. "He gets letters from around the globe from racists and from those who embrace weird cults and Satan worship." He said many who wrote to Manson hoped he would write back and the letter would become a valuable collector's item. "But it's a total con. Charlie has a whole network of fellow inmates forging his signature. They are even peddling autographed glossy photos and souvenir prison garb. How he manages to do all this behind bars baffles me."

In 1989, Manson found himself returned yet again to Corcoran. It was the only state prison with a forty-seven-bed wing to house inmates who needed to be kept in protective custody, separate from the general prison population. The isolation sector housed a handful of other notorious senior-citizen mass murderers. One was Juan Corona, convicted of killing twenty-five migrant farmworkers in 1971 and burying their bodies in shallow graves in peach orchards in a river bed in Sutter County, California; another, Rodney Alcala, known as the "Dating Game Killer," was a smooth-tongued, Texas-born art student-turned-photographer who was convicted of raping and killing seven women in the late seventies. Alcala's victims, including several children, were sadistically tortured before death. Other than mass murder, Alcala's main claim to infamy was that in the midst of the murder spree, he showed up in September 1978 as a contestant on the popular TV show. He was picked by the bachelorette Cheryl Bradshaw. However, intuitively she had second thoughts about going on a date with Alcala, although they shared tickets to Magic Mountain and for tennis lessons. Neither of those two killers was competition for Manson, who remained *numero uno* at Corcoran and studiously avoided personal contact with his fellow jailbirds.

However, Manson did become friendly in November 2003 with his next-door cellmate, Guillermo E. Mendez, who was in his thirties and serving a sixty-eight-year prison sentence for armed robbery and attempted murder. They became a real Mutt and Jeff team: Manson almost seventy, toothless, and a frail-looking five-foot-two, with the strapping, six-foot, 230-pound Mendez. Manson nicknamed him "Boxcar Willie"—supposedly because Manson told him the name Willie reminded him of the singer Willie Nelson—and the two men shared more than just memories. In Mendez's memoir, *Charles Manson Behind Bars: The Crazy Antics and Amazing Revelations of America's Icon of Evil*, written with crime writer Mark Hewitt, he stated: "With the exception of his pasty white skin, he could easily have passed for my tiny grandfather. The old man reminded me of my own mortality. We became friends and confidants, and I came to love Charlie. Our relationship was more as an affable grandfather than a physical threat."

He only lightly touches on most of Manson's well-chronicled history. However, Manson did reveal a childhood story that was not generally known. He told Mendez that when he was eight years old, an uncle he was living with forced him to dress in girls' clothing and sent him to school to confront a boy who had bullied and beaten him up. Togged out in the dress belonging to his cousin, the young Charlie showed up and proceeded to beat up the student who had attacked him the day before.

Mendez also relished basking in the afterglow of his notorious pal and was impressed by how prison visitors reacted to catching a glimpse of Manson: "Every week, there were people who came to tour the prison facility. They came from junior colleges, universities, and different law-enforcement agencies. All these groups visited to learn how the system works, and possibly find employment among the ranks of the Department of Corrections. In addition to these educational visits, some juvenile probation officers brought their charges to participate in a 'Scared Straight' program, designed to scare the living hell out of youngsters to steer them away from a life of crime.

"Part of many visits included a walk past Charles Manson's cell, as a zoo tour would include a trip to the tiger cage. Most participants never approached his cell directly, staying some 30 feet or more away from it as though they could sense danger. They hoped he was not asleep, but if he was, a guard would tap on his window. 'Charlie, you've got some visitors,' they would say, or 'Girls, Charlie, girls!'

"He usually got up to the window and put on a show for the guests. Sometimes, he would wave his arms around mimicking an octopus or he would jump around his cell like a monkey. The visitors usually went away laughing. Once, he put on a fierce expression, and appeared to growl at the spectators. He may have been trying to look like a grizzly bear. Even in his seventies, it was apparent to me that Charlie could still move quickly and be entertaining."

In November 2017, Corcoran was to lose its most famous attraction.

Father Time was finally catching up with Charles Manson.

DEATH TO MANSON

"Mr. Manson once dreamed of stardom, and he assembled a drug-fueled apocalyptic cult along the way. Like a 20th-century Jack the Ripper, his name evokes a legendary tale of violence that has inspired writers, filmmakers and others for decades."
—*New York Times*

"Charlie Manson is dead. Good riddance."
—Mia Farrow, actress and friend of Sharon Tate and Roman Polanski

"Manson's death spells the end of a very evil man."
—Stephen Kay, former LA Deputy District Attorney, 2018

The press release from the California Department of Corrections and Rehabilitation was a no-frills document:

Inmate B33920 Charles Manson, 83, died of natural causes at 8:13 p.m. on Sunday, November 19, 2017, at Kern County Hospital.

Charles Milles Manson's nefarious life was summed up in that meager press release. No specific cause of death was noted. One thing was certain: death did not come as a result of stabbing, shooting, beating, torture, strangulation, or mutilation—the methods that befell many of his victims. Manson had been battling colon cancer and spent four days in the hospital before dying of cardiac arrest and respiratory failure. Apparently, the cancer was something he had been afflicted with for quite some time—nine months earlier it was reported that he was in need of surgery for severe internal bleeding, but prison authorities decided he was "too weak" to go under the knife. So he was sent back to prison to die. And for those most familiar with his dissolute life, his demise was very much a case of good riddance to bad rubbish. Prison authorities alerted Sharon Tate's sister, Debra, who, along with her late mother Doris, had consistently battled to block all the killer's parole attempts, to inform her about the death of "The Prince of Darkness," as some called him— although by no stretch of the imagination could anyone in his right mind feel that Manson deserved being labeled the "prince" of anything! Debra contacted Roman Polanski in Paris and noted: "For me, Charlie was the least of my worries…all the others rallying to get out of prison are my main concerns."

The *New York Post* front page headline declared:

EVIL DEAD
Make Room Satan:
Charles Manson is finally going to Hell.

Manson would not have liked that truncated farewell, particularly exiting without any pomp and circumstance. Definitely not his style, although the line "Finally going to Hell" might have appealed to his twisted sense of humor. His ego was enormous. For almost half a century, the poseur and self-appointed messiah, with no fixed abode, had occupied isolation cells in assorted high-security protective housing units with addresses at San Quentin, Folsom, Vacaville, the innocuous-sounding hellhole known as Pelican Bay, Corcoran, and other assorted state prisons. In fact, as he liked to point out, he had spent nearly seventy years of his misspent life behind bars, with only more of the same expected in his predictably dismal future. He knew he would never be paroled, to roam the freeways of California in his signature black bus, so he finally quit showing up at parole hearings.

He did, however, succeed in making his mark—though not as the rock star he had dreamed would be his destiny. No, his notoriety was, of course, the result of his part in a series of loathsome murders, making him more famous than any of the other serial killers who left their bloody footprints at crime scenes over the past century. Even London's famed Jack the Ripper was an amateur compared to Manson, especially when it came to self-aggrandizement. No serial killer ever exploited the mass media as well as Manson: the ultimate sociopath turned himself into a brilliant media manipulator as he invaded households around the world with his entertaining claptrap and vainglorious rantings—a clown with an unkempt beard, a swastika carved into his forehead, and a lively line of oft-incomprehensible patter. When he died, Manson had 8,620 Twitter followers, according to author Peter Biskind, writing in a May 2019 *Esquire* article. Biskind refers to the "Manson-industrial complex," noting, "In addition to comic books and multiple websites devoted to him and his groupies, jewelry, coffee mugs and T-shirts displaying his image sell on eBay, Etsy and Amazon." Novelists, like Emma Cline, author of the 2016 best seller *The Girls*, biographers, podcasters (the best of which were the 2015 "You Must Remember This" by Karina Longworth, and "My Favorite Murder" with Karen Kilgariff and Georgia Hardstark in 2016), bloggers galore, psychiatrists, and just plain folk have been obsessed by the cult of Manson. He has made appearances and incarnations over the past half-century in multifarious forms of media:

- Unending hours of Manson documentaries;
- Two TV miniseries—in 1976 and then again in 2004—based on

Vincent Bugliosi's book *Helter Skelter*;

- The 2015 series *Aquarius* on NBC with David Duchovny as an LA cop who infiltrates the Manson Family;

- Plays and even television skits poking fun at Manson, including Bob Odenkirk in a series of "Ask Manson" sketches in The Ben Stiller Show in 1992;

- Manson popping up in *South Park*, of all places;

- Manson musicals, including *Charles Manson: The Failed Musician,* described as "a musical trip between LA and Death Valley," which was staged in Germany. *Mean*, a musical comedy about how Charlie met Tex, premiered in Dallas, and more recently, *Girls*, a Hollywood fringe rock musical staged in 2018 featuring, of course, the Manson women; although, in a weird touch of irony, Manson never quite made it onto Broadway, though Lyn Fromme did (off Broadway to be precise) as her character was featured in Stephen Sondheim's 1990 musical *Assassins*, which also played the boards in London's famous Donmar Warehouse in 1992. Fromme's brush with infamy is frequently revived in assorted productions playing in South Africa, Toronto, and (in August 2018) in Sydney, Australia;

- *Manson Family: An Opera* opened as part of the Lincoln Center's Serious Fun festival in August 1990 to flaccid reviews. New York Magazine Critic Peter G. Davis, while admiring the efforts of wunderkind composer John Moran to give it a Greek tragedy twist, described it as, "A shabby collection of shreds and patches...that reworking the material into something more substantial hardly seems worthwhile." But that didn't dissuade another crack at the opera theme done in Leipzig, Germany, in 2017;

- FBI profilers who tackled the Manson phenomenon in books and in the TV series *Mindhunter* in 2017;

- As of the first printing of this book, four movies were scheduled for release to tie in with the August 2019 fiftieth anniversary of the murders;

- Director Quentin Tarantino's *Once Upon a Time in Hollywood*—a $95 million budget, "What if" movie, which rewrites the truth about the killings, with Brad Pitt, Leonardo DiCaprio, and two Australian actors, Damon Herriman as Manson and Margot Robbie as Sharon Tate. It got the thumbs up from Tate's sister Debra after Tarantino sent her a copy of his script; In 2019 Tarantino told *Esquire* magazine that he was six-years-old in 1969 at the time of the murders. "This is my memory piece. This is me. This is the year that formed me. This is my world. This is my love letter to LA."

- *Charlie Says*, from director Mary Harran, focuses mostly on the Manson women. Filmmaker Harran, best known for *American Psycho*, has pulled together an intriguing cast: English actress Hannah Murray (*Game of Thrones*) as Leslie Van Houten; Sosie Bacon, daughter of Kevin Bacon and Kyra Sedgwick, is Patricia Krenwinkel; and Marianne Rendon, fresh from her role as punk musician Patti Smith in the recent biopic *Mapplethorpe,* shows up as Susan Atkins. British actor Matt Smith, who played the controversial artist Mapplethorpe in the same movie, definitely goes down market to play Manson. The Brit is best known for being BBC television's eleventh Dr. Who as well as portraying the Duke of Edinburgh in the, classy, much acclaimed Netflix series *The Crown*;

- Kate Bosworth stars as Sharon Tate in the movie *Tate*, which deals with Sharon Tate's life leading up to but not including the murders. This biopic has also received the blessings of Tate's sister Debra, who also signed on as one of the film's producers. Bosworth's husband Michael Polish directed;

- *The Haunting of Sharon Tate,* with former Disney teen idol Hilary Duff as the doomed actress, received both thumbs down from Debra Tate, telling *People* magazine the film was "classless and exploitative," and "a total fabrication." The movie, which focuses on Tate's premonition that she would have her throat slashed, picked up a best horror film award from a group called the Hollywood Reel Independent Film Festival;

- Singer and songwriter Brian Hugh Warner who, deciding he needed a makeover, helped himself to the names of two vastly different pop culture personalities, emerging as Marilyn Manson, the bizarre and controversial performance artist. Axl Rose, lead singer of the hard rock band Guns 'N Roses, landed in hot water after using a Manson song, "Look at Your Game, Girl," on his 1993 album *The Spaghetti Incident*. (The controversy cooled when David Geffen, boss of Geffen Records, assigned $62,000 for every million albums sold to go to Bartek Frykowski, the son of murder victim Wojciech [Voytek] Frykowski, who was twelve when his father was murdered);

- Some 17,000 photos of Manson on the *Los Angeles Times* website alone;

- There's also a mind-boggling amount of Manson merchandise available (mostly online), from stickers to patches to T-shirts, of course ("I'm Not a Serial Killer," "MAKE MURDER GREAT AGAIN," and "Charlie Don't Surf") to basketball and tennis shoes—although there was never any record of Manson ever playing basketball or tennis.

THE PSYCHOLOGISTS who got a chance to meet and examine the man himself trotted out the predictable diagnoses: he was schizophrenic and paranoid, delusional with an antisocial personality disorder. But whatever the diagnosis, he was our favorite fiend. And his patented credo had been cunningly crafted—merciless, piercing eyes, so mesmerizing in his deranged and menacing demeanor, a killer maybe, but also a crazed TV circus act starring for decades in his one-man freaky Manson Show, rising to the top of the distasteful heap as the half-baked leader of a group of creepy misfits comprised of what could have been your kids...or even mine. Once he got out of prison in the late sixties, he developed his very own adoration machine, carefully calibrated for maximum manipulation. And it worked. Too well.

In her 2017 memoir, *Member of the Family,* Dianne Lake, one of Manson's early conquests, a mere child of fourteen, who was abandoned and dumped off at the Spahn Ranch by her irresponsible hippie parents, writes vividly of how she succumbed to his appealing gibberish: "I have this memory of being on acid and standing in front of a mirror with him. He was showing me how many different people he could become, just by moving his facial muscles and smiling a certain way, shifting his hair or wearing a different hat. He was a chameleon, and he could find people's weaknesses that way. He preyed on them, and he wanted to teach us how to do it too."

Yet, even when death came, the Manson myth did not splutter or fade away. And it probably never will. For, in death, chaos and controversy followed. In a Bakersfield, California, mortuary, his barely cold body was concealed under a fake name, probably to avoid not only tourists and worshipers, but body snatchers. Several so-called relatives and friends and possible seekers of marketable "murderobilia" emerged after his death to take part in a long and acrimonious dispute over the rights to claim his rotting corpse, his paintings, two guitars, and other remnants of his ghastly legacy. "This is a really weird legal case," Bryan Walters, a deputy attorney in the Kern County Counsel's office, told the *Los Angeles Times* as the squabble heated up. "We've had pen pals that claim they have written wills. It's like a circus, and nothing is clear where we should hang our hat on."

The untidy brawl ended in court. The battle raged on for four months, with an intriguing assortment of claimants and combatants. First to be eliminated was building contractor Michael Channels, a longtime Manson pen pal who claimed to be his sole beneficiary in a will filed in 2002 that went out of its way to disinherit Manson's natural-born children. How many children? As far as anyone knows, there are just three, although there was so much unprotected sex with constantly changing partners at the Spahn Ranch that there is no surefire way to really track to whom the children born in 1968 and 1969 belonged.

An avid collector of Manson memorabilia, Channels, who also claimed to have become pals with "Killer Clown" John Wayne Gacy, said he struck up a friendship with Manson after sending him about fifty letters. He told a reporter for *The Vindicator*, a newspaper near his hometown of Youngstown, Ohio, that they finally met in prison in 2002, and that he visited Manson at least twenty times in Corcoran before his death. He also claimed that Manson wrote and signed a will naming him as his executor, authorizing his body to be released to Channels and bequeathing to Channels all of his property. That will, he said, specifically spelled out that he was also to receive all royalty rights to the songs that Manson wrote, as well as image and publishing rights. But Kern County Superior Court Commissioner Alisa Knight rejected Channels' claims, noting a will required two signatures—one of the witnesses who signed was Channels, which constituted a conflict of interest. He quietly went off the air.

Second to go was Matt Lentz, a Los Angeles musician whose somewhat spurious claim was that Manson had fathered him during a Wisconsin orgy—I always thought Wisconsin was famous for cheese rather than orgies. As a result, he had been named as sole beneficiary in a will that Manson purportedly signed shortly before his death. But Lentz, who presented several pages of squiggly handwriting on legal pads from the prisoner, did not provide sufficient proof of their relationship. Lentz said he had tracked down his biological mother—he had been adopted when he was just one week old. But according to law, his adoption meant that his rights to Manson's body were forfeited.

Also joining the fray, briefly, was a genuine Manson offspring: Michael Brunner, son of Manson and Mary Brunner. In the late sixties, while

Manson was freshly out of prison trolling the streets of San Francisco, he happened upon Brunner, then a librarian at the University of California, Berkeley campus. She was his first San Francisco companion/lover and moved with him down to Southern California. On April 15, 1968, she gave birth, with Family members acting as a delivery team; Manson was rumored to have cut his son's umbilical cord with his teeth. Their son, Valentine Michael Brunner, was called "Pooh Bear" by all at the Spahn Ranch. Brunner remained dedicated to Manson—she was present when Gary Hinman was murdered and received immunity after agreeing to testify for the prosecution. However, she kept changing her testimony in an obvious effort to minimize Manson's participation in that killing. On August 9, 1969, she was arrested along with Sandra Good for using stolen credit cards at a Sears store in the San Fernando Valley. It was a blessing in disguise—she was in jail the night Manson sent Watson and the other girls to Cielo Drive.

Brunner was arrested again in August 1971, after taking part in a robbery at the Western Surplus Store, a gun shop in Hawthorne, California. She, along with "Gypsy" Share and other Family members, decided to acquire a stash of weapons in a crackpot scheme that involved hijacking a jumbo jet and blackmailing authorities into freeing Manson. She was wounded in the shootout with police, and in the trial that followed she was sentenced to twenty years to life. She was paroled in 1977 after serving six years. Her rampaging around with the Family resulted in young Michael's eventual adoption by his grandparents, therefore also legally precluding him from acquiring his father's body. He quickly relinquished his corpse claim.

Yet, while the legal fracases unfolded, there was no sign at all of Charles Luther Manson, the supposed second son of Manson, the offspring of his supposed second brief marriage sometime "in the spring of 1959" to Leona "Candy" Stevens, aka Leona Rae Musser. Reportedly she was a prostitute, who met Manson while he was doing his pimping apprenticeship in the late fifties after his release from Terminal Island prison. Author Jeff Guinn writes that the marriage was simply one of convenience and they wed because it meant that she could not testify against him on the serious Mann Act federal charges that he had taken Candy and another woman across state lines from Needles, California, to Lordsburg, New Mexico for the purpose of prostitution. She divorced him in January 1964, and to this day there has been barely been a whisper publicly about the whereabouts of her or her son, who was born in Denver, Colorado, on September 24, 1960, and died in February 2007. In addition, the second Mrs. Manson appears to have opted for anonymity rather than the limelight involving her late, unlamented husband.

Once the "who does the body belong to" dust had settled, Commissioner Knight made her decision: the true claimant, she ruled, was Manson's grandson, Jason Freeman Manson (now known as Jason Freeman), the son of Manson's first child, Charles Manson Jr., the offspring of Manson's first marriage to Rosalie Jean Willis. In fact, Charles Jr. led a tortured life because of his infamous father, despite changing his name to Jay White. In 1993, unable to live with the shame and embarrassment, he put a gun to his head and pulled the trigger. "He couldn't live down who his father was," said Freeman of his father. "He just couldn't let it go."

However, Freeman appeared to have come to uncomfortable terms with his harrowing heredity. Living in Florida with his wife Audrey and their young family, he worked as an oil rigger for several years, then had some experience as a martial arts fighter before turning to religion. He ran the Jason Freeman Manson Ministry, which churned out religious YouTube videos interspersed with claims that the crimes attributed to his grandfather were false and that Charlie Manson killed no one. Freeman has a band of followers who blindly agree with those bizarre postings about the grandfather he hardly knew. One posting, soon after Manson's death, read: "Sad to know he was innocent and couldn't get out of jail. Just praying he's at peace now." Another declared: "Sir

Charles motivated people all over the world to live in harmony with all life on earth. People will still be planting trees in his name many decades from now."

And, in a plethora of old film clips and interviews, Freeman's website featured his grandfather professing his innocence to everything. "I didn't have nothing to do with killing those people, period!" Manson maintained. "I didn't tie anybody up. I was never on the scene when anyone was killed." In those interviews, Manson tries to justify the murder of Gary Hinman by blithely suggesting that the victim brought torture and then death upon himself: "He wouldn't pay the Frenchman [Bobby Beausoleil]," Manson rages on the tape, failing to mention that it was he who sliced Hinman's ear off. And it was he who then ordered his minions to sew the ear back on, and, then "finish him off."

Until almost his dying day, Manson stayed true to his warped ways. In what was probably his last major in-depth interview, with *Rolling Stone* writer Erik Hedegaard ("The Final Confessions of America's Most Notorious Psychopath," which ran in November 2013), he was unrelentingly consistent in his venom toward his victims—particularly Sharon Tate: "It's a Hollywood movie star. How many people did she murder onscreen? Was she so pretty? She compromised her body for everything she did. And if she was such a beautiful thing, what was she doing in the bed of another man when that thing jumped off? What kind of shit is that?"

The day after the Tate murders, Manson randomly drove around several Los Angeles neighborhoods. He then left his disciples waiting in the car and broke into the home of Leno and Rosemary LaBianca. He tied up the LaBiancas, all the while reassuring them that they would come to no harm. Then he drove away with Susan Atkins and Clem Grogan as passengers in the back seat, after instructing the waiting Watson, Van Houten, and Krenwinkel to go back and eradicate the couple. He killed stuntman "Shorty" Shea. He *thought* he had assassinated drug dealer Bernard Crowe; however, he miscalculated that one.

Freeman posted proverbial-style messages about the grandfather he never met. One photograph of a grinning, wild-eyed Manson is accompanied by the words: "Don't let the world change your smile. Let your smile change the world." Another photo of ol' grandad was superimposed with the slogan "Family First." As a staunch defender of his grandfather, he says on the website that his goal is to put to rest "this so-called monster, this historical figure that shouldn't have been blown up as big as it was for all these years."

He did tell *People* magazine that he had frequent phone conversations with Manson while he was incarcerated at Corcoran State Prison. Many of those phone conversations he recorded. He told the magazine that he knew at an early age who his grandfather was—although it was never dinner-table conversation. "People have asked me what was it like to be Charles Manson's grandson. My mom and stepdad did a great job of keeping the past behind closed doors."

Once he took control of his grandfather's body, Freeman—who lives in a Florida community near Sarasota—invited some twenty selected guests to mourn at a Southern California funeral that was held on St. Patrick's Day, 2018. According to the local pastor, Sandra Good attended with a man he said he believed was her husband. While she was not implicated in the 1969 killings, Good served ten years in prison for sending hundreds of threatening letters to corporate executives. As soon as she was paroled, she moved to Corcoran so she could be close to Manson in prison; from there, she ran a website for him. And surely, one of the weirdest twists to emerge in a story where weird twists were commonplace involved an adolescent encounter between Good and Vincent Bugliosi's second-chair prosecutor, Deputy DA Stephen Kay. "I was fifteen, Sandy was fourteen, and we were fixed up on a blind date by my mother's best friend, who was Sandra's godmother," Kay told me. "We met in a pancake house in Burbank and it was a disaster. She was a stuck-up little snob who was living on her rich father's fortune."

Afton Elaine Burton also came to the funeral. She and Manson took out a license to marry in 2014 when he was eighty and she was twenty-six, but the couple never wed. She began writing to him in jail, and then became a regular visitor. Later, the doe-eyed blonde was quoted as saying she wanted to marry Manson, but only because, as his wife, she could inherit his body "and display it in a glass case after his death."

In his last lengthy interview with *Rolling Stone* in November 2013, when he was seventy-nine and ailing, Manson admitted the whole marriage story was pure hokum.

The funeral service was brief. Manson lay in an open coffin; his hands, sheathed in white gloves, were neatly folded. His silver beard was neatly trimmed, and he was heavily made-up. He wore a bright orange shirt under a long gray jacket with a plum-colored handkerchief. Freeman said he tried to put a ring on his grandfather's finger, but he was not able to do so because the body was so badly decomposed. He was unhappy, he said, because his grandfather had been tossed into a gunny sack after his death and refrigerated rather than put into a deep freeze.

During the funeral service, Mark Pitcher, pastor of the Porterville Church of the Nazarene, quoted from what he felt were meaningful scriptures, though none were particularly applicable to Manson. "Greater love hath no man than this, that a man lay down his life for his friends," he said. And, "I can do all things through Christ which strengtheneth me."

The pastor said he didn't dodge talking about Manson's past, but failed to bring up the murders. "He was born into an unhealthy environment to a sixteen-year-old girl who was not prepared for motherhood," he told the assembled. "He never knew his father. He was a product of his environment, and that unhealthy environment followed him. Many choices were thrust upon Charlie as a young boy that had very damaging and destructive consequences upon him, and he made choices later on that were damaging and destructive and negatively impacted many other people for the rest of his life." When asked if he felt Manson was headed for heaven or hell, he diplomatically noted, "From all of his actions we would say he is not heavenly bound. The one thing we know is that Jesus loved him to the very end." It was a savvy answer from a person in a no-win situation. Then again, it's tough to make a case for Manson where redemption and Christ are concerned.

Freeman also hired a camera crew to shoot the funeral—he said he was making a documentary, not about Manson, but about his own tragic father, Charles Jr. While the new documentary, called *CHARLES MANSON The Funeral*, which aired on the REELZ network in April 2019, did touch upon his tragic father, it focused mainly on Freeman and his wife Audrey's efforts to give Manson a decent funeral and is a sympathetic look at Freeman, who is yet another "victim" of his nefarious grandfather. The film also offers an intriguing look into the handful of Manson loyalists who showed up at the funeral and even today still believe he was a hero and not history's archvillain. After the cremation, as the mourners file down a narrow woodsy path by a picturesque stream not far from the funeral home, they are asked to take a handful of Manson's ashes and scatter them into a fast-moving stream. Audrey Freeman—who brings a welcome touch of Greek chorus commentary to the funeral and to the odd assortment of characters who showed up—reacts with horror after she sees what happens after Manson is cremated. The mourners daubed the ashes onto their faces! "This is just insanity," says Mrs. Freeman. "It appalls me that people think this is okay. This is a funeral, not a circus," she angrily notes. In the film Freeman tearfully declares, "I want to give my grandfather a proper burial. I wanna stick him in the ground so we can put the bogeyman to sleep. He has a spiritual side to him that not too many people understand. But I do." Another dramatic segment in the documentary is a meeting Freeman has with former Manson Family member Dianne Lake who, after making life on the Spahn Ranch sound like a jolly holiday resort filled with innocent song and frolics, then tells Freeman the brutal truth about his blue-collar psycho grandfather.

In addition, Freeman produced a "souvenir" funeral program titled "Beyond the Sunset." Because he was hard-up for cash—and noting that he needed to recoup some $11,000 in funeral expenses—he later autographed and sold souvenir Manson funeral pamphlets at $100 a pop. The memento came with a somewhat grisly bonus: small squares cut from the sheet that was used to cover his grandfather's body while it was in cold storage at the morgue. He claimed he found customers in Australia, Argentina, and Scotland willing to fork out the money. "I'm giving a historical moment out to people at a reasonable price," he explained.

Shortly before the funeral, a GoFundMe campaign—supposedly started by friends of Freeman—was launched to request donations so that Manson would be "laid to rest with honor, respect and dignity he deserves. We will not sit back & let them throw Mr. Manson away like trash. His whole life he lived with the pain of feeling unclaimed. We must not let this happen in death. Together we can help Jason bring his grandfather home & prove to the world Charles WAS LOVED & WILL BE CLAIMED!" Within hours some $900 was pledged, but then GoFundMe shut down the campaign.

Funeral home owner Les Peters said that after the service, which he described as having "a hippie vibe," they sang Manson-composed songs, as well as his songs as performed by the Beach Boys, and Guns 'N Roses' "Look at Your Game Girl." Nary a Beatles song was heard—certainly not "Helter Skelter."

The open-coffin funeral and cremation, which featured some mourners kissing the corpse, then putting assorted items ranging from eagle feathers to an Iron Cross, rings and necklaces into the coffin, and then draping the box with an American and a Confederate flag, was not the last to be heard about Manson in death. In October 2018, the TMZ gossip and showbiz news website that earlier had run an exclusive color photo of Manson's last coffin "public appearance," reported that Freeman had "donated" other knick-knacks belonging to his grandfather to Zak Bagans, owner of the Haunted Museum in Las Vegas. Bagans is best known as the host of the Travel Channel series *Ghost Adventures*. A

Facebook posting by Freeman in December 2018 notes that Manson will be the subject of a documentary produced by Bagans. The ghoulish cache—if you can call it that—supposedly included the hospital gown Manson wore when he died, his hospital bracelet, plus electrodes once attached to his ailing body, along with the coroner's toe tag and bone fragments. All were added to an existing Manson exhibit at the museum, which apparently already includes Manson's false teeth and some of his paintings.

Freeman said he decided to make the donations because, after keeping those items in his house, eerie things—like items in his house shifting—began to happen. The paranormal events, he said, scared the living daylights out of him, his wife, Audrey, and their young children.

One might even say this about Manson: death becomes him.

THEN AND NOW

Manson 1969 and 2012

Watson 1969 and 2016

Van Houten 1969 and 2017

Atkins 1969 and 2007

Krenwinkel 1969 and 2016

EPILOGUE

The diabolical history of the incorrigible career criminal, Charles Manson, and his Family still fascinates the public half a century after the murders. Even after death, Manson's dark legend—along with that of his disciples—is being retold in movies, television, documentaries, podcasts, articles, on websites and, of course, in books like this. As of the first printing of this book in August 2019, here is the current status of key figures in this horror story.

THE FAMILY

Charles Manson: The misogynistic mastermind behind the Tate/LaBianca murders as well as those of Gary Hinman and Donald "Shorty" Shea—and likely many others—had been incarcerated in Corcoran State Prison, California, when he was rushed to a Kern County, California, hospital, where he died on November 19, 2017, at age eighty-three. The cause of death was listed as "natural causes" though he was being treated for stomach cancer.

Susan (Sadie Mae Glutz) Atkins: Manson's closest disciple—who eventually disavowed him and found religion in jail—also found love. After a disastrous, quickie marriage to purported Texas millionaire Donald Lee Laisure, while in jail Atkins married a second time in 1987, to James

Whitehouse, a onetime musician and Harvard Law School graduate-turned-attorney living in California. Atkins died at age sixty-one on September 24, 2009, of brain cancer at the Central California Women's Facility in Chowchilla.

Charles Denton (Tex) Watson Jr.: After being convicted in the Tate/LaBianca murders, Watson became an ordained minister while in jail at the California Men's Colony, San Luis Obispo, where in 1979 he married nineteen-year-old Kristin Joan Svege. They divorced in 2003, but not before he fathered four children as a result of conjugal visits. Now seventy-three, he still resides at the Richard J. Donovan Correctional Facilities in San Diego, California. All of his parole requests have been denied.

Patricia (Katie) Krenwinkel: Convicted in the Tate/LaBianca murders, now seventy, Krenwinkle is a model prisoner at the California Institution for Women in Corona, California. All of her parole requests have been denied.

Leslie (LuLu) Van Houten: Convicted of the murders of Leno and Rosemary LaBianca, Van Houten, seventy years old, also is a model prisoner at California Institution for Women in Corona. Three times parole boards recommended she be freed but three California governors denied parole.

Robert (Bobby) Beausoleil: Beausoleil was convicted of the murder of musician Gary Hinman. In 1973, author Truman Capote showed up at San Quentin to interview him and they chatted about topics including the prison's notorious death chamber, Sirhan Sirhan, and Lee Harvey Oswald. In 1981 he married artist/dancer Barbara Ellen Baston and they had four children. She died in October 2012. In jail he continued to write, record music, and paint. At seventy-two, he resides at the California Medical Facility in Vacaville, California. All of his parole requests have been denied.

Bruce Davis: Supposedly Manson's real second in command. Convicted for the murders of Gary Hinman and stuntman Donald "Shorty" Shea, Davis became a born-again Christian, earning a doctoral degree in philosophy of religion while at the California Men's Colony in San Luis Obispo, California, where, at seventy-six, he still resides. All of his parole requests have been denied.

Steve (Clem Tufts) Grogan: Though a member of the Manson family who went along for the ride to the LaBiancas' house, Grogan was not charged with their murder. He was convicted for the murder of stuntman Donald "Shorty" Shea, but was paroled in 1985. Now sixty-six, he is married with a family and was last seen in 2017 performing and singing with a band in California.

Sandra (Sandy) Good: The last Manson faithful, who showed up at his funeral in March 2018, Good was sentenced to fifteen years in prison in 1976 for "conspiracy to send threatening letters through the mail"—she helped write and send death threats to nearly 200 executives of companies that she decided were killing the Earth. She was paroled in 1985, moved to Vermont, and at seventy-four, lives under a different name.

Lynette (Squeaky) Fromme: Fromme was one of Manson's most devoted disciples. She was released on parole from federal prison in August 2009 at age sixty after serving thirty-four years for attempting to assassinate President Gerald Ford in 1975. She claimed she never planned to kill him but pulled the gun to bring attention to Manson and her environmental concerns. Until his death, Fromme kept in close touch with Manson and tried—often in vain—to keep a low profile at her home in upstate New York.

Mary (Mother Mary) Brunner: The mother of Manson's son Valentine Michael, Mary served six years in jail for her role in the August 1971

Hawthorne, California, gun store shootout with police. Upon her release in 1977, she assumed a new name, got custody of her son, and, at seventy-five, lives in the Midwest.

Linda Darlene Drouin Kasabian: She drove the killers to the house on Cielo Drive, but committed no murders. She became a star witness for the prosecution in the 1970 trial. She has struggled with drug and alcohol abuse over the years. Now seventy years old, she lives in Tacoma, Washington, with her husband and children.

Paul (Little Paul) Alan Watkins: Once Manson's right-hand man and chief procurer, Watkins testified for the prosecution in both the Manson and Watson trials. He became a musician and authored the 1979 memoir *My Life with Charles Manson*. The father of two daughters, one of whom, Clair Vaye Watkins, is a successful novelist (the prize-winning *Battleborn*, among others). He lectured widely about the dangers of cults before he died in August 1990 at age forty of leukemia.

Brooks Poston: Along with Watkins, Poston became disenchanted with Manson and fled the Spahn Ranch, testifying for the prosecution in the Tate-LaBianca trial. He later formed the musical group Desert Sun with Watkins and has largely stayed out of the public eye.

Catherine (Gypsy) Share: Share was convicted of participating in the August 1971 gun shop robbery in Hawthorne, California, along with her then husband Kenneth Como, and Mary Brunner and three other lesser-known Family members. Their cockeyed plan was to hijack a Boeing 747 and kill a passenger every hour until Manson and the girls were released. In 1979, she found Christianity, and now, at seventy-six, speaks out against cults, as well as being a regular talking head on Manson family documentaries.

Kenneth (Jesse James) Como: He was arrested August 1971 for robbery at a Hawthorne, California, gun store in a raid carried out to acquire weapons to break Manson out of prison. Four years later, while in Folsom Prison, he attacked Manson in the exercise yard, and armed guards had to break up the fight. He died in September 2004 at sixty-four.

Catherine (Cappy, Capistrano) Gillies: Her grandmother owned the Myers Ranch next to the Barker Ranch, where Manson was arrested in late 1969. While she was not involved in any crimes, she was one of the Manson girls who parked daily on the sidewalk outside the Los Angeles Hall of Justice during the Tate/LaBianca trial. She was present when John "Zero" Haught killed himself, supposedly playing Russian roulette. After marrying and divorcing, she lived in Oregon with her four children. She died of cancer at age sixty-nine in June 2018.

Barbara Hoyt: A prosecution witness and victim of the notorious "hamburger laced with LSD" murder caper—she was fed a burger with ten tabs of acid in it to prevent her testifying against Manson—Hoyt survived to testify. She died of kidney failure at age sixty-five on December 2017.

Nancy (Brenda McCann) Pitman: Pitman met Manson through her Malibu pal Deirdre Lansbury, daughter of British actress Angela Lansbury. After Pitman split with the Family, she became implicated in another crime involving a prison murder. After her stint in jail, she eventually moved to the Pacific Northwest with her four children. She's now sixty-eight.

Dianne (Snake) Lake: When her hippie parents turned her over to Manson at the age of fourteen, Lake had the honor of becoming the youngest of "Charlie's Girls," though she never participated in any Family crimes. After the trial, she worked as a special education teacher, was widowed in 2013, and at sixty-eight, lives in California and has three children. She told her story in a riveting 2017 memoir, *Member of the Family*.

Ruth Ann (Ouisch) Moorehouse: Moorehouse met Manson when her pastor father, Dean Moorehouse, picked up the cult leader and two girls as they hitchhiked in San Jose, California, in 1967. It was Ruth Ann who fed the LSD-laced hamburger to Barbara Hoyt to prevent her from testifying against Manson, but she was never charged. After the murders, she changed her name and, at sixty-eight, lives with her husband and children in the Midwest. Her father died at ninety in May 2010 in Shasta Lake, California.

THE LAW

Vincent Bugliosi: The chief prosecutor of the Manson trial, with Curt Gentry, wrote what has been considered the seminal book of the murders and trial, *Helter Skelter*, which was made into a movie in 1976 with Steve Railsback as Manson and George DiCenzo as Bugliosi. It was remade as a TV miniseries with Jeremy Davies and Bruno Kirby, respectively. A number of other mostly true-crime books followed, including *Outrage*, in which he "explained" the O.J. Simpson verdict. He ran unsuccessfully for the job of Los Angeles District Attorney. He died in Los Angeles of cancer at the age of eighty in June 2015.

Charles Older: Older was the main judge during the Tate-LaBianca trial, after taking over from Judge William Keene in April 1970. The World War II Flying Tiger pilot packed a pistol under his judicial robe after Manson tried to attack him during the trial. He died in Los Angeles in June 2006 at the age of eighty-eight from complications after a fall.

Aaron Stovitz: Best known as the man who lost his job as the lead prosecutor on the Tate/LaBianca trial for talking to the media despite a press gag order, Stovitz continued as a prosecutor until his retirement. He died at age eight-five of leukemia in January 2010.

Stephen Kay: The Deputy District Attorney in Tate-LaBianca trial was on vacation when he was tagged to work alongside Bugliosi on the case, and followed up handling the prosecution in trials involving Tex Watson and Van Houten's retrials. He devoted his professional life to making sure that Family members did not get parole. He also successfully prosecuted Bruce Davis for the murders of Gary Hinman and Donald Shea. After teaching law, he retired in 2005 after thirty-eight years in the DA's office and lives in Southern California.

Irving Kanarek: After the Manson trial, Kanarek battled mental illness and was disbarred in 1990 following client payment disputes. The most recent Kanarek interview in 2014 in the London *Guardian* pictured him in a wheelchair, noting: "I didn't spend much time [thinking about Tate and the other victims] because they were victims of disputes that Charlie had nothing to do with. I think his direct involvement has been woefully extrapolated."

Ronald Hughes: Leslie Van Housten's lawyer, died reportedly of drowning, in March 1971, at the age of thirty-five.

Paul Fitzgerald: Patricia Krenwinkel's lawyer, Fitzgerald died in October 2001 at age sixty-four of a heart attack in his home in Beverly Hills.

Daye Shinn: Susan Atkins' lawyer, Shinn was disbarred from practicing law in September 1992. He died at the age of 89 in June 2006.

THE OTHERS

Roman Polanski: Sharon Tate's actor-director husband, now eighty-five, lives in Paris with actress wife Emmanuelle Seigner and their three children. Lawyers in Southern California are still trying to get him pardoned so he can return to America. Polanski fled from Los Angeles in February

1978, fearing that a judge would send him to prison after he pled guilty to unlawful sexual intercourse with a minor. Mostly retired, Polanski appears publicly to receive awards for his contribution to movies. In April 2019, the Oscar-winning director filed suit claiming he was unfairly expelled from the Academy of Motion Pictures Arts and Sciences, the group that stages the annual Academy Awards, demanding they reinstate him. In 2019 Polanski was seeking an American distributor for his latest film, *An Officer and a Spy* about France's notorious 1894 Alfred Dreyfus affair. The French language film stars Oscar winning French actor Jean Dujardin and Polanski's wife Emmanuelle Seigner.

George Spahn: Four years after his desert ranch was destroyed by a wildfire in September 1970, Spahn died in a rest home in 1974 in Van Nuys, California, at the age of eighty-five.

AUTHOR'S NOTE

"Manson's name is virtually synonymous with mass murder, so for people who are only vaguely aware of his story it often comes as a surprise to learn that he never killed anyone."
—Jeffrey Toobin, *New Yorker,* November 2017

"Why are you writing a book about Charles Manson?" many wanted to know.

From day one, Saturday, August 9, 1969, when I was abruptly tossed into the deep end of a story that started off as "The Sharon Tate Murders" and later was hijacked and metamorphosed into "The Charles Manson Story," I become instantly enmeshed in this bloody train wreck. On and off it was to dog my footsteps for decades.

My last true-to-life memoir was titled *The Beatles and Me on Tour,* and while trying to come up with a title for this book, one that could succinctly encapsulate all that had unfolded over the past half century, some cynic suggested it might be appropriate to call this book *"Manson and Me on Tour"*! No thanks.

The killings, coming when they did, in one foul swoop dramatically transformed the whole psychedelic, druggie culture of the Sixties from love to fear and hate and violence. Over the years I tracked this saga as it snaked from one century into another and often found myself on the "front lines" revisiting the story. Even today I am still trying to make some kind of sense out of these random killings and their horrific fallout. It was a story that wreaked unbearable havoc on so many lives and, even now, there is no rest for the wicked and the innocents.

I must admit, I still have trouble wrapping my mind around the fact that Vincent Bugliosi got a jury to believe that the carnage was blamed on a bunch of lyrics from several Beatles songs. Today, I firmly believe that Manson ordered the look-alike Tate-LaBianca killings to get Bobby Beausoleil off the hook for the Hinman murder.

While Manson is dead and so is Susan Atkins, the story refuses to go away. With regularity, his convicted minions step out into the public eye as they continue to battle for parole and their freedom—and will continue on that path until the end.

So why another book? Shortly before Manson died in November 2017 and before I wrote this book, I was visiting relatives in the Pacific Northwest and got into a conversation with two young men in their late twenties or early thirties who had come to remodel a kitchen.

Over a cup of coffee we got talking about crime, and I asked them what they knew about Charles Manson.

"Wasn't he the preacher who got his followers to drink poisoned Kool Aid?" said one, obviously referring to the Rev. Jim Jones, who persuaded some 900 cult members to swallow cyanide-laced soft drinks in Guyana in 1978.

"No, no," said his workmate, "Manson is a revolutionary like the South American guy Che Guevara who worked with Fidel Castro."

He was on a roll: "All his life Manson fought the US government over things like pollution and destroying the forests and keeping water fresh. Instead they railroaded him, tossed him in jail and threw away the key. They said he was a murderer, although he never murdered anyone."

I listened to these explanations with a mixture of bemusement and horror. Memories and the years do indeed dull the senses; although, of course, in all fairness, both men were not born when Manson reigned over his bewitched, bothered, and bewildered lackeys. Still, it was cause for concern.

And while some may confuse the Manson cult with other cults, what I have also noticed, with increasing alarm, is that since the insurgence of the Internet, there are now countless websites that offer a whole new spin to the Manson story. In this rampaging era of social networking, some are devoted to clearing his name. And, in checking them out, I was stunned at some of this twenty-first century revisionist claptrap that has been foisted on the current generations Y and Z—as well as the Millennials, who have no memory whatsoever of the events surrounding the murders.

I hate to think of what kind of pernicious and pervasive poison Manson would have fed to a gullible audience had the Internet been as prevalent in the last thirty years of the twentieth century as it is now. Retired Deputy DA Stephen Kay says, "He would have attracted a much bigger family if the Internet had been around."

Of course, it is too late for Manson to receive a "get-out-of-jail-free" card.

My own journey back into the period I lived through, and my look back into Manson's iniquitous career, clearly shows that while it is true that, in the high-profile murders at the Cielo and Waverly addresses, Manson may not have plunged a knife into the bodies, he was clearly the architect of the killings, which one writer described as "murder by proxy."

And in an era of the so called "free Internet speech," nobody should ever forget—and certainly not even question—the fact that Manson, despite his abysmal and neglected childhood, was a stone cold killer until his dying day.

ACKNOWLEDGMENTS

Without author/editor Marshall Terrill gently but persistently nagging, there would be no book. He first suggested the idea when we met at a Beatles convention in 2013.

He had read *Five to Die*, which was the first Manson murder book I wrote in 1970 with the late journalist, Jerry LeBlanc. And he insisted it was now time for me to take a fresh look at my fifty-year journey on the case.

Thanks to Lew Harris, my redoubtable former *Los Angeles* magazine editor, who kept me honest. And Cara Highsmith of Highsmith Creative Services, who crossed the t's, dotted the i's, and helped keep my grasshopper mind in line, as did Flo Selfman at Words á la Mode. Pedernales Publishing chief honcho, Jose Ramirez, for steering me on the tricky publishing front.

And so many more.

Louise Sherman (along with Uncle Tom Cobley), as well as Maurina Sherman, weighed in with guidance and fact-checking.

Many others helped me factually focus on the past. Particularly the razor-sharp memory of Stephen Kay, who has gone through the Tate-LaBianca ringer so often and for so long, yet still remains fresh and highly quotable.

Thanks to legal eagles Harland Braun, Kenneth Clayman, Donald Goldsobel, Steve Lipson, Mark J. Phillips, and California Justice Steve Perren.

In London, Diana Wilmot and Poppy Wilmot raided the archives of the *London Daily Express,* and Michael Sarne and Tanya Sarne remembered the awful days following the murders.

Thanks to my "companions at trial": Journalists Linda Deutsch, Sandi Gibbons, Martin Kasindorf, Mary Neiswender, and the late Bruce Russell. LA based author Steve Oney's invaluable *Oral History of the Manson Murders*, which he wrote for *Los Angeles Magazine* in 2009, and writer Simon Wells in England generously shared their knowledge and extensive research as did journalist-author Anthony Delano in France, who provided his Manson coverage memories and notes.

Chris Hillman weighed in with musical memories and Kathleen Kaiser with media savvy. Carolyn Fox, of Hollywood News Calendar, kept me *au courant* with what's going on in Southern California, and Gideon Oscar Ogle Davis provided tech support.

Appreciation also to my European book manager Clive Walters, to John Aes-Nihil, Marilyn Barnes, Rona Barrett, Phil Freed, Phil Kaufman, Joie Gould Gati, the late Julie Payne, Clark Hubbard, Jim Harris, Buddy Fowler, Diane Hubbard, Katherine Lipson, Dr. Charles Murphy, former California prison warden Joe McGrath, Mel Novak, Jon Osumi, Aryn Z. Philips, Irene Seda, Karen Shea, Anthony Strauss, Michelle Strauss, Rebecca Davis Suskind, Jannis Swerman, Michael Terry, Terry Thornton, Julian Wasser, and Paul Whitehead.

On the photo/illustration front, much help was provided by Robert Arnold, Jaime Bailon, Harry Benson, Jim Harris, Paul Harris, David Jacobs, Denise Fox, Cyril Maitland, Dave McTaggart, courtroom artist Bill Robles, Los Angeles Police Museum archivist Bob Taylor, and, from the Museum of Ventura County, Elena Brokaw, Denise Sindelar, Deya Terrafranca, Anna Bermudez, and Charles Johnson. Thanks also to Nancy Masters, director of the Inyo County Free Library.

WORKS REFERENCED

A BIBLIOGRAPHICAL NOTE:

Much of the background for this book came from my own stories and memories written over a fifteen-year period for the London *Daily Express*, along with my diaries and magazine articles I later wrote. For the first few years following the murders I was reporter on the ground, following the story daily, which included the front-row seat at the trial.

In the old days—back in the twentieth century—I would spend endless hours reading through yellowed clippings or looking at library microfilms until my eyeballs complained. And then, reluctantly, antediluvian as I was, I found that the Internet could be a valuable source, but only if handled with care and great caution. There is much rumor, innuendo, and outright inaccuracy to be found on that road. One such reliable site is Scribd.com—a digital library that provides a subscription service along with the court records and transcripts I needed. CieloDrive.com, www.CharlesManson.com, and FamousTrials. com by Professor Douglas O. Linder also provide a large variety of official information as well as transcripts and the original police audio interviews with key witnesses, precious and perfect, to capture the time and mood of the era. Through some of these solid websites I was able to find a real treasure trove of official documents—psychiatric reports, parole hearing transcripts, and other details too numerous to list. And then there was the opportunity to watch documentaries as well as YouTube interviews that had Vincent Bugliosi butting heads with Family members like Sandra Good.

The Los Angeles Police Museum, the LA DA and Sheriff's office also provided valuable archival information, as did publications like *Rolling Stone* magazine, the *Los Angeles Times,* and the *New York Times.* And then a slew of new interviews done over the past two years.

Some of the books used for research were invaluable, many questionable. I read Nuel Emmons' 1986 book *Manson in His Own Words*, which purported to be in Manson's own words. While there was much intriguing stuff, it did not seem to jibe with the Manson voice I witnessed during the trial and heard at parole hearings as well as the multitude of radio and TV interviews. What struck me as particularly outlandish and unreal in the Emmons/Manson book was a remarkable episode that he recounted that stretched credibility to breaking point. Manson claimed that after the Sharon Tate murders, and after his killing crew arrived back at the Spahn Ranch in the wee small hours of the morning, he was so worried they might have botched it up badly that he jumped into his car the same night and drove himself to the Cielo house. There, if we are to believe his story, he walked around the murder scene carefully wiping away any fingerprints and removing other telltale signs!

Another point about the plethora of websites that focus on various elements of the murders: Some are scrappy, others professionally done. I have deliberately avoided mentioning the questionable sites, but what is intriguing is to check out the slicker sites, particularly one done in Leslie Van Houten's name. The site quotes large chunks of dialogue from Charles Denton Watson (no longer known as "Tex" Watson, his site notes) that reduces Van Houten's culpability in connection with the LaBianca murders. All of those quotes were considered valuable in Van Houten's long, fruitless uphill battle for parole.

BOOKS AND STUDIES REFERENCED:

Aes-Nihil, John, Nick Bougas, Adam Parfrey, Boyd Rice, Jimmi Rocket, Nikolas Schreck, and Jack Stevenson, *The Manson File: Charles Manson As Revealed in Letters, Photos, Stories, Songs, Art, Testimony and Documents*, Edited by: Feral House, 1988 and 2011.

Atkins, Susan and Lawrence Schiller, *The Killing of Sharon Tate*, New American Library, 1970.

Atkins, Susan and Bob Slosser, *Child of Satan, Child of God*, Bridge-Logos, 1977.

Bergen, Candice, *Knock Wood*, Simon and Schuster, 1984.

Biskind, Peter, *Easy Riders, Raging Bulls*, Bloomsbury, 1998.

Bravin, Jess, *The Life and Times of Lynette Alice Fromme*, St Martin's Press, 1997.

Bugliosi, Vincent and Curt Gentry, *Helter Skelter*, W.W. Norton, 1974.

Crosby, David and Carl Gottlieb, *Since Then*, Putnam, 2006.

Cullen, William, *The Adolescence of Charles Manson: His origin of Evil*, self-published.

Dalton, David and David Felton, *Charles Manson: The Incredible Story of the Most Dangerous Man Alive*, *Rolling Stone* magazine, June 1970.

Davis, Ivor and Jerry LeBlanc, *Five to Die: The Book that Helped Convict Manson*, Thor Publishing, 2009.

Didion, Joan, *The White Album*, Simon and Schuster, 1979.

Douglas, John and Mark Olshaker, *Mindhunter: Inside the FBI's Elite Serial Crime Unit*, Pocket Books, 1995.

Eliot, Marc, *Nicholson: A Biography*, Crown Publishing, 2013.

Emmons, Nuel, *Manson in His Own Words: The Shocking Confessions of "The Most Dangerous Man Alive,"* Grove Press, 1986.

Evans, Robert, *The Kid Stays in the Picture*, Hyperion Books, 1993.

Gaines, Steven, *Heroes and Villains: The True Story of the Beach Boys*, De Capo Press, 1995.

Geimer, Samantha, and Lawrence Silver, *The Girl: A Life in the Shadow of Roman Polanski,* Atria, a division of Simon and Schuster, 2013.

George, Edward and Dary Matera, *Taming the Beast: Charles Manson's Life Behind Bars,* St. Martin's Griffin Edition, 1998.

Gilmore, John and Ron Kenner, *Manson: The Unholy Trail of Charlie and the Family,* Omega Press, 1971.

Guinn, Jeff, *Manson: The Life and Times of Charles Manson,* Simon and Schuster, 2013.

Hewitt, Mark and Guillermo E. Mendez, *Charles Manson Behind Bars: The Crazy Antics and Amazing Revelations of America's Icon of Evil,* Page Publishing, 2013.

Hoskyns, Barney, *Waiting for the Sun: Strange Days, Weird Scenes and the Sound of Los Angeles,* St. Martin's Press, 1996.

Katz, Burton S., *Justice Overruled,* Warner Books, 1997.

Kaufman, Phil and Colin White, *Road Mangler Deluxe,* White-Boucke Publishing, 1993.

Kolman, John, *Rulers of the Night, A Unit History and Pictorial Record of the Los Angeles County Sheriff's Department's Special Enforcement Detail/Bureau, 1958-2008,* Graphic Publishers, 2009.

Lake, Dianne and Deborah Herman, *Member of the Family: My Story of Charles Manson, Life Inside his Cult, and the Darkness that Ended the Sixties,* William Morrow, 2017.

Martin, Deana and Wendy Holden, *Memories Are Made of This,* Crown Publishing, 2004.

Marynick, Marlin, *Charles Manson Now,* Cogito Media Group, 2010.

Murphy, Bob, *Desert Shadows,* Sagebrush Press, 1993.

Neiswender, Mary, *Assassins…Serial Killers…Corrupt Cops…: Chasing the News in a Skirt and High Heels,* CreateSpace Publishing, 2012.

Oney, Steve, *Manson: An Oral History, Los Angeles* magazine, July 2009.

Phillips, John and Jim Jerome, *Papa John: A Music Legend's Shattering Journey Through Sex, Drugs, and Rock 'n' Roll*, Doubleday, 1986.

Phillips, Mark J. and Aryn Z. Phillips, *Trials of the Century*, Prometheus Books, 2016.

Polanski, Roman, *Roman by Polanski*, William Morrow, 1984.

Sanders, Ed, *The Family*, Da Capo Press, 2002.

Sanders. Ed, *Sharon Tate: A Life*, Da Capo Press, 2015.

Sandford, Christopher, *Polanski*, Palgrave MacMillan, St. Martin's Press, 2008.

Steffens, Bradley and Craig L. Staples, *The Trial of Charles Manson: California Cult Murders*, Lucent Books, 2002.

Stimson, George, *Goodbye Helter Skelter*, Peasenhall Press, 2014.

Terrill, Marshall, *Steve McQueen: The Life and Legend of a Hollywood Icon*, Triumph Books, 2010.

Udo, Tommy, *Charles Manson: Music Mayhem Murder*, Sanctuary Publishing, 2002.

Watkins, Claire Vaye, *Battleborn*, Riverhead Books, 2012.

Watkins, Paul and Guillermo Soledad, *My Life with Charles Manson*, Bantam, 1979.

Watson, Charles and Chaplain Ray Hoekstra, *Will You Die for Me? The Man Who Killed for Charles Manson Tells His Own Story*, Revell Company, 1978.

Wells, Simon, *Charles Manson: Coming Down Fast*, Hodder & Stoughton, 2009.

Wenner, Jann S., *Rolling Stone Interviews*, Back Bay Books, 2007.

Wilson, Theo, *Headline Justice*, Thunder's Mouth Press, 1996.

Young, Neil, *Waging Heavy Peace: A Hippie Dream*, Blue Rider Press, 2012.

PODCASTS AND WEBSITES REFERENCED

Kilgariff, Karen, Hardstark, Georgia, *My Favorite Murder*, 2017
Longworth, Karina, *You Must Remember This,* 2015
Aes-Nihil, John, Manson archives
Brian Davis, StarCityradio.com
California Board of Parole
CieloDrive.com
Law.Justia.com
LAPL.org
Mansondirect.com
MurdersofAugust69
The Crime Victims Action Alliance (CVAA)
The Manson Family Blog (mansonfamilyblog.com)
TheTate-LaBianca Homicide Research blog (LSB3.com)
truthontatelabianca.com
www.history.com

PHOTO AND ILLUSTRATION CREDITS

Page 357: Manson Family transportation by dune buggy — LA County Sheriffs' Museum

Page 357: Ranch hand John Swartz's 1959 four-door Ford — LAPD Museum

Page 358: Polanski with *Rosemary's Baby* star Mia Farrow — Harry Benson

Page 358: Sheriff's raid on Spahn Ranch — James Harris, LA County Sheriffs' Museum

Page 435-436: Then and Now — Dave McTaggart

In the event of any inadvertent acknowledgment omission, Cockney Kid Publishers will insert appropriate acknowledgment in any subsequent printing of this book.

ABOUT THE AUTHOR

As West Coast correspondent for the *London Daily Express,* Ivor Davis covered the Sharon Tate murders and Charles Manson trial from day one. In 1970 he wrote *Five to Die,* the first detailed book about the murders.

He has written for the *Times of London,* penned a weekly column for the *New York Times Syndicate* for 15 years, and was Editor at Large at *Los Angeles* magazine.

His award-winning 2014 memoir, *The Beatles and Me on Tour,* was based on his travels with the Beatles on their first North American tour in 1964. His first children's book, *Ladies and Gentlemen...the Penguins!,* was published in 2018. He is based in Southern California and working on a new memoir.

INDEX